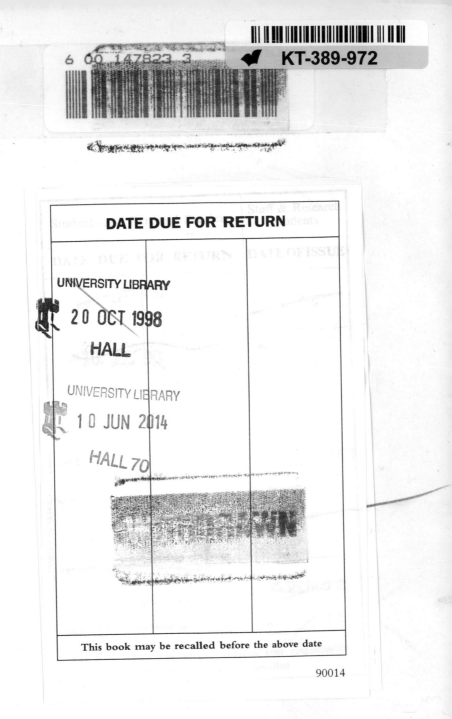

THE PURITAN SPIRIT

THE PURITAN SPIRIT

ESSAYS AND ADDRESSES

by

GEOFFREY F. NUTTALL

LONDON : EPWORTH PRESS

FIRST PUBLISHED IN 1967

BY EPWORTH PRESS

Book Steward
FRANK H. CUMBERS

PRINTED IN GREAT BRITAIN
BY EBENEZER BAYLIS AND SON, LTD.
THE TRINITY PRESS, WORCESTER, AND LONDON

FOREWORD

BY GORDON S. WAKEFIELD
Connexional Editor of the Methodist Church

THE word Puritan, in spite of the careful studies of many historians, secular as well as religious, is still employed to concentrate the antipathies of its users. It stands for harshness, rigidity, iconoclasm, blindness to the beauty of the world, and goodness knows what psychological perversions and abnormalities. Even the renowned and militantly Protestant G. G. Coulton found the 'High Ancestry of Puritanism' in the manichee and all that was most repulsive in the asceticism of the Middle Ages.

These varied pieces of Dr Nuttall's, collected from his published and unpublished output of thirty years, are linked together by a very different understanding of the Puritan spirit. The first essay (his first published paper) defines it as that 'which has driven men at all times to seek a purer way of life, one that was simple and good as opposed to the insincere conventionalities and corruptions in the world around them', and everything that follows is in some sense a variation on that theme. Thus men in some respects so different as Bernard of Clairvaux and William Temple had something in them of the Puritan; and when the young Geoffrey Nuttall describes Chartres in May or pays tribute to Virginia Woolf he evokes a rapture and a humanity which are sensitive to the beauty and frailty of this passing world and which are found also in the Puritans, Baxter, Bunyan, Cradock, Cromwell, and Fox.

'Puritan' as Dr Nuttall understands it is a comprehensive *sobriquet* and in its great age, in seventeenth-century England, it includes many men of differing opinions about theology and politics. In his book *The Holy Spirit in Puritan Faith and Experience* (1946), Dr Nuttall himself distinguishes Puritans of right, left and centre, each party with its own wings. There

5

is no doubt that, finely objective in his historical writing as he tries to be, his own sympathies are with the left and centre, the Arminians rather than the Calvinists, and so it is appropriate that several of these chapters should deal, not only with Quakerism, but with aspects of the Christian social conscience and with the ministry of reconciliation through suffering.

Above all, we have here a living example of the true Puritan alliance between scholarship and devotion. There is great learning and formidable precision in these essays and addresses, though presented with such lucidity and grace as never to be turgid or obscure. (What a contrast with the writing of the great Congregationalist theologian, Peter Taylor Forsyth—the difference between Niagara and Thames (or Rhine), or the lightning flash and the candle of the Lord!)

More than once, Dr Nuttall is concerned with his fellow academics, as when in the Leeds University sermon he utters the opinion—unfashionable among our present *avant-garde* in the churches—that 'the serenity and fearlessness, the liberation from self-concern and self-regard' which Christian faith should bring 'may well help us towards a greater objectivity in our search for truth than would otherwise be in our range'. But he never forgets either the pastoral minister or the simple believer, and this collection represents not inadequately the Church historian whose many works range from an Oxford D.D. thesis to a Lent Book on *The Reality of Heaven*, and whose Puritan catholicity includes Dante, Doddridge, and Dean Church in its ample veneration.

ACKNOWLEDGEMENTS

The author and publishers are indebted to the following for permission to use material which originally appeared under their auspices:

The Times Literary Supplement for the review 'The Letters of Erasmus' (*T.L.S.* 10 January 1948).

The Syndics of the Cambridge University Press and the Library Committee of the Society of Friends for 'George Fox and his Journal', which is the introduction to *The Journal of George Fox* (Cambridge, 1952), a revised edition by John Nickalls.

The Hogarth Press for quotations in Chapter XXIX from the published writings of Virginia Woolf.

The Abingdon Press for Chapter VIII, from *Man's Faith and Freedom*, edited by Gerald O. McCulloh.

The Fellowship of Reconciliation for 'The Justification of War', from *Choose Your Weapons*, edited by Derek Walker, and for Chapter XXV.

The *University of Leeds Review* for the Leeds University Sermon.

The *Journal of Ecclesiastical History* for the review (April 1955) of *A History of the Ecumenical Movement*.

The Independent Press and the Rev. John Huxtable for *The Principles of Congregationalism in their Historical Setting*; for the two pieces on Philip Doddridge reprinted from the 1951 commemorative volume edited by Dr Nuttall; for the study of 'The Church's Ministry of Suffering', from *Studies in Christian Social Commitment*, edited by John Ferguson; and for Chapters II, III, VI, IX, XIII, XIV, XVII, XXIV, XXX and XXXII from the *Congregational Quarterly*, which has now ceased publication.

The *Mansfield College Magazine* for the appreciation of Dr W. B. Selbie.

The *Transactions* of the Congregational Historical Society

for Chapters I, IV and XII and the remainder of Chapter XXXI.

The *Friends' Quarterly* (formerly *Friends' Quarterly Examiner*) for Chapters XI, XIX and XX.

CONTENTS

THE PURITAN SPIRIT THROUGH THE AGES

THE name Puritan, like the names Christian, Protestant, and Methodist, like the names Quaker, Shaker, and Convulsionnaire, and more nearly like the name Cathari, was a nickname bestowed by their opponents on a particular group of people at a particular time in a particular part of the world. When this is granted, however, it is not doing violence to the word to apply it more generally to that spirit in religion which has driven men at all times to seek a purer way of life, one that was simple and good as opposed to the insincere conventionalities and corruptions in the world around them. A passionate desire for righteousness, which demands improvement and reform, and therefore implies opposition from lazy souls, is an essential part of Christianity, and in every, or almost every, century there have been groups of men who have seen this and who have striven to realize their ideal. These men have been Puritans in spirit, if not in name, whether they were the early Cistercians, the early Independents, who came to form the backbone of historical Puritanism, or the early Quakers. That there was an essential sameness of spirit in all these men may be seen from a consideration of some of their chief characteristics—characteristics which have not failed to receive adverse comment from critics who have never tried, or who have at least failed in the attempt, to understand the experiences which inspired them.

Puritanism, we have said, was a movement towards freedom from the corruption in the world around. This naturally expressed itself in the desire to get away from the world. Thus Cîteaux, where the founders of the Cistercian order went when they left Molême, was 'a remote and savage spot almost inaccessible by reason of thorns, and inhabited by wild creatures only',[1] which took its very name from its stagnant

[1] A. M. Cooke, *A Study in Twelfth Century Religious Revival and Reform* (reprinted from the John Rylands Library *Bulletin*, January, 1925), p. 13.

pools.[1] Thus Skeldale, near Ripon, which became the site of Fountains Abbey, was a place 'full of thorns and enclosed by rocks'[2] and therefore pleasing to the monks who had been disgusted by the luxury of St Mary's Abbey at York and had fled into the wilderness. Again, Savonarola, who was in many ways a Puritan, tells us that it was because of 'the great misery of the world, the iniquities of men, the rapes, the adulteries, the robberies, the pride, the idolatry, the cruel blasphemy'[3] that he found such attraction in the line from the Æneid

heu fuge crudeles terras, fuge litus avarum[4]

and eventually betook himself to the Dominican convent at Bologna. A precisely similar spirit is evident in the charter of an Independent church in London in 1571, which runs as follows:

> So we a poore congregation whom god hath seperated from the churches of englande and from the mingled and faulse worshipping therin used, out of the which assemblies the lord our onely Saviour hath called us, and still calleth, saying cume out from among them, and seperate your selves from them & touche no unclean thing. . . .[5]

Lastly, the separateness of Quakerism has been marked from the beginning and needs no illustration. 'By reason of its strangeness and separateness, the Society came to be looked on almost as a monastic order.'[6] George Fox himself had the quality, not indeed of otherworldliness, but, as it has been well said, of overworldliness.[7]

Together with this separateness, which is one of the chief characteristics of the Puritan spirit, there went, almost inevitably, two other things, a simplicity, and a freedom, whether from bishop, priest or State. The Cistercian reform

[1] H. B. Workman, *The Evolution of the Monastic Ideal*, p. 239.
[2] *Ibid.*, p. 241.
[3] W. R. Clark, *Savonarola: his Life and his Times*, pp. 33f.
[4] *Æneid*, III. 44.
[5] Albert Peel, *The First Congregational Churches*, p. 33.
[6] A. N. Brayshaw, *The Quakers: their Story and their Message*, p. 159.
[7] *Ibid.*, pp. 31f.

was, very definitely, a return to a simplicity which was to run through the whole life of the monks and which shows itself even in their architecture. Thus it is at Cistercian abbeys like Fountains and Kirkstall that a blank wall takes the place of an ornamental *triforium*.[1] Similarly, the lofty tower at Fountains is not central, just because, like the meat kitchen at Jervaulx, it was not in the original design and was added only after the first ideals had gone with the first generation of monks. Again, one of the marks of Savonarola's preaching was a natural and straightforward simplicity, which scorned the sophisticated verbal elegancies and ornaments which were fashionable.[2] When we come to the English Puritans of the seventeenth century, their devotion to simplicity is indicated by the modern use of the word 'Puritanical' as a term of disparagement, which, though it may be shown to be unfair in its implication that Puritan simplicity was narrow, must have had reason to grow up. This we will consider in detail later. The early Friends, too, were noted for their simplicity, whether in dress or in speech or in their way of worship.

The spirit of freedom shows itself very clearly in these Puritan movements. The Cistercians were free from the authority of bishops almost from the beginning[3]; and their polity, with their independent chapters, has been compared to an aristocratic republic, as against the monarchy of Cluny.[4] Savonarola was so devoted to freedom that it brought him to the stake. In English Puritanism the name Independents speaks for itself, and here we have the idea of the independence of the Church from the State as well as of the independence of the layman from the priest. Robert Browne's words 'The Lords people is of the willing sorte'[5] struck at the very root of Elizabethan Anglicanism; but they were the strength of the early Independents. Characteristic of the Independents, again, was their firm belief in the doctrine of the priesthood of all believers. The Quakers, once

---

[1] Francis Bond, *Gothic Architecture in England*, p. 534.
[2] C. Silvester Horne, *The Romance of Preaching*, pp. 155f.
[3] H. B. Workman, *op. cit.*, p. 244.
[4] A. M. Cooke, *op. cit.*, p. 39.
[5] *A Treatise of Reformation without tarying for Anie*, ed. T. G. Crippen, 1903, p. 25.

more, are so free that they have no ministers at all, in the ordinary sense of the word, and in their meetings for worship anyone may speak as he or she feels moved by the Spirit. Puritanism has indeed always been opposed to sacerdotalism. The Lollards, who may certainly be considered as Puritans, came to be called 'the lay party' in the Church.[1] Nor must we assume, as we are sometimes prone to do, that the medieval priests had a monopoly of what idealism and spirituality there was. Henri Pirenne, writing of lay religion in the Middle Ages—and it must be remembered that it was from the laity that the ranks of monasticism were filled—says:

> Cet esprit laïque s'alliait d'ailleurs à la ferveur religieuse la plus intense. Si les bourgeoisies se trouvèrent très fréquemment en lutte avec les autorités ecclésiastiques, si les évêques fulminèrent abondamment contre elles des sentences d'excommunication, et si, par contre-coup, elles s'abandonnèrent parfois à des tendances anti-cléricales, elles n'en étaient pas moins animées d'une foi profonde et ardente.[2]

Yet, however much this simplicity and this freedom may be praised, the separateness of Puritanism has often been criticized both as foolish and as selfish and even unchristian. In 1857 an Independent lady, aged seventy-four, thus finished her letter to her grandson, aged sixteen:

> My dear J, may the Lord incline you to walk in the narrow path of life that you may be kept from the sins and vanitys of this wicked world is the sincere prayer of your affte Grandmother Ann Muscutt.

To Ann Muscutt, living securely at Cockermouth all her ninety-six years, the phrase may have been due to a fear of entering into, rather than a desire to flee away from, 'this wicked world'; but her spiritual ancestors had had to suffer much for daring to be independent of the world and of the worldly Church. The cloistered and fugitive virtue which Milton could not praise during the Commonwealth was

[1] James Gairdner, *Lollardy and the Reformation in England*, I. 201.
[2] Henri Pirenne, *Les Villes du Moyen Age*, 1927, pp. 202f.: in the translation by F. D. Halsey from the original lectures given in America, *Mediæval Cities*, 1925, pp. 242f.

under the Restoration the virtue of those 'gathered churches'[1] of the Independents which Milton himself continued to support,[2] no less than the virtue of the Cistercian monks centuries earlier. Many still share with Milton the feeling that to flee from the world is both cowardly and selfish; but too few of them have ever felt the horror, amounting almost to despair, at the corruptions in the world as it is, which alone will enable them truly to understand the reason for such flight. After all, the Puritans have the Apostolic injunction to keep themselves unspotted from the world;[3] and even the disciples were told by Jesus to flee into the next village, rather than to endure, when they were persecuted;[4] and, though Jesus came eating and drinking,[5] He also said that an offending member ought to be cut off.[6] True, it might seem more Christian to stay *in* the world and to try to make it better from within; but, we repeat, most of those who *can* do this have never felt the despair which has sent men out of the world into separateness. If they had, they would not be so quick to use the term 'selfish' when speaking of at least the originators of a religious revival, whether they be the early Cistercians, the early Independents or the early Quakers.

The Puritans are, further, often accused of keeping to the letter rather than to the spirit. Indeed it has been asked whether anything could be 'more characteristic of the timeless Puritan spirit whensoever and wheresoever it appears' than 'an interpretation of the spirit in the terms of the letter'.[7] There is a certain piquancy in the question; but it really applies not to the Puritan but to the Traditionalist, who has lost the right to the name of Puritan. We have seen how closely Puritanism is connected with freedom; and freedom is incompatible with keeping the letter of the law. Simplicity will always be condemned by some as narrowness, which the

---

[1] Some of Watts's less well known hymns give an admirable reflection of the 'We are a garden walled around' spirit of these conventicles.

[2] It is amusing to remember in this connexion the line from Wordsworth's Sonnet 'To Milton':

'Thy Soul was like a star and *dwelt apart*.'

[3] *Jas.* i. 27.
[4] *Mt.* x. 23.
[5] *Lk.* vii. 34.
[6] *Mt.* v. 29f.
[7] A. M. Cooke, *op. cit.*, pp. 24f.

term 'Puritanical' now implies. It may be conceded that men of Puritan spirit do tend to distrust pleasures which are really harmless, and that they are so much the poorer thereby. It is perhaps almost impossible for a man who is impressed by the valuable powers of salt as an antiseptic to remember that it has also the virtue of giving relish to food; and the Puritans, in their very anxiety to be the salt of the earth, have always been in danger of losing their savour.[1] We must not, however, forget the corruption of the society from which they are reacting. Reactions are proverbially violent; and in a time of reaction there are few who have the insight and even courage to distinguish between what is corrupted but in itself good and what is in itself bad—few who, like St. Francis, can decry the immoral purposes to which the emotions are being put by the world around and can yet be free and spontaneous in the joyful expression of their own emotions.

In any case, the Puritans of the seventeenth century are much maligned by those who represent them as disdaining the innocent pleasures of music, sports, and the stage. It is too little known, in the first place, that

Cromwell and nearly all the leading Parliamentarians did their best to prevent actual destruction of instruments and of music. Cromwell himself and many of his chief supporters were ardent music lovers, and the vast body of Puritans never for a moment questioned the lawfulness of ordinary music, confining their prohibitions to profane music on the Sabbath, organs and choirs in churches and stage plays. . . . Cromwell gave State concerts at Whitehall.[2]

Cromwell also

hunted, hawked and played the games of the times as did the royalist country gentlemen . . . and had as real a love for a fine horse as they.[3]

Many of the Lancashire Puritans, and even some of their preachers . . . were mighty hunters, keen anglers, fond of hawking, of shuffleboard, of bowls, of billiards, and . . . of baiting the

[1] I owe this thought to a sermon preached by the Rev. A. J. Costain at Rydal School on 26 July 1931.
[2] Ernest Newman, *A History of Music in England*, pp. 121f., 144.
[3] John Brown, *The English Puritans*, p. 152.

badger, of throwing at the cock, and even occasionally of private theatricals.[1]

With morris dancing and the maypole, it was to their religious association, to their connexion with Church festivals that they objected. The stage they mostly did abhor, in fact, the theatres were definitely closed during the Commonwealth. The reason for this is clear; for

> the drama heaped its bitterest and often coarsest attacks upon whatever savoured of the Puritan spirit; gibes, taunts, caricatures in ridicule and aspersion of Puritans and Puritanism make up a great part of the comic literature of the later Elizabethan drama and of its aftergrowth in the reign of the first two Stuarts.[2]

Further, to speak of the seventeenth-century stage as an innocent pleasure shows either ignorance or a moral outlook that has remained of Restoration date, while the Puritans have gained the day. For

> with the exception of Shakespeare, it was the custom of the comedies of the seventeenth century to introduce adultery as a subject for laughter, and often as the staple of the whole plot, the seducer being let pass as a " handsome gentleman," and the injured husband made the object of every kind of scorn and ridicule.[3]

It is, indeed, high time that the Puritans were rescued from their fate at the hands of popular criticism in this respect. Most people, however, find a coloured picture more pleasing to look at than one of pure white; and the traditional view of Puritanism has been fostered by a romantic novelist like Scott and by a rhetorical historian like Macaulay, for whom it was natural to paint only the decadent Puritanism, caring not that their portraits do but show that

> Lilies that fester smell far worse than weeds.[4]

The error is not made less by the constant vilification of

---

[1] Robert Halley, *Lancashire: its Puritanism and Nonconformity*, p. 34.
[2] A. W. Ward, art. 'Drama in *Enc. Brit.*, 13th edn., 1926, VIII. 526.
[3] John Brown, *op. cit.*, pp. 153f.
[4] Shakespeare, Sonnet XCIV.

Oliver Cromwell in so many English cathedrals. The way in which Lichfield was treated was exceptional; more characteristic was the consideration he showed for Ely, as was pointed out in *The Spectator* last year.[1] In any case, when a Cromwell is to blame, it is far more often Oliver's namesake and relative, Thomas Cromwell, to whom the damage is due.

The extreme simplicity of the early Quakers in their speech and dress may seem nothing but the keeping of the letter of the law. That it became so we shall have to admit; but originally

> it flowed from the principle which pervaded (Fox's) whole conduct, the desire of piercing through the husk and coating of forms in which men's hearts were wrapped up and of dragging them out from their lurking places into the open light of day.[2]

> The witness of Friends on points of speech and dress . . . is not to be treated as an excrescence on their main message. We ought rather to feel that the main message, under the conditions of that age [and it was an age of ostentation and insincerity][3] could not have been uttered in its purity and force if Friends had shrunk from giving it fearless application to these parts of life.[4]

> Fox was, it must be remembered, the incarnation of a sensitive conscience. No matters of right and wrong could ever be trivial in his sight. . . . If formal etiquette expected him to say to a man what he very well knew was not true, then he resolved to have nothing more to do with formal etiquette till the end of the world.[5]

In their ardent Puritan search for reality, it was natural that the early Quakers should have been wedded to this simplicity as opposed to the conventionalities of the day. In time, it must be admitted, the spirit of dead tradition grew up. Plain clothing of a certain type, for instance, became a

[1] E. G. Hawke, 'Cromwell and the Churches', in *The Spectator* of 30 August 1930. The consideration Cromwell showed for Ely, like the consideration Fairfax showed for York, may have been due to the fact that it was the cathedral of his native county.

[2] *Guesses at Truth*, p. 127: quoted in W. C. Braithwaite, *The Beginnings of Quakerism*, p. 494.

[3] See also A. N. Brayshaw, *The Personality of George Fox*, pp. 59f.

[4] W. C. Braithwaite, *op. cit.*, p. 495.

[5] R. M. Jones, *George Fox—Seeker and Friend*, pp. 100, 200.

requirement to which rigid adherence was demanded. Margaret Fox, in her old age, saw the danger and protested against 'this narrowness and strictness entering in'; for, as she added, 'It's the Spirit that gives life.'[1] Her protests were in vain, and the narrowness she feared descended on the Society. Yet it *is* important to realize that it was not there originally. The esoteric distinction between 'gay' and 'plain' Friends, in connexion with which we are told of a member who gave up music, 'but once a year he went to the top of the Monument in London, and there, where his action could do no harm to anyone, he played his flute'[2] was a late development. To keep to the letter in this pitiful way is *not* typical of Puritanism at its best; far more Puritan are Margaret Fox's words 'It's the Spirit that gives life.'

Like them, again, is the anecdotal[3] saying of George Fox to William Penn, when Penn was uncertain whether his newly-adopted Quaker principles would permit him to wear his sword. Fox's advice was, 'Wear it so long as thou canst'— advice which is striking in its Puritan freedom, when we remember the strong and consistent testimony Friends have borne against war.

There is one other objection to Puritanism which we may consider briefly, and that is the disparagement of the intellect. We see it in the controversy of Bernard of Clairvaux with Abelard, we see it in Savonarola's suspicion of his tendencies towards philosophical speculation,[4] and we see it markedly in the Quakers, who had to wait for Penington and Barclay before they made any attempt to work out the theology of their position. Following along the lines of Fox's sound words

> that being bred at Oxford or Cambridge was not enough to fit and qualify men to be ministers of Christ[5]

[1] *Epistles*: quoted in W. C. Braithwaite, *The Second Period of Quakerism*, pp. 518f.

[2] A. N. Brayshaw, *The Quakers*, p. 158, n. 2.
     One is reminded of the Plymouth Brother who never sang another secular song for the rest of his life, through overhearing a carpenter say to his fellow: 'He can zing a zong, zo well's another, though he be a minister.' Edmund Gosse, *Father and Son*, p. 125.

[3] S. M. Janney, *Life of William Penn*, p. 50: quoted in M. R. Brailsford, *The Making of William Penn*, pp. 206f.

[4] W. R. Clark, *op. cit.*, pp. 30, 127f.

[5] *Journal*, 1901 edn., I. 7, 11.

they came to distrust the intellect so much, that it became customary for Friends who spoke in meeting to assure their hearers that what they were about to say 'has occurred to me unexpectedly since taking my seat here this morning'.[1] This was indeed a misunderstanding of the true Quaker position, as is now realized; and that Fox and the early Friends were keenly interested in education is clear from the number of schools they established.[2] In any case, the explanation of the disparagement of the intellect by the Puritans of all ages is that they have had an intense religious experience at first hand. Conscious of this, they cannot help feeling that theological speculations are dry, barren, irrelevant, and unnecessary, and tend to become little more than dialectic and logic-chopping. Once again, if the critics had anything approaching the mystical experience of the revivalists, they would be more sparing in their condemnations.

Thus we have followed the Puritan spirit through the centuries, taking the early Cistercians, Savonarola, the early Independents, and the early Quakers as our illustrations. There are, of course, many others whom we might have chosen. Of especial interest are the Catharist sects of the early Middle Ages, whose very name means Puritan, and who were emphatic in their distrust of this world and in their desperate attempt to be free from it and from the established Church. In their scrupulous simplicity and conscientiousness they were the forerunners of the Friends, since their witness against war and against swearing, to take but two instances, was no less consistent. Like them, also, they preached the doctrine of Perfection in this life and even divided their own ranks into two bodies—the *credentes*, who were in the majority, and the *perfecti*, who, by a still more severe process of abstinence from all things worldly, became true Children of God, very angels in the flesh, separated from Christ only by the thin screen of death.[3]

All these, then, whether Catholic or Protestant—for the same types of piety are to be found in both the great branches of the Christian Church—all these were Puritans in their

[1] A. N. Brayshaw, *The Quakers*, p. 210.
[2] See A. N. Brayshaw, *The Personality of George Fox*, pp. 55ff.
[3] See F. C. Conybeare, art. 'Cathars' in *Enc. Brit.*, 13th edn., 1926, V. 515ff.

search for reality and righteousness, in their desire to get away from the corruptions of 'this wicked world', in their devotion to simplicity and to freedom. All this sprang directly from their religious experience; while their tendencies to narrowness and to the disparagement of the intellect were the almost inevitable defects of their qualities, nor did the narrowness become pronounced until Puritanism had degenerated into Traditionalism.

Note.—It is interesting to see how often the word 'pure' actually occurs in the writings of these men of Puritan spirit. Wordsworth, for instance, has written a poem 'On a Cistercian Monastery' around these words of Bernard of Clairvaux, which he saw inscribed on the walls of the monastery: '*Bonum est hic nos esse, quia homo vivit purius*. . . .' Again, a charter of the Independent church in London in 1571 referred to above states that it 'stryueth for to haue. Fyrste and formoste, the Glorious worde and Evangell preached, not in bondage and subjection, but freely and *purelye*. Secondly to have the Sacraments mynistred *purely*. . . . And laste of all, to have, not the fylthye Cannon lawe, but dissiplyne onelye. . . .'[1] Lastly, Fox's *Epistles* abound in such phrases as 'Mind that which is *pure* in you to guide you to God', 'Wait upon God in that which is *pure*' and 'Obey that which is *pure* in you. . . .'[2]

1931

---

[1] Albert Peel, *The First Congregational Churches*, p. 32.
[2] *Epistles*, pp. 9, 14 and 94: quoted in A. N. Brayshaw, *The Quakers*, pp. 26, 54 and 99. The italics are in all cases my own.

II

ST BERNARD OF CLAIRVAUX
AND HIS IDEAL

THE character of St Bernard of Clairvaux, like that of other great personalities, is one which presents brilliant contrasts, so that, with each facet sparkling, we are apt to be dazzled and to find difficulty in discovering the unity which was the real man. He was a monk, who loved to lose himself in mystical contemplation, yet at the same time he was in more than metaphor the dictator of Europe. He was an orthodox medieval, who (after Beatrice) plays the most important part in the *Paradiso*; he was also respected by Luther as the most pious monk, whom he preferred to all others. At least one biographer rests content with the thought that Bernard's worldly activity was but incidental to his real life; but such a judgement is not borne out by Bernard's writings, and in any case a unity there must have been in fact.

What follows is intended as a study of the things which made Bernard's character and gave him his individuality rather than of his actions and influence. In it an attempt is made to understand something of what was central to Bernard's life, his religion; and briefly to consider, first, its relation to his active secular life as a whole, and secondly, the way in which it affected his attitude in three particular spheres.

First and foremost, Bernard's religion was the mystical love of God. F. D. Maurice ventured the statement that 'no writer of any age has dwelt more upon Love as constituting the very being and nature of God',[1] and the central dogma upon which Bernard seized was the prevenience of God's love. Man may search for God and find Him, but neither in searching nor in finding will he be the first. He may rise in the night to be down before service, but he will not anticipate God's watchfulness; God's love is both greater and prior. It

[1] F. D. Maurice, *Mediaeval Philosophy*, p. 124.

is in close relation to this that we find Bernard expressing Pascal's thought, that no one could search for God who had not already found Him; for, though man searches for God in order to love Him more, he would not search at all unless he already loved Him, nor could he love Him without having found Him. This mutual search, this finding and being found of God, Bernard never wearies of describing, and in the most superlative terms. A sweet intercourse (*dulce commercium*) he calls it, explicitly preferring the word *commercium* to the more legal word *contractus* (covenant), and the erotic language of *Canticles* is freely used by him. This he would have justified, had he seen need for justification, with the claim that no other language can less inadequately express the intimacy of the relationship between the soul and God. For love knows not reverence, so that the soul may converse with God in all familiarity, may become at one with Him, herself become divine (*sic affici deificari est*).

Throughout Bernard's writings this experiential, or experimental, aspect of religion is given prominence. To his own experience he refers constantly, and counts it a sufficient guarantee of the validity of his statements. 'By the revived activity of my heart I know Him.' On one occasion he goes so far as to identify belief with discovery. He also fully appreciates the part played by personal goodness in enabling the believer to understand what Christianity means.

For Bernard's religious experience was a disciplined experience. Too often mysticism is divorced from ethics, but in Bernard's religion there is a strongly ethical element, and it is this which forms the seed in his mysticism from which his whole secular activity springs. When we find that it is by the disappearance of his vices and the suppression of his carnal desires that he recognizes the presence of the Heavenly Lover, by an improvement in morals that His loving-kindness is made known, we are less surprised at Bernard's influence outside his monastery. It is not that he was not contented with the life of mystical contemplation. With those who aspire to be done with meditation and be engulfed in the busy life of abbots and priors he has little patience. He knows too well what it means to be torn away from quietude to those who desire his help or advice. Indeed, he would not go, were it not that love bids him, but in the language of *Canticles*, which Bernard loved so dearly, the kisses of contemplation must yield to the breasts of preaching and of service; not for our own good must we live, but for the good of all.

Bernard thus, no less than Francis, though in a different mode, felt called to secular activity, and to it he called others. *Nolle proficere, deficere est*, has been suggested for his motto[1]; of which the variant might be added, *Praesis, ut prosis*. Certainly Bernard had more than his share of activity and responsibility. Apart from the influence he wielded through the large number of monks from Clairvaux who held sees throughout Europe, including Henry Murdac at York and two bishops in Ireland, he declined three bishoprics himself. To his former pupil, Eugenius, now Bishop of Rome, he wrote that men were saying that Bernard, not Eugenius, was Pope. His power in moulding the order of the Knights Templar, for whom he was long supposed to have written their Rule, was only less than his power in moulding the Cistercian order. Most striking of all, he was actually elected commander-in-chief of the Second Crusade.

Notwithstanding all this, Bernard has hard words for those who take to activity too easily and too soon. In the Church of his day, he remarks, there are too many canals and not enough reservoirs. A reservoir knows that its supplies depend upon its source, nor does it overflow until its banks are full; but our leaders today are eager to give out before they have received, to govern others when they have not yet learned self-discipline. And self-discipline needs learning. Bernard never pretends that it is an easy task, he knows from his own experience that it is not. He also insists that a prior condition of self-discipline is self-knowledge. In his opinion, indeed, knowledge of the soul should come first in all learning. Consequently the faults of youthful priests cause him no surprise; they have yet to understand themselves.

Wherein, then, lies the means of obtaining this self-

---

[1] *Cf.* H. Fechner, *Die politischen Theorien des Abtes Bernhard von Clairvaux in seinen Briefen*, Bonn 1933, p. 85. Mottoes do not lend themselves to translation, but the Latin may be paraphrased 'Not to be wanting to help is to be wanting' and 'Be at hand, to be handy.'

knowledge which is requisite? The answer is interesting, and the more revealing in that it comes in a casual adverbial phrase. It is through humility that man comes most truly to understand his own worthlessness. On the all-importance in religion of humility Bernard never wavers. The humility, which, expressing itself in love, brought him forth in the service of others, he describes explicitly as the foundation of the whole spiritual fabric. In the Virgin Mary, to whom, as a good Cistercian, he was passionately devoted, he rates her humility above her virginity; without her humility her virginity would not have sufficed, nor would the Holy Ghost have rested on her. Seek ye first humility, and all these things shall be added unto you: Bernard says this in almost so many words.

If we turn to consider his attitude to scholasticism, we find that it is controlled by these two factors, his experience of sweet intercourse with God and the humility which is at once the cause and the result of that intercourse. His own discovery of God was not along the paths of reason. Of course he is aware of the place reason must have in life. He can ask a boon because it seems reasonable; he can wish to do a thing since reason demands it; and when he wrote against the dogma of the Immaculate Conception, he gave the ground that reason was against it. But there is all the difference between reason (*ratio*) and reasoning (*ratiocinatio*); and in the latter sphere he was fully aware that disingenuous arguments can depend on impure motives.

> Down Reason then, at least vain reasonings down!

But more. Even Plato and Aristotle and the study of them he could deprecate,

> Though Reason here aver
> That moral verdict quits her of unclean.

The explanation is that Bernard felt, as Dante was to feel, that after the sharp conclusion to which one is brought by the power of the Holy Spirit every logical demonstration must be dull (*ottusa*). Nor should such an attitude be dismissed as obscurantist. To obscurantism it may lead; but so may scholastic reasoning lead to aridity and barrenness. Bernard's position finds sympathetic reflection in his contemporary Walter Daniel's description of Aelred, the Abbot of Rievaulx. After observing that words may lack sense and be no better than dogs barking, Walter praises Aelred for putting the rules of grammar in their place and for despising the vain study of worldly eloquence, out of a love for truth pure and undefiled.

Bernard's antagonism to Abelard was thus in part because Abelard impersonated, as it were, the whole forces of *ratiocinatio* in religion. The outcome of Abelard's teaching, moreover, was as objectionable to Bernard as his approach. To Bernard, as a mystic, the truths of religion, apart from whatever certainty they possessed through being supernaturally revealed, were as indubitably certain as the truth of experience generally. Mystical contemplation he defines as an apprehension of the truth which is certain and leaves no doubt. This is, indeed, the certitude of intuition rather than the certainty of reason—we recall the identification of belief with discovery—a distinction which the poverty of abstract nouns in Latin did not help Bernard to see clearly; but it is certitude. Inevitably, therefore, and not simply as the guardian of orthodoxy, Bernard was bound to condemn Abelard, when Abelard defined faith as opinion. 'I know whom I have believed, and am persuaded (*certus sum*)', Bernard quotes, very justly retorting that opinions are the issue of dons' minds, whose province it is to doubt everything and be sure of nothing.

Such language as Abelard's further revealed a lack of that humility which for Bernard was essential. Abelard was outstepping himself and through the wisdom of words forsaking the Cross. Bernard realized (to use Hooker's phrase) that it were dangerous for the feeble brain of man to wade far into the doings of the Most High; grace, not language, must be the teacher here, and for the present his philosophy would be to know Jesus and Him crucified. Obscurantist this might be, but he was decided. Unless it were in the name of Jesus, he would be party to no discussion.

In the aesthetic sphere Bernard's attitude is of a piece with this. Without an appreciation of natural beauty he certainly was not. His power of detachment, it is true, was so great that, like Calvin, he could pass by the Lake of Geneva without so much as observing it; but there seems no reason to regard as insincere his advice to Henry Murdac that he would find more in the woods than in books, that nature could teach him what might not be learned from his masters. Besides this, there are his many references to flowers: Nazareth he interprets as a flower, the Virgin is a sweetly smelling flower, so is the Virgin's Son, a flower white and ruddy. It was over the place of beauty in religion that controversy arose, especially with the Cluniac order, and here Bernard simply adopts the timeless Puritan position. Some will defend the Cluniac monks as thinking that they could not do too much in using the beauty of art to help them in giving glory to God. That is all very well, but it represents an ideal, and Bernard asks just how the immodest monkeys and monstrous centaurs, which adorned the great Cluniac churches, were to give glory to God. He lays down the Puritan condemnation that these things are a distraction rather than an aid to worship. What is their purpose? he asks; to bring sinners to repentance or to be admired? Beauty is not the same as the numinous, nor is the bringing of a gift to be identified with prayer. Such luxury of externality, an expression, like contemporary scholasticism, of a flowering humanism, was far removed from the simple, austere inner life of religion which Bernard knew. He further condemned it for the wealth it required and the expense it involved. In Catholic, as in Protestant, Puritanism it is possible for the artistic approach to be eclipsed by a utilitarian motive as well as by one more truly devotional; but poverty, simplicity, was an especial ideal with the Cistercians, and it is natural that Bernard should appeal to it as a criterion for the true worship of God no less than for His service in the world.

Here Bernard sharply distinguishes between the regular and the secular priest, between the monk and the bishop. Of the wine Paul counselled Timothy to drink, he quaintly remarks that it was intended for a bishop, not a monk, and he reproaches the monks of Cluny for aping episcopal habits. One might therefore expect that he would deprecate the leaving their monastery by his own monks, in order to become

27

bishops. Yet after 1120, when a precedent was made by the elevation of Peter of Clairvaux to the archbishopric of Tarentaise, the number of sees which were filled by monks from Clairvaux continually increased, in each case enlarging the sphere of Bernard's influence throughout Europe. A solution of the apparent contradiction may be found in the emphasis Bernard lays on poverty. This it is which characterizes, or should characterize, the monk; and if the monk will retain it as a bishop, the episcopate can only be strengthened. Others might advance the common-sense objection to the monk-bishop expressed later by Henry III of England, that the cloister could hardly provide him with much experience in secular activity, but such an appeal to expediency would weigh little against Bernard's otherworldliness. That Master Gilbert should become a bishop is no matter for surprise, he wrote in congratulation to Gilbert the Universal, but that a bishop of London should live in poverty is magnificent. This poverty, of which Bernard makes so much, is, we may see, but the outward expression of the humility which he counted essential. As he says in so many words, it is not poverty which is a virtue but the love of poverty. Blessed are the poor, not in goods, but in spirit.

In this ecclesiastical sphere, no less than in the aesthetic and the academic, Bernard thus strove after an ideal of humility which proceeded directly from the self-knowledge given in his mystical experience of the love of God. He had the faults of other great idealists. He tended on occasion to identify his ideal with himself, as perhaps in parts of the controversy with Abelard or when he commanded the English king to assist the monks who were coming to found the first Cistercian house in this country as if they were the messengers of Almighty God. He was also so passionately devoted to his ideal that he could disregard the sacrifice of human personality to it. The good of the Church must come before people, and his abuse of Abelard may in this way best be explained, though not excused. Bernard had his faults, but it was a noble ideal which he pursued; and he succeeded in being, to use his own image, a reservoir of the prevenient love of God, a reservoir calm and deep, humbly dependent upon his source, overflowing with the simplicity, yet with the unrestrainable power, of a mountain brook, fertilizing and refreshing, till, by the way of loving service, a return was made to the ocean whence in the beginning his waters came, *illi pelago aeterni luminis et luminosae aeternitatis.*

1953

III

A READING OF THE *PARADISO*

NEAR the beginning of his essay on Dante, R. W. Church refers to 'that great gift and power by which he stands pre-eminent even among his high compeers, the gift of being real'. One of the things which contribute to this sense of reality in Dante, making what he writes keenly alive, is the place in it of *desire*. *Disio*: the word comes again and again; there are few cantos without it or one of its cognates. Its connotation is enriched from a number of different spheres of discourse, but it never loses its fundamental meaning of eager longing, whether emotional, intellectual or religious.

To the modern reader *desire* appears an emotional word; and to the modern reader it is an attraction of the *Commedia* that he is rarely left for long without an appeal to his emotions, some incident which, though told with high seriousness and always in relation to the over-ruling purpose of the poem, is as pure romance as he could wish. In this sense Dante's desire is bound up with Beatrice, to whom, as the spirit he has been watching so eagerly vanishes from sight, he turns as to the object of a yet greater desire. Whenever he gazes at Beatrice's eyes, Dante's longing comes to rest; the claim upon him of every other longing falls away.

But not for long; for Dante's intellectual longing, his desire to know the truth, is no less keen than is his desire to gaze at Beatrice. At the very beginning of the *Paradiso* he tells how the first new sight and sound which were vouchsafed to him kindled in him a desire to understand what caused them. Nor can he hide the fact: his desire, this intellectual longing, is painted on his face. Fortunately, there is no need to hide it. The spirits too show desire: Cacciaguida is as eager to answer Dante's questions as is Dante to ask them. Beatrice also, *tutta disiante* herself, recognizes Dante's longing for the truth. His lofty desire to understand what he sees gives her pleasure, and she frequently encourages him to give expression to it, as it swells within him and enflames him.

For Dante, as a good Thomist, there is also another object of desire: God. God, who moves all the heaven with love and desire also moves men, enamouring them of Himself, so that they ever long for Him. By such longing, indeed, everything becomes what it is; and it is in keeping with this that at the end of his pilgrimage, amid scenes of fulfilment which he no longer has the power to describe, Dante tells how the love which moves the sun and the other stars now worked upon his own will and desire without further interruption or irregularity.

This *disio* of many colours, which thus pervades the *Paradiso*, also helps to keep the story in motion. It not only reflects Dante's own eager nature, *pronto e libente* as he was— and the Church Militant, to quote Beatrice, had not a son with more hopefulness than he. It also points to the end, the end which by being the fulfilment of desire is the end of his pilgrimage and the end of the poem.

From the first canto, with its pregnant phrase about the mind's drawing near to its desire, to the last canto, in which we see Dante himself drawing near to the end of all his longings, we are never for long without the sense that desire is meant to be satisfied, and can and will be satisfied. To the mind, Dante says, truth is like the rest which, once gained, its den brings to a wild beast home from its ranging. And gain it it can, he insists; otherwise all longing would be futile. In this last phrase there is an *a priori* flavour; but the conviction it expresses also issues from experience. For Dante quickly finds that Beatrice can set his intellectual longings at peace as well as give rest to his emotions. And what she does by the way, God does always. In the love of God heaven itself is still resting in His love. Here, in the kingdom of truth the mind is stilled by truth. Nor do those in heaven's lower ranges desire to be placed higher: their will is stilled by the love in which they have their being, to be at one with God's will: *e la sua volontate è nostra pace* (iii. 85, a familiar line the force of which is greatly increased when it is set over against Dante's own eagerness). From this Dante realizes that in heaven everywhere is Paradise. But it is part of his skill and triumph that nevertheless he preserves throughout so strong a sense of pilgrimage. We are always being pointed forward to the end, where his lofty desire, with all others, will be fulfilled. There is the life of love and peace, unblemished by either longing or anxiety; which is but another way of saying that every desire has achieved its own faultless maturity and perfection.

The three-fold nature of Dante's desire—intellectual and religious as well as emotional—is reflected throughout the *Paradiso* in the pattern, constantly changing yet fundamentally simple, which gives the poem a certain richness and the charm of variety and which at the same time binds it together. This appears most evidently, perhaps, in Dante's use of the imagery of light. The quality and power of light affect and fascinate most poets; but for Dante pre-eminently, to quote Dean Church again, light is 'his special chosen source of poetic beauty', and not of beauty only.

Truth, for instance, and the understanding of it which Dante so keenly desires, are often described in terms of light and of vision or the seeing of light. Reason's wings are short, and logical argument is a blunted instrument; truth is something which must be seen, shining, self-evident and sure, in its own light. The whole of Dante's pilgrimage is a gradual entering, as his vision becomes progressively less blurred, into eternal light, the deep light which in itself is true. This light, the true light of the kingdom of truth, casts its shadows, and often Dante does not penetrate beyond them. Yet even these are shadowy prefaces to the truth, *ombriferi prefazii*; the reflection of the eternal light early glows within Dante's mind, as Beatrice recognizes; and even where he is misled, it is still some vestige of the light, shining through, which he misunderstands. Dante himself observes that the angelic circles flame forth more brightly as their nature shares more deeply of the truth; and when Beatrice gives him a clear answer to one of his many intellectual problems, the truth appears, he says, like a star in heaven—an image which he applies elsewhere to the shining within himself of the truth of the Christian faith.

This correlation of truth with light is assisted by the double reference, for Dante, of the word *chiaro*. *Chiaro* is the word by which he describes the clarity of Beatrice's answer; elsewhere, 'you have made me glad', he says to Charles

Martel, 'now make me clear (*chiaro*), enlighten me, since you have moved me to doubt'. *Chiarezza*, however, denotes very much more than merely intellectual clarity. It retains something of the force of the Latin *clarus* and hence also means clear-shining or bright. In this sense, together with a number of words which render the shining, flashing, sparkling, glowing, blazing, and burning of light, it is used frequently throughout the poem. *Splendori*, in particular, is a favourite word of Dante's for describing the spirits in Paradise. The glory of a divine *je ne sais quoi* is apparent in them. It is, in fact, through the glowing of God's light reflected in them, the light of that glory which penetrates the universe, glowing more here and less there, that the spirits have their being, and shine; even though the source of their light may be hidden, as, sometimes, the sun is hidden, while its rays are seen to be streaming over a meadow of flowers.

The conception of God as the Light in whom is no darkness at all, and of His creation as in measure partaking in that light, is ancient and, if not universal, is common, though never common-place. What is peculiar in Dante's vision is the delicacy with which the heavenly spirits flash and glow in response to, and in revelation of, their desires and joys and loves. Their *chiarezza*, their shining quality, is fundamentally in direct relation to their vision of the divine light, of God Himself; but never in a mechanical or impersonal way. 'I see the supreme essence', Peter Damiani exclaims to Dante, 'and hence comes the joy with which I flame': the joy of vision, *allegrezza*, is the middle term. So on a lower plane the spirits show their love for Dante and their readiness to answer his questions by shining more brightly and thus growing yet more beautiful. As on earth one may read an absorbing affection written on the face, so Dante can read their wish to please him in their flaming glow: in heaven joy expresses itself in brightness, as on earth it does in a smile.

This last comparison, is especially revealing: in no other long and serious poem, perhaps, are there so many references to a smile. Beatrice's eyes are always smiling, and glowing as they smile. When Dante is only halfway through the heavenly world, her smile so blazes that he thinks Paradise can hold no more for him. He is overcome by the light of her smile: the glow in her laughing eyes can scatter his single-minded love of God. All this movingly reflects Dante's romantic attachment to Beatrice; but hers is also a holy smile, *il santo riso*, and on one occasion Beatrice restrains it, lest its glow prove too dangerous to Dante's mortality. In time Dante becomes stronger again to sustain it; and at last he sees her laughing so merrily that God Himself seems to be rejoicing in her face. So in a sense God is; for it is the rays of God's eternal delight, shining directly upon Beatrice, which are reflected for, and on, Dante in her smiling face. Nor is smiling confined to Beatrice. From among the spirits Piccarda, Justinian, Aquinas, and Cacciaguida are all described as smiling; so is the Virgin Mary. The spirits, in a striking phrase, have each their own smile; while once, with characteristic audacity, Dante says that he saw, as it seemed to him—*O gioia! O ineffabile allegrezza!*—a smile of the universe, *un riso del universo*.

In heaven, however, except in the case of Beatrice, whose figure in this respect remains more earthly, joy is more naturally expressed by brightness than by a smile, a brightness which by its beauty in turn creates joy; and throughout the *Paradiso* such brightness and joy are constant. It would be strange if they were not: for in heaven we are in the happy world, *nel mondo felice*, the kingdom of eternal joy where life is glad and free from care. Moreover, as the journey proceeds, the joy intensifies. The higher they climb and the nearer they are to the eternal beauties, the more beautiful Beatrice becomes, and the freer from any unworthy element is Dante's delight in her beauty. Again, as when a man's ability increases, he feels a growing delight in doing what he does well, so in Paradise there is more delight as the vision of truth becomes profounder. The spirits rejoice in their sweet achievement; and the joy of which Dante is conscious in his final endeavour to describe his vision of the gathering up of all things in the universe into a single light he regards as evidence of the vision's truth.

As, then, God's light is the ultimate source of the brightness which reveals joy, so His beauty and His truth, the spring from which all truth derives, are ultimately the cause of all joy; while a more proximate cause is His own joy, for in joy

God Himself shares, rejoicing over beauty as in the end only its creator can: the angels, indeed, gather joy directly from the contemplation of God's face. The deepest source of joy, however, is in God's goodness and love and self-giving grace. In this way thought and emotion, inquiry and longing and the satisfaction of both, are intertwined with and embraced by religious feeling, and the threefold nature of Dante's desire finds true fulfilment; and, though the poem's philosophical framework is that of scholasticism and consequently owes much to Aristotle, its theology is no less in debt to St Paul and is profoundly Christian.

The fount of all creation is God's goodness and love, the goodness which makes everything what it is, the eternal love which ever unfolds itself in new loves. The greater goodness is, the more it desires the good of others; and God is the Supreme Good, as He is also the Primal Love. More, He is the Primal Lover, desirous that all should become like Him. Hence His goodness is displayed and dispersed and multiplied throughout creation; and as goodness, simply *qua* goodness, when understood, kindles love, so love, thus kindled, of its own nature multiplies, simply by loving.

This is supremely illustrated in the love of God in Jesus Christ. As what is done is more gracious, the more it reveals of the heart's goodness, so in God's giving *Himself* in Christ we see His largeness of heart, courtesy, grace. The spirits' vision of Him, on which their blessedness depends, is all of grace, something freely bestowed upon them beyond their own power. Nor could love so free be satisfied without an element of freedom in the love given in return. The freedom of man's will is in fact God's greatest gift, bestowed *per sua larghezza*, in all His creation. *Larghezza*: it is a rich word for largeness of heart and generosity; it has the feudal and romantic overtones of largesse; while once Dante uses it to compare God's grace to the ample unfolding, to its outermost petal, of a rose. In response to such munificence, the spirits willingly accept the divine providence and disposal of themselves as a necessity dictated by God's love. In His grace to bestow diversities of gifts is part of God's joy in His creation; and in so great a love, and in the amplitude of the kingdom in which they find themselves, the spirits are content

35

to rest. For this is heaven, and their enlightened minds are full of love, while their love, being a love of true goodness, is full of joy.

So, once again, truth and joy and love are all together, united in pure light. *Chiarezza, allegrezza, larghezza*: in these three words, which on occasion Dante rhymes with one another, may be seen something of the *Paradiso's* pattern. Only something; for the poet brings together much not mentioned here, history and philosophy and science, as well as poetry and romantic love and imagination and high theology, as if to lay every treasure known, in adoration, before the Creator. The three words may also suggest the pleasure to be found in reading the poem. A clear-shining happiness and greatness of heart pervade it, a vision of the brightness caused by joy in the largeness of God's love; and such is the intensity of Dante's conviction, such the beauty and precision of his language, that the reader can hardly avoid seeing what he saw and believing as he believed.

1956

IV

BISHOP PECOCK AND THE LOLLARD MOVEMENT

T HE neglect of the Lollards by English historians is
hardly stranger than the neglect of their protagonist,
Reginald Pecock. Pecock's life is interesting (he was
deprived of his see of Chichester on the charge of heresy,
expelled from the Privy Council, and sent to Thorney Island,
there to end his days in obscurity, without even pen or ink);
but the present study will be confined to his thought, and to
his thought in relation to the Lollard Movement. Of his extant
works three have been published since 1920 by the Early
English Text Society; the other two are in the Rolls Series
and in an edition by Professor J. L. Morison respectively.

The controversy between Pecock and the Lollards may be
described as one between rationalism and biblicism. The
biblicism of the Lollards and the faith in inspiration implied
in it are interesting, and must receive attention later; but the
extent of the bishop's rationalism, together with his neglect of
ecclesiastical authority, is far more remarkable. For the
claims of reason he has the most absolute respect: he speaks
of it as the inward book lying in man's soul in contrast to the
outward book of Scripture, quaintly identifies it with the
writing in man's heart of *Jer.* xxxi. 33, and calls it the largest
book of authority that ever God made, the greatest doctor
that is this side God Himself. He admits its fallibility, but
reduces the significance of his admission by pointing out that
our senses are no less fallible and yet we trust them, and by
arguing for the formal infallibility of the syllogism. The
syllogism is, moreover, practically all-inclusive: the truths
which cannot be proved by a syllogism are merely parenthetic
in his thought. It is here, in his blindness to the place of
intuition, that his weakness, in common with other rational-
ists, lies; but one cannot escape a sympathetic admiration
for his never wearying insistence that for the knowledge of
any truth we must have convincing evidence. This principle

continues to hold, he affirms, where faith is concerned: unless we fearlessly examine the evidence for our faith, we shall be misled as often as the bay horse goes between the shafts, and for the examination we have no other power but reason. On reason he is confidently content to rely. In his life, like Erasmus, he found it better in the end to submit to the Church, but in his thought the Church's authority finds no place. It is true that he expects laymen to trust to the conclusions of the majority and of the more knowledgeable of the clergy, but that is solely on the ground that the clergy are better educated. For himself he is not afraid to abandon an article of the Church's faith, where no convincing evidence for its truth can be found. On this ground he rejects not only a basic patristic dictum of St Gregory's but the article of Christ's descent into Hell in the creed: 'it is not al trewe that bi holi men is in parchmyn ynkid'.

It is dangerous to compare men of different centuries, but the two whom Pecock resembles most nearly at first sight are perhaps Peter Abelard and Richard Hooker. Abelard and Hooker, like Pecock, had a great faith in reason; their attitude to authority, particularly ecclesiastical, was similarly negative; and they are objectively connected by their apologetic interest, and by their disapproval of tendencies which appeared to them to be obscurantist. The differences between Pecock and each of the others are still more significant for an understanding of his position. For Abelard reason remained in the sphere of divine inspiration and of the supernatural, while for Pecock it was natural in the fullest sense; with Hooker the contrast is rather in the spirit of the men, in that Pecock's rationalism is proud and contemptuous, whereas Hooker's is combined with a humble acknowledgement of the divine mysteries.

Before proceeding to a consideration of the Lollards and of their conflict with Pecock, it will perhaps be of service very briefly to recall the scholastic development in regard to these matters. The earlier medieval tendency, which persisted so long as the traditional approach with its roots in Augustine was sovereign, was to fuse the two functions of faith and reason as being merely different aspects of the same activity, an activity fundamentally supernatural. The triumph of Aristotle meant the triumph of the humanist theory of reason as natural, and may be called the turning-point of medieval theology. Henceforward faith and reason were more and more separated from each other, until at last their provinces became wholly distinct. Aquinas's attempt to harmonize the new reason with a theology built upon Augustine was magnificent, but it was an unstable harmony of incompatibles which he produced. In Scotus we see a reaction, in which an irrational scepticism demanded a new stress on the supernatural authority of the Church and on the moral autonomy of the will; but reason once admitted refused to be evicted, and in Pecock the wheel is come full circle. *His* scepticism is a rational one, it is in favour of reason at the expense of the Church; and, in that by him faith and reason are brought back into the closest relationship, it is at the expense of faith too, as faith was then understood.

To turn to the Lollards is to find ourselves in a completely different world. Perhaps the most certain thing we know about them is that they were simple, uneducated folk. They had as little of Wycliffe's scholasticism as the early Methodists had of Wesley's learning. What distinguished them from their fellows was that they read the Bible for themselves; and because they read it freely, they were not slow to see how alien to it was much of contemporary religion and to criticize accordingly. Like other undisciplined readers of it, they were prone to be captured by exaggerated ideas, of which Pecock delighted to make mock. If nothing is to be allowed except what is specifically permitted by the Bible, not only clocks and other modern conveniences must be abandoned but the more intimate necessities of life must be omitted. In fairness to Pecock it should be said that his contempt for the Lollards and their folly is tempered by a certain good-humouredness. It was hard for him that his rational preference to argue with them rather than to persecute them should have led to the Church's persecution of himself. He also went some way with the Lollards in his attitude to the Bible: he not only granted that the clergy might err in its interpretation and that only what was 'conteynyd expresseli' in the New Testament was to be regarded as 'catholik feith', he also admitted that Scripture 'ful oft expowneth hir silf', and even that sometimes one simple person may be wiser to declare what is the true sense of Scripture than is a great general council.

The conflict came over the question of authority: by what criterion was the Bible to be interpreted? The Lollards saw no necessity for a criterion. Any man might understand the Bible, they said, and he would understand it better according to his meekness, by which they meant his readiness to receive light from on high. Pecock had naturally no difficulty in showing, with a glance at disturbances in Bohemia, that such an idealistic doctrine provided no means of settling a dispute between differing interpretations by the Lollards themselves: the only possible judge, in fact, was reason, and reason dispassionately regarding the evidences offered. On this issue of evidence Pecock certainly had a case, and a case against the Church as well as against the Lollards, as the Church (to his pain) soon realized. The intensive biblicism of the Lollards evidently tended to produce, as again at the Reformation, a *Schwärmerei* of varying kinds, as the broad conception of individual inspiration, on which the notion of the individual interpretation of Scripture was ultimately based, narrowed to a conception of individual revelation. To Pecock's rationalism such a conception was entirely foreign, and not unjustly. It is amusing to find him deriding a Lollard for claiming a special revelation on the matter of total abstinence; to show sufficient evidences that God wills such an abstinence, he says, is hard, 'but if thou were in state of a prophet'.

This was the cleft which inevitably divided the parties to the controversy. With all the dangers involved in the fact, and without sufficient recognition of them, the Lollards *were* 'in state of a prophet'. Their rediscovery of the Bible had given them a new approach to life, at the root of which was a new prophetic insight. Naturally they could not express it so themselves, but that it was so becomes clear from the theories of faith which Pecock puts into their mouths and condemns. These theories are twofold. One is that faith knows a thing not by evidence judged by the understanding but by assignment of the will, and that faith varies in strength according to the strength of the will to believe; the other is that, even as the sun, by giving light to the eye and to a colour, makes the eye to see the colour, so God, by giving light to the understanding and to an article of faith, makes the understanding to believe the article, and to believe it with 'suerte' though not with 'cleerte'. The first of these theories Pecock stigmatizes as 'abhominable', the second, as 'childeli fantasies'. His cavalier treatment of them is remarkable, and significant either of his blindness or of his small concern for authority, since both theories have a respectable tradition in scholasticism. What is more important is their implication for the Lollards. Probably they would not have expressed themselves just so, as the traditional form of the theories indicates: probably Pecock was throwing into as good a rational form as he could devise the fact that, as he elsewhere complains, the Lollards put all their motive in their affection or will and not in their intellect or reason, 'and in lijk maner doon wommen'. What the Lollards had found in the Bible, as Pecock expressly admits, was an experience as delightful as their life: such an experience was something new, and, because it was new, it would not fit into the normal categories; if normal categories were to be found, Pecock's choice was very just. The Lollards were not theologians but prophets, too content with the light they had found to seek to theorize about it; and, if their biblicism sometimes led to crude absurdities, it also laid the way for an apologetic of inspiration and intuition which in their time still lay implicit.

It may be noticed that in the last resort the authority Pecock advanced for his faith was not so different from that of the Lollards. If pressed, Pecock could only have admitted that the reason, by which articles of faith are to be proved, is its own intrinsic authority, which is a telling illustration of the non-rationalism, ultimately at one with the non-rationalism of a religious conviction, to which the rationalist is eventually driven back; for he would have found it hard to defend the authority of reason by reason. A pragmatic defence he could and did give: 'we han noon other power'; but at least implicit in the Lollards' biblicism, as we have seen, was the assertion of another power, in its own sphere as imperious and impregnable as reason, the power of divine inspiration. Reliance on the one power is in the end on exactly the same footing as reliance on the other; and to live entirely by logic would be as absurd as the life to which an uncritical biblicism also led.

Conflict between the two is still a matter of experience, and the struggle between the logical and the intuitive, the classical and the romantic, the Aristotelian and the Platonic, is written large on history's face. The absorbing interest of this particular struggle is that it was the last occasion before the spirit of emancipation and individualism, which animated the combatants on both sides, revealed itself as single. Within a century Pecock's appeal to reason and the Lollards' dependence on inspiration through Scripture combined, and the combination became part of the breaking of the Middle Ages. This neither side could foresee: the Lollards could hardly divine the part which rationalism would play in assisting and developing the individualism of the Reformation, while Pecock would have scorned to recognize the force brought to the Renaissance movement by the spirit, at once lay and mystical, of the common *bourgeoisie*. Whether they foresaw it or not, it came. When, with a reference to *I Cor.* ii. 15, Luther asserted his right as a Christian to private judgement, both Pecock and the Lollards were behind him, now at one. This is the meaning of the fact that Pecock came to be so closely associated with the Lollard Movement, a fact which seems at first strange, and which, so far as conscious purposes are concerned, is not, indeed, to be justified. The Church was not wrong in recognizing the same ultimate danger in each of them: both rationalism and illuminism have an independent outlook, and, though in their extremes they may degenerate to deism and to ranterism, it was in their fusion, in the recognition of the *Christian's* right to *judge*, that the glory of the Reformation was revealed.

1938

V

THE LETTERS OF ERASMUS[1]

BY 1534 Erasmus was growing weary. He was then sixty-eight, and suspected that he had not much longer to live. 'My health is always getting worse', he wrote to his young Portuguese friend, Damian à Goes, 'my soul is preparing to flit from its wretched abode.' This was in May 1535; but even in the previous summer he had been so un-well as scarcely to go out of doors. Life had become a per-petual struggle with old age and its attendant ills, especially gout, *podagra et chiragra, vel holagra potius*, as he said. The winter was a severe one, and after Christmas he was con-fined to bed for more than two months. My lot, he wrote in February to Peter Tomiczski, the Bishop of Cracow, is the lot usual in that stage of life of which David writes, And what remains is labour and sorrow. More than once in this last volume of his letters he signs, pathetically, *Erasmus Rot. mea manu chiragrica* or *egra manu*. Sometimes he cannot sign at all. In the hope of a better climate, and also in order to see his *Ecclesiastes* through the press, he left Freiburg in the summer of 1535 for Basel (where he was welcomed with a handshake so hearty that he cried out in pain); but he gradually grew worse, till he was largely confined to his room. From a boy, he tells Tomiczski in August, he was *delicati corpusculi, rarissimaeque (ut medici loquuntur) texturae*; now that his illnesses have left him little more than skin and bone, it is natural that he cannot face the fresh air.

Somehow, he dragged through another winter, though there is a noticeable falling-off in his letters. By March 1536, he had become *clinicus pene perpetuus*, unable at times even to study. For the man who three years earlier had written *Fateor absque literis* ἀβίωτον εἶναι τὸν βίον, the end could not be long delayed. He died on the night of 11–12 July 1536.

---

[1] P. S. Allen, *Opus Epistolarum Des. Erasmi Roterodami.* Tom. XI. 1534–1536. Ediderunt H. M. Allen et H. W. Garrod. Oxford: Clarendon Press. London: Cumberlege.

For anyone who has come to know and love Erasmus, it is hard to witness the old man's physical break-up. It is clear, moreover, that he could find no comfort in the troubled world outside. For all his invalidism he remained in close contact with it to the end. As late as May 1535, Caspar Hedio, the Reformer, wrote beseeching him for a swan-song of counsel concerning the calamities *huius fermentati seculi*. In the last three months of his life he had letters from Strasbourg, Besançon, Spires, Nozeroy, Antwerp, Leipzig, Rome, Cologne and Augsburg. It was a troubled world. Gone were the days when he had watched, as he thought, the beginnings of a golden age. As recently as 1531 he still had hopes of it; but now, he writes, *videmus fatalem quandam rerum humanarum mutationem*. The word *fatalis* recurs, significantly. Everything to which he had devoted his life, the renewal of Christianity and the advance of culture alike, seemed to be breaking. *Video morbum plane fatalem.*

Of all the years of that violent period, 1535 has some claim to be considered the most savage. From the middle of 1534 the Anabaptists, with their New Jerusalem established under John of Leiden and Knipperdolling, were holding Münster against a siege by its own bishop. In England, for declining the oath of compliance with the Act of Succession Sir Thomas More and Bishop Fisher of Rochester were in prison. Both troubles came to a head in the same week of June 1535. On 24–25 June Münster fell to its besiegers, and John of Leiden and Knipperdolling were taken prisoner, to be executed later. A day or two earlier, on 22 June, Fisher was executed. More was executed on 6 July. Other terrible things were happening elsewhere. In France the King had suddenly changed his policy and turned on the heretics, burning some and condemning others to the galleys. In Africa the Emperor was at war with the Turk. But it is to Münster, and to More and Fisher, that Erasmus's correspondents repeatedly refer. The fall of Münster and the deaths of More and Fisher are the cardinal points on which the period turns.

Some of the value of contemporary letters lies in their reminder that part of what is now all past was once still future and uncertain. *Extremam porro aleam hisce diebus iacere*, wrote Viglius Zuichemus, who as diocesan Official was well placed for keeping Erasmus informed of developments, *Monasteri-umque, cunctarum haereseon sentinam, omni vi oppugnare principes nostri constituerunt.* It was a risky business. Münster, *infoelix illud anabaptistarum domicilium,* as Tielmann Gravius calls it, proved to be well fortified and quite capable of holding out. In February 1535, the issue was still in doubt, with the Anabaptist plague spreading, so that there was scarcely a town not ἐνθουσιασμῷ *Monasteriensi afflatum.* If things went on like this, it would certainly be the end of all religion and culture. When the city at last fell, Erasmus had letters from both Zuichemus and Gravius, and also an account filling several pages from Conrad Heresbach. Even then, Heresbach wrote, there had been more than a chance that John of Leiden and a faithful few would have been able to hold out for some time longer. It was *non sine fatali omine,* he thought, that the city was captured on St John the Baptist's day.

Both Zuichemus and Gravius, though mainly concerned with Münster, refer also to the troubles in England, which touched Erasmus far more nearly. The editors supply a note on the slowness of the news in reaching Erasmus, 'owing to the danger of sending compromising letters out of the country'. But eventually it did come, from various correspondents in Antwerp, Louvain, Cologne and Padua. All Europe was aghast: *O facinus inhumanissimum ac nostro seculo inauditum!* writes Christopher of Stadion, the Bishop of Augsburg. There is no letter extant between Erasmus and More after June 1533, when More had sent Erasmus a copy of the epitaph he had composed for himself (and then it had been the heretics who were feeling the weight of the king's anger). But in 1535 More is still for Erasmus *unicum illud Angliae sydus,* a man *cui pectus erat omni niue candidius,* and More's execution came as a death-blow to his friend. *In Moro mihi videor extinctus,* Erasmus wrote to Tomiczski, *adeo* μιὰ ψυχὴ *iuxta Pythagoram duobus erat.*

There is evidence that Erasmus's old affection for Bishop Fisher had cooled somewhat, but he recalls it with fidelity in the preface to his *Ecclesiastes.* This volume on preaching, on which he had been at work for twelve years, he had, indeed, intended to dedicate to Fisher; and to whom more suitably?

45

For Fisher, as he recalls, and Fisher's patroness, the Lady Margaret, had held there was no better method of reviving religion *quam si per idoneos concionatores spargatur semen Euangelicae doctrinae*. The phrase, together with his lament at the continuing scarcity of faithful preachers, looks back to those earlier happy days in England when Colet was alive, and when 'the Gospel' was not yet a party catchword. It also looks forward to the Protestant emphasis on preaching, to which, as to other Reformed emphases, Erasmus contributed.

Some of Erasmus's correspondents took him to task for not speaking out more clearly on the death of so dear and so intimate a friend as Thomas More. Erasmus, it seems, considered he had risked his English pension quite sufficiently by saying so much. Fortunately for him Cranmer and Cromwell had not seen the *Ecclesiastes*, when in September they sent him money! Nor was Erasmus above writing to thank Cromwell, and to assure him that much as he valued Cromwell's present, he valued Cromwell's favour still more highly. Erasmus always knew on which side his bread was buttered; and at his death he left 8,000 florins. 'This must be accounted wealth', say the editors, who make interesting comparisons of Erasmus's income with the rates paid in different parts of Europe to university professors. 'Certainly he never learned to live cheaply.'

Four hundred years after the death of More and Fisher, in 1935, the *noui martyres*, as they were called at once, received (within their own communion) the honour of canonization: churches may now be found under their patronage. In the wider sphere of *bonae literae*, the completion of this edition of his letters brings Erasmus into a canon, different but no less real. Few great writers of the world, few great letter-writers even, have had their correspondence edited so carefully and comprehensively and on this scale. The eleven volumes contain more than 3,100 letters (the actual number of the last letter, 3,141, is misleading, since some letters were inserted too late to be placed in sequence, and a few were written neither by nor to Erasmus), and run to nearly 6,000 pages. Of first importance is the amount of previously unpublished material included. In this last volume alone are more than forty letters never before printed, taken from libraries in

France, Germany, Italy, Switzerland, and Denmark as well as in this country—a *diaspora* reflecting in part the international character of Erasmus's friendships. The list of his correspondents fills fourteen and a half pages. Throughout the work new names, whether of correspondents or not, are identified, with bibliographical references; in many cases the biographical notices, which often depend largely on other correspondence, some of it still in manuscript, are extensive. Everything touching Erasmus—and in the years of his prime what did not?—receives attention, pride of place being given to matters literary and scholarly. The notes are in themselves an encyclopaedia of Renaissance and Reformation personalities, publications and events. Such a work could have been entertained in prospect, let alone carried through, only by a very remarkable man, who, moreover, found his life's task early.

P. S. Allen started work as long ago as 1893, under the influence of Froude, who, he always held, 'understood Erasmus as none of his other biographers have'. He continued it 'under the gloom of Indian summers and in high valleys in Kashmir'. In 1906 the first volume was published, from Longwall Cottage, Oxford, where, as Mr Garrod relates in the memoir of Allen prefixed to Vol. VIII, *una mensa capiebat et inlaboratas dapes et laboriosa scripta.* Allen went on to be Fellow and Librarian of Merton, and later President of Corpus Christi. But whatever his other duties, and they were never neglected, *cum Erasmo cenabat, dormiebat, lavabat; omnis in uno animus Erasmo.* In vacations the libraries of every country in Europe were searched; and, gradually, the help of scholars in every country was won—for Allen, as Sir Maurice Powicke has written recently, regarded academic society 'as an unselfish brotherhood with no frontiers except the frontiers imposed by the duty to maintain a high standard'. This standard is exemplified in the return journeys to foreign libraries which Allen made in order to correct the proofs from the original documents instead of from his own copies. He died in 1933; and, just as in 1536 Erasmus, had been *totus in Origene,* so to the end Allen was *totus in Erasmo:* 'the proofs were always near him'.

Those proofs were of Vol. VIII only. The last three

volumes have been edited by his widow, who throughout their married life had shared in all his work with a rare fullness, and by his friend, Professor H. W. Garrod. No pains have been spared to preserve P. S. Allen's high scholarship in every detail. A courageous struggle has been fought against odds which have included a second world war and, latterly, failing health; and it has been won. The appearance of this last volume is thus a moving tribute to unyielding fidelity and friendship, as well as the completion, after more than fifty years, of a work prosecuted with unwavering devotion. The Clarendon Press has been as faithful in its sphere as have the editors. It is good to know that a full and worthy index-volume is to follow.

During his closing years Erasmus's friends comforted him with the assurance of posterity's praise, *commemoratione clari nominis, nec apud posteros unquam intermorituri.* He accepted such comfort as not unwelcome. Had he known some of the by-ways of Christian history along which his influence would flow, he might have felt surprise. Anabaptists, for instance, he compared to the plagues of Egypt; yet by Köhler he has been called one of the spiritual fathers of the Anabaptist movement. When doubts of Christ's divinity were first raised, it was for Erasmus *prodigiosa exordia: qualis futurus sit exitus, nescio*; yet Dr Delio Cantimori, in the Basel *Gedenkschrift zum 400. Todestage,* has drawn attention to Erasmus's influence on the first Socinians, such as Blandrata, who said of him, *primus mouit hunc lapidem.* In New England Professor Perry Miller has shown Erasmus to be as much the Puritan's intellectual progenitor as was Calvin; Erasmus's *De Ciuilitate* has been suggested as the basis of George Washington's *Rules of Civility.* In the last century, the direction of attention in biblical criticism *ad ipsas fontes* and the fresh vision of Christianity as essentially a way of life both owed much to him. More recently, his thought and personality have been newly appraised by Professor Huizinga, of Holland, M. Pineau, of France and Professor Preserved Smith of America, to mention no writers nearer home. Each has drawn largely, as did T. R. Glover in these pages on the fourth centenary of Erasmus's death, on the material made more accessible, when not actually first presented, in this edition of his letters.

Not for the first time in the history of scholarship, accessibility has brought about a new interest, which in turn has brought new understanding.

A key-word for that understanding is friendship. In a society for which, in the sphere of human relationships, the ideal was conceived in terms feudal or monastic, the word inevitably possessed overtones. These are not lacking in Erasmus's use of the word; but for him its setting is less the Middle Ages than the Renaissance. This place of honour which he gave to friendship reflected, of course, his own temperament. As a young man he remarks more than once his readiness and ease in making friends. When he is nearing sixty he is still one for whom any breach in friendship is something which matters deeply—'one of the few'. In 1530 he laments the rarity of faithful friends, and says he has learned from experience both to be more careful and to care less about his friendships. But it is only a year later that a correspondent charges him with being *nimium facilis in amicicia.*

Among friends, he says, he was always inclined to blurt out whatever came into his mind. It is because he wrote as he spoke that his letters are so fascinating. For they are not only a source book for the history of Europe in a period of breathless excitement and lasting significance. They are great *letters*, the true mirror of a living personality. Ingenuousness and spontaneity were among the qualities which drew Erasmus to Colet and More. They are his own qualities also. He has many faults, he admits; but 'I cannot be other than I am'. Such as he is, he gives himself in his letters, wholly. Is not that what friendship means?

1948

VI

TOWARDS AN APPRECIATION OF ERASMUS[1]

Tʜᴇ fascination of the sixteenth century is that in it so many strands are interwoven: among others, the claims of reason and of common-sense, a stress upon personal life and the ethical, and a more direct and individual approach to God. Erasmus's books had an exceptional sale throughout the century; and the reason for his immense hold over men's minds was that he combined, in a quite remarkable manner, the first two of the three strands mentioned. The third strand was distinctly lacking; he was a cold man, temperamentally as well as physically, and the warmth of the religious reformer was not part of his make-up. Yet in him, as in no one else, at least with his gifts of expression, the reasonable and the ethical fused and joined forces.

There is much in Erasmus about *philosophia*, but Erasmus was no *doctrinaire* philosopher. It was the reasonable in its pragmatic sense of what is sensible in action which attracted him; he used *philosophia* as we use the word philosophy also, meaning a way of life. His concern lay never with abstract truth; he confesses that he was not made of martyrs' stuff, and that, even had Luther been in the right, he would prefer to be mistaken rather than to embroil himself in the fight for truth and to run the risk of losing his life on its behalf (Epp. 1218 and 1219). He also asserts his conviction that it is sometimes right to conceal the truth and recalls with approval Plato's policy of deceiving the people with lies for their own good (Ep. 1195). Just as, despite his constant appeals for mercy and moderation, he was ready to sacrifice Luther, esteeming it a little thing that one man should die for the people (Ep. 1192), so he was willing, if need be, to play fast and loose with truth. His endless jeers at the pride and folly of the scholastic philosophers were rooted in a persistent

[1] The references to Erasmus's letters are to Dr. P. S. Allen's edition; acknowledgement is also due to M. Pineau's *Erasme—sa pensée religieuse*.

tendency to a critical scepticism: what is beyond us is no concern of ours, was his opinion (Ep. 1334), and we shall do well to confine our attention to what is reasonably practicable. It is not always realized how deeply Erasmus was influenced by Origen. In 1504 he told Colet that in Origen's works he was finding all the groundwork of theology laid open and made clear (Ep. 181), in 1518 he confessed to John Eck that he learned more of the Christian way of life from a single page of Origen than from ten of Augustine (Ep. 844), and only a year before his death he began upon a Latin edition of the Father. From Origen he learned to be judicious as well as critical: *fortassis* is as frequent and as typical in Erasmus as τάχα is in Origen.

Great as was Origen's influence, Colet's was still greater; nor did that influence express itself only in providing Gibbon with the material for his epigram, 'Erasmus learned Greek at Oxford, and taught it at Cambridge.' In Colet Erasmus found an *anima naturaliter Christiana* (*cf.* Ep. 414), who drew out all that was the best in him. Men of Colet's enthusiasms did not generally attract Erasmus, but fortunately Colet combined with his prophetic fervour (Ep. 116) the saving character of elegance and culture (Ep. 1211). It was from Colet that Erasmus first learned the importance of the Christian life for the Christian, because it was in Colet that he first saw that life being effectively lived.

The time came when he could say that a pure and simple life was all that Christ demanded of us (Ep. 858), that such a spiritual life was in fact Christianity (*Ench.*, ed. 1641, p. 184). No Puritan used these words *pure* and *simple* more regularly: as in the days when the Christian faith found expression in men's lives rather than in their subscription to articles, so still it is only the pure in heart who will see God (Ep. 1334). Simplicity and purity, that is what Christ is, nothing else, in a word just what He taught (*Ench.*, p. 145). The Christ whom Erasmus follows is admittedly Christ the Teacher rather than Christ the Saviour, Erasmus even goes so far as to say that Christ was born and died in order to teach (*ibid.*, p. 194), but that is what is meant in saying that Erasmus was ethical rather than religious. Nor is his acknowledgement of his discipleship dryly intellectual. He had early found it was

51

useless to have anyone to teach you, unless he were your friend (Ep. 56), and it was in terms of friendship that he thought of his relationship to Christ. Christ is, in fact, our especial friend (*De Contempt. Mundi*, c. vii), and Christianity, again, is nothing else than a true and perfect friendship (Ep. 187). It was in His inner life rather than in His outward living that Christ's perfection lay (Ep. 858), and it is for us, with the help of the Spirit speaking to us in Scripture, to be transformed, until our interests are more worthy of Him (Ep. 1304).

The outstanding character of such a view of Christianity was its freedom. Erasmus thought freedom was man's right by nature (Ep. 11), and it was the limits set to freedom which he found objectionable in monasticism. There can be no genuineness about a forced consent, he argued; the surrender Christ desires is a voluntary one (Ep. 1334), and he resented being for ever kept in theological bearing-reins (*Ench.*, p. 192). His critical faculties had always been sharp, and he now had a further justification for using them. If much of the current practice was pharisaism and many of the current theories superstitious *impedimenta*, then an attack on them could only clear the way for a fuller recognition of the one thing needful, the spiritual life.

Erasmus therefore cast about him with a good will. The claims of reason were strong here, and Erasmus felt their strength. His classical education had gone deep, and he saw the Christian religion against the background of antiquity. That the historical sense was well developed in him is apparent from his insistence that the scholastic philosophers wrote each for his own age (Ep. 1334), and that it is important in evaluating their worth to discover in each case the temporal and causal context of their teaching, as well as the bearing of their own personalities (Ep. 1581). So with the Bible itself Erasmus was not afraid to point the likeness between the early chapters of *Genesis* and the stories in Homer, or to suggest that in breaking bread at the Last Supper Christ was following a ceremony of plighting troth common in antiquity. Nor did the similarity he observed between the pagan and the Christian hagiologies remain limited to the lesser figures; the Virgin had probably never left shore, yet

as Star of the Sea she had taken the place of Venus, Child of
the Sea, while weeping evoked by sermons on the Crucifixion
reminded him of the mourning for Adonis. Moreover, his
criticisms went further. He not only complained of the
unreasonableness of credulous devotion to such relics as those
of the Virgin's milk, he regretted that higher honour was
paid to, deeper trust felt in, the Virgin than her Son. He was
also downright in his condemnation of any *opus operatum*
notion of the sacraments. He refused to recognize baptism as
constituting a man a Christian (*Ench.*, pp. 173f.), and remarked that he failed to find any indelible character attributed to the ceremony by the apostles; so also he could allow
no efficacy to the Eucharist apart from the working of the
Spirit.

It is the mention of the Spirit which reminds us of the
double strain in Erasmus, and which forces us to recognize
that his criticisms of contemporary Christianity were by no
means due solely to a half-pagan preference for the antiquity
he so much loved. The rediscovery of the present Spirit of
God was at the root of the greater stress on ethics and human
personality, and, no less than the reasonableness issuing from
antiquity, was responsible for the freedom of Erasmus's
approach. The Spirit, he said, is above all human laws, it is
even above the Pope and general councils; and, ideally at
least, when one is spiritually adult, one needs the law no
longer, however valuable educatively it may have proved.
From such a judgement to the undermining of the prestige
of a sacerdotal and authoritarian Church was but a small
step, and it was a step which Erasmus did not hesitate to take,
in principle. The true Church he defined as the Christian
people; it is for them to hear, with fairness but not uncritically, those who are in name, and should be in fact, their
ministers, and if necessary to reject their teaching. This they
may do, just because of the reality of the Spirit, and just because the possibility of the spiritual life, as outlined above, is
open to all.

So Erasmus taught, in principle: the freedom of the
Spirit, he says himself, was the burden of his message (Ep.
1887); the tragedy is that he came to regret having taught it
(*ibid.*). In 1519 he still thought he could see the beginnings

of a golden age, the world was waking up from sloth and slumber (Ep. 966, *cf.* Ep. 333); only six years later he lamented, not this time, it would seem, in Horatian vein, but in all seriousness, that everyone he knew was becoming not better but worse (Ep. 1887). The age he had seen beginning was the age of the Reformation; theologically his quarrel with the Reformers was over predestination and freewill, but deeper than this, and not unrelated to it, was their disagreement over the freedom of the Spirit. Already in 1523 Erasmus started his withdrawal in admitting to Zwingli that the discernment of spirits was a rare gift (Ep. 1384): as Henry VIII had once remarked to a man who claimed to have been inspired by the Spirit to attack the study of Greek, there was the spirit of folly as well as of Christ (Ep. 948); so now Erasmus, who had always been suspicious of unreasonable spirituality, feared that the Spirit of which the Reformers made so much was the spirit of Satan (Ep. 1483). He found good reason for so thinking, as he believed, in the issue of allegiance to their Spirit; for that issue was not freedom but unharnessed licentiousness (Ep. 1887), which meant in fact an enslavement worse than the old (Ep. 1597). Here, again, the two strands always to be found in Erasmus were at work. Often it is the scholar who appears, ever seeking the will-o'-the-wisp of *tranquillitas*, and wistfully longing once again for the integrity of the monastery library, the years having softened the memories of what he found there without having weakened the ideal with which he first entered it. Yet we see also the Christian, saddened beyond any expectation to find that the free and simple Christianity he had taught, the spiritual life of friendship with Christ, was being not so much overlaid as used and plundered in support of a life of dissension and of licence.

The truth is that Erasmus had himself to suffer for the reasonableness which in the general course of events proved of prime importance. The epigram of the Cologne friars about Erasmus's laying the egg and Luther's hatching it (Ep. 1528) was, in one way, strictly true; Erasmus's own view was that Lutheranism was nourished on the humanities (Ep. 1977), and towards the popularizing of the humanities, with the reasonable attitude towards Christianity which they

54

favoured, no one had done more than himself. It was on the other side of their characters that Erasmus and Luther were as opposite poles. Of Augustine, in whom, after Paul, Luther's storm-tossed soul found the most satisfying teacher of Christianity, Erasmus had the audacity to remark that his conscientiousness seemed a little meticulous, and the remark goes deep: Erasmus was too easily good ever to understand the psychology of the twice-born and the whirlpool of sin, in the escape from which the Lutheran Reformation took its birth. Erasmus went back to Christ the Teacher rather than to Paul; and so late as 1530 we find him expressing a real admiration for St Francis and for those who have *sincerely* sought to follow Christ by walking in Francis's steps (Ep. 2300). This appreciation is revealing, especially to a generation which finds the ideal of St Francis, if not his actual behaviour, so attractive. It should serve to balance Gibbon's other remark about Erasmus, that he was the father of rational theology. This he was; but he was also an influential leader in the succession of those to whom the essence of Christianity has been a life of friendship with the Christ who went about doing good.

1936

55

VII

THE PRINCIPLES OF CONGREGATIONALISM
IN THEIR HISTORICAL SETTING

THE name 'Congregational' was not in use before the 1640's, but the movement has its roots in the Reformation. It is no coincidence that the word 'Reformation' occurs in the title of one of Congregationalism's foundation-documents, *A Treatise of Reformation without tarrying for Anie*, published by Robert Browne in 1582.

For ordinary people, at least in England from 1540 onwards, the main effect of the Reformation was that the Bible was available in their own tongue. Without persecution, they were free to read it, or more often hear it read, and to meditate upon it, and to interpret it, for themselves. With this went also the new practice of worshipping God in the vernacular, and so intelligibly. At first, the impact of the Bible as a document was sufficient, and men were satisfied to read it historically and to treat it as a wondrous story but no more. Soon, however, it began to speak inwardly to the hearts of the most sensitive and conscientious, and men found they were invited themselves to share in biblical religion, to enter into biblical experience. Those to whom this insight was given tended inevitably to grow impatient with what to them seemed the more satisfied, conventional religion of the dominant party in the Established Church. Some hoped in time to bring the Church to fuller reform by working from within. Others in despair felt driven to break away from the Church and the Church's subservience to prelate, parliament, and magistrate, and to form new groups in which they could be free to worship and to live according to their consciences, as these were constrained by the demands of Scripture and by the response of the Holy Spirit in their hearts.

All these men, whether remaining within the Church or not, were nicknamed Puritans, because they passionately desired, and repeatedly urged the need for, purity in worship, church government and personal life. Those who separated from the Church were also called Separatists, but they were none the less Puritans. Their separation was not undertaken lightly or fractiously but only because they felt impelled to seek the way of church life enjoined in Scripture. They called the new groups which they formed 'gathered churches'. They called them *gathered* churches, because they believed they were gathered by the Spirit of God: by the God who called to men, 'Come ye out from among them, and be ye separate, and touch no unclean thing'; who gathered those He had redeemed from the east and from the west, and from the north and from the south; and who through Christ had promised His presence to those gathered in His name. They also called them gathered *churches*, because they believed churches to be just such societies of men and women who knew, and who manifested, the gifts and graces of God's Spirit.

This will be seen at once to have implications for the nature of the Church and of its membership; but two of the principles involved, which in fact were determinative for Congregationalism, may perhaps be less evident now than they were then, when they were revolutionary. One is the voluntary principle: that 'the Lords people is of the willing sorte'; 'for it is the conscience and not the power of man that will driue vs to seeke the Lordes kingdome'. The other is the separatist principle that Christians must separate, not only from the world, but, if necessary, from the Church, if the Church has become so far worldly as to 'haue all aloft by ciuill power and authoritie . . . that men may say, Loe the Parliament, or loe the Bishoppes decrees'.[1] These two principles join in a recognition of the inwardness of true religion, as their exponents rediscovered this in their English Bibles, and of the New Testament's demand for consecrated personalities; and it was from this angle that they approached the nature of the Church. The accepted Reformed insistence on the preaching of the word and the administration of the sacraments as the marks of the Church was not regarded as adequate, 'for the word could be preached and the sacrament administered to "assemblies of unbelievers" '[2]; these marks

[1] Robert Browne, *Treatise of Reformation*, ed. T. G. Crippen, 1903, pp. 25, 21.
[2] Perry Miller, *Orthodoxy in Massachusetts, 1630–50*, Harvard University Press, 1933, p. 57, with reference to John Robinson, *Works*, ed. R. Ashton, 1851, III. 428.

were, in fact, to be found in the Church of England, and yet that Church had been weighed and found wanting. 'He is a christian which is redeemed by Christ vnto holines & happines for ever & professeth the same by submitting him self to his lawes & government'[1]; and the Church is made up of such Christians. It is a high doctrine of the Church, which implies a maximum of seriousness in the desire to serve Christ faithfully. But it is also true, in A. C. McGiffert's words, that 'to Browne . . . the believer is first, and the Church second, for the Church is nothing else than a community or assembly of those already saints'[2]: not in the sense that the believer normally (though he does sometimes) comes to his faith apart from direct contact with the believing community, but that the Church is defined in terms of the believers of whom it consists, and without whom and whose active and professing belief, and whose consequent profession and evident holiness, it cannot exist.

From this angle Congregationalism may be seen as one of the earliest attempts in England seriously to work out ecclesiologically the meaning of the Reformation doctrine of the priesthood of all believers; to give due and continuing weight to the recovery at the Reformation of immediacy in the relation between the soul and God. This is not to say that the early Congregationalists were individualists or isolationists. On the contrary, they rediscovered much of the reality and glow of New Testament *koinonia*. But in that fellowship, and in the presence and will of Christ made known in and through it, they found all they desired, and—more importantly—all they believed He desired. They were called Independents, because they claimed independence of outer control, ecclesiastical control, whether by bishop or presbytery, no less than secular; but they sought such independence only in order to become more fully dependent on the Lord's will made known to them, and sufficiently made known, in their church meetings. Similarly, they came to be called Congregationalists, because they claimed the right of all members of the congregation to a share in the direction of the church's affairs in these church meetings; but they

[1] Robert Browne, *op. cit.*, p. 27.
[2] A. C. McGiffert, *Protestant Thought before Kant*, 1911, p. 136.

claimed this as a right, because they saw it as a duty and a privilege, in response to the movings in all their hearts, as they met together, of the Spirit of Christ.

Such is the rationale of early Congregationalism. Historically, the elaboration of the principles which soon emerged, where they had not been perceived at once, was facilitated by a recurrence of the conditions which first gave rise to the movement, conditions, namely, of persecution by the dominant majority. During the first hundred years persecution was not continuous but came in four main waves of repressive activity issuing from Lambeth during the primacies of Whitgift, Bancroft, Laud, and Sheldon. In each of the first three periods one name stands out among Congregational leaders: in the first, Robert Browne, to whose *Treatise of Reformation* (1582) reference has already been made; in the second, John Robinson, who wrote *A Iustification of Separation* (1610) and an *Apologia* (1619), and who went into exile at Leyden, where he was pastor of the church some of whose members in 1620 sailed to New England in the *Mayflower*; and in the third, John Cotton, who in 1633, likewise removed to New England, and whose most influential works in defence of Congregationalism were *The Keyes of the Kingdom of Heaven* (1644), *The Way of the Churches . . . in New-England* (1645) and *The Way of the Congregational Churches cleared* (1648).

Though three of his contemporaries, Barrow, Greenwood, and Penry, were martyred, Robert Browne, after much suffering, renounced his Separatist principles and conformed. John Robinson was anxious to distinguish those associated with him from the Brownists and Barrowists, and at the end of his life became less extreme in his Separatism. John Cotton's path is described in the introduction to his *Keyes* as 'that very Middle-way between that which is called Brownisme, and the Presbyteriall-government'.[1] Robinson, indeed, does not seem to have been directly influenced by Browne, nor Cotton by Robinson. Both Robinson and Cotton came to their position under the influence, rather, of such convinced but still conformist Puritans as William Perkins and Richard Sibbes; but they came to it independently,

[1] *Op. cit.*, introduction by Thomas Goodwin and Philip Nye, p. vii.

through their own study of Scripture, and also through the pressure of a persecuting Church. When this pressure was removed, as largely in Holland and entirely in New England, it was natural for their claims to grow more moderate and their exposition more conservative. In New England, where there was neither priest nor presbyter to contend with, Congregationalism from the start reverted nearer to the parochial and presbyteral pattern.

Not so, however, in old England, where in the 1640's 'the turmoil of civil war gave centrifugal religious forces a long-sought opportunity'.[1] Then, and still more under the protection of the Commonwealth legislation, Congregational churches sprang up in considerable numbers and with full conviction of their voluntary and separatist principles. 'By 1650 the New Englanders were an isolated faction'[2]; and the Independency of the Commonwealth was of a radical and self-assured type, conscious of its difference from the Presbyterianism which for a time had been established in England and still flourished in Scotland. In September 1658, the elders and messengers of the Congregational churches met in London at the Savoy and issued a *Declaration of the Faith and Order Owned and practised* in those churches, with an appendix 'Of the Institution of Churches, and Order appointed in them by Jesus Christ'. The principles set forth in this document are 'in substance . . . identical with the principles'[3] maintained by Browne and Robinson. Christ calls men out of the world into communion with Himself, it is stated, and commands those thus called to walk together in particular societies or churches. These gathered churches consist of officers and members; the members (who are described first) being 'Saints by calling, visibly manifesting and evidencing (in and by their profession and walking) their obedience unto that Call of Christ'; and the officers, 'Pastors, Teachers, Elders and Deacons', being chosen by the church and set apart for those duties, without thereby excluding from preaching 'others also gifted and fitted by the Holy Ghost for it, and approved'. 'Besides these particular Churches, there is not

[1] Perry Miller, *op. cit.*, p. 269.
[2] Perry Miller, *The New England Mind: the seventeenth century*, New York, 1939, p. 434.
[3] R. W. Dale, *History of English Congregationalism*, 1907, p. 385.

instituted by Christ any Church more extensive or cath-olique.' It was a bold manifesto: and even so was less radical than English practice, for its admission of occasional synods after the New England pattern, carefully defined though these were as 'not entrusted with any Church-Power, prop-erly so-called, or with any Jurisdiction over the Churches themselves', does not seem to have been followed.

Under the novel and experimental ecclesiastical establish-ment set up by Cromwell, some 130 Congregational ministers accepted parochial livings. The number is a small propor-tion of those who were ejected at the Restoration, for these numbered over 1,900, and some of the most outstanding of Commonwealth Congregationalists had abandoned their livings earlier or had never been beneficed. Even so, it is remarkable that in a movement so closely bound up with Separatism there were any who at any time were ready to be incumbents.

With the Act of Uniformity of 1662, and the repressive measures which followed it, there was a return to the *status quo antea*; with the important difference that, though having had less than a generation of favour, the Congregational churches were now consolidated. Crippling persecution and exclusion their members were again to endure, and associa-tions with Holland and New England were renewed, par-ticularly for the education now denied them at home; but there was no fresh large-scale emigration. The outstanding name in this period, as indeed already during the Common-wealth, is that of John Owen, a former chaplain of Crom-well's, who had also been Dean of Christ Church, Oxford, from 1651 to 1660, and Vice-Chancellor of the University from 1652 to 1657. Owen had been converted to Independ-ency by Cotton's *Keyes*, and was thus in sympathy with the less extreme type of Congregationalism: Stoughton, indeed, calls him 'a very decided Conservative'.[1] Between Owen's *Eschol: or Rules of Direction for the Walking of the Saints in Fellowship* (1648) and his posthumous *True Nature of a Gospel Church and its Government* (1689) there is a development com-parable with that noted in John Robinson's thought. In this last treatise, however, as in others of his writings, reappear the

[1] John Stoughton, *History of Religion in England*, 2nd edn., 1881, II. 249.

familiar principles. 'The church is a voluntary society', consisting of 'persons called saints separated from the world', who 'make an open profession' of their subjection to Christ, some of whom are chosen by the church and set apart as officers, and some of whom teach or preach, although they are not pastors. Owen was also in the mainstream of Congregational tradition in writing a comprehensive *Pneumatologia: or a Discourse concerning the Holy Spirit* (1674). In two further *Discourses concerning the Holy Spirit* (1693) he emphasizes the charismatic basis of true ministry.

That the ministry is, on the one hand, thus dependent on the immediate call of the Holy Spirit and, on the other, is dependent on the church's call and choice, has made it as impossible for Congregationalists to define the Church in terms of the ministry as in terms of the word preached and the sacraments administered by the ministry. 'The Church is before the Ministers, seeing the power of choosing Ministers is given by Christ unto the Church'.[1] In accordance with this principle, John Owen lays it down that while the ministry is necessary to render a church 'completely organical', yet men may 'become a church essentially before they have any ordinary pastor or teacher'.[2] The principle is seen in practice in the fact that many small churches have existed, and exist today, without a minister, as did the Pilgrim Fathers for nine years. The fact may be regretted, it may tend to lead to dissolution, but in itself it in no way unchurches them. As recently as 1929 the Assembly of the Congregational Union repudiated with vehemence the phrase that the ministry 'is essential to the being', and not only to the well-being, 'of the Church'.

We have dealt at large with the first century of Congregational history, because it was during those years that the fundamental principles of Congregationalism were first worked out, as the result of deep personal conviction and at the cost of much suffering. In the succeeding centuries the principles have been coloured by other movements within the Church at large, such as the Moravian, the Methodist,

---

[1] [Richard Mather], *Church-Government and Church-Covenant Discussed*, 1643, p. 15.
[2] John Owen, *Works*, ed. W. H. Goold, 1850–5, IV. 496.

the Evangelical, even the Oxford, certainly the Missionary movements. They have also been applied to meet changing circumstances and needs; but they have not been added to. Some of the main applications may now be mentioned.

The insistence on holiness rather than orthodoxy, for instance, has led to interesting results, which have often been misunderstood. Congregationalists have adopted the position of the Dissenting Brethren, who in the *Apologeticall Narration* (1643), wrote: 'We took measure of no man's holinesse by his opinion.' They hold that the formulation of creeds is the proper concern of theologians but not of Christians with little possibility of understanding them, and that living doctrine springs from personal experience of the grace of Jesus Christ as made known to us in Scripture and of His continuing presence in the fellowship of the Church. Their efforts, therefore, have been to bring and to keep experience under the influence of the Holy Spirit. They have customarily asked those desirous of church membership not for formal subscription to creed or catechism, however venerable or widely accepted, but for a statement in their own words of their faith and experience. The disuse of creeds as a test of membership, or even as a confession recited in worship, must lead, many Christians of other communions suppose, to vagueness, if not error, in doctrine. On the contrary, Congregationalists have, in fact, kept very much to the middle path of Evangelical Christianity; and they believe that their freedom on the whole from the heresies and even the latitudinarianism, which have troubled other communions, is due largely to their refusal to trammel the true latitude of Scripture in fixed and narrower formulae, and to their genuinely trusting in the freedom of God's living Spirit. At the same time, such convictions have been accompanied, inevitably, and Congregationalists believe rightly, by a very wide doctrinal tolerance. Philip Doddridge, for instance, in the eighteenth century, and R. W. Dale in the nineteenth, were as outspoken as the early Congregationalists in their determination not to exclude any who doctrinally might be lacking or eccentric or mistaken, but whose devotion to Jesus Christ was equally unmistakable.

In this way, as the Presbyterian Robert Baillie complained

in the seventeenth century, Congregationalism is 'become a uniting Principle'.[1] 'Heads need not breed differences in hearts.'[2] 'Differences, or rather indifferences, . . . in some point of doctrine or discipline . . . need not interrupt the unity of Spirit.'[3] So far from having led to narrowness, the path of Separatism has led into a large room, where, by putting first things first, and only first things, men of varying intellectual gifts and judgements find it possible to be at one. Today, as in 1662, Congregationalists find themselves unable to abandon such unity already gained on a basis of large mutual trust and spiritual freedom for the offer of comprehension in a system limited to particular ecclesiological theories or practice of a narrower nature. They believe rather that they possess a genuine catholicity, the preservation of which eventually will prove in others' interests as well as their own.

The mutual trust, as well as the faith in God, which the practice of Congregationalism demands, originally found expression, as it still sometimes does, in the covenants which church members drew up, especially at the gathering of a new church. In these they gave themselves to God and to one another to walk together before Him in all His ways known or to be made known. The formal importance of the covenant has perhaps been overstressed in some recent Congregational apologia, for the seventeenth century was an age when covenants of all kinds were fashionable; they were not in the least a speciality of Congregational ecclesiology, as might now appear. What the covenant implied was mainly what would now be called committal and mutual trust: it helped to ensure church members' seriousness in their profession, in their care for one another, and in their endeavours to fulfil their duty in the life of the church.

One main duty was to take part in the direction of the church's life at regularly held church meetings. As has appeared, this was in origin a spiritual principle. Though complained of already in the seventeenth century as 'popular' and 'democratic', it was not politically egalitarian in in-

1 Robert Baillie, *A Dissuasive from the Errours of the Time*, 1645, p. 93.
2 John Cook, *What the Independents would have*, 1647, p. 11.
3 John Milton, *Areopagitica*, 1644, p. 38 in Everyman (1927) edition.

tent; it was a practical recognition, rather, of what Troeltsch calls Christians' 'negative equality' before God, that is to say, their common sinfulness and equal unworthiness. It did, however, have important consequences for democratic practice. Englishmen were familiar with habits of discussion, more or less free, in Parliament before the seventeenth century; but the patience in discussion, the respect for others' judgements, the tolerance shown to minorities and the willingness to accept the majority's decision, which had been learned and practised in Congregational church meetings, came to be extended to secular groups, including Parliament itself. In the present state of the world, Congregationalists may still give something here, though not directly except within the context of the Church. Church meetings rest on a basis of unity already reached in a common faith in the guidance of God and in a common desire to discover His will; and in the nature of the case this is not present in a purely secular context.

A further character developed in those taking part in church meetings, developed indeed through the immediate response of the individual soul to God of which church meetings are themselves an expression, has been moral responsibility, both in witnessing to Christ and in being called to the service of men. The stress on visible holiness has not led to pietism of an introverted nature. On the contrary, a much cherished part of Congregational tradition has been that in the day-to-day lives of its members the life of the church should be carried into the life of the world and the Lordship of Christ be proclaimed. Especially in local government and local education, since finally with the repeal of the Test Act in 1828 both these spheres have again been opened to them, Congregationalists have played a not inconsiderable part. Much earlier they supported the Charity School movement, as also the still continuing Sunday School movement. In 1795 they shared in the foundation of the London Missionary Society, and on characteristically broad principles. The Society's purpose is 'not to send Presbyterianism, Independency, Episcopacy, or any other form of Church Order and Government . . . but the glorious Gospel of the blessed God'; and its unsectarian character was a factor in the choice of the

Society by David Livingstone, who was himself a Congregationalist. Again, in the movements against slavery, the exploitation of children, and war, as in turn these have troubled the Christian conscience, Congregationalists, and often Congregational laymen, have taken their full share. They have been accustomed to take a responsible part in church government, and to some extent in the leading of public worship, and this has made it easier for them to take a similar part also in Christian movements in wider spheres.

In every century, Congregationalism, in its doctrine of the Church, as indeed in all else, has thus built upon a foundation of what was once called 'visible holiness': what we should now call 'consecrated personality'. Theologically, this has been an expression of the doctrine of the Holy Spirit, discovered anew in Scripture and sealed by the known continuing activity of the Spirit in men's hearts. If seemingly a slender foundation for an ecclesiology, it is at least Biblical and Hebraic. Congregationalists remark that in much of the best contemporary biblical scholarship the Hebrew genius, the Hebrew insight into God's nature and ways with men, is receiving new attention and exposition. They believe that this may lead in time to a deeper understanding of the spiritual principles upon which Congregationalism rests.

1950

VIII

THE INFLUENCE OF ARMINIANISM
IN ENGLAND[1]

I AM inclined to begin by recounting two recent incidents which together may serve as an interesting pointer. Among the papers set for a higher degree in one of the English universities is an essay paper, with three or four alternative subjects; and one of these, a few years ago, I remember, ran thus: ' "Since Wesley we are all Arminians": discuss.' One of the alternatives that year was an invitation to discuss the dictum, 'Thou shalt not suffer a witch to live'; so we need not assume that the assertion that Arminianism is now universally accepted was regarded as indisputable! It is interesting, nonetheless, that the assertion could be made.

The other incident happened more recently. I was speaking of this Arminius-Symposium to a friend who, though not a minister, has written one or two books on subjects relating to Wesleyan Methodism; and I received the answer, 'Do you know, I never realized that there was anyone called Arminius!' In part, no doubt, this reflects the contented ignorance of theology common among Englishmen; but to a shrewd observer it may suggest the genuine triumph of Arminianism. In the last decades there has been a revival of Calvinism in Europe; but a revival of Arminianism is difficult to imagine. 'Since Wesley we are all Arminians' whether we know it or not, whether we have ever heard of Arminius or not. Arminius has triumphed much as, in a far shorter time, Sigmund Freud has triumphed: all of us think differently because of Freud, even those who have never heard of him.

'The influence of Arminianism in England': it is a vast subject. 'How interesting!' said a clergyman of the Church of England to me; 'Lancelot Andrewes and Archbishop Laud and all those people in their struggles with the Puritans in the seventeenth century.' Truly, the doctrinal transformation of the Church of England in the generation between the Synod of Dort and the death of Laud would amply repay

[1] A paper read to an Arminius-Symposium at Amsterdam in August 1961.

a paper on its own account. The oft-repeated *bon mot* in reply to the question 'What do the Arminians hold?', namely 'The best livings in all England', was by no means devoid of truth; it is a pity, however, if the witticism diverts attention from a change of sentiment which raised genuine theological issues as well as social, political, and financial—not to mention the philosophical issues so attractively presented in Dr Colie's recent study, *Light and Enlightenment* (Cambridge, 1957).

'The influence of Arminianism in England': 'how interesting!' said another friend to me, too. But he is a Unitarian; and he thought of the subject as connoting the dawn of the light of reason in religion: the light which, as the eighteenth century proceeded, would break out into bright sunshine, in Arianism and Socinianism.

Any English Methodist, meanwhile, regards Arminianism as his own communion's peculiar preserve; and not unjustly. Did not the Methodists institute in 1778 a periodical with the brave title, *The Arminian Magazine: consisting of extracts and original treatises on universal redemption*? Even in 1778, apparently, an Arminian could regard the Battle of the Decrees as won. 'Whatsoever was the case in times past,' writes the editor, John Wesley, in the first number, 'very few now receive them (the Decrees) even in Holland. And in Geneva they are universally rejected with the utmost horror. The case is nearly the same in England.' In 1778 Arminius' name was still in use, as a bogey; it was not much more. 'We know nothing more proper to introduce a work of this kind', Wesley continues, 'than a sketch of the Life and Death of Arminius; a person, with whom those who mention his name with the utmost indignity, are commonly quite unacquainted; of whom they know no more than of Hermes Trismegistus.'[1] It is fair to observe that after only one generation the commemoration of Arminius gave place to an eponymous title: in 1805 *The Arminian Magazine* became *The Wesleyan Methodist Magazine*.

Then there are the Quakers, who in the pages of history precede the Methodists by almost a hundred years. They seem always to have been universalists. Arminians without Arminius one might venture to term them, remembering their noted

[1] *The Arminian Magazine*, I, 1778, pp. viii, v.

abhorrence of all 'notions', as they called theology. They would then offer an inviting avenue for exploration in the search for the *anima naturaliter Arminiana* in a century when so little is allowed to be natural. In fact, however, the first Quakers were not wholly in ignorance of Arminius. They were not allowed to be by the writers who controverted their universalism. One of the largest and most effective defences of early Quakerism is to be found in a treatise published in 1660 by Samuel Fisher, the subject of a recent dissertation by Miss Edna Hall. Samuel Fisher had begun his career as a clergyman of the Church of England, and before this he had enjoyed a university education; so it was somewhat ironically that he entitled his book *Rusticus ad Academicos*. It takes the form of a reply to attacks on Quakerism by four eminent contemporaries, Richard Baxter, John Owen, John Tombes, and Thomas Danson. 'These Four', Fisher says, 'do as one man withstand and resist this Truth the Qua:(kers) testifie, concerning the general love and Grace of God in Christ Jesus to all mankind, i.e. every individual man.' 'Arminiana sunt omnia jamdudum profligata', 'they are all Arminius his matters (quoth J.O.), Arminian points (quoth T.D.), thus they stun men's minds; not knowing', Fisher adds, with alliterative emotion, 'that Arminius (though deem'd and doom'd an Heretick by that Divine and domineering denunciation of the Divines at Dort) was as no less learned, so fully as holy and honest as themselves'.[1]

But it is not only in the variegated life of those denominations which make the story of English Protestantism such a multi-coloured picture that the subject, 'The influence of Arminianism in England', is vast. If at all adequately dealt with, it would include, besides the gradual, and eventually almost insensible, adoption of the doctrine of general redemption, consideration of the increasingly large place allowed to reason in religion as over against superstition; and also the growth in mutual tolerance among Christians; and then in the toleration of multiformity in religion by the State, which came to accompany this. All these phenomena, undoubtedly, had other theological, and also other more secular, contributory causes besides what may, broadly

[1] Samuel Fisher, *Rusticus ad Academicos*, 1660, iv. 83f.

speaking, be called Arminianism; but Arminianism played no small part. In the English scene in the seventeenth century the cause of religious liberty owed much, undeniably, to the Independents; but 'it is a natural conjecture', as Douglas Nobbs has written, 'that the Independents were directly inspired by Remonstrant principles, particularly as (Philip) Nye developed theories closely related to the argument of Episcopius', who 'valued the liberty of sects as a moral pearl of great price'.[1]

When the field is so large, it is essential, within the compass of a single lecture, to delimit the part to be ploughed. Now it is worthy of remark that self-confessed Arminianism in England is to be found, in the main, in one or other of two contrasting movements. One of these two movements leads on into Arianism, Socinianism, and Unitarianism and eventually decreases in numbers and influence. The other remains Trinitarian and Evangelical, and increases. Why is this so? It is largely from within the confines of this question that we shall regard the subject. The answer, if we can find one, should be illuminating.

First, let me illustrate the way things went in the eighteenth century, when Arminian tenets were adopted in churches which already existed; and let me do so from the situation in Wales. The history of religion in Wales has its differences from the history of religion in England, but at this point the story is one and the same; and the area of the Principality is sufficiently small and compact to allow a reasonably comprehensive but brief survey.

The first great name here is that of Jenkin Jones, an Independent who, it is interesting to note, appears under the heading 'Arminian minister' in the *Dictionary of Welsh Biography* published last year by the Honourable Society of Cymmrodorion, where he is described as 'the apostle of Arminianism'.[2] Jenkin Jones began to preach the new doctrines in opposition to the Calvinism traditional among the Independents in 1726. In 1733 he built a meeting-house at

[1] Douglas Nobbs, *Theocracy and Toleration*, Cambridge, 1938, pp. 105, 103.
[2] *Dictionary of Welsh Biography*, 1959, ed. Sir John Lloyd and R. T. Jenkins, *s.v.* For the English reader this *Dictionary* provides a convenient account of Arminianism in Wales: see the articles on the ministers mentioned in the following paragraphs.

Llwynrhydowen in Cardiganshire, 'the first Arminian chapel in Wales'. After his death in 1742 he was succeeded in the pastorate by his nephew, David Lloyd. Now David Lloyd, who died in 1779, was apparently an Arian; his assistant and successor, David Davis, certainly was so. Another generation passed and Arianism began to give way to Unitarianism. In 1802 David Lloyd's son Charles, who had declared himself a Unitarian, led a secession of sympathizers from Llwynrhydowen to found two distinct Unitarian churches. This is regarded as 'the official beginning of Unitarianism in Cardiganshire', and thus in Wales as a whole. David Davis, who continued at Llwynrhydowen, remained an Arian; but after his retirement in 1820 the church proved unable to stand against the new trend. His successor in the pastorate, John Davies, was a Unitarian; and today Llwynrhydowen is regarded as the mother-church of Unitarianism in Wales.

A similar development may be watched elsewhere in the Principality. At Cwm-y-glo, Merthyr Tydfil, in Glamorganshire, the first minister to preach Arminian tenets was Roger Williams. In 1730 he died, and his assistant and successor, James Davies, remained a Calvinist; but the minister chosen to assist Davies, Richard Rees, was an Arminian; and in 1747 Rees led a secession from Cwm-y-glo to form a new church at Cefncoedcymer. This church, like Llwynrhydowen, has long since been Unitarian. Later in the century, in 1787, the same thing took place at Glandwr in Pembrokeshire. Seventeen members were excommunicated for Arminianism, and formed a new church across the county border in Carmarthenshire at Rhydyparc. This church likewise in time became Arian, and by 1848 its minister was a Unitarian.

Llwynrhydowen, Cwm-y-glo and Glandwr were all Independent churches. Arminian tenets also appeared at much the same time among the Baptists in Wales who, like the Independents, were traditionally Calvinist. In 1749 Charles Winter, the assistant minister of the church at Hengoed in Glamorganshire, was excommunicated for Arminianism, and with twenty-three sympathizers formed a new church at Craig-y-fargod. By 1792 the minister of Craig-y-fargod, Daniel Isaac, had become a Unitarian. He resigned; but by 1809 the church itself had become Unitarian.

In 1790 Craig-y-fargod was still the only Arminian Baptist church in the Principality;[1] but nine years later a fresh wave of Arminianism broke over the Welsh Baptists, and a number of churches seceded on these grounds. The sequel here is interesting. By this time Evangelical Arminianism, in the form of Wesleyan Methodism, was at last, belatedly, making itself felt in Wales. Those Arminian Baptist churches whose ministers welcomed the Wesleyans are found rejoining before long their former co-religionists, the Calvinist or Particular Baptists. The other Arminian Baptist churches, but three of which are still in existence, Wick and Nottage in Glamorganshire, and Pant Teg in Carmarthenshire, eventually, like Craig-y-fargod, became Unitarian.[2]

In England, as is well known, the same steady movement of those Dissenters who had espoused Arminian tenets towards Arianism and Socinianism took place throughout the eighteenth century. In England the movement affected not so much the Independent and Baptist as the Presbyterian churches; till by 1844, when the present Presbyterian Church of England took its rise, of the older English Presbyterian churches which still existed scarcely one had not become Unitarian. Why, the question I want to ask is, did this development not likewise affect the Methodist Societies which arose in much the same period, since these were equally insistent in their proclamation of Arminianism? By and large Methodism, while remaining unashamedly Arminian, has also continued Trinitarian. It is true that in 1817 there was a small secession in Lancashire, the supporters of which took the title of Methodist Unitarians; but they never spread beyond the district of their origin and they can hardly be said to possess much significance for historical theology (though they may for the history of Chartism).[3]

Let us ask another question. Whence, and why, did the Methodist Societies adopt Arminianism? Or perhaps this

---

[1] Joshua Thomas, *History of the Baptist Association in Wales*, 1795, p. 55.

[2] For this paragraph, see *Dict. Welsh Biog.*, *s.vv.* James Davies (1767?–1860), Evan Lloyd (1764–1847), Benjamin Phillips (1750–1839), William Thomas, (d. 1813), Moses Williams (d. 1810).

[3] See H. McLachlan, *The Methodist Unitarian Movement*, Manchester, 1919.

question is too large. Whence, then, and why, did Wesley adopt Arminianism? Possible answers to this question are many, but I propose to suggest three. The first is that Wesley was born and grew up in a favourable area: Arminianism was in the air he breathed. Lincolnshire was a stronghold of Arminianism in England almost a century before the new doctrine reached Wales. To begin with, the first English Baptist, John Smyth, who also became the first English General or Arminian Baptist, was from the Lincolnshire town of Gainsborough, not far from Wesley's birthplace. True, Smyth did not become an Arminian until after he had removed to the Netherlands in 1608; but his influence may have continued among those whom he left behind him, or have been restored by some of his companions in exile who returned home. This is conjecture; but by 1651 the Arminian Baptist movement in Lincolnshire was sufficiently conscious, organized and vocal for it to supply twelve out of the thirty churches in eight English Midland counties which in that year issued a joint *Faith and Practice;* and by 1673 there were as many as thirty-three centres in the county.[1] The part of Lincolnshire called the Isle of Axholme, moreover, of which Epworth, Wesley's birthplace and early home, is the capital, was particularly Arminian. In 1669 it was reported to the Bishop of Lincoln that the General Baptist conventicle in the parish of Epworth numbered fifty-seven supporters; and a further fifty-seven were reported at Belton, thirty-four at Crowle and twenty-four at Haxey. These villages, three of the other six parishes which with Epworth make up the Isle, also find mention in the manuscript church book of the General Baptist Church at Epworth. In 1673 the church members numbered 126. Their minister, John Norfolk[2], had in 1661 been among the signatories to a *Humble Address from Lincoln* to Charles II.[3] In 1699 the church enclosed a piece of land as a burial ground[4]—always a sign of virility in English Dissent. This was four years before John Wesley's birth.

[1] See *Minutes of the General Assembly of the General Baptist Churches in England*, 1909, ed. W. T. Whitley, I. lxii–lxiii.
[2] A. de M. Chesterman, *Axholme Baptists*, Crowle, Lincs., 1949, pp. 15, 20. There is a copy of this pamphlet in Dr Williams' Library, London.
[3] Whitley, I. xl.
[4] Adam Taylor, *History of the English General Baptists*, 1818, II. 425f.

The strength of Arminianism in the district may be attributed in part to the fact that, during the reign of Charles I, 60,000 acres of the surrounding swamps (which gave the Isle of Axholme its name) had been drained by Dutchmen under the supervision of Cornelius Vermuyden; and that in course of time some two hundred Dutch families had settled here.[1] It is not surprising that some of these were among the Dissenters reported to the Bishop in 1676.[2] Wesley's father, Samuel Wesley, the Rector of Epworth, no doubt had no love for these Baptists among his parishioners, who in general gave him frequent trouble. Samuel Wesley's biographer, writing a hundred years ago, describes the inhabitants of Epworth as 'little better than Christian savages'; although two pages later he quotes an account of them written in 1821 as 'good-natured, simple, sincere, humble, and singularly modest'.[3] Whatever doubt may exist concerning their character, there is none concerning the doctrine of a number of them. It is at least suggestive that the greatest English Arminian was reared in a village and neighbourhood to which active and self-confessed Arminianism had long been no stranger.

It may be convenient here to continue and conclude the story of these English General Baptists. Like the church at Craig-y-fargod in Wales, their churches later turned in the main to Arianism and Socinianism. In 1770 a number of churches which deplored this development formed a separate General Baptist New Connexion. This New Connexion, as a recent Baptist historian remarks, 'was obviously a child of the Methodist Revival'[4]: its founder, Dan Taylor, and others of its originators had come under Methodist influence. In 1815 the church at Epworth joined the New Connexion: this also was under Methodist influence, locally.[5] Like the General Baptist churches in Wales which welcomed the coming of Wesleyan Methodism, the churches of the New Connexion were later absorbed among the Calvinistic or Particular Baptists. The final official amalgamation between the two

[1] L. Tyerman, *Life & Times of the Rev. Samuel Wesley*, 1866, p. 332.
[2] Chesterman, p. 15.
[3] Tyerman, pp. 331, 333.
[4] A. C. Underwood, *History of the English Baptists*, 1947, p. 153.
[5] Taylor, II. 427.

bodies, in the present Baptist Union of Great Britain & Ireland, took place in 1891,[1] and distinctions of origin are now forgotten. The Socinianizing General Baptist churches, on the other hand, are now, in every case where they still exist, Unitarian. Their General Assembly, which first met in 1660, still exists as a legal entity and meets annually, but is now but a shadow of its former self; it includes only eleven churches in England and two of the three churches in Wales mentioned earlier. The third of these, with one or two churches in England of General Baptist origin, does not send representatives to the Assembly.[2]

To return to Wesley. There was indeed no need for him to go to his Baptist neighbours to learn Arminianism. He learned it at home from his parents. As good Anglicans, the Rector of Epworth and his wife were of course Arminians. Of course, but not as a matter of course. Both Wesley's parents were remarkable people, his mother no less than his father. Each of them had grown up in Calvinistic Dissent, in a family which had braved suffering for conscience' sake; for both of them Arminianism was a position fought through to, when, independently of each other, they had abandoned the influence of home and ancestry for the Established Church. Wesley's father 'fearlessly repudiates the doctrines of election and reprobation'[3] in more than one of his published pieces; and in the first number of *The Arminian Magazine* Wesley printed a 'Hymn to the Creator' by his father, which includes the lines:

> No Evil can from Thee proceed:
> 'Tis only suffer'd, not decreed.[4]

In 1725, likewise, when Wesley was just twenty-two, his mother, Susannah Wesley, wrote to him thus: 'The Doctrine of Predestination, as maintained by rigid Calvinists, is very shocking, and ought utterly to be abhorred; because it

[1] Underwood, p. 216.
[2] For these statistics I have to thank the late Rev. Wilfred Waddington, Secretary of the General Assembly of the General Baptists, and Dr Jeremy Goring.
[3] Tyerman, p. 144.
[4] P. 44.

charges the most holy God with being the Author of Sin.' This letter, which Wesley also printed in the first number of his *Magazine*,[1] continues with what Dr John Newton, in a recent prize essay on Susannah Wesley, justly calls 'an exposition of *Rom.* viii. 29f. which breathes the authentic evangelical Arminianism which was of the essence of her son's developed theology'. Whether or not it owed anything to the ambient air of Lincolnshire, Wesley's Arminianism, with much else in Methodism, certainly owed a good deal to his parents.

From his parents, indeed, Wesley not only learned Arminian doctrine directly. He learned something else, which at the time was far rarer and more remarkable, and which, it may be argued, profoundly affected his Arminianism and his reasons for holding to it so firmly. This was a missionary outlook. To quote his father's biographer, 'The missionary spirit was a passion in the Wesley family, when Christian missions to the heathen scarce existed.'[2] This may sound exaggerated, but solid grounds for the statement may be adduced. The first Church of England missionary society, the Society for Propagating the Gospel in Foreign Parts, was founded in 1701; but its original interests were confined to those parts of the world where English colonies and plantations were to be found. In 1705 Wesley's father not only 'suggested a scheme for the conversion of Jews, Mohammedans and heathens',[3] but offered to go himself as a missionary to Abyssinia, India, or China, for the sake of the heathen, whose language he expressed himself willing to learn, as well as of the English colonists and of any existing native churches.[4] One may wonder how far this desire Samuel Wesley had conceived was shared by his wife. At the time she was probably more concerned with his improvidence and imprisonment for debt; but when later her son 'expressed a wish to preach to the North American Indians', that intrepid woman exclaimed, 'Had I twenty sons, I should rejoice, were they all so employed, though I should never see

[1] P. 37.
[2] Tyerman, p. 431.
[3] John Stoughton, *History of Religion in England*, 1881 edn., V. 260.
[4] See Tyerman, pp. 295f.

76

them more.'[1] Nor did Wesley's father allow his own zeal for foreign missions to be cooled by the fact that his earlier scheme had not proved practicable. Eleven months before John and Charles Wesley left England on their mission to Georgia, Samuel Wesley wrote to General Oglethorpe, who had recently brought back to England some Indian chiefs and had presented them to George II: 'I had always so dear a love for your colony that if it had been but ten years ago, I would gladly have devoted the remainder of my life and labours to that place, and think I might before this time have conquered the language, without which little can be done among the natives, if the Bishop of London would have done me the honour to have sent me thither, as perhaps he then might, but that is now over.'[2] John Wesley's missionary zeal, as Stoughton puts it, 'might almost be said to have come to him by inheritance'.[3]

Now, what has all this to do with Wesley's Arminianism? Much, I believe. 'The world is my parish': these famous words on Wesley's memorial in Westminster Abbey have a peculiarly eighteenth-century ring. They breathe the universalism of the eighteenth century in a far larger sense than the theological, and could scarcely have been uttered in any earlier age. But they also breathe the missionary and evangelical concern which was Wesley's overmastering passion. To execute this concern Wesley needed, could hardly have succeeded apart from, Arminianism. If universalism had not existed, one may almost say, he would have had to invent, or discover it. The theology of Calvinism arises, naturally and properly, as a theology of the people of God within the household of God. An Arminian theology arises equally naturally and properly as a theology of mission to the unbeliever.

Among the Puritans of seventeenth-century England not only any missionary enterprise but any missionary concern was almost entirely absent. This is apt to excite to surprise; but our surprise is a measure of the triumph of Arminianism. One of the few Puritans who both put missionary enterprise high among the objects of his prayers and gave ardent

[1] Stoughton, VI. 113.
[2] Tyerman, p. 428.
[3] Stoughton, VI. 113.

77

support to John Eliot's isolated mission to the American Indians was Richard Baxter; and theologically Baxter was so far from finding a rigid Calvinism acceptable that he was frequently charged with being an Arminian. At the end of the eighteenth century missionary concern at last awoke among English Dissenters. Among those then most prominent in establishing the Baptist Missionary Society and the London Missionary Society were the two men who, once again, were also leading the way in reducing or modifying the Calvinism still traditional in orthodox Dissent, Andrew Fuller and Edward Williams. In neither century is the double interest coincidental. Speaking historically, the missionary overspill of Christianity during the last 170 years would hardly have been possible psychologically but for the Arminianism of the Wesleyan Methodist movement, which first broke down the dykes in the fifty years before that; nor in turn, one may surmise, would Wesley have preached Arminianism so fervently but for his missionary passion.

It is here, I submit, that the answer lies to our major question concerning the great divide between the two contrasting types of Arminianism in English religion. The Arminianism of the General Baptists, and of the Dissenters at large, was an Arminianism of the head. The conclusion that all men will be saved was a logical consequence of argument about the nature of God. There was as yet no thought of missions. Within a theology still largely necessitarian, the doctrine that God wills all men to be saved could, in fact, be as inimical to the notion of missions as could the doctrine that God wills only some men to be saved. Such a doctrine of general redemption, moreover, easily came to be associated with a doctrine of general revelation; and this, in turn, with the reduction of the importance of the Incarnation in the plan of salvation.

Wesley's Arminianism, on the other hand, and the Arminianism of the Methodist Societies, was an Arminianism of the heart, a precondition of missionary activity undertaken that all men might be saved by the power of Christ. Hence, while the universalism of the Dissenters tended in a direction Unitarian and rationalist, Methodist universalism by its very nature could not do otherwise than remain Christo-

78

centric, missionary, and evangelical. The Methodist missionary society was founded in 1813; and it is interesting to observe that in 1817, a generation after the founding of the first Dissenting missionary society by the Particular Baptists, the General Baptist New Connexion started a mission of their own.[1] The Socinianizing General Baptists made no such move.

By way of conclusion, let us look again at English Quakerism, which is often useful for correcting, or confirming, such general judgements as have suggested themselves to us. The Baptist historian, W. T. Whitley, states that 'Friends had originated with George Fox from the General Baptist stratum.'[2] This may be suspected of being *parti pris*; but it is a fact that many of the first Quakers were what Fox calls 'shattered Baptists', and this may in part account for Quaker Arminianism. Whether Baptist in origin or not, the first Quakers were at one in being passionately missionary in their outlook. To the scornful comment that Quaker doctrine was fit to be taken to Turks and heathens Samuel Fisher retorts that in truth 'many Quakers have been among them, but few or none of our Chimney-Corner Church-men that I know of'[3]; and the retort was justified. Two years before publishing his book Fisher and another Quaker had, in fact, set out for Turkey; and, though they came no nearer their destination than Venice, a third Quaker did complete the journey and even had an interview with the Sultan.[4]

At the same time, the Puritan divines who attacked Quakerism were not mistaken in perceiving in the universalism of the Quakers' 'light within' a tendency to a reduced Christology, call it 'the light of Christ' though Friends might. Samuel Fisher insists that 'the Salvation of God is freely given in common to all men, so that every man who will may have it'; and in defence of this position he appeals to what he calls the 'strong and serious Asseverations, Complaints, Commands, and seemingly compassionate Compellations'[5] of God in Scripture. This is one thing. His attribution

---

[1] *Encyclopaedia Britannica*, 13th edn., 1926, *s.v.* Missions.
[2] Whitley, I. xvi.
[3] Samuel Fisher, *Rusticus ad Academicos*, 1660, ii. 21.
[4] See W. C. Braithwaite, *The Beginnings of Quakerism*, pp. 420–28.
[5] Samuel Fisher, iv. 93f.

of sufficiency for salvation to what Friends called 'that of God in every man' is another thing. In the course of its history Quakerism does in fact reveal within its own society, and in large measure leave unresolved, the same conflict between the two kinds of Arminianism which, in the wider field of English religion generally, has been our subject. In some periods, as in some contemporary groups, a universalism which is Christocentric and evangelical has been continued, or revived, in Quakerism and has issued in missionary work. In others a more Socinian or humanist universalism is professed, and any genuine missionary concern is then lacking.

I began by suggesting that today we are all Arminians, whether we know it or not; and in a sense this is true. It is also true that, in England Arminianism, or what Arminianism has turned into, where it lacks missionary concern, appears to be dead or dying. Perhaps this is only a particular application of the broader truth that faith without works is dead; and that faith worketh by love.

1961

IX

LAW AND LIBERTY IN PURITANISM[1]

I N Hebrew religion, and in the Christian religion which
has sprung from it, the problem of the relation between
law and liberty has been recurrent and pressing. Are law
and liberty incompatible, or on the contrary, mutually
necessary? If God commands us, and punishes us if we dis-
obey, how are we free? If Christ has made us free, are we no
longer living under law? If, as may be argued, the Old
Testament stands by law, while the New Testament offers
us liberty, is the Old Testament superseded? Yet St Paul also
speaks of the law of Christ; and of the law of the Spirit of life.
But the Spirit bloweth where it listeth; how then is there a
law of the Spirit? In theology such questions can be puzzling
as in philosophy are the problems concerning determinism
and freewill. Those problems are found soluble in experience,
so perhaps these may find an answer in devotion. Our present
object, however, is not to wrestle for the answer. It is to see
these problems at work in the minds of serious Christians in
the late sixteenth and early seventeenth centuries, there
producing a ferment which in this country has permanently
affected our conception of the Christian life, of Christian
worship and church government and of the relations between
the Church and the State.

The Puritan movement was a child of the Reformation. It
has characters in common with earlier movements in
Christian history including those which were given a similar
nickname; but in its own place in history it arose from the
recovery of the Bible in a language which the common people
could understand. The English Bible and Erasmus's *Para-
phrases* in English, together with the English Prayer Book,
made religion and worship intelligible and related them to
everyday life. No longer was the Bible the private property
of the priests, or its interpretation their preserve. The
English Bible was directed to be read in every church, and

[1] A paper read to the Vacation Term for Biblical Study at Oxford in August
1950.

men could have it in their homes without licence or fear of penalty were it discovered. It was new, and they delighted to read it, or hear it read, to ponder its teaching for themselves and to discuss this with their friends. At first its impact as a document was sufficient: they were satisfied to read it historically, to treat it as a wondrous story, but no more. And at once problems were posed; for on the relation of law and liberty, as we have seen, Scripture speaks with many voices.

Soon, moreover, the more sensitive and conscientious among its readers found that it spoke to their hearts with a strange contemporaneity; found that they were invited themselves to share in biblical religion, to enter into biblical experience. In theological terms, the recovery of the Bible brought with it a recovery of the doctrine of the Holy Spirit. ' "Word and Spirit" is the watchword of the Reformation', Paul Wernle has said; and in this Puritanism is true to its parent. But the introduction of the second term at once complicated the problems already present in the minds, now often untrained minds, of those searching the Scriptures for themselves. The relation between the Word of God spoken outwardly in Scripture and the Word of God spoken inwardly by His Spirit is one aspect in which, for the Puritans, the relation between law and liberty presented itself.

Hardly at first, however. The clash came first on a more mundane level, where for Christians it had often come before, between freedom of conscience and the law of the State. The world in which the Puritans grew up, was still nominally a *mundus Christianus*, with the State and the Church ideally one. But the ideal was breaking down—not so much, perhaps, because the sixteenth century was a century of 'religiosity divorced from morality',[1] as Mr Parker would have us believe, as because the Word of God was proving a sharper divider than any two-edged sword, and was revealing who were serious in their Christian profession and who were not. The Elizabethan Settlement might satisfy the more conventional, and pious magistrates and ministers of the Queen might endeavour to honour it. Many Puritans thus continued to hope for further reformation from within the

[1] T. M. Parker, *The English Reformation to 1558*, 1950, p. 18.

Established Church. But the tying of the Church to the wheels of the State was bound to act as a brake (as it still does: think of Charles Gore), which to the more ardent spirits became intolerable. In 1582 Robert Browne published *A Treatise of Reformation without tarying for Anie, and of the wickedness of those Preachers, which will not reforme till the Magistrate commaunde or compell them.*

> They saye, the time is not yet come to builde the Lordes House, they must tarie for the Magistrates and for Parliamentes to do it. . . . They teache that a lawefull Pastour must giue ouer his charge at the discharging, and when they withholde the Church gouernement, it ought for to cease, though the Church goe to ruine thereby . . . doe they not pull downe the heade Christe Iesus, to sett vppe the hande of the Magistrate? yea and more than this, for they firste proclaime the names and tytles of wicked Bishoppes and popishe officers, and the Lordes name after: Seeing also the Bishoppes must discharge the lawfull Preachers, and stoppe their mouthes, though the Lorde God haue giuen them a charge for to speake, and not to keepe silence. . . .
> Ye will haue all aloft, by ciuill power and authoritie: you are offended at the baseness and small beginnings, and because of the troubles in beginning reformation, you will doe nothing. . . .
> The Lords people is of the willing sorte. . . . For it is the conscience and not the power of man that will driue vs to seeke the Lordes kingdome.[1]

This was revolutionary teaching. Of course it was the power of man that should drive men to church, and to their parish church and no other, on penalty of a fine which rose as the opposition to it increased. The Puritans clung to the doctrine of the godly prince. Yet a clash between the rights of even the godly prince and the crown rights of the Redeemer was always possible in theory. In troubled times it was rarely long in coming. Browne conformed after much suffering; but others with his convictions were put to death. They died as loyal to the Queen as the Roman Catholic Sir Thomas More had died loyal to the King. Yet those responsible for government were not astray in smelling potential disloyalty. Fifty

[1] *Op. cit.*, ed. T. G. Crippen, 1903, pp. 18, 21, 25.

years later Puritan action led to the execution of the King, as fifty years after More's death some Roman Catholics were attempting the Queen's assassination. The *Short Treatise of Politique Power*, by John Ponet, Bishop of Winchester in Edward VI's reign, a work which defends tyrannicide, was reprinted in 1639 and again in 1642. The question, 'Is tyrannicide sometimes right for a Christian?' is a question which unfortunately we understand better than our fathers did.

For most of the radical Puritans their revolutionary teaching led not to revolutionary action, but to suffering: suffering for disobedience to the law; for disobedience to the law of men in order to preserve freedom to obey a higher law; but still for disobedience to the law. This is something of which no Christian can be guilty lightly; but Richard Baxter may speak for many who disobeyed, though they could not all express themselves with the clarity and simplicity which he used of a famous occasion.

> When the Plague grew hot, most of the Conformable Ministers fled, and left their Flocks, in the time of their Extremity: whereupon divers Non-conformists pitying the dying and distressed People, that had none to call the impenitent to Repentance, nor to help Men to prepare for another World; nor to comfort them in their Terrors, when about Ten Thousand dyed in a Week, resolved that no obedience to the Laws of any mortal Men whosoever, could justifie them for neglecting of Men's Souls and Bodies in such extremities; no more than they can justifie Parents for famishing their Children to death: And that when Christ shall say, Inasmuch, as ye did it not to one of these, ye did it not to me, It will be a poor excuse to say, Lord I was forbidden by the Law. Therefore they resolved to stay with the People, and to go in to the forsaken Pulpits, though prohibited, and to preach to the poor People before they dyed; and also to visit the Sick, and get what relief they could for the Poor, especially those that were shut up.[1]

Today we repudiate compulsion in religion and accept in its place the voluntary principle. We also claim to respect minorities and to recognize the right of conscientious objec-

[1] *Reliquiae Baxterianae*, ed. M. Sylvester, 1696, pt. iii. sect. 6.

tion. It is proper that we should remember how much suffering was involved in the struggle through which these positions have been established: the more so since the area in Europe where they are honoured even in name grows steadily smaller.

If we ask, 'By what authority did these men act? What was the higher law in obedience to which they disobeyed the law of the State?' the answer, in a word, is that it was the law of God in Scripture. The law of the Church was gone: in the universities the academic study of canon law was prohibited, even—'the fylthye Cannon lawe',[1] as the charter of a Separatist church in London in 1571 calls it. But some law there must be. The sheet-anchor of early Puritanism was that Scripture contained the law of the Lord: a model or pattern for all life, social and national life as well as ecclesiastical, down to the smallest details of the individual's personal behaviour. In the sphere of church government Cartwright and Saravia might wrangle over the question whether presbyters or bishops ruled by divine right; but that there should not *be* a *jus divinum*, and that founded in Scripture, was unthinkable. In the same expectation Congregationalists sought to justify their church covenants, and Baptists their believers' baptism, from the law laid down in Scripture. If these things could be proved to be biblical, the duty to observe them would not be questioned.

At the same time the moral demands found in Scripture grew ever stricter and more precise; till a system of casuistry was needed, evolved and put into use. *The Practise of Piety*, by Lewis Bayly, Bishop of Bangor, first published *c.* 1611, by 1630 was in its twenty-fifth edition. In *A Christian Directory*, published in four parts, containing over 1,200 pages, Richard Baxter enumerates fifteen reasons why it is better to avoid stage-plays, though he will not have the going to see them called a sin.[2] In these easy-going days we smile at churches which took their witness to the world and their responsibility for one another so seriously as solemnly to record in the church book that one member had been admonished for threatening to blow his brother's brains out, and another for

[1] Albert Peel, *The First Congregational Churches*, p. 32.
[2] R. Baxter, *Practical Works*, ed. W. Orme, V. 482.

85

walking over new-mown grass.[1] But here again, though their sense of proportion may have been faulty, we have learned to accept the principle they proclaimed. We no longer seek an infallible law in Scripture, and in the performance of what commands we do find there we think it right to leave considerable liberty; but we agree that Christians must bear their witness to the world, and that they have a responsibility for one another within the local congregation.

This freer attitude towards Scripture and towards life began to appear, in fact, within Puritanism itself. The Sabbatarianism, long sermons, psalm-singing, fast-days and rigid morals which developed came to seem as much a piece of legalistic paraphernalia or abracadabra as the masses, penances and indulgences of unreformed Roman Catholicism had seemed. 'O such a one doth great things', says Walter Cradock, the minister of the Congregational church at Llanvaches in Monmouthshire, 'he prayes, and hears, and reads, and disputes much; I [Aye] but hath he the spirit, or no?' 'I fear our fast dayes are the most smoky dayes in God's nostrills of all the dayes of the year'. In a work entitled *Gospel-libertie*, published in 1648, he says:

> It is convenient to pray at all times: but if you make it an absolute law, there will be guilt upon your conscience when you omit it, though the occasion be never so great. Labour to know your Christian liberty.
>
> Remember, the greatest miserie to an honest heart (next to an Old Testament spirit, that is the rise of all) is this, a misdrawing of rules out of the word of God: you take a word and doe not compare it with other Scriptures, and see whether it be temporarie and doth absolutely binde: but you goe with your book under your arme, and think all wise men are out, and you have Scripture for it: beware of that.[2]

Cradock, and those who thought with him, accepted the truth that the newly regained freedom of the Christian man was a trust and a responsibility which he might not demit.

---

[1] See extracts from the church book of Rothwell Congregational Church, printed in N. Glass. *The Early History of The Independent Church at Rothwell*, 1871.

[2] W. Cradock, *Divine Drops Distilled*, 1650, pp. 209, 4f.; *Gospel-libertie*, 1648, pp. 53, 58.

In principle, the Congregational and Baptist churches today stand where he stood. Thus in public worship it is possible to pray without relying on the forms printed in the Prayer-Book, to pray more freely in dependence on the help of the Spirit of God, whose strengthening of our infirmities has been promised us. As Cradock puts it, with feeling:

> When it may be the poore Ministers soule was full of groanes, and sighs, and he would have rejoyced to have poured out his soule to the Lord, he was tied to an old Service-Booke, and must read that till he grieved the Spirit of God, and dried up his own spirit as a chip, that he could not pray if he would; and he must read it for an houre together, and then it may be come into the Pulpit: but his spirit was gone.

Equally, in the sphere of church government, ordinary Christians, when gathered in Christ's name, are able, and must be free, to discover His will and to perform it. To quote Cradock once more:

> It is base to tie a son as much as a servant. So we being now to be sonnes, truly and really, the Lord hath given us a larger liberty.
> What an abominable thing is it to tie the sonnes of God that are not babies, now under tutors, with paltrie things, when the Spirit of God in the least Saint is better able to determine than all the Bishops.[1]

The Puritans are often thought of as men of the Old Testament rather than of the New; but among the more radical Puritans Cradock's warning against an Old Testament spirit is not unrepresentative. The position of another Congregationalist, John Owen, who during the Commonwealth was Dean of Christ Church, Oxford, and for five years Vice-Chancellor of the University, was a good deal to the right of Cradock's; yet, as James Moffatt observes in his study of him, 'Owen displays comparatively little of that undue predilection for the Old Testament which often threw practical Puritanism out of gear, owing to the obvious fascination

[1] W. Cradock, *Glad Tydings from Heaven*, 1648, p. 29; *Gospel-libertie*, 1648, pp. 18, 48.

exercised by the Jewish Scriptures on men who sought a model for the moral and civil government of a nation. Owen's interests are in the New Testament.'[1] The conservative Puritans would, indeed, feel thoroughly at home with the recent stress on the unity of the Bible and on the continuity of Israel with the New Israel which was the Church. The more radical were inclined, as they have been throughout Christian history, to see the two Testaments more in antithesis. Here is a passage in defence of believers' baptism, drawn from the church book of the Baptist church still at Broadmead, Bristol. The writer complains that paedobaptists

> will have ye Same Law of entrance into ye Church under ye Gospell Administration as it was under ye Law. Because all ye Children of ye Nation of ye Jews had a Right to both ye Seals under ye Law, namely Circumcision and ye Passover, therefore they argue that Children under ye Gospell administration have a right to Baptisme. Yet they themselves will not graunt them a Right to ye Lord's Supper, though under ye Law they had a right to ye Passover; which doth confute themselves, in their keepeing them from one of ye Seales, and not from both, as they should untill they professe their faith in Christ; for soe is ye Law under ye Gospell administration, *if thou believest thou mayest*, Acts viii. 37; it being changed from what it was under ye Law. . . . But there is not a change of ye Moral Law, for that abides as a rule of life for conversation to all generations.[2]

It is no matter for surprise if accompanying this freer attitude to the Old Testament, and sometimes to the element of law in religion, went a strain of antinomianism in the doctrinal sense. A useful guide here, out of much controversial literature, is a small and moderate work from the conservative and disapproving side published in 1643 by John Sedgwick, Rector of St Alphage, London Wall, and entitled *Antinomianisme Anatomized, or, A Glasse for the Lawlesse: who deny the Ruling use of the Morall Law unto Christians under the Gospel*. Like many works of its time, it is written in the form of a discussion, in the manner which *The Pilgrims' Progress* has made familiar to us. The characters are three:

[1] J. Moffatt, *The Golden Book of John Owen*, 1904, p. 48.
[2] *Records of a Church of Christ meeting in Broadmead, Bristol*, ed. N. Haycroft, 1865 edn., p. 34.

Nomist, Antinomist and Evangelist. Antinomist opens by declaring:

> I hold all the Ministers in London, yea and of the whole Kingdom to be but Legall Preachers; for as yet the Light is not revealed to them, and they neither do or can tell how to Preach Jesus Christ, or advance the free grace of God in Jesus; they in their Preaching do hold men to the direction of the Law; tell them that there is an use of it, not onely to unbeleevers, but beleevers; they presse men to dutie, make them Dutie-mongers, as if that Christ had not done all for them.

Nomist challenges this with some passion, and welcomes into their company Evangelist, who explains, more moderately and at length how 'the liberty from justification by the Law, doth not destroy but increase and stir up the obligation of, and obedience to the Law'. Only, he warns Nomist:

> I would have every Minister wary in Preaching the Law; The Chyrurgeon that launceth, may do as much hurt as he that doth not use the Instrument at all; Such as Preach not the Law at all may make dead and loose hearers, and such as Preach the Law too far may make desperate hearers. The golden mean is to be observed; The thing I would do is this. 1. I would not have the Law to be Preached alone by it self, without a mixture of some of the Promises of the Gospel; The fire hath its heat and light, and a Minister should have both Law and Gospel in his mouth. 2. I would have the Law to be Preached, as it was published, for Evangelicall and mercifull intentions and purposes; not for destruction and desparation, but for edification.

Nomist agrees, but urges that 'whereas we have one tender broken-hearted hearer, there are a thousand stubborn-hearted men and women, who need the hammering of the Law'.[1] This was also the conviction of a later Puritan, Giles Firmin, the ejected Vicar of Shalford in Essex, who in a work entitled *The Real Christian*, published in 1670, urges the need of 'Axes and Wedges' 'to hew and break this rough, unhewn, bold, yet professing Age'. To discover to men their sinful state, the Law must still be preached, though 'of late years this kind of preaching is laid by'; 'to convince men of

[1] *Op. cit.*, pp. 1, 26ff.

sin by the Gospel *first*', he says, 'this I look upon as very irrational and immethodical'.[1]

According to Baxter, 'The Antinomians were commonly Independants'.[2] This may be held an exaggeration; but the more radical Independents were not alarmed by the charge. In *Antinomianisme Anatomized* Evangelist makes the sensible distinction between 'two sorts of Antinomians. One Doctrinall' and 'Another practical'.[3] In *What the Independents would have*, published four years later by John Cook, who under the Commonwealth became Solicitor-General, this distinction is taken up. 'If an Antinomian doctrinall doe not prove an Antinomian practicall', says Cook, 'hee (*i.e.*, the Independent) thinks some of those opinions are very comfortable, and learnes hereby, not to exalt duty too much, but to study free grace the more, and believes that the Doctrine of Justification and satisfaction, have never been more cleerly taught than by them that have been so called'.[4] We noticed earlier the Bristol Baptists' similar care to distinguish between the ecclesiastical law which they held abrogated and the moral law which abides as a rule of life to all generations. Unfortunately, Antinomians doctrinal did sometimes become Antinomians practical, or Ranters; for 'a Ranter', wrote John Goodwin in 1655, 'is nothing but an Antinomian sublimated'.[5] Of the Ranters William Penn says:

> they interpreted Christ's fulfilling of the law for us, to be a discharging of us from any obligation and duty the law required, instead of the condemnation of the law for sins past, upon faith and repentance; and that now it was no sin to do that which before it was a sin to commit, the slavish fear of the law being taken off by Christ, and all things good that man did, if he did but do them with the mind and persuasion that it was so. Insomuch that divers fell into gross and enormous practices.[6]

For the understanding not only of Quakerism but of the whole inner articulation of Puritanism there are few docu-

[1] *Op. cit.*, pp. 55, 51f.
[2] *Reliquiae Baxterianae*, pt. i. sect. 162.
[3] *Op. cit.*, pp. 29f.
[4] *Op. cit.*, p. 11.
[5] J. Goodwin, *Catabaptism*, 1655, pref.
[6] W. Penn, preface to G. Fox, *Journal*, 1901 edn., I. xxv.

ments more helpful than Penn's preface to George Fox's *Journal*, published in 1694, from which these words are quoted. His sketches of the different parties within Puritanism are all shrewd; but this reference to the Ranters has an added piquancy from the fact that of the Ranters, as Fox remarks, 'ye people of ye worlde said they was Quakers',[1] and not the people of the world only, but Baxter and Bunyan also. 'The very opinions that are held at this day by the Quakers', wrote Bunyan in 1657, 'are the same that long ago were held by the Ranters. Only the Ranters had made them threadbare at an alehouse, and the Quakers have set a new gloss upon them again, by an outward legal holiness or righteousness'.[2] The identification was untrue and is confusing. We may attempt to place early Quakerism more fairly in its relation to law and liberty.

For this we should recall not only the Sabbatarianism and ecclesiasticism of early Puritanism but also its demand for a strict and rigid morality in private life. Too often this led to an anxious introversion, and this to melancholy and mopishness, until troubled consciences came to be as much a burden as the young Luther's had been. 'I have known one eat but one meal in a week', says Walter Cradock; 'and let them eat little or much, they defile their consciences. One while they must go so in their apparel with lace, and after that, lace damneth them'.[3] This state of strain and anxiety was to prove one seedbed of Quakerism. In Baxter's shrewd words, 'No person more fit for a Quaker, a Papist, or any sectary to work upon, than a troubled mind'.[4] Scrupulosity, if wound too tight, eventually, and suddenly, springs back, or out into a new freedom. There is a revealing passage in the *State Papers* about Margaret Fell, the nursing-mother of Quakerism, as she has been called, and later the wife of George Fox, that 'she is one that is past the cloud, and hath liberty to wear satins, and silver and gold lace, and is a great gallant'.[5] Thurloe's informant here was writing with his tongue in his cheek; but 'one that is past the cloud', could

[1] G. Fox, *Journal*, ed. N. Penney, 1911, II. 125.
[2] J. Bunyan, *Works*, ed. G. Offor, 1862, II. 183.
[3] W. Cradock, *Divine Drops Distilled*, 1650, p. 44.
[4] R. Baxter, *Works*, ed. W. Orme, XII. 500.
[5] J. Thurloe, *State Papers*, ed. T. Birch, VII. 527.

hardly be bettered as a description of an early Quaker. Another Puritan group, now forgotten, was known as the Manifestarians, because, following *Rom.* viii. 19, they awaited the manifestation of the sons of God. Them the Quakers eagerly challenged to disputes, for in Quaker experience men believed that the kingdom of God was come. In modern jargon, theirs was a realized eschatology: 'then are the children free', and free already.

About the beginnings of Quakerism there was something of what has been called 'the ranter swell'[1]; there were even occasional outbreaks of immorality, as in the case of Christopher Atkinson, whom Fox bluntly calls 'yt dirty man'.[2] But Fox and the other leaders took care to check their followers' temptation to run out into imaginations, after the fashion of the Ranters, by constantly urging them 'to think soberly, according as God hath dealt to every man the measure of faith'. A comparison of the Quaker doctrine of *measure*, in its charismatic context, with the connotation given to *canon* in Catholic usage is an inviting field for study. With regard to Scripture, the Quakers followed the Baptists in seeing the two Testaments in antithesis. Their literal and complete acceptance of Christ's words in the Sermon on the Mount compelled them to take this position. In Fox's words:

> I shewed ym ye types & figures & shadowes of Christ in ye time of ye law & shewed ym how yt Christ was come yt ended ye types & shadows & tyths & oaths & denyed swearinge & sett uppe yea & nea Insteade of it & a free teachinge: & now hee was come to teach people himselfe:[3]

Alongside this passage must be set another, from a tract published by Fox and James Nayler in 1654, with the title *A Word from the Lord, Unto all the faithlesse Generation of the World*. In this the Ranters are addressed thus:

> You had a pure convincement, I witness, which did convince you; but having fled the Crosse, and now to it are become

[1] A. Gordon, *D.N.B.*, *s.v.* G. Fox.
[2] G. Fox, *Journal*, ed. N. Penney, 1911, I. 187; the words were omitted from earlier editions of the *Journal*, though Penney has neglected to insert the square brackets inserted elsewhere to indicate passages so omitted.
[3] *Ibid.*, I. 256.

enemies, . . . you never come into the Sons doctrine; had a convincement under the law, then start up to be as Gods; and never came through the Prophets, nor Moses house, nor Christ who is the end of all oathes.[1]

While insisting that Christ had ended certain Old Testament usages, the Quakers saw the wisdom, indeed the necessity, of coming 'through the Prophets', if 'the Sons doctrine' was ever to be reached. They did not repudiate the Old Testament, but saw it as introductory to the New Testament, introductory in our experience as well as in history, our *Paedagogus*, as St Paul calls it. The moral law they then magnified rather than belittled. Throughout Fox's *Journal* the term 'Christianity' is used with a strongly ethical connotation, as something which rude people shame by their drunkenness and violent behaviour and persecution. Outwardly, the first Quakers were thus at one with the earlier Puritans in observing, as Baxter admits, 'a Life of extream Austerity'.[2] But inwardly, the spring was different. A passage often quoted or referred to in early Quaker apologia is the last two verses of *Rom.* ii: 'He is not a Jew which is one outwardly; neither is that circumcision, which is outward in the flesh; but he is a Jew, which is one inwardly; and circumcision is that of the heart'. It was words spoken from this text by Fox which first 'convinced' Margaret Fell; and when at the end of the century a uniformly sober dress was first being demanded of Friends, she would have none of it. 'We are now coming into Jewism', she protested; 'Legal ceremonies are far from gospel-freedom. . . . It's the Spirit that gives life.'[3] Inwardly, that is, the early Quakers walked at liberty, as those for whom the law was no longer law, because they loved it. So today the Quakers' testimony against war, for instance, is seen by themselves not as testimony to an idealist law which leads inevitably to despair, because it cannot be fulfilled; they believe rather that the royal law of love is one of the new laws of the new age, which Christ's new men are made able and free and happy to obey.

This is a position at some remove from that of those earlier

[1] *Op. cit.*, p. 13.
[2] *Reliquiae Baxterianae*, pt. i. sect. 123.
[3] *Cf.* W. C. Braithwaite, *The Second Period of Quakerism*, pp. 518f.

Puritans, whom Penn describes as being 'rigid in their spirits'. With it we may conclude our study. What we have seen has been a period of acute sensitiveness to the elements of law found in Scripture followed by a series of attempts by radical Puritans to reduce the sphere and the influence of law in Christian faith and experience, and to increase the sphere of liberty. All Puritans, conservative as well as radical, were a minority demanding further reformation and thereby were forced into a certain degree of independence with regard to the law of the State. The Congregationalists and Baptists sought what they believed to be the implications of a fuller liberty of the Spirit in the form and government and worship of the Church. The Quakers found inspiration in freedom from a legal scrupulosity. All three groups tended to see the two Testaments as in antithesis and to show sympathy towards an Antinomianism doctrinal. The Ranters, or Antinomians practical, claimed liberty from the moral law. Many Puritans moved from one position to another, generally in the direction of a larger liberty. Some thought it right to stop at one point, some at another; as within the modern Free Churches we still do, though we are none of us Ranters. A Catholic may regard the story as illustrating the slippery slope which Protestantism becomes through the initial mistake of rejecting the known and definite law of the Church for what proves to be an uncertain law of the Lord written in Scripture and in the heart. It is probably truer that Puritanism reveals in little, but with some intensity, the same problems and the same variety of answers as are to be found in Christian history more at large.

1951

X

THE HOLY SPIRIT IN PURITAN PIETY[1]

FUNDAMENTAL to the Puritan (as to any deeply biblical) understanding of the Holy Spirit is the remembrance that the Spirit of God is a living Spirit, a life-giving Spirit, the Spirit of the living God. 'My soul thirsteth for God, for the living God.' At the heart of Puritan piety is thirst for the living God, who has given us mortal life; who sent His Son that we may have immortal, eternal, abundant life; and whose Spirit may be known in a living community now. It is as living stones that we are to become a spiritual house.

The living Spirit of the living God new-creates through Christ both individual and community; is known in both by what lives and moves and is effective; by power and energy (two characteristic words in St Paul's epistles); by faith, but a faith active in love. 'The power of the Lord was over all': these words recur throughout George Fox's *Journal* and well describe the man and his piety. Fox could walk cheerfully over the world, a match for every occasion, as William Penn remarked of him, because he lived in the Lord's power; finding, by sensitiveness and obedience to His Spirit, doors opening for creative, redemptive work for Him where before, or otherwise, there was only a blank wall; finding himself, moreover, released, strikingly, from the power of fear; released, even, to a recognizable degree, from the power of sin; for the Holy Spirit is not only life-giving but, insofar as He gives Himself to us, which is precisely what God in His love is always seeking to do, is also, by the very name, holiness-giving: 'sin shall not have dominion over you'.

To the more orthodox Puritans, who, as Fox quaintly puts it, 'roared up for sin in their pulpits', this was a point at issue, where Fox and the Quakers overreached themselves. 'I am one that is sick and hath need of the physician' was Richard Baxter's comment, and one recognizes, gladly, the humility.

[1] The substance of a paper read to a Lutheran-Anglican conference at Hamburg in September 1951.

Yet Fox's assurance of triumph over sin through the Spirit's help equally represents something without which Christian experience would be shorn of a major glory—and too often is shorn. To speak as if the best one can do is to sin, be forgiven, and then sin as badly as before, to a Puritan seems as unreal, and as unChristian, as to a Lutheran seems what he often regards as Anglo-Saxon perfectionism or perfectibilitarianism. The Puritan is always concerned to call men to 'serious holiness' (Baxter's phrase), and he has faith in the reality of *some* degree of maturity or fulfilment, of becoming what the A.V. misleadingly calls perfect, even on earth, where we are to *grow up* unto Him who is the head. Without the controlling sanction of the Holy Spirit this conviction can peter out into the thinnest humanism, with the assumption that progress is automatic; but Puritanism is no more to be judged by this than Catholicism is by the superstitions which may be found breeding in its decay. *With* the Spirit's help the Puritan finds himself, even on earth, delivered from darkness into glorious light; brought into the liberty of the sons of God; and in the New Testament Christians are called sons of God, just as Jesus is, though for theological reasons translators think it wise to differentiate between the Son of God and the children of God. The Puritan, in a telling phrase used of an early Quaker, is 'past the cloud'; still struggling, but struggling with an energy that powerfully activates him. The Puritans recovered something of what Professor Cullmann means when he writes of the early Christians as believing that the moment of decision has already taken place, and as believing it because its spiritual effects are powerfully present in their experience. Something is *happening*, and happening to *them*; they have an existential faith. 'They were changed men themselves before they went about to change others', Penn says of the first Quakers; and they did go about to change others, for they had a treasure which they could not keep for themselves alone.

We shall see later the resultant place of witness in Puritan piety. First we must recall that the Spirit creates, and constantly new-creates, the community as well as the individual. If in the Bible as a whole the Spirit is found correlated with life and increasingly with holiness, in the New Testament there is as close a correlation with community, communion, partnership, sharing, having in common and bearing others' burdens. God's Spirit seeks, and creates, community, for God is love; and the community with one another which the first Christians had, taking its character from, as indeed it was made possible by, their community with the Spirit, was something so different from their ordinary intercourse with men, that they used the word as one of their names for the Church. This also the Puritans rediscovered; and consequently differed from the accepted doctrine of the Church. Even Word and Sacrament could not be the marks of the Church, though they might still be *sine quibus non*; still less could intellectual assent to formulae credal or liturgical or such a requirement of uniformity as ordination by bishops alone. All these things, as John Robinson observed, may be present and the Church be yet no Church, be dead, because knowing nothing of the Spirit and the community of the Spirit. The marks of the Church are, rather, the gifts and graces, the grace-gifts as Paul calls them, coining (it seems) a new word to describe a new reality, of the Spirit which creates it. Long-suffering with joy (a conjunction hardly to be found in any other community), willingness to suffer and take the humbler part, faith in others' faith and intentions, a tender carefulness not to quench the smoking flax in others' aspirations, these are among the marks whereby the community of the Spirit which is the Church may be recognized. Without *them*, and the presence of the Risen Christ making them possible, there may be notions but no faith; an institution with outward rites, but no Church.

With such a conception of the Church the conception of the ministry also naturally differs from the conventional. Not that ministry is lacking: even the Quakers, lacking ministers in the accepted sense of separated, ordained, full-time and paid, professional ministers had (and have, and highly value) ministry. But ideally and primarily ministry is conceived not as an office, with status attached, not even as a function, but more prophetically as itself a grace-gift of the Spirit, one among many; not the irrevocable possession of a particular man or group of men but something to be shared as widely as possible; to be neither scorned when given only occasionally or temporarily nor yet honoured above what is right. Among Baptists and Congregationalists, alongside of a trained and ordained ministry, occasional ministry was (and is) encouraged in those now misleadingly called 'lay preachers' but originally known more correctly as 'gifted brethren'. In Quakerism those called elders and overseers are appointed for a limited period to care for worship and oversight, respectively. In Quaker worship there is, ideally, *nothing but* a waiting together upon the Spirit until one or another, anyone, man or woman, is inwardly moved to minister vocally in exhortation, exposition, testimony or prayer—vocally, because by Quakers the sharing of silent prayer and meditation is itself, rightly, regarded as ministry. What is demanded, and demanded of all present, is expectancy, sensitiveness, obedience: 'to go to meeting determined to speak or determined to keep silence are both unquakerly': the Spirit's leading will be given *in coetu fideli*; therefore, though the mind and heart should be prepared, the decision to minister vocally must not be taken beforehand. In this Quakers only apply to worship a principle widely recognized as wise in other spheres of the Christian life.

From one angle this may be seen as a laicizing, a universalizing, of Christianity, and thus as a continuance of what was begun in the Reformation. 'Would God that all the Lord's people were prophets' is a favourite and characteristic Puritan text. From another angle it may be seen as an idealizing, a sectarianizing of Christianity; since the demands made, or implied, may be considered too great for flesh and blood to bear. To this a number of things may be said, more in comment than in retort.

Those in the Puritan tradition, while for the most part no longer holding to the doctrine of election in the strict Calvinist form to which once they were wedded, find much in biblical religion to suggest that the people of God are likely always to be a remnant, or a leaven, a little flock, who must strive to enter in by the strait gate. Nor, it may be said, are flesh and blood supposed to be going to inherit the kingdom of God; 'the flesh and the Spirit are opposed to each other' and 'they that are Christ's have crucified the flesh' (a strong expression). In any case, it may be urged, to treat Puritan piety in terms of *demand* at all is a misunderstanding from without; since, in Augustine's phrase, what is demanded is *given* by the new-creating Spirit of power and love.

It may also be claimed that the actuality of Puritan piety is its own best witness in convincing others: that here is something which, because of its universal element, is felt as *open* for all men; which, because of its ideal element, is seen as *desirable*; and which, because it is also actual, can be accepted as possible *now*. In Puritan piety the local church, the worshipping community, is conceived as itself bearing a large share in the witness to Christ, in the missionary outthrust which is a mark of the true 'apostolic succession'. To come, for instance, into a meeting of Quakers sitting with bowed heads in silent waiting upon, and for, the Spirit is to be faced, at once, with an unmistakable and striking witness to *faith*.

The unexpected effect upon himself of joining in such worship Robert Barclay expresses thus: 'I found the evil weakening in me and the good raised up.' For all Puritans, Quakers included, worship is deeply ethical, touching the will as well as the heart and mind. The Light, Fox would say, brings a man to see the evil in himself—though then also, he characteristically adds, to see *over* the evil. Few Christians have greater power in upbuilding and winning others than those who in worship have learned thus to discern evil *and* to see over it, first in themselves and then in others also. They breathe out to others something of the forgiveness of sin and of the reconciliation of the sinner which they have known at God's hands themselves. They desire above all not to grieve His Spirit; consequently they cannot despise the most despicable of men, for 'he who despises, despises not men but God who has given us His Holy Spirit'. Quakers follow this line further in believing that Christians are brought into that life and power which takes away the occasion of all wars. Christian Pacifism is but an extreme example of what from within is seen not as an impossible moral demand but as part of the liberation of the sons of God: an empowering of men so to live in the Spirit, the Spirit of the crucified but forgiving Lord, the crucified but triumphant Lord, that fighting, war, is just not possible for them.

We turn to consider, in the light of Puritan piety, two contrasts or inter-relations which appear when the Spirit is under discussion. The motto of the Reformation, in Paul Wernle's phrase, is Word *and* Spirit. The copula is important. The Word without the Spirit, even the preached word, let alone the written word, if the Spirit attend not the preaching, can be as near death as the Spirit without the Word can be near mere humanism. The Puritan urges us to be on our guard against allowing 'the Word' to degenerate into 'the letter;' for 'the letter' is not only dead but killeth, is death-bearing whereas the Spirit giveth life. The fear of this is one reason for many Puritans' disinclination to be tied too closely to the verbal formulae of creeds ancient or modern. The primitive confession, Jesus is Lord, is enough; and this no man can say, and mean what it is intended to mean, 'but in the Holy Spirit'. Again, Puritans seek to guard against allowing 'the Word' to degenerate into 'the law'; for 'the law' can enslave, whereas the Spirit makes free. 'Thou art no longer a slave, but a son': 'we are no longer under a tutor; for ye are all sons of God'; 'I call you no longer slaves . . . but I have called you friends'. We may still do but that which it was our duty to do, but the spring, the inner motive, is different; there is a freshness and expectancy which only the Spirit gives.

When, as many of them did, the Puritans covenanted with the Lord and with one another to walk in all the ways of the Lord, it was in His ways known or to be made known to them: 'the Lord hath yet more light and truth to break forth from His Word'. Still from His Word. Despite a tendency to antinomianism, Puritan piety in general held fast to the conjunction between the Spirit and the Word; but it insisted on a *continuity* of the Spirit's action which to other Christians was often unwelcome. It is the same Spirit that worked in those who wrote the Bible and in the first Christians which still works in us. We cannot understand God's word there to them unless we also are 'in the Spirit'. Puritans were unsympathetic to the comfortable argument that there was an extraordinary manifestation of the Spirit among the first Christians which is no longer to be expected by ourselves. While accepting the conception of the biblical revelation as necessary and as sufficient, they disliked the conception of it as final, as if the number of the redeemed had long been a *numerus clausus*. God still speaks 'as well without the written word as with it, though according to it'—a phrase of Oliver Cromwell's. God still inspires (as a Prayer Book collect seems to allow).

What of the antithesis mentioned earlier between the Spirit and the flesh, between spirit and matter? At all times Christians sway uneasily between the attractions of the natural man and the baleful influence of Gnosticism. Of late years much has been heard, much made, of William Temple's assertion that 'Christianity is the most materialistic of all great religions': an assertion made by him with reference to the Johannine phrase 'and the Word became flesh', in which, Temple says, 'is implicit a whole theory of the relation between spirit and matter'. The phrase hardly justifies the assertion. *Sarx* does not mean 'matter', it hardly (in the context) means 'flesh'; rather, as *basar* over against *ruach*, it stands for the human personality as a whole; for this there was as yet no special term, and the Johannine phrase means much the same as the Pauline description of Christ as 'being found in the likeness of men'. A correspondence may indeed be found between the Incarnation of the Son in Jesus and the Indwelling of the Spirit in men; but it remains true that 'in my flesh', as the figure of my human personality treated as in abstraction from God, 'dwelleth no good thing'. It is the Spirit's work and triumph to *transform* my human personality, till I become less unworthy of calling on Christ, and calling on Him not simply as only-begotten but as the first-born among many brethren: to transform me even outwardly somewhat as Jesus Himself when at prayer was transformed, transfigured: 'we are being changed into the same image by the Lord Spirit'.

This stress on transformation, metamorphosis, whereby matter is *redeemed*, is a very different thing from describing Christianity as materialistic, as if matter in itself, or the natural man in himself, were holy. Puritanism, like monasticism, tends to swing towards the opposite pole, towards Gnosticism, and to treat matter, flesh, as in itself sinful. Yet most Christians, if honest, acknowledge that they understand what Paul and the Hebrew tradition in general mean, when they say that in the animated matter which our flesh is seems to dwell an evil impulse which 'lusteth against the Spirit'. There is a realism and an effectiveness about asceticism which wins respect even from those who do not practise it. Puritans, while witnessing gratefully to the Spirit's transforming power, also know that a continuing and lifelong discipline is called for, and that at times the body must be browbeaten if it is to be servant and not master.

It is in keeping with the foregoing considerations that Puritans are not easy over the parallel drawn by others, which doubtless was not absent from Temple's mind, between the Incarnation and the Sacrament. The belief that in the man Jesus the Spirit dwelt uniquely, and in His brethren in lesser degree, transforming their personality, and the belief that, whether by sacerdotal word or intention or by the faith of the recipient, the Spirit transforms, transubstantiates into Christ's flesh, bread, which is not animated matter in the sense that man's body is, do not run on all fours. For the Puritan the former belief in fact precludes the latter. It is not possible to stress faith, and the place of personality in the Spirit's economy, and at the same time to stress what are called 'the elements' or any ritual deliberately dissociated from what are felt to be the dangerously subjective, or inhibiting, conditions of personality. For Puritans the sacraments are seen not so much as channels, conferring grace or even conveying it (this distinction was discussed), but rather as declaratory of grace always in the giving, grace given already, given now and to be given. Likewise in ordination the laying on of hands, where this is observed (and by Congregationalists it has not been required as of necessity), indicates no tactual 'apostolic succession', for the succession is prophetic, through the Spirit's moving in the heart; no special grace is given now and only now, but there is recognition, as in *Acts* vi and *Numbers* xxvii, of those already 'full of the Spirit', in whom beforehand 'the Spirit was', and prayer for them, as they begin their life's work.

This aspect of Puritanism may be summed up in words of Zwingli: 'for the Spirit a vehicle is not necessary; if we think otherwise, Judaism is coming in again'. Zwingli, it is important to recall, was no Gnostic or Manichaean but a Christian humanist; nor does he say that the Spirit does not normally use some *vehiculum*, only that this is not necessary. In Puritanism what religiously and theologically springs from concentration on the doctrine and experience of the Holy Spirit may be seen more philosophically or psychologically as a concern with immediacy, as an insistence on the non-necessity of a *vehiculum* or medium. Historically this arose in reaction against, indeed in horror at, a religion throughout which, in priesthood, in sacrament, in invocation of saints, mediation was dominant. It is possible for the reaction to lead, as von Hügel fairly remarks, to dispensing with the Mediator. Originally, it is equally fair to remark, it was the outcome of joy and liberation in a new, direct, personal faith in Christ and a new, direct, personal experience of His Spirit. Only in Quakerism was opposition to all mediation carried so far that separated ministry and sacramental observance were both abandoned. In all Puritan piety, however, there is a ready response to the principle of non-necessity. The principle is negative only in appearance. Positively, like the doctrine of predestination, it calls attention to, and safeguards, the freedom and supremacy of God's grace. 'Where the Spirit of the Lord is, there is liberty.'

1951

XI

THE PERSONALITY OF RICHARD BAXTER

SOME years ago Dr. F. J. Powicke put his hand on my shoulder and said, 'Read Baxter; read Baxter; read Baxter. He touches every point at issue in the seventeenth century, and you will never regret time spent on him. He has a flowing, easy style which makes him pleasant to read, and you will find he grows upon you, until you come to know him and to love him.' I did not forget the old man's exhortation; but it was not until last year, that in the course of some more general researches into Puritan piety, the opportunity arose to do as he suggested. During that year there was a growth of Baxter's stature in my mind (if I may put it so) more than of anyone else's, and this although I was studying radical Puritanism more especially, and did not expect to find Baxter too sympathetic. In the first place, there is something about Baxter's writing which I find peculiarly affecting: the style, the self-expression, is so direct, penetrating, sure, yet so sincerely modest, almost ingenuous, and produces a strange feeling that the man is personally present, at least that he wrote this only yesterday and wrote it to *you*. Next, Baxter does combine, in a most remarkable way, intense caring and concern with judiciousness; there is in him a true blend of the spiritual and the rational. And lastly, he is a signal example of the kind of influence for good which a man can have through what he *is* rather than through what he *does*. Baxter never held any higher position than that of Vicar of Kidderminster, yet Alexander Gordon, who was likely to know and is not given to extreme statements, says 'Richard Baxter, in his best days, was a stronger power with the religious people of England, than either the Westminster Assembly or the Parliamentary leaders.'[1]

1615–91 are his dates, so that he just about covers the seventeenth century, being almost an exact contemporary of George Fox, who died in the same year. Baxter was born at

[1] A. Gordon, *Heads of English Unitarian History*, p. 65.

Rowton, near High Ercall, in Shropshire, and lived there till he was ten years old with his maternal grandfather. He was educated at Wroxeter School, and later by Richard Wickstead, the Chaplain to the Council of the Welsh Marches at Ludlow. He never went to the university—very noteworthy, considering the influence he had, and has continued to have, with university-trained men—but he evidently read voraciously for himself: he speaks of 'my natural Inclination to Subtlety and Accurateness in Knowing",[1] and says 'I could never from my first Studies endure Confusion.'[2] Little is known of his childhood and youth, but of the following passages the first is of some psychological interest, while the second is characteristic in its revealing power.

> When I was younge (yea till 20 yeares of age) I durst not have gone into a darke roome alone; or, if I did, ye feare of it would have made me even tremble.[3]
>
> God knoweth, that I never hurt a Man in my Life, no never gave a Man a stroke (save one Man, when I was a Boy, whose Legg I broke with wrestling in jest; which almost broke my heart with grief, though he was quickly cured).[4]

He mentions various books which played a part in his adolescent religious development, in particular Edmund Bunny's edition of the Jesuit Parsons' *Resolutions*, but 'whether sincere Conversion began now, or before, or after, I was never able to this day to know': 'God breaketh not all Men's hearts alike.'[5] Walter Cradock, when sheltering from episcopal pursuivant at Shrewsbury, was one whose warm piety had a permanent influence on Baxter; and in 1638 he was ordained deacon by the Bishop of Worcester (Thornborough),[6] and became master of the new school at Dudley. Two years

[1] *Reliquiae Baxterianae* [hereafter referred to as *R.B.*] ed. M. Sylvester, pt. i. sect. 212 (3); there is an abridgement in the Everyman series.

[2] *Ibid.*, pt. i. sect. 5.

[3] MS. letter of 1657, cit. by F. J. Powicke, *Life of R. Baxter*, i. 150.

[4] *R.B.*, pt. ii. sect. 258.

[5] *Ibid.*, pt. i. sects. 3, 6 (4).

[6] 'The known facts preclude the possibility of his having proceeded to the priesthood', but 'there can be no doubt that he did celebrate Holy Communion', and 'no question of "status" was raised . . . when he was offered the See of Hereford': F. J. Powicke, in *The Times Literary Supplement*, 22 January and 5 February 1925.

later he went to Bridgnorth, 'the second Town of Shropshire', as assistant minister, but in 1641 he accepted a unanimous invitation to a lectureship at Kidderminster.

> My mind was much to the place as soon as it was described to me; because it was a full Congregation, and most convenient Temple; an ignorant, rude and revelling People for the greater part, who had need of preaching; and yet had among them a small Company of Converts, who were humble, godly, and of good Conversations, and not much hated by the rest, and therefore the fitter to assist their Teacher; but above all, because they had hardly ever had any lively, serious preaching among them:[1]

During the next few years he was away from Kidderminster a good deal, at one time as army chaplain at Coventry, where he declined an invitation from Cromwell to become pastor of the 'gathered church' to be formed by 'that famous Troop which he began his Army with', and also in Colonel Whalley's regiment; but between 1647 and 1660 he was at Kidderminster, where he was persuaded with some reluctance to accept the position of Vicar, and it was at Kidderminster that he made his name, and that, in a sense, his life's work was performed. Of this, more in detail in a moment.

By the time of Charles II's restoration, Baxter was sufficiently prominent to be made a chaplain to the King, and, further, to be offered the see of Hereford, which for reasons of conscience he refused, modestly suggesting several names of others whom he considered suitable for such a position. His tolerant mind, which made him unable to declare his unfeigned consent and assent to everything contained within the Book of Common Prayer, made him also unable to retain his living at Kidderminster. Although 24 August 1662 was the date fixed for the ejection, he preached his farewell sermon in a London pulpit as early as the preceding May, 'because I would let all Ministers in England understand in time, whether I intended to Conform or not'[2]; and for the rest of his life he was outside the Established Church, and often suffering fines or imprisonment for preaching. His

[1] *R.B.*, pt. i. sect. 29.
[2] *Ibid.*, pt. ii. sect. 278.

longest imprisonment, after a trial by Judge Jeffreys, of which Macaulay has a famous description, lasted a year and a half, when he was seventy years of age. What seems to have troubled him more was the loss of 'my Books (which I have not seen these ten years, and pay for a Room for their standing at Kiderminster, where they are eaten with Worms and Rats)'[1]; and it is pathetic to find him at the end of his life having to part with what books he had in London, to satisfy distraint for preaching.

> If Books had been my Treasure (and I valued little more on Earth) I had been now without a treasure. . . . But God saw that they were my Snare. We brought nothing into the World, and we must carry nothing out. The Loss is very tolerable.[2]

His death took place in 1691, when he was seventy-six.

Something must be said of his marriage with Margaret Charlton in September 1662, the month after his ejection, when he was forty-six and she twenty-five. Margaret was a woman of strong character and religious views, who had been in his congregation at Kidderminster, and had found herself unable to stay behind when her minister left for London; she was also a woman of private means, which must have been useful for providing a home in the difficult days which followed, when they were not living with one or another friend. Baxter has several *obiter dicta* on women, as that 'it is Style and not Reason which doth most with them',[3] and 'Women are usually less patient of Suffering than Men.'[4] These suggest, perhaps, the detachment of a naturally celibate mind, and one of the 'conditions of our marriage' was 'that she would expect none of my time which my ministerial work would require',[5] but there is no question that he was passionately devoted to his wife, who, he says, 'was never so Chearful a Companion to me as in Prison, and was very much against my seeking to be released'.[6] After her death in

---

[1] *R.B.*, pt. iii, sect. 171.
[2] *Ibid.*, pt. iii. sect. 309.
[3] *Ibid.*, pt. i. sect. 159 (4).
[4] *Ibid.*, pt. iii, sect. 13.
[5] R. Baxter, *Breviate*, ed. J. T. Wilkinson, p. 110.
[6] *R.B.*, pt. iii. sect. 119.

1681, he wrote a most moving *Breviate* of her life, from which two quotations may be permitted:

> If I carried (as I was apt) with too much neglect of Ceremony or humble Complement to any, she would modestly tell me of it; if my very looks seemed not pleasant she would have me amend them.
>
> For near these 19 years that I have lived with her, I think I never heard her thrice speak a doubting word of her salvation, but oft of her hopeful perswasions, that we should live together in Heaven.[1]

Baxter also found expression for his grief at her death in some *Poetical Fragments;* parts of one of which, 'He wants not friends that hath thy love', find a place in the *Congregational Hymnary* (no. 335) and carry an unexpected poignancy when the occasion of their publication is known. Considering the happiness of his married life, it is the more remarkable to find Baxter claiming as one reason for the success of his labours at Kidderminster that 'my single life afforded me much advantage: For I could the easilier take my People for my Children, and think all that I had too little for them'.[2] He also offers this and other grounds for commending celibacy in ministers, in his *Christian Directory*,[3] written shortly after his marriage. The ability to give objective judgement, even though his own practice was inconsistent with it, is one of his most striking characteristics.

Baxter's work at Kidderminster may perhaps be said to be without parallel in the religious history of this country. For its effect at the time, there is his own statement in 1658 that 'among Eight Hundred Families, Six Hundred Persons are Church-Members',[4] and his remembrance that 'those People that had none in their Families, who could pray, or repeat the Sermons, went to their next Neighbour's House who could do it, and joined with them'.[5] The memory of it is perceptible to anyone who goes today to Kidderminster,

[1] R. Baxter, *Breviate*, pp. 129, 128.
[2] *R.B.*, pt. i. sect. 137 (16).
[3] R. Baxter, *Practical Works*, ed. W. Orme, IV. 20.
[4] *R.B.*, App. iii, p. 63.
[5] *Ibid.*, pt. 1. sect. 137 (6).

where Baxter's communion-table is preserved in the Congregational church (called by his name), his pulpit in the Unitarian church, and his chair in the parish church, where the town library has a collection of his books and a manuscript letter by him, and where one ward of the urban district is called Baxter. There is also a statue of him, unveiled by Dean Stanley in 1875, and not far off on Kinver Edge is an obelisk also to his memory. When I went to see this last year, an evacuee and a member of the Forces, whom I questioned about him, had both heard of him, one saying he had been burned at Kidderminster, the other that, from the way the people talked about him, he had evidently been very good to them. This, after three hundred years, says a good deal.

First of all, there was his preaching. His constant ill-health, he says, 'made me study and preach things necessary, and a little stirred up my sluggish heart, to speak to Sinners with some Compassion, as a dying Man to dying Men'.[1] This last phrase, which he repeats later in his autobiography, was evidently a favourite with him, for it recurs in his *Poetical Fragments*, whence it finds a place in Bartlett's *Familiar Quotations*. It is hardly credible that so much could be done by one suffering from as many complaints and disabilities as dogged Baxter perpetually. He describes them with all the loving detail of a hypochondriac, admitting that 'the Physicians call'd it the Hypocondriack Melancholy', but praising God that 'I was never overwhelm'd with real Melancholy. My Distemper never went so far as to . . . damp me with sinking Sadness'.[2] He also describes the various remedies with which he experimented, showing a scientific tendency reminiscent of Bacon's catching his death of cold through stuffing a fowl with snow. At all events, the ill-health produced in him an intense seriousness, which must have been never more evident than in his preaching. What this was like can be imagined from his remarks on preaching, as that men 'are greatly taken with a Preacher that speaketh to them in a familiar natural Language, and exhorteth them as if it were for their Lives'.[3]

[1] *R.B.*, pt. i. sect. 32 (4); cf. sect. 137 (2).
[2] *Ibid.*, pt. i. sect. 9.
[3] *Ibid.*, pt. i. sect. 49.

I know not how it is with others, but the most reverend preacher, that speaks as if he saw the face of God, doth more affect my heart, though with common words, than an irreverent man with the most exquisite preparations.

In preaching, there is a communion of souls, and a communication of somewhat from our to theirs.[1]

Secondly, there was the catechizing, for which he was specially concerned. He regarded it as 'the unquestionable duty of the generality of ministers in these three nations, to set themselves presently to the work of catechizing and instructing, individually, all that are committed to their care, who will be persuaded to submit thereto'. He spent 'Monday and Tuesday, from morning almost to night in the work . . . and I cannot say yet that one family hath refused to come to me . . . And I find more outward signs of success with most that do come, than from all my public preaching to them'.[2] These passages are taken from his *Reformed Pastor*, a book which it is not easy for a minister to read without deep shame at the shallow, easy-going methods with which we content ourselves today. Baxter's deep pastoral concern finds expression also in his missionary interest: 'no part of my Prayers are so deeply serious, as that for the Conversion of the Infidel and Ungodly World'.[3]

Thirdly, Baxter 'was forced five or six years by the Peoples Necessity to practise Physick. . . . And because I never once took a Penny of any one, I was crowded with Patients, so that almost Twenty would be at my Door at once'. He confesses, very sensibly, that 'the very fear of miscarrying and doing anyone harm, did make it an intollerable burden to me', so that, as soon as he could procure 'a godly, diligent Physician', he turned them all off, and 'never medled with it more'; but he also confesses that his practice helped his ministry, 'for they that cared not for their Souls did love their Lives, and care for their Bodies . . . And doing it for nothing so obliged them, that they would readily hear me'.[4]

[1] R. Baxter, *The Reformed Pastor* (1835 edn)., pp. 183, 223.
[2] *Ibid.*, pp. 81f.; it may be noted that George Herbert devotes a chapter to *The Parson Catechizing* in his *Country Parson*.
[3] *R.B.*, pt. i. sect. 212 (23).
[4] *Ibid.*, pt. i. sects. 135, 137 (17); Herbert, again, has a section on the parson as physician.

Baxter also busied himself with matters of ecclesiastical discipline and organization, being 'almost constant Moderator' at local ministers' meetings. The 'voluntary association' of ministers of different denominations, inaugurated by the 'Worcestershire Agreement' of 1652, had 'no previous precedent in England', but, largely through Baxter's influence, within a few years came to be adopted by about half the counties. Baxter himself, though often miscalled so, 'was never a Presbyterian'; he called himself 'a meer Catholick', and personally preferred the old-established system of churchwardens for parish ordering.[1] It is the tolerance of his scheme for 'voluntary association' which is most noticeable.

In addition to these multifarious associations, there was always correspondence. At Dr Williams' Library there are about 800 letters, covering almost every year from 1652 to his death, to or from Baxter, who counted sixty-eight correspondents among ejected ministers alone. In the cases of conscience which so troubled Puritan piety everyone seems to have turned to him for his powers of analysis and perception in giving spiritual advice. He was ahead of his age in recognizing the effect on conviction of temperament and education. Matthew Sylvester relates in his funeral sermon that Baxter

> had as rational satisfaction as they (others) have, that his soul was safe: and yet could never feel their sensible consolations. And when I asked him, whether much of this was not to be resolved into bodily constitution? he did indeed tell me that he thought it might be so.[2]

On another occasion Baxter wrote to the scholar Henry Dodwell as follows:

> I must say that our different educations, I doubt not, is a great cause of our different sentiments. Had I never been a Pastor nor lived out of a Colledge . . . I might have thought as you do. And had you converst with as many country-people as I have done, and such country-people, I think you would have thought as I do.[3]

[1] A. Gordon, op. cit., pp. 64f.
[2] M. Sylvester, Funeral Sermon, printed in R.B., ad fin., p. 15.
[3] R. Baxter, An Answer to Mr Dodwell and Dr Sherlocke, p. 93.

To such sanity Baxter added a rare spiritual warmth and intimacy. To the wife of a certain Thomas Lambe, who had left John Goodwin's church for a Baptist church, and was now unsettled over Quakerism, he wrote:

> There is a Connaturality of Spirit in the Saints that will work by Sympathy, and by closing uniting Inclinations, through greater Differences and Impediments than the external Act of Baptism: As a Load-Stone will exercise its attractive Force through a Stone Wall. I have an inward Sense in my Soul, that told me so feelingly in the reading of your Lines, that your Husband, and you, and I are one in our dear Lord, that if all the self-conceited Dividers in the World should contradict it on the account of Baptism, I could not believe them.[1]

When he began thus, is it a matter for wonder that he could go on to do what he liked with people? Nor did he fail to be faithful in rebuke. To Lambe's concern against 'gay Apparel and following of Fashions . . . a Sin in my Apprehension (at least) that few are sufficiently sensible of', Baxter replies with pungency, 'O that we had no sorer Diseases to encounter, than fine Cloaths:' and refers him to sixty poor families of whom he says, 'when they have sat by me to be instructed in my Chamber, they sometimes leave the Lice so plentifull that we are stored with them for a competent space of time'.[2] The kind of advice Baxter offered on almost every possible question may be studied in detail in the four volumes of his *Christian Directory*. Almost always there is the combination of sanity with deep concern. He gives fifteen reasons why he thinks it better to avoid stage-plays, yet he will not have the going to see them called a sin.[3]

We are not yet finished with his work, for 'all these my labours (except my private Conferences with the Families), even preaching and preparing for it, were but my Recreations, and as it were the work of my spare hours: For my Writings were my chiefest daily Labour'.[4] According to the Rev. A. G. Matthews' *Bibliography*, Baxter published 141 volumes and

[1] *R.B.*, App. iii, p. 54.
[2] *Ibid.*, pp. 59, 63.
[3] R. Baxter, *Practical Works*, V. 482.
[4] *R.B.*, pt. i. sect. 135.

contributed to forty others, while there is still much in manuscript at Dr Williams' Library. It may be doubted whether anyone has ever read them all, unless it were Dr Johnson, who, in reply to Boswell's query 'what works of Richard Baxter's I should read', said 'Read any of them; they are all good',[1] a notable commendation from so pronounced an abhorrer of Dissenters. The autobiography, memoir of his wife, poetry, *Reformed Pastor* and *Christian Directory* have been mentioned already; but the most famous of Baxter's works is undoubtedly *The Saints Everlasting Rest*, on the strength of which he has been called 'the creator of our popular Christian literature'.[2] Of this Baxter says:

> Indeed for the Saints Rest I had Four Months Vacancy to write it (but in the midst of continual Languishing and Medicine) : But for the rest I wrote them in the Crowd of all my other Imployments, which would allow me no great Leisure for Polishing and Exactness, or any Ornament; so that I scarce ever wrote one Sheet twice over, nor stayed to make any Blots or Interlinings, but was fain to let it go as it was first conceived. . . . the Apprehensions of Present Usefulness or Necessity prevailed against all other Motives.[3]

Looking back, Baxter regretted the *ad hoc* character of much of his writing, but this differs from most work of the kind in escaping ephemerality: further, the style was benefited through an expression often terse and always pointed of what was heavy on his heart.

In the not very satisfying article on Baxter in the *Dictionary of National Biography*, Archbishop Trench is quoted as remarking of *The Saints Everlasting Rest*, 'In regard, indeed, of the choice of words, the book might have been written yesterday. There is hardly one which has become obsolete, hardly one which has drifted away from the meaning which it has in his writings'. This is an interesting observation and invites comparison with the forthcoming translation of the Bible by Mgr. Knox, which is said to be made on this principle of using only 'changeless' language; but it remains

[1] J. Boswell, *Life of Johnson*, s.d. 29 May 1783.
[2] A. B. Grosart, in *D.N.B.*, *s.v.*
[3] *R.B.*, pt. i. sect. 212.

merely literary criticism from without. We penetrate farther with Wesley's observation of 'that loving, serious Christian', that he wrote 'dipping his pen in tears'.[1] Baxter himself, in controversy with John Owen over the place in worship of read, as against extempore, prayers, says, 'I doubt you lay too much on words; . . . Words must be used and weighed; but the main work is heart work';[2] and elsewhere he says, 'the Transcript of the Heart hath the greatest force on the Hearts of others'.[3] His style is flowing and pellucid, the transcript of his heart and a very plain transcript of a very warm heart; it carries the reader on easily, and includes sufficient epigrammatic *aperçus* to relieve any tedium.

> Overdoing is the ordinary way of undoing.[4]
> Education is God's ordinary way for the Conveyance of his grace.[5]
> The Gratefulness of the Person doth ingratiate the Message.[6]
> Whoever be the Sect-Masters, it is notorious, that the Prelates (tho' not they only) are the Sect-Makers.[7]
> When Christ shall say, Inasmuch as ye did it not to one of these, ye did it not to me, It will be a poor excuse to say, Lord I was forbidden by the Law.[8]

There is no getting round a man who can express truth like that; and Baxter did not lose either his conviction or his power of expression when under hardship. He used to tell people who visited him in prison, he says, that

> it much more concerned us, to be sure that we deserved not Suffering, than that we be delivered from it. . . . If Passion made me lose my Love, or my Religion, the Loss would be my own. And Truth did not change, because I was in a Goal.[9]

After an excursion among the more radical Puritans, who, at one extreme, shade off into what can only be called the

---

[1] J. Wesley, *Journal, s.d.* 4 May 1755.
[2] R. Baxter, *Account* . . . (printed in his *Catholick Communion Defended*), p. 21.
[3] *R.B.*, pt. i. sect. 157.
[4] *Ibid.*, pt. i. sect. 40.
[5] *Ibid.*, pt. i. sect. 6 (3).
[6] *Ibid.*, pt. i. sect. 137 (5).
[7] *Ibid.*, pt. iii. sect. 99.
[8] *Ibid.*, pt. iii. sect. 6.
[9] *Ibid.*, pt. iii. sect. 125.

lunatic fringe, it is immensely reassuring to return to someone who is as sane as Baxter. One could wish he had come to
a more sympathetic understanding of the Quakers, with
much in the best of whom he had unrecognized affiliations.
His reply, for instance, to Owen's claim 'that there could be
no other way of Saving Revelation of Jesus Christ' than by
Scripture, that 'he was savingly revealed by Preaching many
years before the New Testament was written'[1] might have
come from any Quaker disputant. What Baxter, surely
rightly, found offensive in the Quakers was their insistence
that perfection and sinlessness were attainable in this life.
'Can that man that hath one spark of grace believe that he
hath no sin?' he asks. 'Can he have so little knowledge of
himself? For my part, I am one that is sick and have need of
the Physician.'[2] Today we can appreciate both Baxter's
humility and human insight and Fox's assurance of triumph
over sin through God's Spirit; but in their own day these
seemed incompatible. From Baxter's point of view, moreover,
the Quakers were irresponsible intruders, and he probably
cared much less about their abusive disturbance of his services than about their disturbance of minds already none too
well balanced in 'an age of excitement'.[3] 'No person more
fit for a Quaker, a Papist, or any sectary to work upon', he
says, 'than a troubled mind'.[4]

His controversies with the Quakers and others have somewhat concealed his truly extraordinary tolerance, the
genuine tolerance which arises not from indifference, but
from a deep desire for as close a unity as possible among all
who sincerely love the Lord Jesus. To Owen, again, who
wished to have the creed as expounded in the first four
Councils established as a rule of faith, Baxter wrote 'I can
readily subscribe myself, but it's better let them all alone,
and not to be so fond of one onely Engine, which hath torn
the Church for about 1200 years'.[5] To the end of his life he
remained faithful to this principle of tolerance, going to the

[1] *R.B.*, pt. ii. sect. 54.
[2] R. Baxter, *The Quakers Catechism*, p. 29.
[3] T. B. Macaulay, *Essays*, 1863 edn., I. 136.
[4] R. Baxter, *Practical Works*, XII. 500; *cf.* F. J. Powicke, 'Richard Baxter and
the Quakers', in *Friends' Quarterly Examiner*, 1919, p. 182.
[5] *R.B.*, pt. iii. sect. 143.

parish church or to 'the privater Minister and Worship', whichever was 'most spiritual, powerful and profitable' in the place where he happened to be, but in either case going occasionally to the worship which he did not regularly attend, 'yea, tho it were to one that is against Infant Baptism by mistake',[1] that he might not seem to disown either communion. It was, ultimately, the same tolerance, the same concern for all God's children, good and bad, learned and unlearned, whether in the right or mistaken, which made him oppose all Separatism so vigorously. The case against the 'gathered church' can hardly be put more cogently than in the following passage:

> I will never join with them that will have but one Form in Christ's School. I would have the A B C there taught as well as the profoundest Mysteries. 'Tis no Sign of the Family of God to have no Children (what if I said Infants) in it, but strong Men only: Nor of the Hospital of Christ, to have none Sick; nor of his Net to have no Fish, but good; nor of his Field, to have no Tares: Flesh and Blood hath ticed me oft to Separation, for Ease; but its too easy a way to be of God.[2]

With these convictions it must have been peculiarly difficult to stand firm against the blandishments of the Establishment, and to be forced into a false position, involving some form of the very separatism which he disowned. Baxter's position, in fact, was so central as to be eccentric. It allowed him, however, the advantages, which are not negligible, of the 'free lance', and possibly all men trusted him the more just because he was so openly of no party but Christ's, and could see both sides of most issues, or more than two, and had some sympathy with all. To the student desirous of direction in his reading, he could send a long list of the most useful books in every faculty, for he seemed to read everything. Of the ignoramus he could write:

> Thousands believe savingly, that have not wit enough to tell you truly what believing is; and many thousands have the

[1] R. Baxter's *Unnecessary Separating Disowned* (printed in his *Catholick Communion Defended, ad fin.*), p. 11.
[2] *R.B.*, App. iii, p. 62.

Spirit that know not what the Spirit is. . . . I can give a truer description of any county in England, and distance of one town from another by my maps, though I know not the places, than most men that live in those counties can do, because they know but a smaller part of it; and yet they know their own homes better, and their knowledge is more sensible and experimental, and beneficial to them.[1]

They know their own homes better: there is the saving modesty which will not intrude into either home or heart, yet which longs to be the bearer of the light of Christ into every place which has an open door or window. In an appeal for reverence in his *Reformed Pastor*, Baxter says that 'we should, as it were, suppose we saw the throne of God, and the millions of glorious angels attending him';[2] and the secret of his influence was that he *did* see the throne of God, and the glorious angels attending Him, and his people saw that he saw (as his readers may see still), and they wanted to see too. Moreover, because, 'when he spake of weighty Soul-Concerns, you might find his very Spirit Drench'd therein',[3] his people did see something of what he saw, till 'we were fain to build five Galleries' in the church, and on Sundays 'you might hear an hundred Families singing Psalms and repeating Sermons, as you passed through the Streets'.[4] Nothing in all Baxter's writings is more revealing than, at the end of a lengthy, argumentative work on *The Reasons of the Christian Religion*, his sudden outburst, as if he was weary with forbearing, and could not stay:

Thy presence makes a crowd a Church; Thy converse makes a closet, or solitary wood or field, to be kin to the angelical choir.[5]

1945

[1] R. Baxter, *Practical Works*, XX. 189.
[2] *Id.*, *Reformed Pastor*, p. 184.
[3] Matthew Sylvester, Funeral Sermon, printed in *R.B.*, *ad fin.*, p. 14.
[4] *R.B.*, pt. i. sect. 136.
[5] R. Baxter, *Practical Works*, XXI. 391.

XII

WALTER CRADOCK (1606?–1659):
THE MAN AND HIS MESSAGE

SOME years ago Dr Selbie wrote in the *Congregational Quarterly*[1] that belief in the doctrine of the Holy Spirit was the acid test of a living Church: it is in this high tradition, now so unfashionable, that Cradock takes his place. Together with this emphasis in his approach goes, I think inevitably, an appeal to religious experience, a faith in the possibility of fresh light from God, and a recognition of natural as well as biblical revelation; it is interesting to observe this, if only as a reminder that, despite the attacks of the dialectical theologians, natural revelation (as perhaps it should be called rather than natural theology) is not a nineteenth-century invention nor confined to Catholic mysticism, and that faith in new light is not a product of the theory of evolution nor the appeal to experience a result of the 'new psychology'. Cradock further insists on the central-ity in Christian doctrine of the Fatherhood of God; this also, then, is not simply a 'pre-War emphasis, initiated by Fair-bairn, and dependent on an undue regard for the Synoptic Gospels'. The fact, of course, is that all these tendencies—Holy Spirit, natural revelation, experience, fresh light, God's Fatherhood—form a definite tradition in Christianity, and a tradition of which there seems no reason to be ashamed, either because it has been the tradition of the Sects rather than of the Church, or because it is now out of fashion. Part of the historical interest of Congregationalism is in its inter-weaving of the Calvinist and Anabaptist strands; in the quater-centenary year of the *Institutio* it has been natural to stress the Calvinist strand, but in the classical Puritans, of whom Cradock may justly be counted as one, the other strand, the texture of which I have suggested, is often as markedly present. I have called it Anabaptist for want of a better name, but I believe that certain of its threads may be discovered already in the Lollard Movement, while in

[1] July 1926, p. 357.

Cradock's day it was becoming strongly represented by the Quakers, with whom his sympathy, at least potentially,[1] will be evident. Since I am personally in sympathy with the Anabaptist strand, it may be as well to say plainly that I did not study Cradock on this account, but came to him for his own sake, not knowing what I should find. I thought it best, however, to indicate the general orientation of my paper, before retiring and allowing Cradock to speak for himself.

His dates are usually given as 1606?–1659, he succeeded William Wroth as minister of the first Congregational church in Wales, and he was appointed a Trier; otherwise there seems little in his life which calls for remark.[2] Yet on his contemporaries his influence was sufficiently great for them to bring him from Llanvaches in Monmouthshire to London, to preach at All Hallows and before the Parliament. A perusal of his sermons[3] reveals a most attractive personality, that of a humble, earnest, deeply spiritual preacher, whose Celtic[4] origin appears in the warm, tender style of his appeals and illustrations, but who shows above all simply a longing to bring men to Christ. 'I doe verily believe, that he preached these Choise Lectures from the bosome of Jesus Christ, that these things were the very experiments[5] of his owne soule, and the lively actings of the spirit of God within him': so writes John Robotham to the reader, very justly.

Cradock was a Congregationalist, and he could say a word in defence of the Independent polity, of the theocratic nature of which he was not unconscious: it was his complaint against Papacy and Prelacy that under them 'the people never had

[1] He was not the only man of that age who showed at once a sharp antagonism to the Quakers and a partial sympathy with their outlook; cf., e.g., Henry More.
[2] His son-in-law Thomas Jones, of Abergavenny (T. Rees, Prot. Noncon. in Wales, p. 57), should perhaps be identified with Thomas Jones, of Bedwellty, who obtained a licence to teach at a Baptist conventicle in his own house (G. L. Turner, Orig. Records, II. 1227).
[3] The original quarto edition of his collected sermons was republished in 1800: both editions are in the Congregational Library. I am indebted to Dr Sippell of Marburg for the loan of the original edition and of other Puritan texts from which I quote.
[4] Cradock is English for Caradoc.
[5] This use of experiment and experimentally is significant for Cradock's type of piety. Geo. Fox's 'And this I knew experimentally' (Journal, 1901 edn., I. 11) is well known, but the word is also to be found not only in a mystic like John Everard but in such a sober Puritan as John Owen.

yet liberty to choose men according to God's own heart, that would feed them with knowledge and understanding'. It was evidently the freedom of Congregationalism which attracted him, for he was no sectarian. For him

> Presbytery and Independency are not two religions: but one religion to a godly, honest heart; it is only a little rufling of the fringe.

In contrast with the army, where 'there is abundance of sweet love', he laments:

> We are the most miserable men in the world, this poor City: if a man had as much grace as Paul had, if some Independent see him, and say he is inclining to Presbytery, or if a Presbyterian see him, and say, he is inclining to Independencie, then let him go, and cut his throat.
>
> When I have communion with a Saint, I must not looke so much whether he be of such an opinion, or whether he have taken the Covenant, or have been baptized once or twice or ten times, but see if he have fellowship with the Father, and with Jesus Christ.[1] I speake not this as if my opinion were for rebaptization or against the baptizing of the infants of beleevers, the contrary appears by my practise: but only, that such difference of opinion should not hinder their mutuall receiving each other to fellowship and communion, who are in fellowship with God and Jesus Christ.

In keeping with this attitude is his condemnation of undue scrupulosity and of the formal fastings which were the order of the day:

> I have known one eat but one meal in a week; and let them eat little or much, they defile their consciences. One while they must go so in their apparel with lace, and after that, lace damneth them. . . . This shews that they are defiled; for to a good man everything is pure.[2]

[1] *Cf.* Joshua Sprigg, *A Testimony to Approaching Glory*, 1649, p. 127:

Is there no unity, but where there is uniformity? Because we have not still one form, have we not therefore one Father (*sic*), one Lord, one Baptism, or one common condition of suffering?

[2] Margaret Fox had the same criticism to make, when Quakerism began to stiffen (*Works*, p. 535):

they can soon get into an outward garb, to be all alike outwardly; but this will not make them true Christians. It's the Spirit that gives life.

The first thing that I fear highly provokes God among us
. . . is our formall humiliation, and repentance, and fasting,
and such like things. . . . I feare our fast dayes are the most
smoky dayes in Gods nostrills of all the dayes of the yeer. . . .
There is a great deal of stirre about the Sacrament, and the
mixed multitude, and the Service-Book, and I know not what
. . . and people think there is a glorious reformation, but God
knows where it is, only there is a great stirre about it.[1]

He reveals very clearly the Puritan's passion for integrity, his
hatred of all sham:

How hatefull, how abominable hypocrisie is to God.
It is a principle in Religion that Christians should observe
(and a principle, that is a generall grand rule) to call things as
they are, to call a Spade a Spade.

With a firm hand Cradock strikes at the root of scrupulosity,
when he warns against an exaggerated biblicism:

Remember, the greatest miserie to an honest heart (next to
an old Testament spirit, that is the rise of all) is this, a mis-
drawing of rules out of the word of God: you take a word
and doe not compare it with other Scriptures, and see whether
it be temporarie and doth absolutely binde: but you goe with
your book under your arme, and think all wise men are out,
and you have Scripture for it: beware of that.[2]

The question to ask of a man was not, or not only, 'Has he
Scripture for it?' but 'Has he the Spirit?'[3]

[1] *Cf.* John Everard, *The Gospel-Treasury Opened*, 2nd edn., 1659, II. 253:
Truly they make a great deal of stir about the Outward Baptism more
then need: for outward Baptism is but a Type and Shadow of the True
Baptism.
[2] *Cf.* Everard, *op. cit.*, I. 370:
there are Too, Too many such children (who indeed think themselves Tall
men) who have most of the Scriptures at their fingers ends; who Because
they can answer or discourse of any Catechistical Point in Divinity, they
must be accounted The greatest Proficients and Tallest Christians.
[3] The nearness of this to the Quaker approach appears, *e.g.* from a comparison
with the following from William Penn's *Summons or Call to Christendom* (*Select
Works*, 1825 edn., II. 338):
You profess the holy scriptures, but what do you witness and experience?
. . . Can you set to your seal they are true, by the work of the same Spirit
in you, that gave them forth in the holy ancients?

O such a one doth great things, he prayes, and hears, and reads, and disputes much: I [Aye] but hath he the spirit, or no?

The greatest difference (that I know) in all the Book of God, between Saints and Sinners is, that the one hath the Spirit, and the other hath not.

The spirit is all in all in religion.

Like others with experience of spiritual religion, he speaks of its self-authenticating nature:

A man may know the spirit in himself clearly by the evidence of the same spirit, And a man that hath the spirit may know the spirit in another by the spirit . . . How can a poor lamb know the dam among a thousand?

For as in naturall things, you know, that by the same light whereby I see the Sun, by the same light I know that I see him[1]: So there is in the very manifestation of God to the soule, it carries a witnesse in it self, it is so cleare, that when I have it, though I never had it before, and I cannot demonstratively speak a word what it is, yet I know as it is Gods sight, so I know I see him.

With John Robinson, Cradock believes that 'the Lord hath yet more light':

One maine cause of contention among us is, God comes now with more light than wee had before; we have more, and more; but this light is not a full light, I mean thus, this light comes, and shines but in part of the will of God to us.

Goe on in love, and when it comes to that wee shall see more light.

If you endeavour to do that which is pleasing in Gods eye, God will reveale himself more and more clearly and fully to your soules.

---

[1] It is interesting to find Bp. Pecock accusing the Lollards of using precisely this simile (which has a long history) to explain the nature of faith; *cf.* also John Owen on Scripture (*Divine Originall*, 1659, pp. 72f., 80):

Let the Sun arise in the firmament, and there is no need of Witnesses to prove and confirme unto a seeing man that it is day. . . . Doth it not evince its selfe, with an Assurance above all that can be obteined by any Testimony whatever? . . . It is all one, by what meanes, by what hand, whether of a Child or a Church, . . . the Scripture comes unto us; Come how it will, it hath its Authority in it's selfe . . . and hath it's power of manifesting it's selfe . . . from it's owne innate Light.

With the 'jangling' of 'proud Professors' he has no more sympathy than has George Fox:

> There are many men, I [Aye], and many Professors, that doe not love to heare a man in a few modest words to commend the spirit of God: but all must be by studie, and reading, and learning, and for the spirit of God it is a plaine meere Cypher, and there is an end. But my life on it (if I had a hundred I would say so) they shal be beholding to the spirit of God, and extoll him before they be taught spiritually; they shall be willing to lay downe all their learning (as I have seen a learned godly man of late) even with the Plow-boy.

Of the original Gospel

> we see the Lord chose simple people to go, and preach it, he chose generally fisher men, and such poor men, and women[1] sometimes. Rude men, in a manner without learning, these were to goe and tell a simple story of Jesus Christ, and him crucified, &c.

So of their successors

> it may be he hath Greek, and Latine, and not Hebrew, though he be full of the Holy Ghost, and yet the people must be starved.
>   and shall we raile at such, and say they are Tub-Preachers, and they were never at the University? Let us fall downe, and honour God.

How much better that such Tub-Preachers should help in 'the most glorious work that ever I saw in England . . . the Gospel is run over the Mountaines between Brecknockshire, and Monmouthshire, as the fire in the thatch' than that the Spirit should be restrained, as in former days. Of the days of 'stinted prayers' Cradock's memories are bitter:

> When it may be the poore Ministers soule was full of groanes, and sighs, and he would have rejoyced to have poured out his

[1] This perhaps with a glance at the revival of preaching among women in Cradock's time, and not only in Quakerism, though only in Quakerism was this particular form of the freedom of the Spirit permanently retained.

soule to the Lord, he was tied to an old Service-Booke, and must read that till he grieved the Spirit of God, and dried up his own spirit as a chip, that he could not pray if he would; and he must read it for an houre together, and then it may be come into the Pulpit: but his spirit was gone.

This is not to say that Cradock underestimated learning. He was evidently familiar with Hebrew as well as Greek, and could quote a Latin poet where it suited. He knew his history too: more than once he refers to 'Queen Maryes time', and of the part played by the Lollards he is fully aware. Nor does his enthusiasm for spiritual religion imply a contempt for the ordinances of Christ's Church:

> The devil . . . hath brought us from repetition of the word, and from singing of Psalms, and many from baptizing the infants of the godly, and divers from the supper of the Lord,[1] and from hearing the word of God preached.
>
> There is a people that throw away the ordinance of prayer, and they professe to live immediately upon God without ordinances, without prayer, and without all the rest. I do not know what their perfections may be, therefore I cannot judge; but this I know as far as ever I had experience, that the chiefest way of communion with God is spirituall prayer.

Elsewhere he says:

> I speak not this as if the Spirit were contrary to the Word, as some men to advance the Spirit, set the Word and Spirit by the ears; but the Spirit leads by the Word.

That his idealism was not a spurious one, that he understood men's frailties well enough, is apparent from the following:

> But you goe home when Sermon is done, and say there was a great Company, a throng, and he Preached a little too long, and we must goe to him againe after Dinner, and so you mind not, the Lord Jesus pittie you; that is the reason that you are ignorant, and will be World without end, because you mind not spirituall things.

It is his pure spiritual idealism which is Cradock's most marked characteristic, and which is the grandest thing about

---

[1] This is interesting in view of the date (1650).

him. The grace of God is a reality to him in his own life, and he longs for it to be so in the life of others. The Saint, he tells us, can say:

> God hath appeared two hundred times, two thousand times to my soule. I have seene him one while in the Sacrament, I have seene him among the Saints, I have seene him in such a country, in such a condition, in such a place, in such a medow, in such a wood, when I read his word, and called upon his name.[1]
>
> I remember, in such a Countrey, in such a Chamber, in such a place, where God shew'd himself to me, and I was satisfied; I saw everything vanish before me, and I desired nothing but that.
>
> God may be out of sight, and ken, and yet you may be Saints: but there is a more glorious life, when a man always walks in Gods sight, God seeing him, and he seeing God. These things are not for the head, but for the heart. Now talk with thy heart a little, and see what is thy temper, and thy way, and if thou finde it not thus, tell God: the minister said that there be Saints that live gloriously, that are fond of God, that are always with him, sleeping, and waking, at bed, and board, they are never out of his sight. Lord, make me such.

Cradock would have agreed wholeheartedly with Joshua Sprigg that 'the glory of our moderne Orthodox Divinity' was that 'The Father himself loves us, That the enmity is on the creature's part, not God's'.[2]

> Ye are Come to mount Sion, to the glorious state in the new Testament; and there is nothing but what is amiable, and what is beautiful.
>
> It is ordinary with the Saints, that they have a little adoption, they can cry Abba father, a little, and low, and at some-times: but there is a great deale of the spirit of bondage mingled

[1] *Cf.* Agnes Beaumont (a member of Bunyan Meeting, Bedford), *Narrative . . . in 1674*, ed. G. B. Harrison, pp. 6f.:
> And, the Lord knowest it, their was scarce A Corner in the house, or Barnes, or Cowhousen, or Stable, or Closes vnder the hegges, or in the wood, but I was made to poure out my soul to god.

[2] J. Sprigg, *op. cit.*, Preface; John Smyth also taught that Christ's sacrifice 'doth not reconcile God unto us, which did never hate us, nor was our enemy, but reconcileth us unto God and slayeth the enmity and hatred which is in us against God'; cit. by R. Barclay, *Inner Life of Religious Societies of the Commonwealth*, p. 111, n.

with it, there are sometimes feares, secret whisperings in the heart. . . . Now in the New Testament we should labour for a full spirit of adoption. . . . If thou come below this, if thou call on God with feare, and canst not cry abba, abba, that is as much as daddie, daddie, as our babes use to say, if thou doe not come so high, thou art spoiled, and undone, desire God to teach you this Lesson also.

From this filial relation to God Cradock is not afraid to draw the conclusion that the Christian has a freedom not known before:

It is base to tie a son as much as a servant. So we being now to be sonnes, truly and really, the Lord hath given us a larger liberty.

What an abominable thing is it to tie the sonnes of God that are not babies, now under tutors, with paltrie things, when the Spirit of God in the least Saint is better able to determine than all the Bishops.

More often, however, it is the peace and trust and security of the Christian upon which he dwells: 'we must suffer: talk of Reformation, and what you will; all honest hearts inevitably shall have tribulation'; but

our trouble is not a little imprisonment, or poverty: Paul, or Sylas, were in prison, and were to be hanged the next day, for ought they knew; yet they could sing.[1] The man is as his minde is.[2] . . . There is (saith the Apostle) a peace of God that shall keep you, or as the word in the Greek is, garison you.

As if you should see a Plowman, or a countrie man come to a Mathematician, that were at his Globe, and his compasses, and were drawing lines from one to another; the Countrie man knowes nothing of this: but he would not therefore say the other is a foole, and doth he knoweth not what. He would rather say, I warrant you he is a Scholler, and hath had good breeding: but allas what simple people are we in the Countrie, we know not what belongs to the Globe, and compasses. So a Christian when he is in affliction, he doth not say, God doth he knows not what, and he plagueth me: but sayth he, God

[1] So could Fox (*Journal*, 1901 edn., I. 171f.).
[2] A good Puritan sentiment; *cf.* Milton, *Paradise Lost*, I. 254f.; Cromwell, *Letters and Speeches*, Speech V.

hath wisdome, and love, in all this; only I am a simple poore creature that know not this.

When a mans ways please God, the stones of the street shall be at peace with him. Did you ever see the stones of the street angry with you? but the meaning is, when a mans ways are cross with God, and he hath a guilty conscience, a guilty soul hath no true peace, he is ready almost to fall out with the stones in the street, he quarrels with his servant, with his horse, with everything, because he hath an unquiet spirit within; when a man pleaseth God, the stones shall be at peace with him, that is, he shall be at peace with everything. Why so? because there is an infinite, unspeakable quiet in his own soul.

One might fear that this quietistic strain would imply a certain self-centredness in religion, but the passion with which Cradock preaches to others shows that it need not be so; he also says expressly that 'a strong, fond saint takes less care for his owne salvation, but he cares much for the service of Jesus Christ'. What it does imply is a tolerance, a slowness to judge others, springing from a humble gratitude for God's mercies to oneself. So Cradock interprets Jesus's words:

but many that are first shall be last, and the last shall be first. As if he should say, I would not have you to be proud, and to crow over that poor man that is run from me, because you are old Disciples; it may be that man may come back again to me, and be my best servant when you may run away: for many that are first shall be last, and the last shall be first.

With this in mind, he cannot bring himself either to be proud towards sinners or to condemn those who are wanderers in the faith:

It may be because of my fleshliness I think him to be an heretick or a Schismatick, and it may be he is a Saint, and childe of God, and one of his hidden ones.

And indeed Beloved, I doubt not but that there is many a poore sinner that now follows the ale-house, and drinking, and swearing, and whoreing, that yet may be in Heaven before thee and me.

The right thing, therefore, is not proudly to condemn sinners but humbly and gently to invite them to come to Christ:

We are not sent to get Gally-slaves to the Oares, or a Bear to the stake: but he sends us to wooe you as spouses, to marrie you to Christ.

I am the doore: But some may say, wee love not to go in at such a doore, unlesse wee know when it is locked, and when it is not. No, saith he, I am not a doore that hath locks and bolts, that will bring you into straits; but I am a doore that you shall goe in and out, and find pasture for your soules.

This is Cradock's characteristic note. It reappears in a passage with which we must end and which may be quoted *in extenso*, that the appeal of his simple sustained rhythms may be felt —they are simple, but is it fanciful to be reminded by their swayings and swellings of John Donne?

For your comfort, this is one thing; thou that hast but little grace coming in so many yeers: I tell thee, God saith that grace is like the springing of the sea; or the springing of the yeer. Now in the springing of the sea, when men would have a tide for their passage, a man is glad to see a little turning of the water first, it is so much the nearer: then he observes, and is glad to see the Sea rise, and cover a few stones or marks, though it be little: but stay till it be almost full Sea, when it is high tide, then every thing almost is covered on a sudden, the tide over-runs all. Take it in the spring of the yeer (for we should learn something from the creatures) about February, you are glad to see the buds of Haw thorn; you look a week together, and it grows a little, and you see no other, it is a signe that Summer is coming. In the beginning of March it may be there are two or three things more, and they come slowly, and you are glad to see them, and look on them every day. In Aprill or May, the Gardens are full of Flowers, and the fields full of grass; you know not what to observe. So it is in experience, in the beginning the Lord makes a Saint glad of a Primrose, of a little turning of the water, that the flood, that the stream is turned; if he begin to hear the word, that hated it, and to rejoyce in the company of good neighbours, that hated it, two or three little Primroses. But grace comes as the tide; stay a while, and thou shalt see such a flowing of grace in thy soul, that thou knowest not where to look; such a tide of love, and joy, and knowledge, such innumerable lessons, that thou knowest not where to look. Therefore wait upon the Lord, and thou shalt see grace come in as the tide.

128

Lastly, thou dost not (it may be) make use of the experiences thou hast had of God. Thou hast had abundance of experience of the Lord; and we are apt to forget: As Christ saith, do you now doubt whether you have bread? O ye of little faith[1]! Truly the very creatures will rise in judgement against us, that having had so many experiments of God, we are so shie of trusting God, and thinking well of God. Didst thou ever see a Dog (let me instance in that vile creature) (for God would have us learn from the creatures, and God hath cast them so that they should not be onely for our use, but every thing in reference to his Gospel, that we may not only occasionally draw such things that hap hazzard fall out, but to observe their nature, and qualities, and learn somewhat from them) you see in a Dog when he hath abused you, it may be against his will, and it may be you have beat him; he runs away, or he comes with fear, and is very shie, and will hardly come to you: but take him in your arms, and stroak him, and all his fear is gone; when you smile, he thinks you mean him no hurt, he hath no thought of your former anger. So we come many times to the Lord, and are shie, and tremble, and fear, and think he means to hurt us; and what are his thoughts? How oft hath God taken us in his arms and stroaked us, and laid us down again, and yet we fear again, and are worse in many respects than the bruit creatures. When the Master hath the Dog, he may kill him if he will; but he stroakes him, and the Dog thinks his master means well to him; so, many times God might kill us, and throw us into Hell, and catch us at advantage, yet in stead of that he loves us, and imbraceth us, and layes us down again; and yet we are so shie, we fear, and distrust him. We have not that plainnesse of heart as that old Martyr said, I have lived eighty yeers, and he never did me any hurt: So God many times hath had advantage to have thrown us into hell, yet he hath kissed, and stroaked us. Why should we be so fearfull, when afflictions, and troubles come upon us? These things procure sadnesse, because we do not trust in that God, that in our extremity hath been friendly, and fatherly to us. The Lord help you to lay up these few broken words in your hearts.

1937

[1] *Cf.* John Everard, *op. cit.*, I. 319:
why murmur you, O you Of little faith? . . . Let me ask you, do you not believe that God is your Father?
Prof. P. Smith points out, in *The Age of the Reformation*, p. 696, that the subject of the Prodigal Son was treated by twenty-seven German dramatists in that period.

XIII

THE LORD PROTECTOR:
REFLECTIONS ON DR PAUL'S LIFE OF CROMWELL

O LIVER CROMWELL'S life demands a retelling in every generation; and fortunate is he who is called to the task—called he must be, else the task were too formidable—for of popular interest he is assured. The framework of Dr Paul's book[1], as the twenty chapter-titles at once indicate, is straight biographical narrative; and very good narrative it is, palling a trifle at times with the cumbersomeness of the detail, but never for long: the interest is well sustained. While availing himself of the great four-volume edition of Cromwell's *Writings and Speeches* issued from Harvard University by Professor W. C. Abbott between 1937 and 1947, Dr Paul would seem to have discovered no facts unknown to previous biographers. He would not, I think, claim to have done this. His intention was, rather, to concentrate on the mutual relationship of religion and politics in Cromwell's life. To some extent no serious student of Cromwell can do otherwise; but Dr Paul's especial purpose is to resolve the 'contradiction' which he sees between 'the Independent who held "democratic" ideas in ecclesiastical matters' and the man who 'ended by becoming an absolute dictator'. Cromwell's 'Independent or Congregational churchmanship', he says, 'appears to run counter to so much within his life'.

This carries the promise, which is not belied, of a fascinating study. Dr Paul's resolution of the problem, put briefly, is as follows. Cromwell had the courage and the consistency to carry into public and political life the doctrine of Providence which as a guide for private life was shared by all Puritans—and by others also, for it was 'no Puritan monopoly'. He believed that the God whose mighty acts are declared in Scripture still makes His will known in and

[1] Robert S. Paul, *The Lord Protector: Religion and Politics in the Life of Oliver Cromwell*. Lutterworth Press, 1955.

through events; and that His intervening and overruling will is especially plain when what has happened for good is strange, unexpected and undesigned by human wills, and when the persons He has used as His instruments are weak in themselves but free from self-seeking in the desire to serve Him. In the power of this conviction Cromwell mounted high; or, in biblical language, went from strength to strength. 'I sought not this place', he constantly avers; 'I speak it before God, angels and men; I did not.' 'I called not myself to this place; I say again, I called not myself to this place.' 'There is ne'er a man within these walls that can say, Sir, you sought it.' Cromwell knew himself to be 'a miserable and wretched creature', 'a poor worm'; but 'I do feel myself lifted on by a strange force, I cannot tell why.' 'By the providence of God it is perfectly come to pass, not by our wisdom, for I durst not design it, I durst not admit of so mixed, so low a consideration.' 'I profess his very hand has led me. I preconsulted none of these things.'

This assurance that the course of his own career fulfilled God's will, and this criterion for the assurance, Cromwell felt equally strongly and applied with equal vigour in relation to the career of the army. 'Wherever they engaged the enemy', he said of his men, 'they beat them continually;' and it was true: in Frederic Harrison's words, 'no single operation of war that he ever undertook had failed'. 'Sir,' wrote Cromwell, 'what can be said to these things? Is it an arm of flesh that doth these things? . . . It is the Lord only . . . Sir, you see the work is done by divine leading'. 'Because of our weakness,' he wrote of his victory at Dunbar, 'because of our strait, we were in the Mount, and in the Mount the Lord would be seen'. Of the whole course of events he claimed that there was 'a remarkable print of Providence set upon it, so that he who runs may read it'.

In relation to the career of the nation, in its civil and parliamentary aspect after the battle of Worcester, the assurance proved more difficult to hold, the criterion to apply. The weakness of successive Parliaments seemed something nearer 'weakness and folly'; and the only way God seemed to over-rule their incompetence was by further magnifying Cromwell himself. In C. H. Firth's words, 'it sufficed for him to remain passive, and power came back to his hands by a sort of natural necessity'.[1] Cromwell found himself increasingly over against the other leaders of the people, even in opposition to them. But had not this been regularly the case with the prophets and with those set over the Lord's people? 'Be not afraid of their words, nor be dismayed at their looks, though they be a rebellious house', he read in *Ezekiel*. 'The paradox which exists between Cromwell the Independent and Cromwell the Lord Protector . . . was resolved in the "prophetic" function of Cromwell's political mission.' Increasingly he saw himself prefigured by Moses or by David. 'In place of the Divine Right of Kingship, a new Divine Right of Vocation was asserted', still 'founded squarely upon the doctrine of Providence'.

This is well argued. It was well argued in less compass, more than fifty years ago, by R. F. Horton, whose *Oliver Cromwell: a study in personal religion* was in its tenth thousand in 1899; but Horton's book is forgotten—Dr Paul does not mention it—and it is good to have the argument set out afresh. How far, I want to go on to ask, does Cromwell's fundamental conviction correspond to any conviction we hold ourselves?

'There was a direct N and halfe of M providentially made upon my breeches plaine to view in any mans sight, made of mire with leaping', a Puritan wrote in his diary in 1663, at a time when the object of his desires bore the name of Mary Naylor; 'I looked upon it to be from providence and fortold somethinge in my apprehension, the smallest of God's providences should not be past by without observation.'[2] I remember another Puritan diarist who sought to interpret the 'providence' manifested in the cat's jumping on to his mother's lap. The underlying attitude of mind, and consequently the faith, expressed here is evidently different from anything common among us today. Whether it is for 'natural law' or for chance or for both that we make room, we are shy of seeing divine intervention in the natural or the trivial. Yet

[1] C. H. Firth, *Oliver Cromwell and the Rule of the Puritans in England*, 1935 edn., p. 340. I add references only for passages from modern works not in Dr. Paul's book.

[2] Roger Lowe, *Extracts from a Lancashire Diary, 1663–1678*, Manchester, 1876, p. 11.

we still, most of us, believe that we may have God's hand upon us for good, and may know when we have it; and we are still inclined to think that a call to a pastorate, or an invitation to some other task, is more likely to be of God if it is one we did not seek.

Probably, although in theological circles the difference between God's ways and men's ways has of late been made sharper, in day-to-day practice we make it less sharp than did Cromwell and his contemporaries. I fancy we allow reason and 'the normal' a larger place in our deciding what course is right; although Cromwell could say, 'what God would have us do, he does not desire we should step out of the way for it'. We see that too pronounced a dualism, too keen a fear of reason, may lead paradoxically through the atrophying of the critical faculty, to something near an identification between God's ways and men's. To 'suffer others to magnifie him' might acquit Cromwell of all self-seeking and yet lead him into as strange a place, as far from lowliness, as it led James Nayler, when Nayler suffered others to pay him Messianic honours, for it is of Nayler (as well as of St Bernard) that one thinks when one reads that Cromwell 'completely identified his cause with the Will of God'.

Probably, for these and other reasons, we are more aware of the difficulties and perils in interpreting God's will in events than Cromwell was; although Cromwell, again, could say, 'How easy is it to find arguments for what we would have'; 'uprightness, if it be not purely of God, may be, nay commonly is, deceived'; and 'mercies should not be temptations; yet we too oft make them so'. Certainly, we are more aware of the particular danger in equating God's will with success, in the unredeemed sense of the word. We feel the force of the words of a Republican which Dr Paul quotes: 'God in his providence doth often permit of that which he doth not approve; and a thief may make as good a title to every purse which he takes by the highways.' Even more penetrating is the comment of another of Cromwell's contemporaries, a conforming clergyman:

For a long time their talk was of providence, and their successes. First, their cause was God's cause, which he would prosper for their sakes (his people, his secret ones) and for his promises, whereof they had a large stock in the Old Testament and the Revelations. This had a strong smack of prophaneness. Then God prospered their cause, therefore it was God's cause, a pure Mahometan conclusion. Now that it's at a loss, the note is (and mark it, I beseech you) God in the ways of his providence towards us walks in the dark.[1]

This may be regarded as too unsympathetic; yet we cannot help being stirred uneasily by Richard Baxter's judgement that Cromwell 'meant honestly in the main . . . till Prosperity and Success corrupted him'. We cannot forget, moreover, that the success in which Cromwell primarily saw God's will revealed was a military success. Few of us today can say as easily as he, 'War is good when led to by our Father.'

The paradox is that it was not until after his last battle was won that Cromwell 'began to doubt'.[2] It is true that victorious generals are not normally good civilian administrators. How should they be? Yet, unless Dr Paul's whole thesis is mistaken, Cromwell was not just another victorious general; he was fundamentally a man of God, seeking and (till now) finding God's will and way. Why is it that, after the dissolution at the end of 1653 of the Nominated Parliament, which S. R. Gardiner justly calls 'the high-water mark of Puritanism',[3] Cromwell stumbles and never really recovers himself, so that the title of this book, *The Lord Protector*,[4] is in a sense the label of a tragedy? 'The failure of the Nominated Parliament', Dr Paul observes, '. . . meant disillusionment'.

[1] John Shaw, *No Reformation of the Established Religion*, 1685, as quoted in *Memoirs of . . . Ambrose Barnes*, ed. W. H. D. Longstaffe, Surtees Soc., L, 1867, p. 410. Over the offer of the Crown in 1657 Cromwell said, 'who can love to walk in the dark? But Providence doth often so dispose'.

[2] C. H. Firth, *Oliver Cromwell*, p. 335.

[3] S. R. Gardiner, *History of the Commonwealth and Protectorate*, 1903 edn., II. 340.

[4] Was the title meant to refer back to the Protector Somerset? and did Cromwell admire, and even imitate Somerset, who had many characteristics similar to his own? cf. A. F. Pollard's summing up of Somerset in *Dict. Nat. Biog.*: 'Strength of conviction and purity of motives admirably fitted him to lead a religious movement. . . . As a general he was successful in every military operation he undertook. . . . He lacked patience, hated compromise and consistently underrated the strength of the forces opposed to him. . . . Under his sway there was less persecution than there was again for a century. . . . Naturally warm-hearted and affable, the possession of power rendered him peevish and over-bearing.'

In Cromwell's speech opening the following Parliament, 'the note of something even akin to despair was not entirely absent'. Later, over the offer of the Crown, Cromwell is 'obviously perplexed in his own mind', 'a bewildered man': 'was this the Supreme Call or the Great Temptation?' In language which Cromwell would have understood, if James Nayler had used it to him (as Nayler came to do of himself), Cromwell can be seen to have 'lost his guide', to be 'running before his guide'. Why was this?

Apart from the providence of God as revealed in events, Cromwell's guidance, like that of most of the Puritans, came from a three-fold source: it came from the word of God in Scripture, from the answering word of the Spirit in his own heart, and from the support and restraint of God's people. Throughout his book Dr Paul has done a most valuable service by indicating many of the biblical references which underlie all Cromwell's thought and language; but he offers no critique of Cromwell's use and application of Scripture. What justification had Cromwell for seeing himself pre-figured by Moses or David, for believing that 'they were passing through the events foretold in the 110th Psalm' and that Psalm 68 was prophetic of 'the existing condition of the Church', or for holding that 'the dispensations of the Lord have been as if he had said, England thou art my firstborn?' We feel uneasy about such 'British-Israel' applications of Scripture. Yet we continue to believe that the Bible has an immediate relevance to ourselves and our day; that Christ's words to John, say, are also to every man Jack among us. This is a subject which requires a study to itself, or at least a chapter to itself in a study of the use of Scripture by the Puritans in general, including the Quakers. Perhaps Principal Cunliffe-Jones will one day write it for us?

Secondly, Cromwell formed the habit of 'a waiting posture, desiring to see what the Lord would lead us to'; he feared to tempt God by 'acting before and without faith', and conse-quently often retired 'for a quarter or halfe an hower' before coming to a conclusion. 'I can be passive and let it go, know-ing that innocency and integrity lose nothing by a patient waiting upon the Lord.' This 'period of inactivity' 'before making a big decision' Dr Paul, who is inclined to play down

135

what he calls 'the mystical element in Cromwell's religion', finds 'very difficult to explain'. It did not seem so to T. H. Green, who in a letter to Scott Holland in 1869 could describe 'what Cromwell used to call "a waiting spirit" ' as 'the highest'.[1] Whether difficult to understand or not, it was certainly fundamental to Cromwell's piety, and, together with recourse to Scripture, continued to be so to the end.

What after 1653 was increasingly lacking was the third source of his guidance, the support and restraint of God's people. Dr Paul brings out clearly the significance of Cromwell's loss of the 'intimate Christian fellowship' which he had known in the army. At the same time, many of Cromwell's friends and supporters, the same who later vehemently opposed his acceptance of the crown, were already opposed to his accepting the title of Protector. This may be illustrated from a text in no way extreme, the church book of Broadmead Church, Bristol: 'Oliver Cromwell, called Lord Protector when as God alone was ye Protector of his people; but we sinned.'[2] It is tragic that parliamentary incompetence and Cromwell's consequent supremacy thus synchronized with his friends' alienation and his consequent isolation, but so it was: the one thing which might have saved him was missing. The occasion when George Fox went to see him and, as Fox puts it, 'he catcht mee by ye hande & saide these words with teares in his eyes, Come againe to my house', has an added poignancy from its date, March 1655, when his sense of isolation was growing acute. Thereafter the hardness of heart which he actually discussed with Fox at their meeting quickly descended upon him: later that same month another Friend wrote, 'his heart is hardened, and he cannot believe'. Nor is this simply the biased judgement of a Quaker; 'a hard heart had further hardened' is the judgement on him at this time of Lambert's biographer.[3] So fatal for him was separation from the fellowship of God's people.

Cromwell's isolated position from 1654 onwards has been commented on from another angle by one of the most per-

[1] Stephen Paget, *Henry Scott Holland*, 1921, p. 32.

[2] *Records of a Church of Christ meeting in Broadmead, Bristol*, ed. N.Haycroft, 1865 edn., p. 37.

[3] W. H. Dawson, *Cromwell's Understudy: the life and times of General John Lambert and the rise and fall of the Protectorate*, 1938, p. 286.

ceptive students of English religion, John Stoughton. 'It is very remarkable', Stoughton writes, 'that no ecclesiastical personage appears controlling the affairs of the Commonwealth. . . . We strive in vain to detect any clerical guidance'.[1] Dr Paul makes out that Cromwell 'relied on the advice and services of . . . clergymen like John Owen, Philip Nye and Thomas Goodwin' and calls Owen 'Cromwell's chief adviser in ecclesiastical affairs'. While it is true, in general terms, that 'Owen and his friends took the lead in the ecclesiastical affairs of the country', I think that in relation to Cromwell and the administration Stoughton's judgement is sounder: 'Independents were about his person, but no evidence exists of his constituting any of them ecclesiastical advisers. . . . Owen and Goodwin were too much engaged at Oxford to have many opportunities for conference at Whitehall. Philip Nye . . . was not the person to carry weight with Oliver.' Over the cardinal issue of liberty of conscience, moreover, Cromwell certainly went much further than Owen and the 'Dissenting Brethren' thought desirable. 'They who are for a Congregationall way, doe not hold absolute liberty for all religions', Dr Paul quotes from Jeremiah Burroughes. To Cromwell, on the other hand, the remarkable saying is attributed, 'I had rather that Mahometanism were permitted among us than that one of God's children should be persecuted.' Dr Paul quotes this too; he does not observe, however, that the tract from which it is taken, like Milton's *Sonnet* to Cromwell, which he also quotes, was written directly in opposition to the 'Fundamentals of Religion' which Owen had put out with a view to excluding, as Baxter complained, both Papists and Socinians.

This inclination to claim for Owen too great a share in Cromwell's ecclesiastical administration arises, I think, from Dr Paul's keen desire to claim Cromwell as a Congregationalist, which appears throughout his book. He admits that Cromwell's name is never 'connected with any particular local Church'; but he points to Baxter's words in his autobiography, the *Reliquiae Baxterianae*, that Cromwell's 'Officers purposed to make their Troop a gathered Church, and they all subscribed an Invitation to me to be their Pastor', and

[1] John Stoughton, *History of Religion in England*, 1881 edn., II. 88.

also to the reference to this passage in the index to the *Reliquiae*, which reads, of Cromwell, 'he invites Mr. Baxter to be Chaplain and Pastour to his Regiment when he was forming it into a Church'. This, Dr Paul claims, 'resolves the mystery of his churchmanship'. Is that really the case? It is, surely, dangerous to build on an isolated piece of phrasing, especially since the form of words in the index to the *Reliquiae* would not be chosen by its editor till as late as 1696. C. H. Firth, in a careful consideration of the passage and its significance, sums up more cautiously: 'in spite . . . of all that Baxter and other Presbyterians say against Cromwell's troopers, it must not be supposed that all, or even the majority of them, belonged to the extremer sects of Independents'.[1] Baxter attributes his invitation to become the troop's chaplain to his friend, James Berry, then Cromwell's captain-lieutenant and later one of the Major-Generals; and of Berry's religious affiliation his biographers write: 'like his leader, Cromwell, Berry, although he may be classified as an Independent, seems never to have identified himself very closely with any one particular sect'.[2] Lambert's biographer says much the same of Lambert: 'ecclesiastical labels and doctrinal shibboleths had no attractions for him'; 'he was never known to have openly avowed adhesion to any one of the many rival ecclesiastical systems of the day'.[3] Milton is another who, from the section on the nature of the Church in his *De Doctrina Christiana* as well as from the passionate plea for liberty of conscience in his *Areopagitica*, may be ranked with the Independents, yet who is not known to have been a member of any church.

It is true that as early as 1644 Cromwell is called by Robert Baillie 'a known Independent'; while in 1658 Hugh Peter writes to Henry Cromwell, 'Your father dyed as he lived an Independent'.[4] The difficulty is that, while all Congrega-

[1] C. H. Firth and Godfrey Davies, *The Regimental History of Cromwell's Army*, 1940, II. 35. Firth also sensibly asks, 'who became chaplain of Cromwell's regiment when Baxter refused?', but says the answer 'is uncertain'.

[2] Sir James Berry and S. G. Lee, *A Cromwellian Major-General: the career of Colonel James Berry*, Oxford, 1938, p. 270.

[3] W. H. Dawson, *Cromwell's Understudy*, p. 167.

[4] *Letters and Documents by or relating to Hugh Peter*, ed. R. P. Stearns, Essex Institute Hist. Coll., lxxiii. 1, January 1937, p. 143.

tionalists were Independents, not all Independents were Congregational; and, although there was a fully organized Congregational church worshipping regularly as close to Whitehall as the Abbey, no contemporary, so far as I know, ever placed Cromwell among 'the Congregational men' or charged him with being of 'the Congregational way'. The appointment of the 'Triers' and other ministerial Commissions reflects the same position and purpose as Cromwell's frequent calling of ministerial conferences for discussion: while the Congregational men are in a majority, neither Presbyterians nor Baptists are excluded. What Cromwell sought to be, as Dr Paul well brings out, was, in Cromwell's own words, 'a good constable to keep the peace of the parish'; and the constable must be of no party. Unfortunately Cromwell's being the sole constable made him appear to be, in the eyes of others and perhaps increasingly in his own, above the law. The very real Christian fellowship which may be found among men with a common, but special and temporary purpose, such as the troopers of Cromwell's army, is not the same as that of a church, which consists of both men and women, all living their ordinary lives, with nothing to bind them together except their faith.

Cromwell's *not* being a Congregationalist, in the sense of being a member of a particular church, and (I believe) his never having been one, was in fact a contributing factor in the tragedy of his eventual isolation and bewilderment and in the consequent hardening of his spirit.

The critical reader may therefore be justified in questioning Dr Paul's initial premisses; and, while it is doubtful if he succeeds in his attribution to Cromwell of 'Congregational churchmanship', it is still stranger that he should say, even by way of introduction, that Cromwell 'ended by becoming an absolute dictator'. Fortunately, in the last sentence of the book, in a bold criticism of W. C. Abbott's interpretation of Cromwell, Dr Paul writes that 'whatever else Cromwell was, he was not a dictator in our modern understanding of that word'. Even from the constitutional aspect, as he shows, this is true. 'The Lord Protector had no right to veto'; 'Parliament should be summoned should the Lord Protector fail to summon it himself'; and 'although it was usual for the wishes of the Protector to be obeyed, it was not an invariable rule'. At a deeper level the charge of dictatorship is undercut by the whole argument of the book. It is this, the careful and sympathetic interpretation of Cromwell's 'prophetic mission' and 'Divine Right of Vocation', which, with certain qualifications, evokes admiring assent, and by which the book will live; and live I think it will.

1955

XIV

JOHN BUNYAN THROUGH FRENCH EYES

A MAJOR study of John Bunyan[1] by a Frenchman is something of an event. For a foreigner *The Pilgrim's Progress* must be almost as hard to assimilate as Boswell's *Life of Johnson*. French, especially, has difficulty with the names of the characters—which are so much more than names: Giant Despair's wife, for instance, Mrs Diffidence, would hardly recognize herself as Mme Manque-de-Confiance-en-Soi.

Such difficulties, which inevitably attend any study of a literature other than one's own, M. Talon has not entirely overcome. His book contains a considerable number of misprints or misspellings of English names; a smaller number of misstatements, such as calling Thomas Cartwright (the Lady Margaret Professor at Cambridge) Professor at Margaret College, Oxford; and an occasional wrong attribution of an anonymous work or inexact wording of a book's title, brought about by reliance on a secondary authority. His quotations from Bunyan himself and the references he gives for what he quotes prove sometimes inaccurate. His knowledge of Bunyan's contemporaries is shallow compared with his knowledge of Bunyan, and at times misleads him into attributing to Bunyan's genius what in fact was common form; and his knowledge of the Bible, at least in the Authorized Version, while remarkable in a Frenchman and a Roman Catholic, is not such as to prevent him from missing its influence in a round dozen of passages, which again he attributes rather to Bunyan himself, occasionally with some misunderstanding of their drift. When all is said, these are minor blemishes in comparison with M. Talon's knowledge of Bunyan's own works, and of volumes which influenced Bunyan, such as Arthur Dent's *Plaine-Mans Pathway to*

---

[1] *John Bunyan: L'Homme et L'Oeuvre*. Par Henri A. Talon. Etudes de littérature, d'art et d'histoire. Paris: Editions 'Je Sers'.

Heaven and Samuel Clark's *Mirrour or Looking-Glass both for Saints and Sinners*. Some of the most valuable pages in the book are those in which light is thrown on *The Pilgrim's Progress* from passages in Bunyan's treatise *The Strait Gate* ('in some respects the allegory appears as the poetical development of several abstract themes in' this) and in his autobiography, *Grace Abounding*. By this means, the unity of Bunyan's personality is seen, and his work receives added depth.

M. Talon's special interest and gifts are in the literary and psychological field; but he is well aware that for Bunyan his faith was essential and the conversion or edification of others his main purpose. In contrast with *a notional and historical assent in the head*,[1] Bunyan's faith is *a principle of life, by which a Christian lives, a principle of motion, by which it walks towards heaven in the way of holiness*; it is 'the intuition of God as present'. *Hast thou not sometimes as it were the very warmth of his wings overshadowing the face of thy soul?* In Bunyan's writing this expresses itself in what M. Talon calls his ' "contemporaneity" with Jesus'; 'Bunyan hears Christ's voice as if he were His contemporary.' *Methought I was as if I had seen him born, as if I had seen him grow up, as if I had seen him walk through this world, from the cradle to his cross.* In his sermons Bunyan 'is present at the Creation', even. As M. Talon perceives, this implies a special quality of faith as well as imagination.

The intimate personal character of Bunyan's faith demanded that it be shared and enjoyed with others. For Bunyan 'one of the highest joys of heaven will consist in the fellowship of those truly one in heart and soul'. A foretaste of these joys is to be found in the fellowship of the saints on earth, and here M. Talon makes good use of Professor G. B. Harrison's facsimile edition of the *Church Book of Bunyan Meeting*, the church at Bedford of which Bunyan was a member and latterly the minister. He also sees its relevance to the Palace Beautiful in *The Pilgrim's Progress*. 'The Palace Beautiful is the Church as Bunyan conceives it: a sort of "home", where one finds refreshment in communion with God and in friendship with one's fellows. His Church is

[1] Quotations from Bunyan are in italics, to distinguish them from M. Talon's comments, which are in inverted commas.

social, if this use of the word may be allowed.' For those who are Bunyan's spiritual heirs there is no need to apologize for the use of the word, or indeed for the idea, which is a New Testament idea, though evidently still strange to a Roman Catholic. M. Talon's description of the Church as for Bunyan 'a sort of "home" ' receives an illuminating comment in a later quotation from J. R. Green that 'the "home", as we now think of it, was the creation of the Puritans'. Elsewhere M. Talon cites what he calls John Geree's bold saying in his *Character of an Old English Puritane* (1646) that 'his family hee endeavoured to make a Church'. For Bunyan likewise 'the family is the cell of all Christian society'.

Again, because Bunyan's faith is so deeply personal, its heart is to be found in prayer—his own prayer. *I am sure . . .*, he wrote in his treatise *I Will Pray With The Spirit* (1663), *that it is impossible that all the prayer-books that men have made in the world should lift up or prepare the heart*. In this treatise M. Talon sees the peak of Bunyan's religious thought. *When the Spirit gets into the heart, then there is prayer indeed, and not till then.* 'True prayer is always personal and spontaneous': *there is in prayer an unbosoming of a man's self* and *the whole man is engaged. Right prayer bubbleth out of the heart . . . as blood is forced out of the flesh.*

The strength of the metaphor here—it may be compared with George Fox's phrase, 'If they should be moved to bubble forth a few words'—is highly characteristic of Bunyan. M. Talon rightly seizes on Robert Louis Stevenson's admiration for his 'energy of faith', and for the 'energy of vision' which accompanied it. Quite normally, if paradoxically, what from without is seen as *energy* is felt from within as *effort*: we touch theological knots of Augustinianism and Pelagianism here, but they are daily soluble in Puritan faith and experience. For Bunyan, with all his sureness of God's energizing grace and help, 'the immediate end of human life is effort', and it is effort which must endure to the end. *The will is all*, writes Bunyan, who, like most Puritans, has his place in the tradition of voluntarist theology worked out by William Ames[1];

[1] An illuminating study of Ames and his importance in this connexion may be found in K. Reuter, *Wilhelm Amesius: der führende Theologe des erwachenden reformierten Pietismus* (Beiträge z. Gesch. u. Lehre d. Ref. Kirche, iv), Neukirchen, 1940, esp. pp. 48f., 138ff.

therefore *inflame thy will.* For *O it is hard continuing believing, continuing loving, continuing resisting all that opposeth; we are subject to be weary of well-doing.* M. Talon finds this element of continual conflict and anxiety unsympathetic. He feels in Bunyan 'an unconscious uneasiness', and adds, 'Catholicism or High Anglicanism would perhaps have chased away the winter of his soul'. But it is true, as he says elsewhere, that it is one of Bunyan's 'strongest convictions, that, for a Christian, the absence of all disquiet is already a danger'.

In all this, as in so much else, Christian in *The Pilgrim's Progress* is at one with Bunyan himself in *Grace Abounding*: each figure illustrates the other. 'Christian's disquiet draws part of its strength from his imagination. While still on earth, he lives already in the invisible world; he sees the City at the end of his journey, and walks towards it with the energy of certitude—a passionate energy into which enters a fanatical pride in not giving up. The greater his solitude and the harder his way, so much the greater is the effort he makes. In the Slough of Despond, before the lions, the giants and the monsters it is always his will and his courage which are in evidence'.

So much is fairly clear. Where M. Talon excels is in showing the intimate links between Bunyan's faith and purpose and his style. Bunyan's, Christian's, energy and effort reappear in his way of writing and its effect. In his pages on '*The Pilgrim's Progress* as a work of art', M. Talon remarks how by the rhythm of his sentences Bunyan takes the reader with him, giving the reader not only the sensation of move-ment ('which is perhaps why *The Pilgrim's Progress* conveys so effectively the idea of space'), but creating in him as he reads 'something like the sense of muscular effort'. Writing of the evocative power of Bunyan's imagery, and of 'the charge of energy' which is accumulated in it with a force sufficient to last to the end of the book, M. Talon says 'Balzac or Flaubert could not have done better'—high praise from a Frenchman. And the same energy is in Bunyan's style as in his imagery: his 'phrases carry right through to their end', M. Talon quotes from Mr Bernard Shaw. To this the mono-syllabic vocabulary, with the 'serried ranks' of the conso-nants, contributes much; and in this connection M. Talon

shows how skilfully Bunyan uses initial monosyllabic inter-
jections (*What! more fools still?*) to help in building up his
characters in a way which makes him 'the forerunner of
modern novelists', 'the father of the modern English novel
before Defoe'.

Give up ourselves, lay down our arms, and yield to so horrid a
tyrant as thou, we shall not; die upon the place we choose rather to do.
In its monosyllabic simplicity and in its combination of a
sense of energy with a sense of effort how characteristic of
Bunyan is this passage from near the end of *The Holy War*!
Bunyan, Cromwell, Fox have their 'tones' as recognizably as
has Milton, and it is perhaps a greater accomplishment in a
prose-writer than in a poet. What M. Talon observes here is
the 'calculated vigour', which so evidently delighted Bunyan
himself. For all the instinctive quality of his art, which could
produce with perfect naturalness a rhetorical figure of speech
such as that just quoted, its effect cannot have been lost on
Bunyan; and elsewhere M. Talon catches him employing a
tautological repetition (*what a turn, what a change, what an*
alteration) 'for the mere pleasure of the trochaic rhythm'.
'Bunyan hears his phrase rather than sees it'; is this not usual
with the greatest writers, in prose no less than in poetry?
Bunyan considered bellringing one of the worst pleasures of
his sinful youth, but he could not get the bellringing out of
his writing—any more than out of his heaven, as M. Talon
acutely remarks. At the pardoning of Mansoul by Emmanuel
in *The Holy War the bells did ring*, and at the pilgrims' approach
to the Celestial City in *The Pilgrim's Progress they thought they*
heard all the bells therein to ring, to welcome them thereto. After all,
what better image than bellringing for the outpouring of
joy, by a number of people together, in a way demanding
continuous energy and disciplined effort? In Bunyan's
writing it is the Elstow bells we hear, the village carillon in
which each bell still rings distinctly.

1950

DODDRIDGE'S LIFE AND TIMES

PHILIP DODDRIDGE was born in London on 26 June 1702. In March Queen Anne had come to the throne, and it was noticed that, when the Dissenting ministers of London presented their Loyal Address, she vouchsafed no reply. In November the Occasional Conformity Bill was brought in. This was intended as a stiffening of the Test Act. Its purpose, that is, was to exclude from civil office not only those whose principles precluded them from ever receiving the sacrament at their parish church, but also those who were prepared on occasion thus to conform but would worship thereafter as usual in a Dissenting congregation. For Nonconformity the times were not auspicious.

'The eminent children of the clergy considerably outnumber those of lawyers, doctors and army officers put together.' 'The average size of genius-producing families is found to be larger than that of normal families.' 'There is a special liability for eldest and youngest children to be born with intellectual aptitudes.'[1] In all these ways, as also in his constitutional delicacy from infancy, Doddridge qualified for eminence. He was the youngest child in a family of twenty. His father, it is true, was known as an oilman, but both his grandfathers were ministers, and ministers with the courage of their convictions. His paternal grandfather, John Doddridge, a graduate of Pembroke College, Oxford, had been Rector of Shepperton, Middlesex, from 1647, but following the Act of Uniformity had thrown in his lot with the Nonconformists and ministered to a congregation gathered in his own home. Doddridge's maternal grandfather, John Bauman, had fled from Prague during the Thirty Years War, and had found a refuge in this country, where he kept a school at Kingston-upon-Thames. Doddridge thus had the advantage of a foreign admixture in his blood, as well as of a willingness to suffer for conscience' sake which he always honoured. His father's family hailed from the West Country

[1] Havelock Ellis, *A Study of British Genius*, pp. 69, 96, 102; *cf.* p. 118.

and had a Nonconformist tradition, for one of them, a Recorder of Bristol, left legacies to several of the ejected ministers. This tradition was continued not merely by Doddridge himself but by the only one of his brothers and sisters who survived childhood, his sister Elizabeth, for she married a Nonconformist minister.

All this probably helped Doddridge to take the courageous step of declining a generous offer from none other than the Duchess of Bedford for the provision of a university education, on the condition that he would conform to the Church of England. Doddridge's uncle was steward to the Bedford estates, and the Duchess seems to have taken a kindly interest in the boy, who by the time he was entering his 'teens had lost both his parents. It must have been a tempting offer, and Doddridge could hardly know that, even without going to Oxford or Cambridge, by the time he was forty he would be *persona grata* with the Heads of Houses at both the universities; or that he would receive an honorary D.D. from Aberdeen. The decision was his own, but some part in it was played by the influence of Samuel Clark, the Dissenting minister at St. Albans, where Doddridge was then at school. Clark not only persuaded him to remain true to 'the dissenting interest, which', as Doddridge wrote a few years later, 'I take to be the interest of Jesus Christ'[1]; he received the lad into his own home, assisted him financially as well as morally in training for the Dissenting ministry, and ever afterwards remained his firm friend. Clark delivered the charge to the minister when Doddridge was ordained at Northampton; and it was on his way to Clark's funeral, at which he preached the sermon, that Doddridge caught the chill which led to his own death ten months later.

The academy to which Doddridge went in 1719 to train for the ministry was at Kibworth Beauchamp, in Leicestershire. It had been opened four years previously by John Jennings, the minister at Kibworth, as his father, a graduate of Christ Church, Oxford, and an ejected minister, had been before him. The years spent at this academy were undoubtedly of the first importance in forming Doddridge. In particular, the influence upon him of Jennings can hardly be

[1] *Correspondence* (see p. 159, n. 1, below), I. 278.

exaggerated. In July 1722 Jennings left Kibworth for Hinckley, and a year later Doddridge succeeded him as minister at Kibworth.

Pastoral duties in the Leicestershire village, and in the neighbouring town of Market Harborough, where Doddridge lived after October 1725, were not onerous. The next five years he spent wisely in consolidating his position by wide and critical reading. 'I must not pin my faith upon the sleeve of any person or persons upon earth, though never so holy or learned, as not knowing whither they may carry it; the best of men are but men at best.'[1] This critical attitude Doddridge had inherited from the Puritans, and the eclectic spirit of John Jennings had reinforced it. His correspondence in these years is full of judgements on the books he was reading, and they are by no means always favourable.

During these years a number of larger congregations sought his services as their minister, but to no purpose; his times were in God's hand, and his hour was not yet come. Particular interest attaches to the invitation he received from the Independent church at Castle Gate, Nottingham (founded in 1655), partly because it still flourishes, and partly because of the circumstances in which Doddridge declined the invitation. There were two Dissenting churches in Nottingham, the one in Castle Gate, which was and is Congregational, the other in High Pavement, which was then Presbyterian and is now Unitarian. After a visit to Nottingham Doddridge wrote thus of the Castle Gate church:

> ... though I discerned a great many most affecting evidences of their very tender friendship and high esteem, yet I saw some other things relating to the high orthodoxy of some of them, as well as to the circumstances of the High Pavement congregation, which confirmed the fears I had before entertained, and fully convinced Mr. Some, who was before urgent for my accepting their call, that it would neither be necessary nor safe for me to fix amongst them.

In his intuition that he would not have been happy at Castle Gate Doddridge proved perfectly right. In 1736 the

[1] Thomas Goodwin, quoted in the anonymous *Independency accus'd and acquitted*, 1645, p. 1.

church excommunicated a member who, on the point of the deity of Christ, 'would give no other answer than in such expressions of Scripture as the Arians take in an unsound sense, and would not declare to us that he took these expressions in any other sense than the Arians did'. Three years later the church further resolved 'that no person be received from the High Pavement congregation as a member of this congregation without giving in their experience, unless they have been received members of that Church before' 1735,[1] when its theology first became unsound. This would not have suited Doddridge at all. When 'some narrow-minded people of his congregation' at Northampton wanted, similarly, to excommunicate 'a professed Arian', Doddridge declared that 'he would sacrifice his place, and even his life, rather than fix any such mark of discouragement upon one, who, whatever his doctrinal sentiments were, appeared to be a real Christian'.[2] It was characteristic of Doddridge, as of the Independency which he inherited and transmitted, that, while himself keeping to the middle paths in Christian doctrine, he was desirous in principle not to exclude any whose theology might be mistaken but whose devotion to Jesus Christ, for all that, was unmistakable. 'He conceives variety of opinions in circumstantials is but as one star differs from another; heads need not breed difference in hearts'; so John Cook, the Solicitor-General, in *What the Independents would have*, in the previous century. 'Nothing, therefore, should be required of an applicant for membership but personal faith in Christ; this may exist, and there may be decisive evidence of its existence, in persons who have no clear intellectual apprehension of many of the great truths of the Christian Gospel; it may exist, and there may be decisive evidence of its existence, in persons by whom some of these truths are rejected': so Dr R. W. Dale, in *A Manual of Congregational Principles*, in the following century.

It was in December 1729 that Doddridge moved to Northampton, there to be the minister of the church on Castle Hill. This church traced its origin to the ministrations of

---

[1] A. R. Henderson, *History of Castle Gate Congregational Church, Nottingham, 1655–1905*, pp. 146ff.
[2] A. Kippis, in *Biographia Britannica, s.v.* P. Doddridge, V. 307.

another ejected minister, Samuel Blower, who, during the Commonwealth, had been a Fellow of Magdalen College, Oxford, and a Lecturer at Woodstock. Originally including Presbyterians, in 1707 the church had become more strictly Independent. Even so, it continued to represent the more conservative type of Nonconformity in Northampton. From 1697 there was another church in College Lane (now College Street), which practised believers' baptism, though not making this a condition of membership, and which had drawn off a number of those in membership at Castle Hill.

It was the custom for Nonconformity in Northampton to be thus radical. In Elizabeth's reign the exercise of 'prophesying', which was to lead into the practice of preaching by laymen, began in Northampton. In Mary's reign two Protestants were burned at the stake there. As far back as 1392 the Mayor of Northampton was found to be harbouring a Lollard preacher, and to be in touch with Lollards in London, Oxford, Bedford, and elsewhere. 'The flourishing state of the Dissenting interest in Northamptonshire' was, indeed, called 'the glory of our cause in England'.[1] Such was the tradition which Doddridge entered into at Northampton. He added to it, became one of its chief lights, and bequeathed it—there are now over a dozen Baptist and Congregational churches in Northampton, two of them calling themselves after Doddridge—but he did not create it. What he actually said of Northamptonshire when he went there was that he had never expected he would be called to minister in a county so delicate and polite—no doubt as compared with his Kibworth congregation, which he described as 'the most impolite I ever knew, consisting of shepherds, farmers, graziers, and their subalterns'.[2] The epithet may serve to remind us that, whatever the traditions of his family or his church, Doddridge's own century was the eighteenth.

For the rest of his life, that is to say for twenty-one years, for he was not yet fifty when he died, Doddridge's work was in Northampton or at least radiated from it. The academy he had recently opened at Market Harborough went with him to Northampton, and proved as famous a nursery of Non-

<hr />

[1] David Jennings in Doddridge's *Correspondence*, III. 186.
[2] *Correspondence*, I. 245.

conformity as in Archbishop Laud's eyes Emmanuel and Sidney Sussex had been as 'nurseries of Puritanism'. Too famous, in fact; for, at the instance of the Vicar of Kingsthorpe, the Chancellor of the Diocese of Peterborough summoned Doddridge to appear before the Consistory Court, there to answer objections 'to Your teaching and instructing Youth in the Liberal Arts and Sciences not being Licensed thereto by the Ordinary of the Diocese'. Doddridge refused to apply for any episcopal licence, and the case became something of a *cause célèbre*, for it was carried to the House of Lords, and eventually proceedings against Doddridge were stayed only by the personal intervention of the King. But it was not otherwise exceptional: 'near twenty such attempts', Doddridge wrote at the time, 'have been made within less than so many years, upon dissenting schoolmasters in this diocese'.[1]

Then, Dissenters were excluded from the English universities, and, if some churchmen could have had their way, would have been excluded from education altogether. If they were determined on a university education, they had to go to Scotland or to Holland; and on their return they might still meet with efforts to exclude them from the professions. 'A resolution to renounce all foreign physicians or learned persons of our own country because bred abroad is, I think, a mere CABAL', wrote Doddridge in 1744; 'it is evidently excluding all dissenters from the possibility of being physicians'.[2] His bold stand over his academy is worthy of an honourable place in the long struggle for the freeing of education from ecclesiastical restrictions—a struggle not yet completely won. At home, it was not till 1871 that it was possible for Nonconformists to receive degrees at Oxford or Cambridge. *Divinity* degrees were first opened to them at Oxford as recently as 1920, largely through the efforts of Dr W. B. Selbie and Dr A. C. Headlam, later Bishop of Gloucester. Divinity *chairs* are still mostly closed to them at Oxford, Cambridge and Durham.

A comparison of Doddridge's achievement, and of the authors read at Northampton, with the education to be had

[1] *Correspondence*, III. 131.
[2] *Ibid.*, IV. 336.

contemporaneously at Oxford or Cambridge would make an interesting study, but must be left to another writer.

Though prominent as an educationist, Doddridge was first and foremost a minister, and he took care not to allow his academic responsibilities to interfere with his duties at Castle Hill, where, as he recorded in the church book, he was 'solemnly set apart to the Pastoral office by Prayer & Fasting & Imposition of Hands'. Within three months of his ordination new members began to join the church, and by 1748 these additions totalled close on three hundred, seventy-eight of whom had been students at his academy and were not, therefore, permanently attached to the church. Besides his preaching and visiting there was church discipline to attend to, which in those days was taken seriously. Some members had to be 'cut off' for drunkenness, bankruptcy or adultery or as 'gone to Church'. On these occasions also a lead would be expected from the minister; but, as Doddridge wrote in the church book: 'Those Ministers who will rule by Love & Meekness need no Laws or Canons to rule by other than those of the Holy Scriptures.' He also realized the importance of winning Christians young. In 1741 he wrote to Dr Isaac Watts of the success he was having with Watts' *Catechism*, which he was using as a means of instruction to '92 Children most of them between the ages of 6 & 12'; and added that he had:

. . . never poured out my Soul before GOD with such earnestness for the Rising Generation as since I have been once a week praying over them & talking with them on religious Subjects in their own way, & many a Tear has I seen dropt from their dear little Eyes while they have stood with an Air of Attention & Pleasure which it gives me inexpressible Delight to recollect.[1]

Then there were his hymns. The singing of hymns in Dissenting churches was but beginning to be introduced, and many were the objections to be overcome, objections to singing (as to praying) from a book, to singing 'conjointly', to singing words other than Scripture (as passages from the *Psalms* were), and so on. 'In some cases churches were split and ministers ousted over the issue of church song.'[2] The hymns

[1] See *Transactions* of Congregational Historical Society, XIV. 4, pp. 240, 217.
[2] A. P. Davis, *Isaac Watts*, 1948 edn., p. 207.

sung at Northampton were frequently Doddridge's own, and 'composed by him for the occasion'. After he had finished writing his sermon, that is to say, he would throw what he wanted to convey to his hearers into the form of a hymn, which he hoped would drive the message home. This may be considered a misuse of hymns; but, especially in a day when, through shortage of books and inability to read those there were, hymns were given out line by line and consequently were sung with attention, it may well have proved useful homiletically. Doddridge's method of composition lies behind the warmth which characterizes so many of his hymns; it also explains why, when they were published, each hymn was headed by a text.

Texts are printed before the hymns in the *Congregational Hymnary*, but here we have texts attached to the hymns rather than hymns attached to texts; moreover, the texts printed before Doddridge's hymns are not necessarily those he had chosen himself. 'Hark, the glad sound', for instance, was not set to *Luke* i. 68, nor, indeed, was it intended as the Advent or Christmas hymn it has become; it was set to *Luke* iv. 18f. (the verses from *Isaiah* read by Jesus when he entered the synagogue at Nazareth), of which, in fact, it is a paraphrase. 'My gracious Lord, I own thy right', again was set to *Phil.* i. 22 (it is headed 'Christ's Service, the Fruit of our Labours on Earth'), not to *Rom.* xiv. 8 ('We live unto the Lord'), as in the *Hymnary*. This last text, nevertheless, has the genuine Doddridge ring about it. *Dum vivimus vivamus* was his family's motto, and the lines he wrote on it won warm commendation from a critic so unfriendly to Dissent as Dr. Johnson.

> Live, while you live, the epicure would say,
> And seize the pleasures of the passing day:
> Live, while you live, the sacred preacher cries,
> And give to God each moment as it flies.
> Lord, in my views let both united be;
> I live in pleasure while I live to thee.

The best of Doddridge's hymns have come into universal use, and Dr. Routley gives good grounds for putting Doddridge high among English hymn-writers. 'My God, and is thy table spread' was for long a regular and recognized communion hymn in the Church of England and was printed in the Prayer Book. Bishop Knox in his *Reminiscences* (1935) looked back regretfully to the days when communion services were held only monthly, as still in most Free Churches, and always after morning worship, and when the communicants were 'marked out by the fact of remaining, and to some extent objects of criticism for not following the outgoing throng'. Then, he says, one could feel the force of the words:

> Why are its dainties all in vain
> Before unwilling hearts displayed?
> Was not for them the Victim slain?
> Are they forbid the children's bread?[1]

This seems to be the only hymn to which Doddridge gave the heading 'Applied to the Lord's Supper'; but he wrote two hymns round the passage in *Eph.* iv. 11–16 about what is there called 'the body of Christ':

> Thy saints on earth, and those above
> Here join in sweet accord;
> One body all in mutual love,
> And Thou, our common Lord.

Certainly the sweet accord of saints on earth was a preeminent interest of Doddridge's. In Northampton itself there was no longer ill feeling between Castle Hill and College Lane. The Independents, on occasion, would lend their minister's vestry to the Baptists, for the convenience of a neighbouring brook in which believers might be immersed; the courtesy was continued after Doddridge's death, and William Carey himself was baptized from Castle Hill. College Lane, in return, was the scene of a regular Thursday evening lecture by Doddridge, whom the Baptist minister addressed as 'Dear and Honoured Father in Christ and Beloved of God.' Today such friendly relations between

[1] E. A. Knox, *Reminiscences of an Octogenarian, 1847–1934*, p. 60; the bishop's version, it may be noted, retains 'dainties', for which 'emblems' is usually substituted, but makes his point by altering Doddridge's 'you' to 'them' and 'they'.

ministers of different Free Church congregations might be expected, but in Doddridge's time the case was often very different.

The present Northamptonshire Congregational Association was not founded till 1812, but this does not mean that the Congregational churches of the county and their ministers were not in touch with one another before that date. At Doddridge's own ordination the ministers of the churches at Kettering, Oundle, Daventry, and Welford were among those taking part. At many later ordination services, at some of which the new minister was one of his own pupils, Doddridge would give him 'a very affectionate and important charge',[1] or preach, or 'ask the usual questions', and afterwards sign a certificate recording the events of the day. When a minister came to settle in Northamptonshire, Doddridge was among the first to welcome 'my dear brother and friend—for so, though personally unknown, I will take the liberty to call you'. When a minister died, Doddridge would sometimes preach his funeral sermon, and even compose the lines to be engraved upon his tombstone. If a church 'had a day of prayer appointed, and invited several sister churches in communion with us to join in seeking a blessing upon us', as likely as not 'Dr Doddridge spake to the people'.

On other occasions Doddridge preached the sermon at meetings of ministers, such as that from *Phil.* ii. 1f., published as *Christian Candour and Unanimity stated, illustrated, and urged*, with a dedication to the Countess of Huntingdon. Such meetings were held in other counties also, as in Leicestershire, where it was at a meeting of ministers at Lutterworth that the opening of an academy by Doddridge was first broached; or in Norfolk and Suffolk, where a visit from Doddridge led to the founding of a regular association in the year of his death. Doddridge describes this visit as 'one of the most delightful days of my whole life',[2] and adds: 'We held a kind

[1] For passages quoted in this paragraph, *cf.* T. Coleman, *Independent Churches in Northamptonshire.*

[2] One of those present stated later, in a funeral sermon for Doddridge, 'not myself only, but many others have with pleasure owned, it was one of the best days of our lives': Richard Frost, *The Stars in Christ's Right-Hand*, 1752, p. 26. For the passage from Doddridge, see *Correspondence*, V. 38.

of council afterwards concerning the methods to be taken for the revival of religion; and I hope I have set them on work to some good purpose.' Doddridge did not originate such meetings, then; but it was Alexander Gordon's judgement that he did 'more than any man in the eighteenth century to obliterate old party lines, and to unite nonconformists on a common religious ground'.[1]

Doddridge's dedication of his sermon to the Countess of Huntingdon is itself another example of his eagerness for Christian association and unity beyond the bounds of Independency as well as the bounds of Northamptonshire. The newly rising societies of Arminian Methodists under John Wesley and of Calvinistic Methodists under George Whitefield and the Countess were included in his ardour. Wesley writes in his *Journal* that, when on 9 September 1745, he called on Doddridge, 'It was about the hour when he was accustomed to expound a portion of Scripture to the young gentleman under his care. He desired me to take his place.' It showed no small breadth and independency for a Dissenting minister thus to be Wesley's friend and to admit George Whitefield to the pulpit at Castle Hill. Dr Payne has drawn attention to Doddridge's still wider interest in Count Zinzendorf and the Moravians, and assesses his influence in sowing the seeds of the whole modern missionary enterprise.

Nor was the Church of England beyond the scope of friendly relations. Thomas Secker, who after Doddridge's death was to become Archbishop of Canterbury, had been educated at the Dissenting academy at Tewkesbury and was on cordial terms with Doddridge, all of whose works he ordered for his library. In 1743, when he was Bishop of Oxford, he went so far as to allow in a letter to Doddridge that 'the dissenters have done excellently of late years in the service of Christianity'.[2] Another product of the Tewkesbury academy was Isaac Maddox, Bishop of St Asaph and later of Worcester. He also retained a good understanding with Dissenters, and when Doddridge was ill at Bath, called and offered the use of his carriage. Nor could the Archbishops of Canterbury under George I and George II be considered as

[1] *D.N.B.*
[2] *Correspondence*, IV. 272.

156

ill disposed to Nonconformity. Wake 'advocated some modifications of the Book of Common Prayer, if by that means the just scruples of protestant dissenters might be removed'[1]; Potter had ordained the Wesleys and remained friendly to the early Methodists; and Herring often attended the services conducted by Dr Samuel Wright, a Dissenting minister in Carter Lane, in admiration for his preaching. With such tolerance in high places, Doddridge was not altogether without hope of some measure of comprehension with the Established Church; and, when Herring invited him to Lambeth for private conversations on the subject, he gladly accepted. He suggested to the archbishop that clergy might be permitted 'to officiate among us, if desired; which he must see had a counterpart of permitting dissenting ministers occasionally to officiate in churches'. This struck the archbishop 'as a new and very important thought'[2]; but the conversations went no further. The archbishop would have demanded reordination; and to this Doddridge would have answered, in the words of his beloved John Howe, that it hurt his understanding.

It is always the men who do most who have time to do more. It is part of Doddridge's fascination that, despite all his religious activities, in the narrower sense, his energy was in no way confined to these. In the spirit of his family motto he gives one the feeling that he enjoyed life and thought it right to enjoy it. In his recommending for publication Blair's *Grave*, which Edmund Gosse considered the 'best of a whole series of mortuary poems',[3] we see the taste of his century. He 'received some entertainment' from Akenside's *Pleasures of the Imagination*, and Akenside, again, has been pronounced by Saintsbury 'an incarnation of the more specifically eighteenth-century qualities, except playfulness'.[4] Nevertheless, Doddridge's enjoyment was his own and no mere fashion. He was out of period, for instance, as his friend Wesley was, in being able to appreciate Gothic architecture. Salisbury Cathedral he thought 'fine', and Ely 'very fine';

[1] *D.N.B.*
[2] *Correspondence*, V. 76.
[3] *D.N.B.*
[4] G. Saintsbury, *The Peace of the Augustans*, p. 84.

'King's College and Trinity are both charming, and I think beyond anything in Oxford.'[1] Doddridge came to know both universities well. At Cambridge he would be entertained by the Master of St. John's or the Master of Jesus; at Oxford, at Trinity or Wadham, or at Christ Church, with the Regius Professor of Hebrew. When Hart Hall was refounded as Hertford College, Dr Richard Newton, the first principal, submitted the new statutes to Doddridge before publishing them. Doddridge's contemporary eminence as an educationist could hardly have received more notable recognition.

Newton was at one with Doddridge in other schemes besides those of education; for he sent him £50 towards the opening in Northampton of the County Infirmary. This has the honour of being among the earliest of such institutions. The first to be established (in 1736) was at Winchester, largely through the efforts of Dr Alured Clarke, then a prebendary of the cathedral there, who, after he became Dean of Exeter, laid the foundation-stone of the Exeter Infirmary in 1741. The Northampton Infirmary was opened in 1744, and the (now more famous) Radcliffe Infirmary at Oxford, and the infirmaries at Worcester and Salisbury,[2] soon followed it. The Bishops of Oxford and Worcester both wrote to Doddridge expressing their interest and their desire to have similar institutions in their cathedral cities. It was one further example of Doddridge's desire for what would now be called 'Christian Action'; and also of his modesty. He knew too well that 'among some even charity grows odious when recommended by a Dissenter'[3], and the sermon at the formal opening of the infirmary was preached at All Saints by a clergyman of the Church of England. But the energy behind the scheme was Doddridge's, with the support of his friend, Sir James Stonhouse, M.D. Stonhouse had been a freethinker, but under Doddridge's influence was won over to Christianity; and when, eventually, he was about to take orders in the Established Church, Doddridge had no qualms about writing to commend him to the Lord Chancellor, who, then as now, had many livings in his gift.

[1] *Correspondence*, IV. 104, 339, 27; for Wesley *cf.* H. Bett, *The Spirit of Methodism.*
[2] Also the Royal Salop Infirmary at Shrewsbury, 1746–7.
[3] *Correspondence*, IV. 307.

It will already have become evident that Doddridge was a great correspondent. On one occasion, after writing with his own hand between fifty and sixty letters within a fortnight, he found he had still 106 left to answer. Fortunately, a large quantity of this correspondence has been preserved and published[1]: it has been drawn on heavily by most writers about Doddridge. Several of the letters were to or from men in high position in Church and State, as has already appeared. As usual, however, it is for the more intimate and personal letters that the correspondence is to be treasured. Mercy Maris, whom Doddridge married just a year after his settlement at Northampton, was not his first love; indeed, she caught him on the rebound a month or two after his former tutor's daughter, Jenny Jennings, had declined him; and there had been earlier flutterings over a Kitty Freeman. But in Mercy he found 'the dearest of all dears'. Whenever he left her he was constantly writing to her, and several letters in the long series which passed between them, often playful and always breathing the intimacy of a deep and unbroken mutual confidence, would not disgrace an anthology of such love letters. Of their nine children as many as five died in infancy. Their only surviving son, Philip, did not marry; but their daughter, Mary, became the ancestress of a line of Congregational ministers proudly preserving the great name, of whom the Reverend Philip Doddridge Humphreys, of Liverpool, is the present representative.

At the end of September 1751, after unavailing visits to the hot wells at Bristol, then in fashion, and to Bath, where he stayed with the Countess of Huntingdon, and met Dr Oliver (of 'Bath Olivers'), Doddridge sailed from Falmouth to Lisbon,[2] in the hope that a winter in a warmer climate might assist in the recovery of his failing energies; but on 26 October 1751, he died, and there, in the English cemetery, he was buried. It would not have been amiss if the simple

[1] Philip Doddridge, *Correspondence and Diary*, ed. J. D. Humphreys, 1829–31, 5 vols. Unfortunately, the MSS. of some of the letters preserved at New College, London, show Humphreys' editing to have been most faulty; where possible, quotations here have been corrected from the MSS.

[2] Lisbon also was in fashion for invalids: Professor Craigie, of Glasgow University, died there the month after Doddridge, and Henry Fielding two years later.

words inscribed on the tomb of John Howard, another eighteenth-century figure, who was also a Congregationalist, and who also died abroad, had been inscribed on Doddridge's, likewise: 'Whoever thou art, thou standest at the tomb of thy friend.'

When Charles Stanford published his life of Doddridge in 1880, he would have liked to compare Doddridge with Bishop Berkeley, but lacked the courage. The *Life* of Berkeley by Dr A. A. Luce suggests several points at which the comparison would not be ridiculous. Berkeley was older than Doddridge, for he was born in 1685, the same year as Handel and Bach; but the years of his fame were the years when Doddridge was a grown man. Berkeley, says Dr. Luce, 'tolerated dissent, but disliked it'; but in America he 'went to Quakers' assemblies and preached, discarding the surplice'. He had, moreover, 'the intellectual courage that marks the Protestant'. One of the two main influences on his thought, as on Doddridge's, was John Locke. Dr. Luce presents a deeply sympathetic account of Berkeley's scheme for a college in Bermuda which should combine education with a missionary purpose. It was, in fact, the missionary expedition of General Oglethorpe and the Wesleys to Georgia which excited keen interest in Doddridge, that contributed in part to the failure of Berkeley's plans. The New World held its attraction for Berkeley, none the less, and the thousand books which he presented to Yale University compare interestingly with those in Doddridge's academy, which included the second edition of Berkeley's *Principles*. In 1745 both men were active in raising and equipping a force in readiness for the advance of the Young Pretender, who did, in fact, reach Derby, only sixty miles from Northampton. Berkeley, again, like Doddridge, was concerned for men's bodies as well as their souls. In his day three voluntary hospitals had recently been opened in Dublin, but in Cloyne, where he lived, there was neither doctor nor nurse, and he did his utmost to relieve the sick. Once more, though no philosopher, Doddridge was not unlike the bishop in combining 'extraordinary powers of fascination' with extreme modesty. Within the Church of Ireland Berkeley was even further from the centre of things as Bishop of Cloyne than was

Doddridge, within English Dissent, as the minister of Castle Hill, Northampton. Finally, both men were accustomed to the practice of piety in the secret places. According to his widow, Berkeley habitually 'struck a light at twelve to rise and study and pray'[1]; Doddridge wrote to his wife of awaking 'before it is light' and of praying 'when I am lighting my candle and putting on my clothes'.[2]

Certainly to possess the influence Doddridge did possess, an influence extending, as we have seen, to high places within the Established Church, would have been impossible apart from its sure foundation in his own personal religion. It is no coincidence that Doddridge's best-known book, which has been translated into nine languages, including Welsh, Gaelic, Tamil and Syriac, bears the title, *The Rise and Progress of Religion in the Soul*.

1951

---

[1] A. A. Luce, *Life of George Berkeley, Bishop of Cloyne*, 1949; the passages quoted are from pp. 42, 119, n. 1, 38 and 182.

[2] *Correspondence*, IV. 124.

XVI

PHILIP DODDRIDGE:
A PERSONAL APPRECIATION

O happy day, that fix'd my choice
On thee, my Saviour, and my God!
Well may this glowing heart rejoice,
And tell its raptures all abroad.

IT was as the writer of these lines that Doddridge first
became known to me. I was a small child learning to play
the piano and eager to be able to play hymn tunes such
as my mother played for us to sing on Sunday evenings. At
the time I was more intent upon the tune set to the hymn in
Golden Bells, for its marked repetitiveness made it one of the
simplest in the book. But it was a good introduction to
Doddridge, and perhaps especially for a child. Like Richard
Baxter, Doddridge's master and (now) mine, 'whether sincere Conversion began now, or before, or after, I was never
able to this day to know'[1]; but Doddridge helped me from
the beginning to regard devotion to Christ as a happy thing,
and a thing to rejoice about.

It is probably true that Doddridge began with the advantage of a happy temperament. In a letter written in his early
twenties he does, in fact, refer to 'the natural gaiety of my
temper'. What is noteworthy is that, amid all the cares and
responsibilities of his adult life, the gaiety remained. Hannah
More reports his friend, Sir James Stonhouse, as saying, 'he
never knew a man of so gay a temper as Doddridge'.[2]
Doddridge would have agreed with the old Puritan who
approved 'a chearful, affable, courteous behaviour in
Christians', adding that 'chearfulness (especially when not
defiled by sin) is the Sun-shine of a man's life'.[3] But in

---

[1] *Reliquiae Baxterianae*, ed. M. Sylvester, 1696, pt. i. sect. 3.

[2] Philip Doddridge, *Correspondence and Diary*, ed. J. D. Humphreys, 1829–31,
I. 405; William Roberts, *Memoir of Hannah More*, II. 450. I owe both these
references to notes made by Joshua Wilson in his copy of Doddridge's *Correspondence*, which his widow presented to the library of New College, London.

[3] Giles Firmin, *The Real Christian*, 1670, pp. 67, 69.

Doddridge's life we may see God at His work of using, transforming, new-creating the gifts a man is born with. We
recall Doddridge's own phrase in his epigram on his family
motto:

> Lord, in my views let both united be;
> I live in pleasure while I live to thee.

This sunny cheerfulness, this Christian joy, is a prime
characteristic of Doddridge's hymns. 'I would not breathe
for worldly joy'; for 'Thou art our joy, and Thou our rest.'
At baptism men are to bring their children to the Lord,
'Joyful, that we ourselves are Thine.' At the Lord's Supper
Doddridge longs for the table to be 'furnish'd well with joyful
guests'. It is apparent even from these few quotations that the
happiness which Doddridge is always celebrating is the joy
of a personal relationship between the soul and its Maker
and Redeemer. 'We live unto the Lord'; that is the secret.

> He drew me, and I follow'd on.
> Charm'd to confess the voice divine.

The word 'charm'd' here is also characteristic of Doddridge,
and is a reminder of his century. In 'Grace! 'tis a charming
sound' he can allow himself the suspicion of a pun. But, as
in the lines just quoted, it is Christ's captivating power which
is uppermost in his mind.

> Jesus, I love thy charming name;

and at baptism:

> See Israel's gentle Shepherd stand
> With all-engaging charms.

From any serious study of Doddridge it soon becomes
abundantly clear that this 'experimental' piety, as it used
to be called, was in no way introverted or pietistic in a bad
sense. Few men have shown the spirit of practical Christianity
with more vigour or effectiveness than Philip Doddridge.
This might indeed be expected by someone who knew

nothing of him besides his hymns from the place in them
given to obedience.

> Ye servants of the LORD,
> Each in his office wait,
> Observant of his heav'nly word,
> And watchful at his gate. . . .

> O happy servant he
> In such a posture found!
> He shall his Lord with rapture see,
> And be with honour crown'd.

And again,

> My gracious Lord, I own thy right
> To ev'ry service I can pay;
> And call it my supreme delight
> To hear thy dictates and obey.

What is remarkable, however, is not the obedience but the
appearance, even here, in the servant on the watch, of happiness, of rapture and delight. In the nineteenth century
Thomas Binney and George Macdonald may be found
singing of 'calm delight', but for Doddridge delight is not
calm, it is rapture, transport, even ecstasy. The *Times Literary
Supplement* reviewer of Professor John Butt's book on *The
Augustan Age* quoted with approval his dictum that 'The Age
of Reason was also the Age of Rapture', and added that this
was a truth 'familiar enough to students of the eighteenth
century'. The stream of writing which sought to express
strong feeling never wholly dried up, it is true, and in that
stream Doddridge's verse has its place, albeit a modest one.
His

> Well may this glowing heart rejoice
> And tell its raptures all abroad

with which we began, or his less well known

> Now let my soul with transport rise
> And range thro' earth, and mount the skies

carry back to Joseph Addison's

> Transported with the view, I'm lost
> In wonder, love, and praise

(a phrase which reappears at the end of Wesley's 'Love divine, all loves excelling'), with its reference, in a verse often omitted in modern hymn-books, to the gratitude 'that glows within my ravish'd heart'. And if we are to look forward instead of backward, it is worthy of note that one of Doddridge's hymns,

> Ye golden lamps of heav'n, farewel,
> With all your feeble light:
> Farewel, thou ever-changing moon,
> Pale empress of the night

though no longer sung, has been included in Mr Geoffrey Grigson's anthology, *The Romantics*.

Within the sphere of literary criticism such observations have their place, but they do not carry us far, or rather they carry us too far from the source of Doddridge's rapture and bliss (to use another favourite word of his), from the intercourse between his soul and GOD, as he always wrote the divine name. 'We live unto the Lord'; he chose this, not for the first time surely, but very deliberately, for the text of what he knew might be his last sermon at Northampton, as in fact it proved to be. For descriptions of what he meant by this text, of the inner devotion which it implied for him, more intimate descriptions than would be possible or proper in hymns intended for what those who disapproved of them called 'conjoint singing', we have to go to Doddridge's letters, and particularly, as is natural, to his letters to his wife. In October 1742, for instance, he wrote to her:

> I have more of the presence of God with me than I remember ever to have enjoyed in any one month of my life. He enables me to live for him, and to live with him. When I awake in the morning, which is always before it is light, I address myself to him, and converse with him, speak to him while I am lighting my candle and putting on my clothes, and have often more delight before I come out of my chamber, though it be hardly

a quarter of an hour after my awaking, than I have enjoyed for whole days, or, perhaps, weeks of my life. He meets me in my study, in secret, in family devotions.[1]

Some may comment on this that, self-evidently, it was but a passing phase, and that in any case it was dangerously removed from the worship of the Church and from the appointed means of grace. Such comment would only betray paucity of understanding. Two years earlier, when the news had been brought to him that 'the doctor had hardly any hopes at all' of his youngest daughter, Cecilia, who had smallpox and had been seized with convulsions, he wrote to his wife that he still found 'a most lively sense of the love and care of God', enabling him 'to pray with that penetrating sense of God's almighty power, and with that confidence in his love, which I think I never had before in an equal degree', and 'with an ardour of soul, which had it long continued would have weakened and exhausted my spirits extremely'.[2] Again, six months later than the date of the first of these two letters, Doddridge wrote to his wife:

> It was our sacrament day; and, indeed, it was a most comfortable one to me; my joy at that ordinance[3] was so great that I could not well contain it; I had much ado to forbear telling all about me, as well as I could, for it would have been but in a very imperfect manner, what a Divine flame I felt in my soul, which, indeed, put me greatly in mind of Mr. How's 'full stream of rays.' Were it possible to carry such impressions through life, it would give the soul a kind of independence far too high for a mortal existence. It was, indeed, in the most literal and proper sense, a 'joy unspeakable, and full of glory'![4]

The reference here to John Howe is worth pursuing. Doddridge was a confirmed admirer of Howe. In 1726 he wrote to Samuel Clark of St. Albans: 'I have lately read

[1] *Correspondence*, IV. 124.
[2] *Correspondence*, III. 501.
[3] The place of the ordinance in the piety of the congregations among whom Doddridge moved—both the value set upon it and the freedom to regard it as but one means of grace—is tellingly revealed in an anecdote he relates in a letter to Isaac Watts: 'when one of the company said, "What if Dr Watts should come down to Northampton!" another replied, with remarkable warmth, "The very sight of him would be as good as an ordinance to me!" *Correspondence*. III. 74.
[4] *Correspondence*, IV. 211.

How on the Spirit . . . I think one may see more of the man
. . . by this, than by any other of his works which I have yet
perused.'[1] Twenty years later in a letter to John Wesley he
wrote of Howe, 'I cannot but say that he seems to me to
have understood the gospel as well as any uninspired writer
I have ever read, and to have imbibed as much of its spirit',
and especially commended Howe's 'two posthumous volumes
on the Spirit, which pardon me if I say you must read.'[2]
'Mr. How's "full stream of rays" ' in Doddridge's letter to
his wife refers to an autobiographical passage (in Latin)
found after Howe's death in the frontispiece of his study
Bible. It tells how, after realizing that 'besides a full and un-
doubted assent to the objects of faith, a vivifying, savoury
taste and relish of them was also necessary', Howe 'awoke out
of a most ravishing and delightful dream, that a wonderful
and copious stream of celestial rays, from the lofty throne of
the Divine Majesty, did seem to dart into my open and
expanded breast'.[3]

This experience of Howe's evidently deeply impressed
Doddridge. There is another reference to it in the account of
his conversation with Benjamin Ingham some five and a half
years earlier than the date of the letter to his wife:

> This gentleman told me of a baptist he met with in Penn-
> sylvania, who was a very holy man; who, after having been
> eighteen years under the hidings of God's face, had a miracu-
> lous vision of a stream of light sent down on his breast, not
> much unlike that of good Mr. Howe; was raised to an extra-
> ordinary nearness to God, and lived often many days and
> nights without sleep, having such extraordinary refreshments
> from inward communion with him.[4]

Again, in 1745, after a violent illness, Doddridge wrote to
one friend: 'It is impossible to express the support and com-

[1] *Correspondence*, II. 230.
[2] *Ibid.*, IV. 488.
[3] Both the original Latin of the passage and the English translation made by
Howe's colleague in the ministry, John Spademan, who preached his funeral
sermon, are printed in Edmund Calamy's *Memoirs . . . of . . . John Howe*, 1724,
pp. 229ff., and again in Henry Rogers' *Life and Character of John Howe*, 1863
edn., pp. 356f., with note *.
[4] *Correspondence*, V. 387.

fort which God gave me on my sick bed. His promises were my continual feast. They seemed, as it were, to be all united and poured into my heart in one stream of glory'; and to another:

> I have lately been, by a violent fever, on the borders of eternity, but O how shall I express the unutterable goodness of our condescending God! He was near me continually, he embraced me in the arms of his everlasting love. I know not, that ever in my life, I enjoyed more exquisite pleasure than in that illness. It seemed as if all the promises had been united in one, and let down in a golden stream of celestial light, into my expanding, rejoicing bosom.[1]

There is no explicit mention of Howe here, but the reference is unmistakable.

John Howe died in 1705, when Doddridge was still an infant; but Howe's second wife survived him till the end of February 1743, when her death is mentioned in a letter written to Doddridge by his wife. In his reply (it is the letter referring to 'Mr. How's "full stream of rays" '), Doddridge writes: 'I am pleased to think what a meeting good Mrs. Howe has had with that glorious spirit above, whose memory is so precious to us both. Oh, what are dukes or princes when compared with such persons!' It is the more affecting to observe that when, at the end of his own life, Doddridge was about to set sail from Falmouth on his voyage to Lisbon, John Howe was still with him. 'We may yet know many cheerful days', he wrote to a friend. 'We shall at least know (why do I say at least) one joyful one, which shall be eternal'; and then he added: 'If I survive my voyage, a line shall tell you how I bear it—if not, all will be well; and (as good Mr. How says)[2] I hope I shall embrace the wave, which, when I intended Lisbon, would land me in heaven! I am more afraid of doing what is wrong than of dying.'

[1] This passage is from a letter not included in Humphreys' edition of Doddridge's *Correspondence* but printed in *The Stars in Christ's Right-Hand*, 1752, p. 27, a funeral sermon for Doddridge by Richard Frost, to whom the letter was written.

[2] *Cf.* John Howe, in Henry Rogers, *Life of John Howe*, 1863 edn., p. 144: 'I think I should joyfully embrace those waves that should cast me on an undesigned shore, and, when I intended Liverpool, should land me in heaven.'

Cheerfulness and joy; they thus accompanied him to the end despite increasing weakness; indeed delight still, and even transport, as of old. ' I cannot express to you', he said to his wife while on board ship, 'what a morning I have had: such delightful and transporting views of the heavenly world is my Father now indulging me with, as no words can express'; and after his death his widow said that the look on his face reminded her of the following verse from one of his hymns:

> When death o'er nature shall prevail,
> And all its pow'rs of language fail,
> Joy thro' my swimming eyes shall break,
> And mean the thanks I cannot speak.

The hymn is not one of those still sung,[1] but we may accept Mercy Doddridge's insight into its aptness as an expression of her husband's ardent spirit. Its last verse may serve as a fitting conclusion to this acknowledgement of the inspiration still to be found in his life more than two hundred years after its earthly close.

> The chearful tribute will I give,
> Long as a deathless soul can live;
> A work so sweet, a theme so high,
> Demands, and crowns eternity.

1951

---

[1] It is still, however, in print as no. 429 in the *Methodist Hymnbook*.

XVII

THE QUAKERS AND THE PURITANS

IF one studies the history of the Puritans at all closely, it is not long before one is struck by their unmitigated abhorrence for the Quakers; and it is natural to wonder why it was that they had such a feeling. Seen from a distance of nearly three hundred years the Quakers appear at first sight very much of a muchness with the Puritans, at least with the extremer, more radical Puritans, and with the Separatists, the borderline between whom and the Puritans was becoming increasingly narrower. If sincerity, simplicity, and separateness be marks of the ageless Puritan spirit, they are surely no less marks of Quakerism: what was it which set the Quakers and the Puritans so at loggerheads?

Before trying to answer this question, it may be admitted that there *was* much in common between them. Indeed, their antipathy was probably partly homoeopathic, like the antipathy between Communism and National-Socialism today. George Fox is only like other pioneers in belittling those who made his pioneering possible; many of his characteristic phrases may be analysed, and his conscious or unconscious dependence on individual and social strains of thought and piety made clear. It would be strange if this were not so, especially in a century like the seventeenth, when the mental seething of Renaissance and Reformation was at last affecting the common people, and men's minds were preternaturally sensitive to influence in the things of the spirit. The overthrow of the medieval securities brought a mental unrest and a wistful seeking, and these in turn created a spiritual suggestibility. The success of Quakerism in its earliest years can be explained only on the supposition that it answered and satisfied the seeking spirits among the Puritans, not that it was a bolt from the blue: there was a fullness of time here too. The parallels and influences of thought can be left to the learned,[1] but it is of interest to note that even in

[1] *Cf.* especially Theodor Sippell, *Werdendes Quäkertum*, 1937.

their differentiating outward characteristics the Quakers were often anticipated. The Quakers, for instance, observed silence before meals, instead of saying grace; so did the early Independents.[1] The Quakers called a church a steeple-house; so did the Anabaptists.[2] The Quakers did away with the outward sacraments; Barrow, Robinson, and Milton had already declared them not indispensable: 'many thousands that never attained the symbol of the Supper yet do feed of the body and blood of Christ unto eternal life'—that is Barrow speaking,[3] not a Quaker. The ministry of the Quakers was open to women; so was that of the Brownists. It is true that in Quakerism alone was the ministry of women preserved, but there was as much objection to the practice among the early Quakers as there is today in some circles of Congregationalism, where the practice has been revived.

In these and in other things there is a real, if little noticed, affinity between the Quakers and the Separatists and extremer Puritans; yet the fact remains that they lost no opportunity of flying at one another's throats. There were, I think, three reasons for this, or three aspects of the same reason: psychological, political, and religious.

In the things of the spirit, as in everything else, there is a rhythm, an ebb and flow. Quaker enthusiasm happened to come in in full flood at a time when Puritan enthusiasm was receding; and every reformer is inevitably the bitterest opponent of further reform. Puritanism had been a positive revivalist movement within the Church, Separatism had sought to hasten reformation 'without tarying for Anie', and in both there had been the heightened sense of the value of the individual and the conviction of God's accessibility to the individual which mark them true children of the Reformation. But by the 1650's much of their original enthusiasm had evaporated; returned exiles and the sons of the persecuted are notoriously conservative, and the second generation is by nature doctrinaire. A Protestant scholasticism had grown up, Puritan theology had been systematized, and God was

---

[1] J. Lydius, *Historie der Beroerten van Engeland*, 1649, p. 78 cited by R. Barclay, *Inner Life of Religious Societies of the Commonwealth*, p. 86 n.

[2] *Cf.* D. Featley, *The Dippers Dipt*, 1647, p. 15 *et alibi*.

[3] H. Barrow, *Discovery of False Church*, ch. xxviii.

in danger of becoming the Deist god of argument again instead of the living God of Christian experience. One of the Puritans says the Quakers scoffed at their imagined God beyond the stars,[1] and that throws a penetrating light. At the Restoration Quakerism was mockingly but not unjustly termed the fag-end of the Reformation,[2] and to the Quakers God was a living near reality, and religion a passion. *Actuel* is the note of Quakerism, and its overpowering excitement and vitality could not but grate on the staider, soberer Puritans. Milton was not alone among the Puritans in believing he was living in an age of ages, wherein God had manifestly come down to do some remarkable good[3]; but it is a far cry from his restrained confidence to Perrot's description of the Quakers as God's chosen Generation, His Royal Priesthood, of whom and of whose time the Holy Apostles prophesied.[4] One of the things which connects Fox's *Journal* with the New Testament is the frequency in it of the word *power*: 'but the Lord's power came over them', Fox writes on almost every page, 'the Lord's power came over all'. To some of the Puritans this claim to direct dealings with the Almighty would seem almost as obnoxious as Methodism seemed to the eighteenth-century divines. Quakerism was to ebb itself, as appears from contrasting Fox's singing in prison fit to drown his gaoler with Elizabeth Fry's fearing to hum to her baby lest haply she instilled into him a love of music; but in its flood-tide beginnings there was every reason for its psychological detestation by those whose religion was settled in a sober quietude and who were satisfied with the settlement.

It may be seen how easy it was for the early Quakers to be misunderstood and feared politically as well. In the seventeenth century in England religion and politics were inextricably interwoven, and the Puritans in the 1650's stood to a man for the *status quo*, for the Commonwealth *régime*. What the Quakers stood for was uncertain, and uncertainty made men uneasy. Because it was then eccentric not to be politically minded, the Quakers' very detachment from politics made

---

[1] C. Mather, *History of New England*, VII, iv. 1.
[2] 1671 treatise cited by F. Bate, *Declaration of Indulgence*, p. 3, n. 7.
[3] J. Milton, *Prose Works*, Bohn edn., III. 69.
[4] J. Perrot, *A Wren in the Burning-Bush*, 1660, p. 5.

them suspect, and their refusal to submit the principles of their religion to the demands of political custom was regarded by statesmen, as always, only as evidence of disaffection. A people who would not take an oath in a court of law seemed an obvious danger to the public security; their refusal to pay tithes looked like incipient disloyalty, their contempt of court in the matter of hats a snapping of their fingers at civil government. In the person of Oliver Cromwell it is true that they had a Protector: 'they would have me to disown these people', he said once, 'shall I disown them because they will not put off their hats?'[1] Fox's interview with Cromwell, who had Quaker maids in his household,[2] when Cromwell, says Fox, caught him by the hand with tears in his eyes, shows the readiness of his sympathy: personally Fox found him the tender man which at heart he shows himself to have been in his *Letters*—in his *Letters* the word *tender* comes almost as often as in Fox's *Journal*. Cromwell, however, believed, like other men, that the Quakers as a body were against both magistracy and ministry,[3] and even came to regard them as his most considerable enemy.[4] Fox might have had more sympathy for Cromwell had they been able to change places, like Dick and Mr Bultitude in *Vice Versa*: between the two of them lay all the gulf between idealist personal conviction and practical social government. Professor Hamilton Thompson considers that in Yorkshire the Quakers did in fact present a serious menace to the *status quo*,[5] and by the men of the time it was hardly to be expected that the Quakers should be distinguished from the Fifth-Monarchy-Men, who *were* politically dangerous. When the Quakers met in the ruins of their burned down meeting-houses, and when their little children continued to go to meeting after their parents had been sent to prison, men could not but fear within them at a spirit so insistent and so invincible. The eventual political activity nurtured in later Nonconformist conventicles shows, moreover, that Cromwell was not wrong,

[1] W. Dewsbury to M. Fell, Swarthmore MSS., IV. 144, cited by N. Penney in note to his edn. of G. Fox, *Journal*, I. 400.

[2] N. Penney in note to *Journal*, I. 427; cf. *Journal*, 1901 edn., I. 210, 332.

[3] R. Hubberthorn to G. Fox, 16 March 1657: *Letters of Early Friends*, p. 50.

[4] H. Cromwell to J. Thurloe: J. Thurloe, *State Papers*, ed. T. Birch, IV. 508.

[5] A. H. Thompson, in *Victoria County History, Yorkshire*, III. 64.

any more than Hitler is, in suspecting sectarian meeting-houses of potential disaffection: those who claim freedom and the right to criticize in religion may well come to claim it in politics.

So far we have considered the psychological and political repercussions of the Quaker spirit on Puritanism; we come now to the motive power behind the repercussions, which was, rather, theological and religious. The root of the quarrel between the Puritans and the Quakers was that the Quakers went, or seemed to go, behind and beyond the Bible. The rediscovery of the Bible by the Puritans had brought a great releasing power, but to only a few of the Puritans had come home the implied activity of the Spirit of God in the power thus released. Catholic modes of thought had tended to substitute an infallible Book for an infallible Man, and the hardening process already mentioned had brought about a reliance on the letter rather than on the spirit of Scripture. The enthusiastic 'prophesyings' of Elizabeth's days had yielded place to what Fox, and the more radical Puritans with him, termed mere 'janglings', and the sweetness the Lollards had found in the Bible had grown dry and tasteless. George Fox knew his Bible as well as any Puritan, and could at times argue as janglingly as any Puritan, but under him Scripture became again thrillingly alive, because answering to and borne out by the witness of the Spirit in man. 'You will say', cried the Quakers, 'Christ saith this, and the apostles say this; but what canst thou say?'[1] Are the Scriptures 'true by the same Spirit in you which gave them forth in the holy ancients?'[2] To the Quakers the Puritans seemed mere 'professors', professing but not living their religion. To the staider Puritans, on the other hand, the Quakers seemed but dangerously wild fanatics. The Presbyterians called the inner light, of which the Quakers made so much, Jack-in-the-Lantern and Will-o'-the-wisp, some called it a beggarly scrap.[3] The Puritans, immersed in the epistles of St Paul, were convinced of the irreparable depravity of man's nature, born in sin: even William Edmundson, the apostle of

[1] G. Fox (M. Fox's Testimony), *Journal*, 1901 edn., II. 512.
[2] W. Penn, *Summons or Call to Christendom*, in *Select Works*, 1825, II. 338.
[3] MS. at Friends House, cited in *Journal* of Friends' Hist. Soc., 1932, p. 62.

Quakerism to Ireland, whose children were born after he became a Quaker, called then Trial and Hindrance. To men of this way of thinking the Quaker claim to constant victories over evil, their constant appeal to the good, the pure, the that-of-God in man, could seem nothing but vilely anti-biblical blasphemy. What had become of their theology of sin and salvation? Karl Holl remarks on the absence of the word *grace* from Fox's *Journal*.[1] To the Puritans, who allowed no creative power in religion outside the Bible, it was highly distressing that the Quakers denied its initial activity in the belief and behaviour they claimed to be right. The soberer Quakers did allow the Bible a checking power, to try whether what they did and thought were right or no, but the initial activity, they said, belonged to the Spirit at work in themselves[2]; and in a time of excitement the checking might too easily be neglected or overridden.

It is here that the ultimate conflict between Puritanism and Quakerism lay, in the conflict between the Spirit and the Word, the mediate and the immediate. 'As well without the Written Word as with it God doth speak to the hearts and consciences of men'[3]: that is Cromwell, but it is a Quaker sentiment; and if without the Word, how can men know, asked the Puritans, that it is God's voice in very truth which speaks? It is the same question at bottom and the same criticism as that levelled at the Groups' doctrine of Guidance today. What is to be the criterion? There is no need to point to Nayler's Messianic entry into Bristol as the extreme example of a disordered spirituality, disastrously remote from external criteria; it was as difficult for the ordinary Puritan to distinguish the Quakers ethically from the Ranters, whose pseudo-spirituality *was* openly immoral, as politically from the Fifth-Monarchy-Men, and the practice of going naked for a sign by the Quakers themselves must have condemned their doctrine of immediacy in the eyes of those whose less imaginative religion made them blind to what it was meant to signify.

---

[1] K. Holl, *Luther*, Gesamm. Aufsätze zur K.G., I. 444, n. 5.

[2] Hackness Parish Register, 12 September 1653, cited by J. W. Rowntree, *Essays and Addresses*, p. 16.

[3] O. Cromwell, *Letters and Speeches*, Speech IV.

As was perhaps inevitable, this same conflict, in a slightly different form, soon developed within Quakerism itself. Together with his vital convictions Fox combined great organizing and administrative powers, and as he aged the latter grew stronger, at the expense of the former, some thought, who found Fox too much of an autocrat. By the end of his life Fox had moulded his Society into a regularly and efficiently organized body, the further reformation of which was as abhorrent to him as his own Quakerism had been to the Puritans. As early as 1673 a minority who felt a concern not to uncover the head in prayer received no sympathy from 'the Body' of Quakers, and consequently accused 'the Body' of the same error in setting up themselves above the Spirit and in making their own dictates the rule, as others before them had made in setting up the Scriptures above the Spirit.[1] It is saddening to see how in less than a generation the tide had ebbed again, and how those of the earlier leaders who had not been put to death were so much at enmity with the new enthusiasts as the Puritans had been with themselves; but it excellently illustrates the original quarrel. Enthusiasts rarely have an easy time, even today when recognized criteria are out of fashion; in the 1650's men had found in the Bible their criterion and were wanting, with the cessation of the Civil Wars, at last a little quiet and security. It was natural enough, after all, that the Quakers, with their spiritual enthusiasm, their unyielding thoroughness and their claims to immediacy in religion, should have seemed to the Puritans nothing more than fanatical, dangerous blasphemers.

1938

---

[1] (W. Mucklow), *The Spirit of the Hat*, 1673, p. 21. I am indebted to Dr Theodor Sippell of Marburg for transcripts of the works mentioned by Perrot and Mucklow, and for the loan of other works mentioned.

XVIII

GEORGE FOX AND HIS JOURNAL[1]

'THE power of the Lord was over all.' If George Fox's personality is to be expressed in a single phrase, then this is it. Throughout his life Fox walked cheerfully over the world in the power of the Lord, finding it, as William Penn was to say of him, a match for every service or occasion.

One immediate and obvious effect was that he was fearless. 'I never feared death nor sufferings in my life.' 'One of the parliament men told me they must have me to Smithfield to burn me as they did the martyrs, but I told him I was over their fires and feared them not.' Nor was this a vain boast, either in the sense that it was an idle threat or in the sense that he would retract if suffering came. At Lichfield, where to Fox's vision the market place was like a pool of blood, Edward Wightman was burned for blasphemy only a few years before Fox was born; nor would Wightman have been the last, had Archbishop Laud had his way. Witches, moreover, were burned till a much later period, and by some Fox was said to be a witch. Nor was persecution long in coming. By 1659, a bare twelve years from the beginning of Fox's ministry, twenty-one Quakers are known to have died in prison or as a consequence of ill usage.

Of these sufferings, rough handling and imprisonment alike, Fox bore a full share, and never shrank from them. When a man came with a naked sword and set it to Fox's side, 'I looked up at him in his face and said to him, "Alack for thee, it's no more to me than a straw." ' Not for nothing was his mother of the stock of the martyrs. In prison, like Paul and Silas, he would sing in the Lord's power, and sing till the fiddler who had been brought into the dungeon to drown him was drowned himself and silenced. When the news reached Fox that at Evesham stocks had been set up against his coming, to Evesham at once he went. On another

[1] The introduction to George Fox, *Journal*, ed. J. L. Nickalls, Cambridge University Press, 1952, from which are taken the passages quoted without further reference.

occasion, when he had been banished from Perth, 'it was upon me from the Lord to go back again . . . and so set the power of God over them'. To our sophisticated detachment such behaviour seems to have more than a touch of exhibitionism; but it bore a witness which was unmistakable. It also set a noble example. At Reading and elsewhere this was reproduced even by the children, who, when their parents were all in prison, themselves kept up the meeting for worship. In Penn's words: 'We are the people above all others that must stand in the gap.' And as in the beginnings of Christianity, such courage proved powerful in convincing others. 'Many turned Quakers', says Richard Baxter, 'because the Quakers kept their meetings openly, and went to prison for it cheerfully'.

Together with this physical courage, as will already be clear, went moral firmness and fidelity to truth. In the writings of the early Quakers, who sometimes called themselves Friends in Truth, truth is a word which recurs constantly, and with a meaning which goes far beyond mere truthfulness, high though Friends rated this. 'The truth can live in the gaols', wrote Fox from one of them.[1] The connotation of the word is emotional and moral rather than intellectual. For Fox as for Isaac Watts, because for the Hebrew poets who inspired them, 'Thy truth for ever firmly stood, and shall from age to age endure.' It is natural that a life devoted to truth should itself bear something of this steadfastness. Fox's father did not become a Quaker but he knew his son's quality here. On one occasion, after a dispute between Fox and some ministers of religion, Fox writes that his father 'thwacked his cane on the ground, and said, "Well", said he, "I see he that will but stand to the truth it will carry him out." ' It had always been so. When Fox was still a child, it was a common saying among people that knew him, 'If George says "Verily", there is no altering him.' So it remained. 'If formal etiquette expected him to say to a man what he very well knew was not true, then he resolved to have nothing more to do with formal etiquette till the end of the world.'[2]

The kind of situation into which Fox was brought by this

[1] G. Fox, *Epistles*, 1698, p. 199.
[2] R. M. Jones, *George Fox—Seeker and Friend*, p. 200.

resolve may be illustrated from the story of his imprisonment at Launceston. He was taking exercise in the castle green when Peter Ceely, the Justice of the Peace who had arrested him, came by. Ceely doffed his hat, and said, 'How do you, Mr Fox? Your servant, Sir.' 'Major Ceely', replied Fox, 'take heed of hypocrisy and a rotten heart, for when came I to be thy master and thee my servant? Do servants use to cast their masters into prison?'

In the trial which followed, Fox requested the judge to let his mittimus be read.

> The judge said it should not. I said it ought to be, seeing it concerned my life and liberty. And the judge said again it should not be read. And I said, 'It ought to be read; and if I have done any thing worthy of death or bonds, let all the country know of it.' So I spoke unto one of my fellow prisoners, 'Thou hast a copy of it. Read it up,' said I. 'But it shall not be read,' said the judge. 'Gaoler, take him away. I will see whether he or I shall be master.' So they did and after a while they called for me again, and I still cried to have my mittimus read up, for that signified my crime. And then I bid William Salt read it up again, and he read it up, and the judge and justices and whole court were silent, for the people were mighty willing to hear it.

In the end Fox got his way. He almost always did. What could one do against a spirit so indomitable? Fox was always determined to have justice. It was part of his fidelity to truth. 'I desire nothing but law and justice at thy hands,' he told a judge once; 'for I do not look for mercy'. For the same reason, he could not agree to be released from prison on a pardon. He had not done wrong, and he could not pretend that he had.

Courage and moral strength are always impressive, and especially so when combined. In Fox's case they were accompanied by a distinctive attitude to persecutors, or, perhaps it would be truer to say, to some of them. Towards officials, such as 'priests' (as he called all ordained clergymen and ministers) and Justices of the Peace, he was commonly resentful and sharp of tongue. In his eyes religion and justice were but mocked by them: they were not living according to what they professed. Towards publicans and sinners, on the other hand, he often showed a remarkable forbearance. To a drunken fellow-prisoner in Scarborough Castle, who had challenged him to a fight, Fox said, 'I was come to answer him, with my hands in my pockets, and . . . there was my hair and my back, and what a shame it was for him to challenge a man whose principle he knew was not to strike; . . . and one of the officers said, "You are a happy man that can bear such things." ' Nor was this an isolated case. On an earlier occasion, in London, Fox heard a rude Irish colonel threatening to kill all the Quakers; so he went to him and said, ' "Here is gospel for thee, here is my hair, and here is my cheek, and here are my shoulders", and turned them to him . . . and the truth came so over him that he grew loving.'

Fox's explicit equation here of the gospel with behaviour, and with behaviour of a certain kind, is worth noting. It is characteristic of him, and is a key to much in Quakerism. It is also worth noting that he later records of the man who had challenged him to fight, 'the Lord soon cut him off in his wickedness'. This is one of several similar observations. Fox's evident satisfaction in thus recording what he believed to be the Lord's judgements reveals a certain hardness in him and has sometimes disturbed readers who have failed to perceive his intense devotion to justice. It is more to the point to remark that he could behave towards a man with forbearance and could yet record the man's bad end; for it is typical of a realism in him which is often apparent. On another occasion, when he was in court, he observed, as he puts it, that 'the power of darkness riz up in them like a mountain'. Nevertheless, he looked the judge in the face, 'and the witness started up in him and made him blush'. Fox is peculiarly sensitive, that is to say, to the evil in men *and* to the good in them; and he can be sensitive to both at one and the same time.

'And the truth came so over him that he grew loving.' We are still in the context of the Lord's power coming over all. The phrase shows, further, the motive of Fox's forbearance. Outwardly, his behaviour can sometimes appear mere passiveness, as when, on being attacked by a rude wicked man, 'I stood stiff and still and let him strike.' But the motive is through the power of the Lord to win men, and in particular to win them to be loving. Now most men, rude and wicked men anyway, are not in a way of loving. 'We love, because he first loved us', Fox read in his New Testament. Ideally, therefore, his forbearance was an endeavour to express a spirit of love through which others' hearts might grow gentle. He was human, and did not always love his persecutors; that he ever did so is sufficiently remarkable. At Ulverston, in 1652, he was beaten with stakes and clubs till he had fallen unconscious. When he recovered, 'I lay a little still, and the power of the Lord sprang through me, and the eternal refreshings refreshed me, that I stood up again in the eternal power of God and stretched out my arms amongst them all, and said again with a loud voice, "Strike again, here is my arms and my head and my cheeks." . . . and I was in the love of God to them all that had persecuted me.' It is a striking scene, and vital for gauging the quality of the man.

Who was this man? and why was he so bitterly persecuted? As for who he was, the answer is short. He was a nobody: a weaver's son from an utterly undistinguished village in Leicestershire; with how little schooling can be seen at a glance from the big, bold scrawl and erratic spelling in what few scraps of his handwriting are still preserved. The reason why he was persecuted is more complicated; but in a word it was because he was a revolutionary in religion at a time when religion dominated men's minds. *Primitive Christianity Revived* was the title which William Penn gave to one of his books, and nothing expresses better what Fox was after. His was not the first but the last of a series of endeavours in this direction, and because it was the last it was both the most extreme and the most keenly resented by those who were concerned for reformation but were satisfied with the limits already reached. Fox was in no way peculiar, for instance, in belittling university education as equipment for the ministry. In 1653 alarm was felt in more than one quarter lest Parliament should destroy the universities altogether; and a majority of the members were for abolishing the payment of tithes in support of the ministry. Fox was not only steadfast in bearing testimony against the system of tithes, he wanted to abolish a paid ministry altogether; for he could find none in the New Testament. Oaths, likewise, were forbidden in the New Testament; then they were forbidden to

Christians still; and if oaths in a court of law were an accepted foundation of contemporary society, so much the worse for contemporary society.

It is thus not surprising that Quakers were said to be against both magistracy and ministry, and were feared; or that, because they were feared, they were persecuted. Fox says himself that his purpose was 'to bring people off from all the world's religions, which are vain'. Men's fears might not have come to anything, had he remained an isolated figure with no following, like many another harmless fanatic of the time. But Fox quickly became the leader of a widespread, closely-knit community devoted to him personally and in sympathy with his revolutionary outlook; and of this the authorities were fully aware.

He began, however, alone; and he had a right to be proud of this. As the Quaker movement grew, it owed much to other leaders also: in particular to James Nayler, a man of temperament more ethereal than Fox always understood, and to the fervent and lion-hearted woman whom eventually Fox married, Margaret Fell. It is true that Fox sometimes unduly magnified his own share in the convincing of others, of whom Nayler was one. But nothing can rob him of the glory of having founded Quakerism, and of having done so alone, by the sheer force of personality and of faith in his mission. Like Paul, he was anxious to claim independence of others in the discovery of his message; and in fact no substantial dependence has been established. For centuries weavers had borne a name for independence and radicalism in religion. In Leicestershire Lollard traditions had lingered since Wycliffe was Rector of Lutterworth, not so far from Fenny Drayton, where Fox was born. To the atmosphere of his own time he owed more than he knew or would allow. To all intents and purposes, nevertheless, Fox was, what Penn calls him, 'an original, being no man's copy'; and in this lay much of his strength. If, as a Quaker historian observes, Friends have been steady 'to step out as pioneers of worthy causes without waiting to make sure of any large band of followers'[1], they have themselves but followed where Fox led. To refer this, with Carlyle, to his 'enormous sacred

[1] A. N. Brayshaw, *The Quakers: their Story and Message*, p. 194.

Self-confidence'[1] is to miss the mark. It is truer, as well as kinder, to see in him something larger, something nearer to what Godwin calls 'that generous confidence which, in a great soul, is never extinguished'.[2]

'All must first know the voice crying in the wilderness, in their hearts.' In this characteristic utterance of Fox we may see an accepted expression of genius, namely, the assumption that what is true for oneself is true also for others, and for all others; its universalizing. We may also see something more. The Reformation principles of justification by faith and of the priesthood of all believers had already introduced a universalizing element into religion; but it was possible for this to become but a theory of universalism, held only by the few who had the wit, and the desire, to theorize. Experience, however, is open to all to share; and in treating his own experience as possible for all Fox also provided a surer basis for the universalizing element in Reformed religion.

What, then, was it which was distinctive about his own experience? Something like this. With the recovery of the Bible in the vernacular, Christians had come to hear the voice of God speaking not only to the prophets and apostles of old but through these to themselves. The word of the Lord endureth for ever, and what was written in Scripture was found to possess contemporary significance and power, and to provide a message which could be preached to others with conviction. 'You will say, Christ saith this, and the apostles say this; but what canst thou say?' These words of Fox proved effective in convincing Margaret Fell, but many were asking questions of this kind besides Fox. Fox, however, went further. He held, with Oliver Cromwell, that God speaks without a written word sometimes, yet according to it. He urged men to attend to the words of the Spirit of Christ still speaking within their hearts, 'Christ within you, the hope of glory.' He argued, moreover, that, unless men first did this, they could not hope to read Scripture with any genuine understanding. 'They could not know the spiritual meaning of Moses', the prophets', and John's words, nor see their

---

[1] *Letters and Speeches of Oliver Cromwell*, ed. T. Carlyle, Everyman edn., III. 341.

[2] William Godwin, of Mary Wollstonecraft, in *Memoirs of Mary Wollstonecraft*, Constable's Miscellany, p. 101.

path and travels, much less see through them and to the end of them into the kingdom, unless they had the spirit and light of Jesus.' This is a position familiar to most of us today, but it was very far from familiar then. Fox also held that by hearkening to the voice of the living Christ latter-day Christians, and all Christians, might live in the power of Christ's endless life as Christ's first disciples had done; and, furthermore, that Christ's power could transport men, even in this life, into paradise, such a paradise as Adam and Eve knew before they fell, thus giving men triumph over their sinful propensities. This proved more than most men could accept, or can; but we can see its place in the context of the power of the Lord being over all.

On the relation of the voice, or the light, of Christ within the heart to the figure of Jesus of Nazareth, Fox did not succeed in satisfying the theologians of his day; but then they rarely satisfied one another. Later Quaker history, it is true, shows that they were not altogether astray in fearing a divorce here rather than an association of some kind. For Fox himself, however, there was the closest association, in whatever terms it was to be expressed. His principle of loving forbearance, to take a single but telling instance, was clearly influenced as much by the example of Jesus in the Gospels as by any inward voice. No one, in fact, knew his Bible better than Fox did, or could quote it in argument more devastatingly. His use of Scripture, together with the nature of the books and passages from which he quotes, or which affect his imagery, most frequently, remains an inviting field for research.

Later Quaker devotion, again, shows a tendency so to concentrate on the light within that in meetings for worship at some periods prayer, in the normal sense of prayer addressed outside oneself, prayer which can thus be expressed vocally, fell into relative desuetude. This also was in no way true of Fox. Fox knew how, as well as when, to be silent, how 'to famish them from words', as he puts it; but normally he was as great in prayer as in preaching, so great that Penn says he excelled here above all. 'The most awful, living, reverent frame I ever felt or beheld, I must say, was his in prayer. And truly it was a testimony (that) he knew and lived nearer to the Lord than other men.' George Fox's Lord was no mere light within.

Nevertheless, the light was there, shining steadily and welcomingly, the light of Christ; and it was to this that Fox pointed men unwearyingly. 'Mind that which is pure in you to guide you to God', he would say.[1] Even in childhood, he tells us, he had been taught how to walk to be kept pure; and he had kept his childhood's vow not to be wanton when he grew to manhood. Here again he universalized his own experience. If he could be kept pure, so could others. He claimed no special grace for himself, no gift that was not for all men to receive who would. Nor did he pretend that it was possible to live in purity without persistent watchfulness, in utter dependence on the power of God. That which was pure had to be minded. 'Friend', he wrote to Oliver Cromwell's favourite daughter, Lady Claypole, 'Be still and cool in thy own mind and spirit from thy own thoughts, and then thou wilt feel the principle of God to turn thy mind to the Lord God, whereby thou wilt receive his strength and power from whence life comes to allay all tempests, blusterings and storms.' Later in the same letter he writes:

What the light doth make manifest and discover, temptations, confusions, distractions, distempers, do not look at the temptations, confusions, corruptions, but at the light which discovers them, that makes them manifest; and with the same light you will feel over them, to receive power to stand against them. . . . For looking down at sin, and corruption, and distraction, you are swallowed up in it; but looking at the light which discovers them, you will see over them. That will give victory; and you will find grace and strength: and there is the first step of peace.

His letter, Fox says, settled and stayed Lady Claypole's mind for the present, and proved useful for the settling of others' minds also. Yet in a day when, in Fox's quaint phrase, popular preachers would 'roar up for sin, in their pulpits', it sounded strange teaching; as to many weighed down with the world's evil it still sounds strange. It is, indeed, a teaching which, unless Fox's Christian presuppositions are realized

[1] G. Fox, *Epistles*, 1698, p. 9.

and accepted, can easily bring a man into peril and has often done so: the peril, for instance, of being more like the Pharisee than the publican. Yet Fox was not wrong in finding in his New Testament the promise that over Christians sin should not have dominion. That he took this promise seriously shows him entirely in character. The Lord's power was over all, sin included.

Had he not held this conviction so strongly, he would never have had the heart to go through either with his forbearance to those who persecuted him, or, more particularly, with his refusal to take up arms. For himself, he had early 'come into the covenant of peace which was before wars and strifes were', as he told those who pressed him to fight for Parliament in the Civil Wars. He had found what it meant to live 'in the virtue of that life and power that took away the occasion of all wars'. But he was far too shrewd an observer of his fellow men to suppose that this was true generally. Nothing could be further from the truth than to see Fox's testimony against taking part in war as idealistic and up in the air. It was exactly the opposite. Fox moved constantly among rude and wicked men, and was keenly sensitive to the evil in them, to the lust, as he found it called in the New Testament, from which all wars arose. His object was to overcome this lust by going among men in the power of the Lord and behaving towards them in the way *the most likely* to reach the inward witness and so change the evil mind into the right mind'.[1] It was essentially a missionary gospel which he preached, the gospel of Christ's power to meet evil and to overcome it; and it had its origin and seal in his own experience. There, before starting out on his ministry, he had seen an ocean of darkness and death, but also an infinite ocean of light and love, which flowed over the ocean of darkness. What he now sought was to be the Lord's instrument in bringing about a similar vision and a similar triumph in the lives of others. And with this we are back at the courage and fidelity and forbearance which first attracted us in him.

But Fox not only lived a remarkable life, he was also the author of a remarkable *Journal*. It is not a journal at all in

[1] A. N. Brayshaw, *op. cit.*, p. 131.

the strict sense of an account written, if not daily, at least shortly after each incident described, when the future is still dark. It is, rather, an autobiography or book of memoirs, written in retrospect in order to illustrate the power of the Lord as shown in his servant's 'Sufferings and Passages', as earlier, briefer accounts by other Quakers were often entitled.[1] Also, although we possess the original manuscript of the *Journal*, it is not in Fox's hand. It was not written by Fox but dictated, and was taken down mainly by his stepson-in-law, Thomas Lower. This makes the effectiveness with which it conveys his personality the more remarkable. Even so, it was not given to the world in its original form until the present century. Fox did not issue it during his lifetime but left instructions for its publication after his death. When he died, it was nearly twenty years after he had composed the *Journal* and more than fifty since the incidents recounted in its earlier sections. Toleration had come, and the missionary exaltation of Quakerism had grown cooler. Consequently, it was thought wise not only to omit or tone down many passages which to a politer age might seem wild or fanatical, but also to smooth out Fox's rugged style and occasionally outlandish vocabulary. This was a pity, though one can see broadly why it was done. A detailed study of the alterations made, and of the additions and omissions, with the reasons for them, so far as these can be ascertained, is another subject demanding research. It would throw light on the aesthetic as well as the ethical canons of editing in the 1690's.

Not that Fox was a man of one book only. Although he composed no other work of comparable length, he published within his lifetime some two hundred tracts and other writings, while the number of unpublished papers by him, now often lost but known from a manuscript catalogue in a contemporary hand, runs into thousands. Many of his earlier published pamphlets have never been reprinted, or much regarded even by his biographers. Though ephemeral in the sense that they were essentially tracts for the times, they

---

[1] A brief narrative by Fox himself bearing a similar title is still extant. It brings his story only to the year 1653 and adds nothing substantial to the *Journal*. See the *Bulletin* of the Friends Historical Association, Philadelphia, xxxix, 1 (Spring, 1950), pp. 27–31.

deserve attention: their systematic study would throw light on the times as well as on Fox. Some of them, mainly those with an interest primarily homiletic rather than social or political, were gathered together after Fox's death and republished in a single volume entitled *Gospel-Truth Demonstrated*. This was preceded by a collected volume of some four hundred of his *Epistles*, most of which were written to groups of Friends or others and are in the nature of exhortations or warnings rather than personal letters. In this country *Gospel-Truth Demonstrated* has never been re-issued; nor have the *Epistles*, though there is a modern anthology of selections from them.[1] Only the *Journal* has been continually republished, till by 1891 it was in its eighth edition. With its appearance twenty years later as first taken down by Thomas Lower,[2] fresh interest was aroused and has been maintained. The nature and purpose of the present edition is explained in the Editor's preface.

Fox might not have been altogether pleased, had he foreseen the reasons for which his *Journal* would come to be valued; for it now interests, even delights, readers who have little or no sympathy with his faith in the power of the Lord. Fox lived in an age when literary self-expression could still be direct and naïve: the sophistication and self-consciousness of the following century were not yet felt. In his *Journal*, like Bunyan in *Grace Abounding*, and Baxter in his autobiography, Fox is so absorbed in the spiritual purpose of his narration that he does not stop to think whether he is giving himself away, or to add touches of artistry with the purpose of bringing out how things should have happened or even of heightening the effect of things as they were. Things as they were were quite sufficiently remarkable; and in any case his devotion to truth demanded a straight narrative. That this did not result in a bald narrative is one of the mysteries of creative writing. All we can say is that Fox's personality was so well integrated, so dominant and pervasive, that what he dictated was, like himself, alive.

Nor is it only himself that he reveals so ingenuously. He had the skill to sketch many a character or situation in a few

---

[1] *A Day-Book of Counsel and Comfort from the Epistles of George Fox*, ed. L. V. Hodgkin, Macmillan, 1937.

[2] *The Journal of George Fox*, ed. N. Penney, Cambridge University Press, 1911.

short vivid phrases. Take this paragraph, which follows closely on the scene of violence at Ulverston, when, though mazed with the blows he had received, he was in the love of God to all his persecutors.

> And so I was moved of the Lord to come up again through them and up into Ulverston market, and there meets me a man with a sword, a soldier. 'Sir', said he, 'I am your servant, I am ashamed that you should be thus abused, for you are a man,' said he. He was grieved and said he would assist me in what he could, and I told him that it was no matter, the Lord's power was over all.

The conversation here is highly characteristic. These are real people, speaking naturally.

> As soon as I came to the door, a young woman came to the door. 'What! Is it you?' she said as though she had seen me before, 'Come in,' said she: for the Lord's power bowed their hearts.

Or again:

> And it being in the evening there being a company of serving men and wild fellows, they met me and encompassed me about and had an intent to have done me some mischief. And it being dark, I asked, 'What! are you highwaymen?'

The syntax is loose; but one can see and hear, almost feel, it as it happens.

Or take Fox's description of the situation which brought about his being belaboured so roughly at Ulverston: the picture of the minister who was 'blustering on in his preaching', when 'of a sudden all the people in the steeplehouse were in an outrage and an uproar'; 'so that people tumbled over their seats for fear . . . and the blood ran down several people so as I never saw the like in my life, as I looked at them when they were dragging me along'.

This last phrase explains something of the *Journal's* power. Fox possessed the detachment to look at men. He had need to do so, it is true. At Aberystwyth 'I turned but my back from the man that was giving oats to my horse, and I looked back again and he was filling his pockets with the provender that was given to my horse'. Fox looked at men, and he remembered what he saw. Small wonder men cried 'Look at his eyes!' and 'Don't pierce me so with thy eyes! Keep thy

189

eyes off me !' He looked at them, and knew what was in them. Sometimes he saw them not only as they were but as they would be. 'As I parted from him', he says of James Nayler in 1655, 'I cast my eyes upon him, and a fear struck in me concerning him.' Within a year Nayler had run out into imaginations, as Fox calls it, and had brought shame upon Friends generally.

Fox was thus not only always minding a light within. He was also, as Penn says of him, a discerner of others' spirits. That he should have been given to visions more generally is hardly surprising. Such visions as, on various occasions, he had of 'a bear and two great mastiff dogs, that I should pass by them and they should do me no hurt', of 'a desperate creature like a wild horse or colt that was coming to destroy me: but I got victory over it', of 'a black coffin, but I passed over it', of 'an ugly slubbering hound', are all presumably to be regarded as but the projections into concrete symbols of a presentiment of danger which often came to him and seldom without cause. He had, however, at least one vision of a more meditative kind, his account of which contains some exquisite dream-language, especially in its closing sentences.

And I had a vision about the time that I was in this travail and sufferings, that I was walking in the fields, and many Friends were with me, and I bid them dig in the earth, and they did and I went down. And there was a mighty vault top-full of people kept under the earth, rocks and stones. So I bid them break open the earth and let all the people out, and they did, and all the people came forth to liberty; and it was a mighty place.

And when they had done I went on and bid them dig again. They did, and there was a mighty vault full of people, and I bid them throw it down and let all the people out, and so they did.

And I went on again, and bid them dig again, and Friends said unto me, 'George, thou finds out all things,' and so there they digged, and I went down, and went along the vault; and there sat a woman in white looking at time how it passed away. And there followed me a woman down in the vault, in which vault was the treasure; and so she laid her hand on the treasure on my left hand and then time whisked on apace; but I clapped my hand upon her, and said, 'Touch not the treasure.'

And then time passed not so swift.

Something of Fox's secret is in this passage. Much, no doubt, cannot be explained. The whole passage was omitted from the *Journal* as first published. The self-satisfaction of 'George, thou finds out all things', as well as the visionary nature of the whole, were not welcomed in 1700. Today, perhaps, we are more ready to understand. 'There is no great leadership where there is not a mystic. Nothing splendid has ever been achieved except by those who dared to believe that something inside themselves was superior to circumstances, and in the pursuit of the great secret the follower finds that detachment which to the world around savours of mystery.'[1]

This vision of Fox's may well throw light upon his mental processes generally. At least we may say that attention to the eye of faith, looking on the things which are not seen but eternal, is likely to foster insight and intuition more at large. 'The strength of her mind lay in intuition,' wrote William Godwin of Mary Wollstonecraft; 'she was often right, by this means only, in matters of mere speculation. . . . She adopted one opinion, and rejected another, spontaneously, by a sort of tact.' To compare George Fox with Mary Wollstonecraft may seem fanciful, but the passage is suggestive; as are the words with which Godwin continues: 'In a robust and unwavering judgment of this sort, there is a kind of witchcraft; when it decides justly, it produces a responsive vibration in every ingenuous mind.'[2]

May we not have here something that explains George Fox's leadership? For not his least remarkable faculty was his ability to draw men to himself and to claim their entire and life-long devotion. That he could do this is, at the same time, the best evidence that he was no mere visionary. He also possessed a robust common sense and had considerable organizing powers. If the Society of Friends has had a continuing existence, while other bands of Commonwealth enthusiasts were forgotten before the century was out, it owes this in no small measure to the system of monthly and quarterly meetings for business which Fox established. His

---

[1] Professor John Fraser, on 'The Influence of Lister's Work on Surgery', in *Joseph, Baron Lister*, ed. A. Logan Turner, 1927, p. 105.
[2] W. Godwin, *op. cit.*, p. 125.

shrewdness, not to say his humour, may be illustrated from the occasion when he was sent up to London after being tried at Lancaster. First he persuaded the authorities at Lancaster to save themselves the expense of sending the gaoler and bailiffs with him as guards, and to trust him to travel with one or two of his own friends only. Then, when he appeared in London on the charge of plotting to imbrue the whole nation in blood, he said, 'I had need to have had two or three troops of horse to have come along with me if such things could be proved,' and was soon set free.

Yet more than shrewdness and common sense are needed to win men as Fox could win them. Despite the central place in his life of forbearance to enemies, it is all too easy to miss his tenderness and gentleness. His courage is more evident; but his tender side was equally essential to his make-up. The scene in which the Lord Protector catched him by the hand and said, with tears in his eyes, 'Come again to my house', says something for Fox as well as for Cromwell. Soldiers, too, 'took me by the hand very friendly, and said they would have me alongst with them'. 'Nathaniel', said Fox to a minister with whom he had been disputing, 'give me thy hand'; for, he added, he would not quench the least measure of God in any, much less put out his starlight. It was the same with Quaker meetings for worship. Fox had no greater praise for a meeting for worship than to call it a tender broken meeting; and if any, in bubbling forth a few words of ministry should go beyond their measure, he bade Friends bear it: 'that is the tender'.

So it was that the men and women whom he gathered round him not only believed in him but loved him. One Friend, John Banks, who had a withered arm, dreamed one night that he was with 'dear George Fox', and felt such faith in Fox that he believed Fox could heal his arm; he accordingly sought Fox out, and received the healing he desired. However the 'miracle', as Fox would have called it, is to be interpreted, and many similar incidents are recorded during his life,[1] the story says much for the relation between the two men. 'George', wrote another Friend when in prison at

[1] See *George Fox's 'Book of Miracles'*, ed. H. J. Cadbury, Cambridge University Press, 1948.

Lancaster, 'sometimes when I think on thee, the power rises and warms my heart. Bonds and fetters (are) ready to burst asunder, for it is not possible that they can hold me.'[1] Robert Widders, the writer of this letter, was a husbandman; John Banks was a glover; not many mighty, not many noble, were called. But when they were, their relation to Fox was just the same. It was so, for instance, with William Penn, the courtier of gentle birth who became the founder of Pennsylvania. In the whole of Penn's carefully balanced character-sketch of Fox printed in his preface to the first edition of Fox's *Journal*, a sketch which is still the best and which has continually been drawn on in the present study, nothing is more moving than the start of affection with which it closes. 'I have done', Penn writes, 'as to this part of my Preface, when I have left this short epitaph to his name: "Many sons have done virtuously in this day; but, dear George, thou excellest them all." '

Out of the strong came forth sweetness. By few has Samson's riddle been better resolved.

1952

---

[1] Swarthmore MSS. (Friends House), IV. 41.

XIX

'UNITY WITH THE CREATION': GEORGE FOX
AND THE HERMETIC PHILOSOPHY

READERS of George Fox's *Journal*, as edited from the MSS. by Norman Penney in 1911, are familiar with Fox's account of his first meeting with John Storey, at Crosslands in 1652.

> & there came Jo: Storey to mee & lighted his pipe of Tobacco: & saide hee will you take a pipe of Tobacco sayinge come all is ours: & I lookt upon him to bee a forwarde bolde lad: & tobacco I did not take: butt It came into my minde yt ye Lad might thinke I had not unity with ye creation: for I saw hee had a flashy empty notion of religion: soe I took his pipe & putt it to my mouth & gave it to him again to stoppe him least his rude tongue shoulde say I had not unity with ye creation.[1]

The passage is amusing alike for its picture of Fox's putting the man's pipe to his mouth for a moment and for the naïve manner of its telling. The more attentive reader will note the striking phrase 'unity with the creation', which Penney prints as a page-heading. Most readers will be content to be amused, and will pass on. Already in 1694, when Fox's *Journal* was first published, its editor, Thomas Ellwood, evidently thought the passage too trivial to be printed, for he omitted the whole of it. Neave Brayshaw with greater insight perceived that the phrase 'unity with the creation' was the key to the passage's significance, and in his study of *The Personality of George Fox* there is an extended discussion of this and similar phrases of Fox's. This book, like many others, suffers, however, from a tendency to study its subject in too narrow a context: its interpretation by cross-references within Fox's own writings is excellent, but reference to the prevailing *Zeitgeist* not so good. Thus, interpreting Fox's use on this and other occasions

---

[1] G. Fox, *Journal*, ed. N. Penney, I. 44. (Hereafter referred to as *C.J.*)

of the phrase 'unity with the creation', Neave Brayshaw is satisfied to see it as 'part of his intense perception of the divine harmony, of the need for all things being in their right place, and being put to their right use'.[1]

This it was, but it was much more. For this conception of a 'divine harmony' in creation was not peculiar to Fox; it was intensely fashionable in his time. It was a fundamental element in a strange complex which it is not easy to reconstruct, though with imagination this may be done, the complex of astrology, alchemy, and herbalism in which so many of Fox's contemporaries were interested. At its lower end it shaded off into Rosicrucianism, magic, and quackery; at its higher into astronomy, chemistry, metallurgy, botany, and medicine. These lines of study, which are not thought of by us as directly related to religion, were about to issue into maturity as independent manifestations of the new experimental spirit in science. In the middle of the seventeenth century, however, they were still largely pursued by men of a religious character, who believed in 'the unity of the world in God and the interpenetration by the Divine spirit of all created things, whether animate or inanimate,' and who held that 'the secrets of nature . . . could be revealed only to the God-fearing.'[2]

In 1650 Thomas Vaughan published his *Anthroposophia Theomagica, Or a Discourse of the Nature of Man and his state after Death; Grounded on his Creator's Proto-Chemistry and verifi'd by a practicall Examination of Principles in the Great World*. Five years later his brother Henry Vaughan, the poet, published a translation of Heinrich Nolle's *General System of Hermetic Medicine*. The title 'Hermetic' was taken from the early pseudonymous writings named after the Egyptian god commonly known as Hermes Trismegistus, whose *Poimandres* (today studied for its relation to the Fourth Gospel) had appeared in 1650 as *The Divine Pymander of Hermes Mercurius Trismegistus, translated out of the original into English by that learned divine, Dr Everard*.[3] These, and many other, works depended on the conviction that everything in Nature has

[1] *Op. cit.*, 1933 edn., pp. 177 f.

[2] F. E. Hutchinson, *Henry Vaughan* (Clarendon Press, 1947), pp. 153, 185.

[3] The extent to which John Everard prepared the way for Quakerism is discussed by R. M. Jones, *Mysticism & Democracy in the English Commonwealth*, pp. 63ff., 77ff., and more fully in ch. I of T. Sippell's *Werdendes Quäkertum*.

its place in the divine ordering, that beasts and birds, trees and herbs, even stones 'are all held together in

> That busie Commerce kept between
> God and his Creatures, though unseen'.[1]

That Fox was in sympathy with this way of thinking will become abundantly clear from what follows.

In the sphere of chemistry and medicine, which were not yet entirely separate, the chief seventeenth-century representative of what is known as the astro-chemical school was the Belgian Jean Baptist van Helmont. His son, Francis Mercurius van Helmont, became the private physician of the celebrated invalid and blue-stocking, Lady Conway of Ragley, whose *entourage*, together with her interest in Quakerism, can be studied in detail in Professor M. H. Nicolson's *Conway Letters*. It was known earlier that George Keith had visited Ragley and had been influenced by van Helmont, from whom he gained his 'belief in the pre-existence and transmigration of souls';[2] also that Fox himself 'struck to Ragley in Warwickshire, to visit the Lady Conway' in March 1678, when he found her 'tender and loving'.[3] It was not until the publication in 1925 of what is known as Fox's Haistwell Journal that it was known that Fox and Keith went together, accompanied by the Quaker doctor of Worcester, Edward Bourne (of whom more anon), 'and Van Helmont & ffrds there was very glad yt G ff came,'[4] van Helmont actually helping Fox and Keith to answer an attack on Quakerism by the rector of the parish, Thomas Wilson. That van Helmont even became a Friend would seem to be implied in a letter by Lord Conway, in which he says that 'all the women about my wife and most of the rest are Quakers, and Mons. Van Helmont is governour of that flock, an unpleasing sort of people, silent, sullen, and of a removed conversation'; Lady Conway also says that he 'goes every Sunday to the Quakers meetings'.[5]

[1] F. E. Hutchinson, *op. cit.*, p. 173, quoting Vaughan's poem, 'The Stone'.
[2] *Dict. Nat. Biog.*, *s.v.* Geo. Keith.
[3] *Journal*, 1901 edn., II. 319.
[4] *Short Journal & Itinerary Journals of George Fox*, ed. N. Penney, p. 267.
[5] *Rawdon Papers*, p. 254, quoted by M. H. Nicolson, *op. cit.*, p. 434; *ibid.*, p. 409.

The Worcester doctor, Edward Bourne, was an old acquaintance of Fox's. They had had a memorable conversation when Fox was in the district some twenty-two years earlier, in 1656. Fox, writes Bourne,

> speake of many Heavenly things in discourse, wch were delightfull & pleasant ... Hee speak of the Glory of the first body, and of the Egiptian Learning, & of the Language of the birds, & of wt was wonnderfull to mee to heare, soe that I believed he was of a Deep & wonnderfull vnderstanding in naturall, but especially in sptuall things, whose works, wch Hee have left behind him, doe demonstrate the same.[1]

'The Egiptian Learning' here is undoubtedly the Hermetic philosophy, in which the young doctor—also, significantly, described on his marriage five years later as a chemist—would naturally be interested. Fox may well have read John Everard's translation of Hermes, for we know that he possessed another of Everard's translations, Sebastian Franck's *Hidden Fruit*.[2] The meaning of the other two subjects mentioned we will leave for a moment.

That Fox himself had an early and a continuing interest in medicine is plain from his *Journal*. He says, in fact, that as a young man 'I was at a stand in my mind, whether I should practise physic'.[3] Neave Brayshaw rightly associates with this remark the occasion at Lyme Regis in 1657 when Fox 'drew uppe some Queryes: Off ye grounde of all diseases'.[4] He seems, however, to accept W. C. Braithwaite's treatment of the two passages as examples of 'a certain parade of learning', which was 'one of his (Fox's) weaknesses'.[5] The context is worthy of closer attention. It reads as follows:

> And att night we came to a place caled Lime: & wee went to an Inn & ye house was taken uppe with mountebankes: & there was hardly any roome for us or our horses: & att night wee drew uppe some Queryes:
> Off ye grounde of all diseases:

[1] *First Publishers of Truth*, ed. N. Penney, pp. 276, 278.
[2] Cf. *Journal of* Friends' Historical Society, XXVIII, 1931, 18.
[3] *Journal*, 1901 edn., I. 28.
[4] *C.J.*, I. 269.
[5] W. C. Braithwaite, *Beginnings of Quakerism*, pp. 301f.

And whether Adam or Eve had any before they fell:

And whether there was any in ye restoration by Christ Jesus againe:

And whether any knew ye virtue of all ye Creatures in ye Creation whose virtue & nature was accordinge to Itts first name except they was in ye wisdome of God by which they was made & created.

And many other particular queryes wee sent to ym & told ym if they woulde not aunswer ym wee woulde sticke ym on ye crosse to morrow. . . .

Ellwood, once again, omits the passage about Adam and Eve and the restoration, and telescopes the fourth query to 'and the natures and virtues of medicinable creatures',[1] but it is 'Adam or Eve' which gives the key.

For the general view among the Hermeticists was that creation, apart from man, had not been involved in Adam's fall. Hence birds and beasts and trees and herbs are regarded with admiration and envy as still fulfilling the divine purpose of their Creator. Man alone is out of order, out of unity with the creation, restless and ineffectual through his sin. This is, for instance, Henry Vaughan's approach to Nature, as is shown in the Tredegar Memorial Lecture for 1944 by W. R. Childe,[2] and more recently in Dr Hutchinson's admirable study of the poet, to which this paper is much indebted. To compare Vaughan and Fox is less fanciful than it may seem. They were almost exact contemporaries, Vaughan being born in 1621, three years before Fox, and dying four years after him in 1695. Moreover, Vaughan's mysticism, though it is the mysticism of a poet, not of a prophet, has many points of similarity with Fox's. His poem on the seed growing secretly[3] is an example of the popularity of this image in religious minds of the time outside Quakerism. He has a true appreciation of the value of silence, 'the soul's dumb watch', and of 'joys active as light, and calm without all noise'.

The Hermetic writers place particular emphasis upon light as the source of life, and Henry Vaughan is for ever using such

[1] 1901 edn., I. 359.
[2] Published in *Essays by Divers Hands* (being the Transactions of the Royal Society of Literature of the United Kingdom), new series, xxii, 1945.
[3] *Works of Henry Vaughan*, ed. L. C. Martin, II. 510.

words as *light, white, ray, beam*, with fuller connotation than most of his readers recognize. He has passed the Hermetic ideas and terms so integrally into the common language of Christian tradition that they do not disconcert the reader; they are not resented as the technical terms of an unfamiliar philosophy, but are accepted as the poet's individual way of expressing his conviction of the 'commerce' between earth and heaven.[1]

The observation may not be altogether irrelevant to the study of Fox. The difference between their conceptions of this 'commerce' is, however, even more illuminating than the similarity.

For Vaughan is always lamenting the fall of man in Adam, and ever since:

> In Abr'hams Tent the winged guests
> (O how familiar then was heaven!)
> Eate, drinke, discourse, sit downe, and rest
> Untill the Coole and Shady Even;
>
> Nay thou thy selfe, my God, in fire,
> Whirle-winds, and Clouds, and the soft voice
> Speak'st there so much, that I admire
> We have no Conf'rence in these daies . . .[2]

Again, writing of Adam, after the fall,

> He sigh'd for Eden, and would often say
>   Ah! what bright days were those?
> Nor was Heav'n cold unto him; for each day
>   The vally, or the Mountain
> Afforded visits, and still Paradise lay
>   In some green shade, or fountain.
> Angels lay Leiger here; Each Bush, and Cel,
>   Each Oke, and high-way knew them,
> Walk but the fields, or sit down at some wel,
>   And he was sure to view them.
> Almighty Love! where art thou now? . . .[3]

---

[1] F. E. Hutchinson, *op. cit.*, p. 155.

[2] *Works*, II. 404.

[3] *Ibid.*, II. 440; for *Leiger*, *cf. C.J.*, I. 110, 273; for walking in the fields, *cf. C.J.*, I. 48, 110; *Journal*, 1901 edn, i. 35; *et alibi*.

All that is left for the modern man is to long to be as the rest of creation, still unfallen.

> I would I were some Bird, or Star,
> Flutt'ring in woods, or lifted far
>   Above this Inne
>   And Rode of sin!
> Then either Star, or Bird, should be
> Shining, or singing still to thee.[1]

Again,

> I would (said I) my God would give
> The staidness of these things to man! for these
> To his divine appointments ever cleave . . .[2]

Vaughan also wrote a poem on *Romans* viii. 19, 'for the earnest expectation of the creature waiteth for the manifestation of the sons of God'.

> I would I were a stone, or tree,
>   Or flowre by pedigree,
> Or some poor high-way herb, or Spring
> To flow, or bird to sing![3]

Romans viii. 19 was the foundation test of a contemporary group who were called the Manifestarians, because they awaited such a manifestation together with the rest of the creation. With them the Quakers entered into vigorous controversy, for in Quakerism the manifestation of the sons of God was not to be waited for, it was already here.

In the same way, Fox has none of Vaughan's nostalgia for unfallen creation. For Fox it is a prime conviction that through Christ man may be restored to the condition of Eden, and be again in full 'unity with the creation'. The passage in which he says 'I was at a stand in my mind whether I should practise physic' follows his assertion that 'it was showed me how all things had their names given them, according to their nature and virtue', *because* he had been

[1] *Ibid.*, II. 442.
[2] *Ibid.*, II. 477; for *staidness*, *cf.* Fox's letter to Lady Claypole, quoted later.
[3] *Ibid.*, II. 432.

'renewed into the image of God by Christ Jesus, to the state of Adam, which he was in before he fell'. Conversely, because they 'were out of the wisdom of God, by which the creatures were made', ordinary physicians 'knew not their virtues'. This probably explains Fox's behaviour in 1670 when he says 'severall freindes yt was Doctors came & they would have given me physicke but I was not to medle with there thinges'.[1] Even though they were Friends, they may be presumed to have offered the conventional remedies, which Fox repudiated.

At the same time, the common sense which was so marked in Fox prevented him from supposing that the knowledge about 'the creatures' which he had received by revelation (as we should say) could not be taught. It not only could, but should. What he intended by his advice that in the Quaker school established at Walthamstow in 1668 'whatsever thinges was civill & usefull in ye creation'[2] should be taught, appears from directions of his for other schools, that a garden should be planted 'with all sorts of physical plants for lads and lasses to learn simples there'[3] and that 'the nature of flowers, roots, plants and trees' should be taught. The textbook Fox used himself was Nicholas Culpeper's *The English Physitian Enlarged*: . . . *Being an Astrologo-Physical Discourse of the Vulgar Herbs of this Nation* (1653), for we know that this was among his books.[4] The full title, together with Culpeper's known associations[5] makes the connexion with the Hermetic way of thinking evident.

Fox's drawing up of the queries at Lyme was thus no 'parade of learning'. A mountebank, such as those to whom the queries were addressed, to be stuck on the market cross if not answered, is defined in Webster's *Dictionary* as 'one who mounts a bench or stage in the market or other public place, boasts of his skill in curing diseases, and vends medicines which he pretends are infallible remedies'. On such an occasion it was right for Fox to make plain the medical relevance of his prime conviction. The last query at Lyme

[1] *C.J.*, II. 166.
[2] *C.J.*, II. 119.
[3] *Cf.* A. N. Brayshaw, *op. cit.*, p. 114.
[4] *Cf.* *J.F.H.S.*, XXVIII, 15, with facsimile of title-page on p. 2.
[5] *Cf.* *D.N.B.*, *s.v.* N. Culpeper.

virtually repeats the phrase quoted earlier, following his original mystical experience.

Nor was the conversation with Edward Bourne a 'parade of learning', either. It was a similar expression of his faith in regard to the concerns of his companion, a Quaker doctor. What he meant by 'the glory of the first body' was the glory of the restoration to Adam's condition before the fall. This is not a matter of conjecture, for he used the phrase twice in the wonderful letter which he wrote two years later to Oliver Cromwell's daughter, Lady Claypole, when she was 'very sicke & troubled in minde & nothinge coulde comforte her'.[1]

> Friend,
> Be still and cool in thy own mind and spirit from thy own thoughts, and then thou wilt feel the principle of God to turn thy mind to the Lord, from whom cometh life; whereby thou mayest receive his strength and power to allay all storms, and tempests. That is it which works up into patience, innocency, soberness, into stillness, staidness, quietness up to God, with his power . . . When thou art in the transgression of the life of God in thy own particular, the mind flies up in the air, the creature is led into the night, nature goes out of its course, an old garment goes on, and an uppermost clothing; and thy nature being led out of its course, it comes to be all on fire, in the transgression; and that defaceth the glory of the first body.[2]

What Fox meant by 'the language of the birds' may be more disputable, but it is not unlikely that he had some such conception of the birds' praising God as we have seen already in Henry Vaughan's poetry. Vaughan has a poem called 'The Bird', in which he writes:

> And now as fresh and chearful as the light
> Thy little heart in early hymns doth sing
> Unto that Providence, whose unseen arm
> Curb'd them, and cloath'd thee well and warm.
> All things that be, praise him; and had
> Their lesson taught them, *when first made*.[3]

[1] *C.J.*, I. 328.
[2] *Journal*, 1901 edn., I. 432.
[3] *Works*, II. 496 (my italics).

Or again,

> heark! in what Rings,
> And Hymning Circulations the quick world
> Awakes and sings;
> The rising winds,
> And falling springs,
> Birds, beasts, all things
> Adore him in their kinds.
> Thus all is hurl'd
> In sacred Hymnes, and Order, The great Chime
> And Symphony of Nature. Prayer is
> The world in tune, . . .[1]

For Fox, we may recall, such a glorious conception was not spoiled, as it was for Vaughan, by the continued necessity of human sinfulness and disunity.

When Fox put John Storey's pipe to his mouth, therefore —to return to our starting-point—'least his rude tongue shoulde say I had not unity with ye creation', he intended, presumably, to make it plain that he had no testimony to bear against smoking. 'Tobacco I did not take', but it had its place and use in the creation. Later, as we know from the *Household Account Book of Sarah Fell*,[2] Fox did take tobacco. This may have been for medicinal purposes rather than for normal smoking; but in either case we may be sure that his taking it would be in accord with the position made known to him in principle even in childhood,

> using the creatures in their service, as servants in their places, to the glory of Him that created them; they being in their covenant, and I being brought up into the covenant, as sanctified by the Word which was in the beginning, by which all things are upheld; wherein is unity with the creation.[3]

As Penn says of him in what is still the best memoir, so weighty is almost every word, Fox was 'a divine *and a naturalist*, and all of God Almighty's making'.[4]   1947

[1] *Ibid.*, II. 424.
[2] Ed. N. Penney, p. 583; the statement here, from *C.J.*, I. 21, that Fox 'decries smoking in others', is hardly correct.
[3] *Journal*, 1901 edn, I. 2.
[4] *Ibid.*, I. 1 (my italics).

XX

EARLY QUAKERISM AND
EARLY PRIMITIVE METHODISM

THE similarities between early Quakerism and early Primitive Methodism and the influence of the former upon the latter appear very largely to have escaped observation and comment. It may be easier for one who is neither Quaker nor Methodist to perceive the filiations. The following notes are the outcome of reading the biographies of Hugh Bourne[1] and William Clowes,[2] the founders of Primitive Methodism, by J. T. Wilkinson. They may serve to provide hints for that comparative study of revivalism in religion which awaits its author.

Even before his conversion, he tells us in his manuscript autobiography, Hugh Bourne had read various books on religion, 'of different denominations, Quakers and others'[3]; and while he was still a seeker after truth he was deeply impressed with some 'large volumes containing the annals of the first race of Quakers', lent him by his employer, which his biographer suggests were probably Besse's *Sufferings*.[4] Bourne's comment on these volumes, looking back, is this:

> The first race of the Quakers were endued with the spirit of martyrs to a most extraordinary degree. And they exhibited examples of faith, patience, and sufferings not often equalled . . . many went through afflictions and imprisonments to crowns of life, even in the most dreadful of persecutions; their zeal for open-air worship was great: it could not be conquered.

'Probably here', his biographer comments,[5] 'is one of the first springs of Bourne's later commitment to open-air preaching

---

[1] *Hugh Bourne, 1772–1852.* By John T. Wilkinson. Epworth Press. Hereafter abbreviated as *B*.
[2] *William Clowes, 1780–1851.* By John T. Wilkinson. Epworth Press. Hereafter abbreviated as *C*.
[3] *B.*, p. 22.
[4] *B.*, p. 24.
[5] *Ibid.*

and praying'. Bourne says himself, in fact, that it was in part through 'the writings of the first Quakers' that 'the desire of open-air worship was so implanted in me that nothing could shake it. I was in that respect quite primitive'.[1] A little later, after his conversion, while he was suffering from some reaction of anxiety about his soul, Bourne attended Quarterly Meeting at Leek, at which a Friend spoke 'of the readiness of Christ to build up again those that had backslidden'. 'I felt the word applied to my heart by the Spirit', Bourne writes, 'and was restored to peace again.'[2] One wonders if the un-named Friend knew how his words had reached the visitor (attending presumably by permission) and had helped to steady him for the great work which lay ahead of him? Probably not.

Hugh Bourne evidently continued to read Quaker litera-ture. For on Christmas Day in the following year (1800), when going, despite great timidity, to visit his cousin Daniel Shubotham, with the express purpose of converting him, he took with him 'a book written by R. Barclay, the Quaker'; and knowing Shubotham 'to be hindered by an erroneous notion, I read him a piece out of Barclay, with which he de-clared himself satisfied. So the way was open. . . . And Daniel afterwards told me that when I was talking to him that morning, every word went through him. . . . The "seed of God" word was sown in Daniel Shubotham's heart.'[3]

Another influence upon Bourne in early days was that of the 'Quaker Methodists' of Warrington. There was no other Methodist society in the immediate vicinity of Warrington, and the society there had consequently grown up in an iso-lation which had led it to adopt vagaries from what had come to be common form within the Methodist Connexion. Especi-ally did the authorities frown upon the continuance of, and satisfaction with, the original cottage-meetings, in which all

[1] B., p. 34. The choice of the appellation 'Primitive Methodists', taken from the words of the aged John Wesley, 'And this is the way the primitive methodists did' (B., p. 92; C., p. 32, n. 15) may be compared with the Quaker desire to show forth, in Penn's phrase, 'Primitive Christianity Revived'. The early Primitive Methodists, like the early Quakers, were called Ranters, but Clowes does not seem to have objected to the name: cf. C., p. 48 ('he knowing that I was a ranter preacher').

[2] B., p. 26.
[3] B., pp. 30f.

present shared the responsibility of ministry, without the oversight of an ordained and paid minister.[1] These 'Quaker Methodists' at Warrington, and the district round about, Hugh Bourne often visited, and he was 'much edified among them'. Of the branch society at Rizley he wrote in his Journal: 'Here each one does that which is right in his own eyes. They stand, sit, kneel, pray, exhort, &c., as they are moved. I was very fond of their way.'[2]

Some of these 'Quaker Methodists', it is recorded, attended the great open-air camp-meetings on Mow Cop and at Norton-le-Moors in July and August 1807, which led to Bourne's exclusion from the Methodist Connexion and so to the founding of Primitive Methodism. Also present at Norton was a doctor of medicine from Dublin named Paul Johnson, whose 'powerful preaching impressed the company and greatly encouraged Bourne'.[3] Johnson was 'much in the Quaker way', Bourne writes, and in the following year 'honestly tried to convert me to Quakerism, but could not succeed'.[4] Bourne's brother William, however, did join Friends about this time, and became a travelling minister in America.[5]

Considering the variety of these contacts with Quakerism, literary and personal, it would be strange if Bourne had failed to come across Fox's *Journal*. In his description of what he felt immediately after his conversion, the words 'I was as if brought into another world; creation wore a fresh aspect'[6] are reminiscent of Fox's words at a comparable point in his own life, 'All things were new, and all the creation gave another smell unto me than before'.[7] For such an occasion phraseology of this kind is perhaps inevitable; but the following passage is more telling.

> I went into the minster. . . . I saw much lightness and sin

<hr />

[1] For the circumstances in which 'Quaker Methodism' arose, *cf.* W. J. Townsend, H. B. Workman and G. Eayrs, *A New History of Methodism*, 1909, I. 558f. It is today represented by the Independent Methodist Church, which has continued to have friendly relations with the Society of Friends.

[2] *B.*, p. 53, with n. 76, where the year-date given is 1809; *C.*, p. 25, n. 22, where it is 1807.

[3] *B.*, p. 56.

[4] *B.*, pp. 56, 60.

[5] *B.*, p. 38, n. 30.

[6] *B.*, p. 26.

[7] George Fox, *Journal*, ed. J. L. Nickalls, 1952, p. 27; hereafter abbreviated as *F.*

among the parsons. It seemed like gross idolatry in them to spend their time in such a manner. . . . I then thought to go out, and a voice came: 'Escape for thy life' . . . I took my hat as soon as they had done, and went out, and the burden was removed. It looked as if judgments hung over that place. I stopped all afternoon . . . and such a travail of soul came upon me as I never before experienced—it was for the city. I mourned greatly . . . I trembled for the place and people. O my God! have mercy on them![1]

When the name of the city is found to be none other than Lichfield, one can hardly doubt that Bourne knew of Fox's experience and behaviour in 'the bloody city'[2] and was influenced by it (perhaps subconsciously). With this in one's mind, one may further wonder whether the great meeting on Mow Cop was not in part imitative of Fox's meeting with the Seekers on Firbank Fell as its prototype? 'On the slopes of Mow Cop the purpose was to seek comparative seclusion for prolonged approach to God'[3]; and 'to see thousands hearing with attention solemn as death', writes Bourne, 'presented a scene of the most sublime and awfully pleasing grandeur my eyes ever beheld.'[4]

Whether Bourne knew Fox's *Journal* or not, there were certainly similarities between the personalities and experiences of the two men: 'Mr. Hugh Bourne makes me think of George Fox, the Quaker', as a contemporary once remarked.[5] Like Fox, Bourne had a good voice and all the courage of his convictions. On one occasion he was standing on the foredeck of a steamer plying between Liverpool and Whitehaven, preaching to all who would hear. 'The music people attempted to play me down, but my voice was too strong for them, and after wearying themselves, they gave it up and went to the other end of the vessel.'[6] Just so did Fox sing 'in the everlasting power of the Lord God', when a fiddler was brought in to drown him in gaol; 'and my voice

[1] *B.*, pp. 50f.

[2] *F.*, pp. 71f. Bourne's biographer draws attention to the parallel.

[3] W. E. Farndale, *The Secret of Mow Cop: A New Appraisal of the Origins of Primitive Methodism*, Epworth Press, 1950, p. 29.

[4] *B.*, p. 47; for the gathering of 'above a thousand people' on Firbank Fell to whom Fox spoke for 'about three hours'. *cf. F.*, pp. 108f.

[5] *B.*, p. 134, n. 49.

[6] *B.*, p. 138.

drowned them and struck them and confounded them and made the fiddler sigh and give over his fiddling'.[1] But, again like Fox, Bourne could also be quiet. 'I had that sacred awe that dares not move', in a phrase reminiscent of Charles Wesley, 'and all the silent heaven of love.'[2] On another occasion, after being 'set upon by a few abandoned people', 'I looked unto the Lord,' he writes, 'till such a spirit of love came upon me that it appeared impossible for me to feel any resentment to anyone, except I first cast away my faith. If a man were to rob or murder me I believe I should only feel tenderness, pity, and love.'[3] This is strikingly reminiscent of Fox 'in the love of God to them all that had persecuted me' after being beaten down and mazed at Ulverston.[4]

Before continuing with this comparison between Bourne and Fox, we will turn to look more briefly at William Clowes, whose own associations with Quakers and Quakerism, though less marked, are by no means lacking: 'Come let us go and have some fun with yon Quaker,'[5] said a man of Clowes one day when Clowes was preaching in the open air.

No evidence is provided by his biographer of Quaker influence upon Clowes, but that he was not unsympathetic to Friends appears from the record of two occasions when he was travelling by coach in Devon and found a Quaker in his company. On the one occasion he had a 'very profitable' conversation with his companion, 'involving practical and experimental religion'[6]; on the other he took sides with the Quaker in a discussion with a sceptic, with the result that 'all the passengers were very attentive' and 'the sceptic was considerably pensive'.[7]

In personality Clowes seems in some ways to have been more like Fox than Bourne was. Like him in being 'a bulky person',[8] for he is described as being 'somewhat portly',[9] Clowes also had 'large prominent eyes, remarkable for their

[1] *F.*, p. 164.
[2] *B.*, p. 69.
[3] *B.*, pp. 68f.
[4] *F.*, p. 128.
[5] *C.*, p. 53.
[6] *C.*, p. 60.
[7] *C.*, p. 70.
[8] Penn, of Fox: *F.*, p. xlviii.
[9] *C.*, p. 76.

penetrating power'. 'Nobody can stand your look'[1] was said to him, just as 'Keep thy eyes off me'[2] was said to Fox. When Clowes preached, 'his speech . . . had little unity or logical cohesion; it seemed rather a series of spontaneous utterances struck off at the moment by the fervour of the speaker'.[3] Fox's sentences about divine things, likewise, 'would fall from him' 'abruptly and brokenly', and 'might seem uncouth and unfashionable to nice ears'.[4] In his dealings with his brethren, Clowes was 'unpretending, unassuming', with a 'perfect naturalness' of manner;[5] Fox, too, possessed 'a most engaging humility and moderation' and was 'civil beyond all forms of breeding'.[6] Both men excelled especially in prayer. 'We never heard prayer like his,' men said of Clowes: 'he lived and moved as though he were on the borders of the heavenly world.'[7] 'The most awful, living, reverent frame I ever felt or beheld, I must say,' writes Penn of Fox, 'was his in prayer. And truly it was a testimony that he knew and lived nearer to the Lord than other men.'[8] Once more, Clowes, like Fox, had his early struggles: 'sometimes I used to walk in solitary and unfrequented places, wishing that I was a bird or beast',[9] he writes, just as Fox tells how he 'walked abroad in solitary places . . . and went and sat in hollow trees and lonesome places'.[10] But after his conversion Clowes was as sure and untroubled as Fox was: 'I have never had a doubt for forty years,'[11] he declared. At his funeral it was stated that he 'went to God through Christ for entire holiness of heart and obtained it, and lived in its blessed enjoyment to the end of his life'.[12] In like manner Fox could say 'Now I am clear, I am fully clear'[13] two days before he died.

[1] *C.*, pp. 81f.
[2] *F.*, p. 157.
[3] *C.*, p. 76.
[4] Penn, of Fox: *F.*, p. xliii.
[5] *C.*, p. 82.
[6] Penn, of Fox: *F.*, p. xlvii.
[7] *C.*, p. 85.
[8] Penn, of Fox: *F.*, p. xliv.
[9] *C.*, p. 17. So too Bourne 'wished thousands of times that I had been a bird, or beast, or anything but a man': *B.*, p. 20.
[10] *F.*, p. 9.
[11] *C.*, p. 85.
[12] *C.*, p. 84.
[13] *F.*, p. 759.

If some of Fox's qualities may be seen in Hugh Bourne, others, and these the more mystical, are thus to be found in William Clowes, much, it may be observed, to Bourne's admiration; for Bourne considered Clowes 'very solid . . . such a man for faith I scarcely ever saw'.[1] On one occasion Bourne records that 'Clowes has fasted now four days'[2]—a practice not unknown to Fox,[3] which Bourne adopted himself: 'to fgain time for concentrated faith Hugh Bourne frequently asted'.[4] On another occasion he tells how Clowes' 'eyesight Seemed for a time to be taken away'[5]—a psychopathic experience which also befell Fox.[6] Both Bourne and Clowes, it may be noted, shared Fox's[7] implicit belief in witchcraft. 'I visited Clowes,' Bourne writes; 'he has been terribly troubled with the woman we saw at Ramsor. I believe she will prove to be a witch. . . . For the witches throughout the world all meet and have connection with the power of the Devil.'[8]

All three men, however, were sure that 'the Lord will give us the victory'.[9] 'Clowes touched me with his hand,' Bourne writes, 'and power came from him and it was a great blessing.'[10] *Power*, or *the Power*, was, indeed, a keyword, not to say a catchword, in the early Primitive Methodist movement as in the early Quaker movement. 'She got well into the power'[11] is how Bourne describes the preaching of Elizabeth Evans (George Eliot's aunt). For preaching by women as well as by men Bourne supported no less than did Fox, even writing a tract entitled *Remarks on the Ministry of Women*, in which he 'urges the sanctions of Jesus'.[12] 'Primitive Metho-

[1] *B.*, p. 43.
[2] *B.*, p. 75.
[3] *Cf. F.*, p. 147: 'I was in a fast about ten days.'
[4] W. E. Farndale, *op. cit.*, p. 68.
[5] *B.*, p. 43.
[6] *Cf. F.*, p. 570: 'I lost my hearing and sight so as I could not see nor hear.'
[7] *Cf. F.*, pp. 155f.: 'I was moved to speak sharply to her and told her she was a witch.'
[8] *B.*, p 80.
[9] *Ibid.*
[10] *B.*, p. 68.
[11] *B.*, p. 71. On 'the power' in early Quakerism, *cf.* my *Studies in Christian Enthusiasm*, Pendle Hill, Pa., 1948, p. 60. 'The power' plays a similar part in the early Irvingite movement: *cf.* P. E. Shaw, *The Catholic Apostolic Church*, King's Crown Press, 1946, pp. 34, 38f.
[12] *B.*, p. 192.

dism began with the belief practically held that there was no sex limitation in Church work.'[1]

Early Primitive Methodism, like early Quakerism, had also its extravagant side, its visions and ecstasies. This was especially marked among the societies in the area round Delamere Forest, who as a consequence gained the sobriquet of 'Magic Methodists'. At their meetings it was usual for some present to 'go into vision'. 'Usually the persons concerned were pious women',[2] such as one Nancy Foden, whom Bourne describes as 'struggling, as if in distress . . . she appeared to have fainted away' and then as 'speaking occasionally without stopping or opening her eyes. She spoke of "a fine green meadow . . . of a fine river . . . of trumpets..."'.[3] 'Never on any occasion did Bourne experience such "vision" himself,' his biographer tells us, although once he admits in his Journal that 'I felt a desire to look and feel more after the visionary power'; but 'for a time,' says his biographer, 'it seems that he accepted both the genuineness and usefulness of these manifestations'.[4] It was, moreover, a meeting with Nancy Foden after he had witnessed her ecstasy which, in determining him to preach 'whatever the cost', 'marked one of the most extraordinary events in my whole life'.[5]

The leader in this group, James Crawfoot, also had a considerable influence on both Bourne and Clowes. On one occasion Bourne writes: 'Crawfoot was looking at me: his face shone: I could not bear it, but was near to fainting away'[6]; and two years later: 'I stayed with Crawfoot . . . and had a most extraordinary opening in faith through his instruction'.[7] Alas, later he has to record that 'James Crawfoot declined from the faith and fell into sin'; that 'J. Crawfoot has gone on worse than ever, and has made cruel work, so things are now come to a point'; and that 'I have never been in full liberty to rest for above a year, chiefly through old J.C.'s

[1] Quoted without source by W. E. Farndale, *op. cit.*, p. 48.
[2] B., p. 79.
[3] B., p. 49; *cf.* P. E. Shaw, *op. cit.*, p. 50.
[4] B., p. 79, with n. 37. On Fox's visions, *cf.* pp. 190 f., above.
[5] B., p. 54.
[6] B., p. 65. *Cf.* Charles Marshall's description of John Audland as 'full of dread and shining brightness on his countenance. . . . Immortality shined in his face', quoted by W. C. Braithwaite, *The Beginnings of Quakerism*, pp. 167, 89.
[7] B., p. 73.

wickedness'.[1] It is impossible not to think of another James, James Nayler, whom the following remarks by Bourne's biographer fit as neatly as they fit James Crawfoot:

> His earlier labours, particularly in personal persuasion of others to the faith, were invaluable: his instruction, especially of Bourne and Clowes, concerning the nature of inward spiritual conflicts, deepened their own mystical experiences, though the visionary aspect of his own mysticism constituted a danger to the rising community, the seriousness of which was fortunately averted by the spiritual insight and common sense of Bourne himself. Crawfoot's contribution was real, but it must not be exaggerated.[2]

In conclusion, we may notice some similarities between early Quakerism and early Primitive Methodism as they sobered and settled down. Bourne, like Fox, was skilful in working out a discipline and an organization which should hold the developing life of the movement together; and on his head, as on Fox's, 'bitter opposition descended as a result'.[3] Quaker influence may perhaps be seen in some of the nomenclature chosen by Bourne, who published *A Treatise on Discipline chiefly as it respects Meetings for Business*; for until 1825 the Primitive Methodists met as a body for 'Annual Meeting', not (like other Methodists) for 'Conference'.[4] It is also of interest to observe that in the earliest days 'we had conferred by conversation', till 'the company was too numerous', and that Bourne describes 'moving, seconding, and voting'[5] as new to him, though he took no exception to it.

The Primitive Methodists were also like Friends in soon turning towards the expression of simplicity in their garb and in accepting something like a uniform. In 1811 Bourne felt that a 'hat-whim' of Crawfoot's 'injured the work by attaching importance to what he felt were secondary matters',[6] but about the same time Clowes spoke to a farmer's daughter 'in the name of the Lord on the subject of laying her curls aside

[1] *B.*, pp. 93ff.
[2] *B.*, p. 95.
[3] *B.*, p. 128.
[4] *B.*, p. 112, n. 87; *C.*, p. 47, n. 7.
[5] *B.*, p. 111, n. 78.
[6] *B.*, p. 94, n. 30.

and becoming plain in dress, as a Christian ought', and 'when she came downstairs, she had stripped off her curls'.[1] By 1819 it was laid down under Bourne's leadership that all travelling preachers were to wear a 'plain' dress: 'the men to wear single-breasted coats, single-breasted waistcoats, and their hair in natural form: and not to be allowed to wear pantaloon trousers, nor white hats'.[2] Was any Primitive Methodist found to protest, like Margaret Fell, against 'this narrowness and strictness entering in'?[3] Bourne's biographer does not say.

Primitive Methodism developed along different lines from Quakerism and has now been absorbed into an undifferentiated Methodism, in which, some may think, its distinctive character has been lost; but in its beginnings and in the personalities of its founders there were clearly elements also characteristic of early Quakerism and George Fox. *Plus ça change, plus c'est la même chose*, one may say, regarding the two movements as variant expressions of revivalism, two moments in one movement of the spirit. Nor need one say it cynically; for this sameness with difference, this repetition with change, is the very stuff of which history is made. One may also perhaps venture the observation that, even when the salt has lost its savour, as (to some extent) Quakerism had done about 1800, if *records* are preserved of earlier saltiness, then fresh salt may appear to take its place.

1953

---

[1] *C.*, p. 34.

[2] *B.*, p. 112, n. 84; *cf.* p. 123, with n. 11. For similar Quaker legislation, *cf.* W. C. Braithwaite, *The Second Period of Quakerism*, pp. 510ff. At this time, furthermore, 'all travelling preachers were required to keep written journals', thus once more emulating Quaker itinerants.

[3] W. C. Braithwaite, *op. cit.*, p. 518.

XXI

THE UNDERSTANDING OF HISTORY AND
ITS APPLICATION IN THEOLOGY[1]

JUDAISM and Christianity are both essentially and distinctively historical religions. Both Jews and Christians believe that God reveals Himself through personalities in history; through writings in history; and through the historical process itself. This paper has three main divisions:

    I. A chronological sketch of the study and understanding of history in the West.
       Principles emerging.
       Some applications of these principles; as in biblical studies.

   II. The present-day anti-historical reaction in theology; especially in biblical studies.
       Four suggested causes.

  III. The need for fresh insistence on the historical character of biblical religion; and for fresh consideration of the application of historical understanding in theology.

I

We may begin with a brief chronological sketch of the study and understanding of history in the West. In Western civilization, it is hardly an exaggeration to say, there were no 'histories' before the Reformation. There were 'chronicles', records; but hardly 'histories' revealing in their writers critical reflection or conscious interpretation in the selection of what was significant.

The lack of historical sense in the Middle Ages may be seen in their paintings, which, though largely of biblical subjects, are either 'modern' in approach or symbolistic. In such matters as dress and buildings it is current fashion which they portray, not the clothes and houses of ancient Palestine. As for their figures, in the fifteenth century these were often

---

[1] A paper read to the London Society for the Study of Religion on 15 June, 1948.

portraits of living persons; earlier, they followed tradition, were conventionalized, 'dehumanized' 'types'. In either case, the Middle Ages were not interested in historic portraiture or representation.[1]

The same lack of historical sense may be seen in another form in the medieval cut of clothes, which differed according to rank, profession or habitat rather than according to century.

> The knight can always be distinguished from the burgess, but only the expert can tell the difference between the lady of 1100 and the lady of 1200. It needs no expert to distinguish between 1912 and 1930; and this change is nothing less than the difference between two conceptions of the Universe.[2]

Where theology was concerned, there was an additional reason for the absence of any historical sense. 'To the medieval mind religion had no history. It was either true or false; if it were true, it was the truth once and for all delivered to the saints.'[3] Not until the unity of sentiment and of faith, which characterized the Middle Ages as a whole, had been broken was the critical detachment of historical perception possible. We see this beginning to appear in the fifteenth century in such a resolute inquirer as Bishop Pecock, who, insisting that 'it is not al trewe that bi holi men is in parchimyn ynkid', is prepared to repudiate a patristic dictum fundamental in scholasticism and even a clause of the Apostles' Creed.[4] We see it more clearly in the sixteenth century in Erasmus' concern to return to the original sources, *ad ipsas fontes*, rather than to merely traditional accounts and interpretations. Erasmus is one of the first to show historical understanding in an appreciation of the importance of context: his *scripsere suo seculo* is a new principle. One must ask of the scholastic dogmas, he insists, by whom, when and on what occasion they were proclaimed.[5] Calvin carries the

[1] E. Kitzinger and E. Senior, *Portraits of Christ*, p. 17.
[2] J. Laver, 'The Triumph of Time', in *Contemporary Essays*, ed. S. Norman, pp. 132f.
[3] *Ibid.*, p. 130.
[4] R. Pecock, *The Book of Faith*, ed. J. L. Morison, pp. 151, 146, 297–305.
[5] *Opus Epistolarum Erasmi Roterodami*, ed. P. S. Allen, Epp. 541. 145; 1229. 11; 1334. 916; 1581. 577–9, 590–1.

inquiry further when he applies the same principle to the findings of the Councils of the first centuries A.D.[1]

As indicated, it is within the sphere of theology that this new sense of history first appears. Their very differences in religion made men study anew and in a new way the documents which to both sides were authoritative. Then, in their new concentration on Scripture, there was, for the Protestants at least, the influence of the philosophy of history to be found in Scripture and especially in the Old Testament. Crude though it may be by later standards in its readiness to alter facts to fit theory, the Hebrew theory of history and of historiography has a significance even yet, perhaps, inadequately perceived, in that it contains, if only implicitly, principles of criticism and interpretation elsewhere hardly visible till modern times; and 'the Old Testament was necessarily the chief history text-book of that age'.[2] It is not surprising that a new interest in the Bible led to a new interest in history. Among other contributing causes were the new interest in secular antiquity for its own sake[3] and the new patriotic interest in the past of one's own nation. '. . . On the whole, the appeal to history was more emphatic in England than it was elsewhere. The serious study of English history had begun . . .'.[4]

We are nevertheless still far from anything like the modern understanding of history. The seventeenth-century historians of whom, in their way, we may be proud, are antiquarians rather than historians. They have not reflected on first principles, they have not sought to establish any regulative ideas about the nature of history and of its presentation by historians. For this we have to wait for Giambattista Vico's *Scienza Nuova*, first published in 1725. For Vico the presentation of history 'becomes an affair neither of accepting nor rejecting

[1] *cf. Institutio*, IV. ix. 8.
[2] Lord Eustace Percy, *John Knox*, p. 177.
[3] There is a brilliant paragraph on the 'clear and interesting curve in the assessment of the ancient Romans' in J. H. Whitfield, *Machiavelli*, pp. 111f.: 'Livy is the Roman historian for the fifteenth century' and not until after the emergence of the absolute monarchies of Europe is there 'the preoccupation with Tacitus instead of Livy, so marked at the end of the sixteenth century'. The only sixteenth-century English translation from Thucydides (1550) was not from the Greek.
[4] F. M. Powicke, *The Reformation in England*, p. 133.

what the "authorities" say, but of interpreting it. The centre of gravity of historical thought is thus placed in the *principles* by which the historian interprets documents.'[1] Gibbon's famous conclusion to his *Decline and Fall*—'I have described the triumph of barbarism and religion'—unconsciously exemplifies Vico's proposition. Gibbon's achievement, indeed, is not only in his attention to the sources but in the fact that his work is consciously and unashamedly interpretative. The interpretation is one-sided: he 'ignores the existence of countervailing facts over which modern scholars have spent years of investigation'[2]; but after Gibbon no worthy presentation of history is anything but interpretative. Nor can it be. The genuine historian does not 'first collect data and then interpret them. It is only when he has a problem in his mind, that he can begin to search for data bearing on it'.[3] Even of Ranke, with all his concern for the impartial discovery and record of how 'things actually occurred', it has been said that 'no historian is less objective, for in his greatest works the whole narrative is coloured by the quality of his mind'.[4]

We have watched the gradual establishment of a dependence on the sources, and of the study of their context, of the conditioning *Zeitgeist*; and also of a frank recognition that the historian's motive, as well as his writing, is bound to be interpretative. These two principles combine in 'the critical spirit, which endeavours to make each age *its own interpreter*'. Than this, Bryce wrote in 1864, there is 'nothing more modern'.[5] More recently, Sir Maurice Powicke expressed the same principle thus: 'A vision or an idea is not to be judged by its value for us, but by its value to the man who had it'.[6] Or again, in R. G. Collingwood's words: 'History did not mean knowing what events followed what. It meant getting inside other people's heads, looking at their situation

[1] R. G. Collingwood, *The Philosophy of History*, p. 7.
[2] E. L. Woodward, *British Historians*, p. 35.
[3] R. G. Collingwood, *op. cit.*, p. 14.
[4] *Encyclopaedia Britannica*, 13th edn., *s.v.* Ranke, Leopold von; *cf.* D. Ogg, *Herbert Fisher, 1865–1940*, p. 172: 'Acton, the most erudite man of his generation, was also the most credulous.'
[5] J. Bryce, *The Holy Roman Empire*, 1928 edn., p. 271 (italics mine).
[6] F. M. Powicke, *Stephen Langton*, p. 161.

through their eyes, and thinking for yourself whether the way in which they tackled it was the right way.'[1]

These principles are concerned with the study and presentation of history. There is the further question: what is history? how is its nature to be conceived? It is, above all, on this level of reflection again, about history itself, that, to quote Collingwood again, 'since 1800 history has passed through a Copernican revolution'.[2] Looking back, we can see first the influence of the attitude known as romanticism.

> In the early nineteenth century Christianity became for the first time the religion of the past, or rather . . . the fact that it was the religion of the past became one of its chief attractions. . . . Religion has taken on something of the quality of a 'period piece.'[3]

But the past as thus recreated 'was largely a creation of the imagination; or a reality so highly idealized as to have become the likeness of a vision'.[4] Thus Chateaubriand's *Génie du Christianisme* has been called 'at least as much a monument to romanticism as a monument to Christianity'. 'Romanticism is Time grown self-conscious',[5] and self-consciousness arrests and petrifies. Hence romanticism's fondness for ruins and, in history, for all that is 'insulated':

nothing
Can touch him further.

In the course of the nineteenth century this desire to *pin down* the historical butterfly (or rather chrysalis) soon gave place to the fascination of watching the chrysalis *turning into* the butterfly. We see here the evident influence of the theory of evolution, which (in England) was confirmed by the discoveries made in natural science. Thought in terms of evolution, of development, was 'in the air', was itself, that is to

[1] R. G. Collingwood, *An Autobiography*, p. 58.
[2] *Ibid.*, p. 79, n. 1.
[3] J. Laver, *op. cit.*, pp. 127f.
[4] A. M. Fairbairn, *Catholicism: Roman and Anglican*, pp. 105f.
[5] J. Laver, *loc. cit.*; the influence of romanticism is still clearly to be seen in Renan's *Vie de Jésus*.

say, the contemporary historical context. In the sphere of theology it may be seen reflected even in book-titles, such as Newman's *Essay on the Development of Christian Doctrine*[1] or, more recently, Caird's *Evolution of Religion* or Workman's *Evolution of the Monastic Ideal*.

This influence fostered reflection about history of a kind which, so far, was realistic and fruitful; only so far, however. History has no need of standing under the tutelage of the natural sciences. The application to history of scientific terms is, indeed, misleading. Theories of development and evolution, which imply growth or increase, if not improvement or progress, with or without a maximum or optimum point, after which decay or deterioriation sets in, are not applicable in history. History is to be seen in terms of its own nature as *process*: i.e., as a *complexio oppositorum*, embracing at once sameness, or continuity, and difference, or change. A clear exposition of this principle is in a comparison made by Collingwood between the *Republic* and the *Leviathan*:

> Plato's *Republic* is an attempt at a theory of one thing; Hobbes's *Leviathan* an attempt at a theory of something else.
> There is, of course, a connexion between these two things; ... That is not in dispute. What is in dispute is the kind of sameness and the kind of difference. . . . The sameness is the sameness of a historical process, and the difference is the difference between one thing which in the course of that process has turned into something else, and the other thing into which it has turned. Plato's πόλις and Hobbes's absolutist state are related by a traceable historical process, whereby one has turned into the other; any one who ignores that process, denies the difference between them.[2]

This quotation from Collingwood has the virtue of indicating the living, moving thing which history is for the modern historian: of suggesting the attraction of the *pattern* in history, a pattern moving and no more capable of analysis in immobility than the pattern cast by sunlight on the waves of the sea or through the wavings of the trees. 'The poetic

[1] *Cf. D.N.B.*, *s.v.*: 'his adoption of the theory of evolution in his essay on "Development" is extremely significant'. It may be noted that Newman's *Development* preceded the publication of *The Origin of Species* by fourteen years.
[2] R. G. Collingwood, *op. cit.*, p. 62.

element in history,' Sir Maurice Powicke has said, 'has probably been revealed in the last fifty years as it was never revealed before', and 'the historical imagination has been roused in hundreds of people who had never realized that they possessed it.'[1] Should not this bode well for a religion distinctively historical, and for those who believe that God reveals Himself through the process of history?

In reflection upon the nature and study of history, several principles have now emerged. History is most truly conceived as process. The historian must depend, so far as possible, upon sources; must study them in their context and under the influence of the contemporary *Zeitgeist*; and must allow the subject studied to be its own interpreter. His own presentation also, however, will inevitably be interpretative.

During the last hundred years this new understanding of history has been applied in theology very largely and with very considerable effect; especially in the sphere of biblical studies. We are now so used to that effect that we hardly realize how new it is or what alarm was felt on its first appearance.

> The present generation (wrote Maude Petre) can scarcely conceive the effect on traditional belief of the—almost sudden —emergence of a new historic conception of the documents of Christianity.
>
> The impact of historical criticism on the traditional teaching of the Church was terrifying. . . . Not perhaps since the startling revelation of Copernicanism, had the shock been greater.[2]

It may be well briefly to run over the change which has taken place. Formerly, Scripture was treated as an undifferentiated unity. The early Church devised a scheme of prooftexts from Old Testament prophecies, conceived as virtually controlling Jesus' behaviour; and a similar method of treatment, which has been called 'uncritical, unhistorical and vicious',[3] came to be applied generally, any text (almost) being treated as applicable to any situation. For such treat-

---

[1] F. M. Powicke, *Three Lectures*, pp. 71f.
[2] M. D. Petre, *Loisy: His Religious Significance*, pp. 41, 112.
[3] T. R. Glover, *The Disciple*, p. 18.

ment much ingenuity in allegorical interpretation was often required; indeed, as Dr Homes Dudden said of the method as used by St Ambrose, one of its greatest exponents, 'it was too subjective, capricious, and arbitrary. It could, and did, make anything mean anything.'[1] Thus a verse from the *Song of Songs* might be definitive for ecclesiastical polity; or Rahab's scarlet thread in the window signify Christ's passion in the window of our minds.[2] 'That this sort of thing should ever have carried conviction to anybody,' says Mr Aldous Huxley in comment on the latter example, 'seems now completely incomprehensible. The fact that it actually did so is a salutary reminder that the frames of reference within which men do their reasoning and feeling do not remain the same.'[3]

In these last years, the historical study of the Bible has greatly altered our understanding of it. The divine revelation has been seen as given not all at once nor once for all, but 'at sundry times and in divers manners' in the course of history. In the Old Testament there has appeared a process, a progress, as we believe it to be, from animism through henotheism to monotheism, and so to a religion at once ethical and universal. Within such progress have appeared, also, the advances and retrogressions, both intellectually and morally, of the men to whom, and through whom, the divine revelation was given: sometimes they understood more, sometimes less. Their understanding, furthermore, has been considered in relation to their own time and environment and its conditions. The dogmatic purpose of the writers upon whose accounts we depend has been studied: in order that we may understand both the interpretation of history which was theirs in their own historical setting, and the actual historical process which they describe. For the divine revelation, it has been urged, is to be found alike in the process itself and in the interpretation of it.

The New Testament as well as the Old Testament has received a historical treatment. A new differentiation has been made between the Epistles and the Gospels, between the

---

[1] F. H. Dudden, *Life and Times of St. Ambrose*, II. 459.
[2] These are both seventeenth-century examples: the first from the Congregational John Cotton, the second from the Roman Catholic Augustine Baker.
[3] A. Huxley, *Grey Eminence*, p. 74.

first three Gospels and the fourth, and still more narrowly. *Mark* has received special attention as demonstrably the earliest Gospel. Determined efforts have been made to separate Jesus' *ipsissima verba* and actual actions in history from the sayings and actions distorted, or even erroneously attributed to Him, for dogmatic purposes. Since the lives published by Strauss, Renan and Seeley to Glover's *Jesus of History* and many more recent studies there has been a continuous stream of attempts at historical biography. Their authors have honestly sought to allow the earliest sources to interpret themselves; at the same time they would not pretend to have escaped the limits of an interpretation also personal to themselves, even perhaps to have sought to escape it.

The corresponding change in the study of the history of doctrine and of the life of the Church has not, perhaps, been so great. At first sight this may appear paradoxical; but in a sphere, in which, if anywhere, some kind of historical method has always been applied, the new understanding of history would be likely to have a less startling effect than in a sphere to which it was altogether strange. The book-titles mentioned earlier, containing the words 'evolution' and 'development', show at least an approach to the new method, even if still dominated by the influence of natural science.

The one sphere in which the new understanding of history seems to have been applied hardly at all, at least in any fullness of careful exposition, is that of theology in the strict sense: the nature of the divine revelation, and the implications of this for our understanding of the nature of God Himself. The most fruitful indications here have to be sought largely in the works of a biblical scholar such as H. Wheeler Robinson, and there largely in reflections by the way on the implications of historical understanding in the sphere of Old Testament studies.

II

That the application in theology of the understanding of history has had such effects as have been sketched is common knowledge. Yet no less so is the fact, frankly admitted by Professor Norman Sykes in his Inaugural Lecture at Cambridge, that 'the contemporary vogue in theological study is not wholly favourable to the historical method'; that today 'the dominant claims proceed from an aggressively dogmatic theological system, which is apt to show impatience of both the slow processes and modest results of the historical method'.[1]

This is nowhere more pronounced than in the sphere in which the understanding of history has already made its most notable triumphs, in biblical studies. By many the Bible is again studied with little or no attention to the differentiation effected by the varying times and circumstances in which its books were written, or in which the events described took place. The Christian heritage from the Old Testament, the continuity between Israel and the Church, is so stressed as virtually to exclude any element of newness in the New Testament. The New Testament itself, like the Bible as a whole, is seen as expressing a single dogmatic purpose, without regard to the writers' personalities, periods or environments. Biblical interpretation has again become allegorical or, as the term is, typological. Thus Jesus' crossing the brook Kedron in *John* xviii, 1 is to be regarded in the light of the brook in *Psalm* cx, 7 and of David's crossing the brook Kedron in *II Samuel* xv, 23 rather than in the light of the natural history of Jerusalem.[2] Any distinction between 'the Jesus of history' and 'the Christ of experience' is denied; any attempt, such as Glover's, to describe 'the Jesus of history' is derided. We are told that it is not possible to penetrate behind the Gospel stories to the events which they relate. We are even told that 'the search for Jesus-as-He-really-was is meaningless'.[3] Where the historical understanding of the biblical revelation is accepted, it is conceived as secondary, or as on a lower level and needing to be 'taken up' into the theological.[4]

For this remarkable reversion four main causes may be suggested:

(1) a dislike, often a fear, of the tendency to rationalism and agnosticism, believed to result from the application in theology of the new understanding of history;

(2) misunderstanding arising from inadequate expressions of the nature of history;

[1] N. Sykes, *The Study of Ecclesiastical History*, pp. 28f.
[2] *Cf.* L. S. Thornton, in *The Apostolic Ministry*, ed. K. E. Kirk, p. 97, n. 2.
[3] K. Grayston, in an early number of *The Presbyter*.
[4] The phrase recurs throughout H. Cunliffe-Jones' *The Authority of the Biblical Revelation*.

(3) the influence of a particular trend in biblical studies; and
(4) a desire for greater certainty, proclaimed with greater
authority, than history is found to yield. We may consider
these briefly, in turn.

A sentence in a letter written by a Congregational minister
in 1773 is illuminating:

> The scheme of exalting the Evangelists above the Epistles was
> first begun by Thomas Chubb (the Deist). . . . I never knew a
> minister make this distinction, but the reason was apparent:
> he was a Socinian.[1]

Were such a verdict to be passed upon modern biographers
of Jesus (and it is sometimes implied), it might be dismissed
as a generalization which could easily be exploded. Yet the
statement has a certain penetration. For it is true that one
result of applying the new understanding of history in New
Testament studies has been a concern with the Gospels, and
an interest in Jesus as a man, which was previously associated
only with Socinians and Unitarians, where known at all.
Furthermore, this new interest in Jesus' humanity has often
seemed, as in many of the lives of Jesus and still more in the
writings and utterances of those influenced by them, to involve a virtual, even an explicit, repudiation of His divinity
as conceived by traditional orthodoxy.

An example of the tendency which is feared may be found
in our attitude to biblical miracles. An increasing unreadi-
ness to give these unhesitating or undiscriminating credence
has been observed. That this has arisen on other grounds
beside the historical is true. Psychologically, we no longer
expect contemporary miracles, as did earlier generations, to
whom the biblical miracles were not exceptional. Philosophically, we accept natural law rather than the unpredictable
variation of 'prerogative' as, at least normally, expressive of
the Father Who makes His sun to rise on the just and on the
unjust. But historically, also, we are conscious that the miracles related, and believed in, by biblical writers are similar
to the miracles related, and believed in, by contemporary
and subsequent writers, in which no one now believes, or is
expected to believe. In respect of the miraculous, says Mil-

[1] J. Orton, *Letters to Dissenting Ministers*, 1806, I. 135f.

man, 'the life of the Saviour is far surpassed by that of St Francis'.[1] Again, 'in the long series of ecclesiastical history,' asks Gibbon, 'does there exist a single instance of a saint asserting that he himself possessed the gift of miracles?'[2] Historians have observed similarly that in the Bible the power of working miracles is not claimed but attributed. The more historical understanding of Church history gained at the Reformation made Protestants doubtful of medieval miracles. The more historical understanding of the Bible has made men similarly doubtful of the miracles related within its pages. And, as at the Reformation, traditional orthodoxy has been offended.

A second cause for antagonism to the historical approach has been a misunderstanding of it, due largely to the baneful influence of the scientific and political conceptions prevailing in the nineteenth century. By some, history was conceived as inevitable 'progress' (which was only the translation to politics or sociology of the scientific concept of evolution or growth docked of its concomitant, decay). For these, the Old Testament was an inviting subject for historical treatment, at least by Christians. This approach led to difficulties, however. For, if Christ be conceived as the climax, the optimum point, of history, no basis is left for the interpretation of the New Testament and the Church in succeeding centuries, since these are not conceived of as having 'progressed' beyond Christ. (The contrary idea that since Christ there has been a perpetual *regression* has never commended itself to any save extreme sectaries, and they have generally been careful to exempt their own generation, or at least themselves.)

Other nineteenth-century theologians, under the influence of natural science, conceived the history of the New Testament and of the Church in succeeding centuries in terms of the seed and the flower. This conception is as unsatisfactory as the other in the arbitrary nature of the decision *when* the flowering takes place.[3] It would also seem, as already observed, to demand a corresponding decay.

[1] H. H. Milman, *History of Latin Christianity*, VI. 33.
[2] E. Gibbon, *Decline and Fall*, ch. xv.
[3] *Cf.* J. V. Bartlet, *Church-Life and Church-Order during the first four centuries*, ed. C. J. Cadoux, pp. 2f.

In neither of these expositions was the nature of history as process, including in itself, but itself transcending, both progress and regress, both growth and decay, clearly expressed. In each case the application of the historical method in theology was clearly open to grave objection.

The historical approach has suffered further through an influential trend in biblical criticism, begun by Loisy's description of the Gospels as 'catechetical' literature, and continued by the *Formgeschichtlicheschule*. This trend in biblical criticism, though itself dependent upon the historical method, is anti-historical in intention and in effect. It first uses the historical method in order to establish the position that the New Testament literature is not a merely factual record, written in detachment of spirit, but was written with a controlling dogmatic purpose. It then argues, with strange inconsistency, that it is not possible to go behind the written account to the events as they actually took place; as if such activities as making allowance for the writers' purposes, weighing the interpretative element in their descriptions, and estimating their reliability were not all part of the regular practice of any student of history and historiography. Combined with this scepticism of the historical method, so soon as it has served the Form-critics' purpose, is a more serious scepticism of the power of Jesus' personality to transcend the New Testament writers' interpretative accounts and to make its own impact upon the reader.

In this school of biblical criticism the theory of Strauss, that 'instead of the real Christ hitherto assumed to be represented in the Gospels, there remained nothing but a later conception of him',[1] has reappeared, but with a paradoxical difference. For, whereas Strauss regarded the Christian creation as no more than an ideal 'exemplar of man as he is destined to be',[2] Loisy and the Form-critics regard it as to be accepted uncritically as the object of faith. That we cannot discover the actual events of history behind the records of them is, they argue, not to be regretted; for the New Testament and the Christ of faith proclaimed in it were created by the Church: there never has been any other. In this way, as

[1] D. F. Strauss, *A New Life of Jesus*, I. 34.
[2] *Ibid.*, II. 436.

Maude Petre penetratingly observed, there has been 'an effort to constitute what I venture to term a kind of theological *by-pass*, for the passage of orthodoxy round the findings of history'.[1]

It is significant that Loisy's background was Roman Catholic. His perception of the catechetical nature of the New Testament literature eventually led him, personally, to be excommunicated; but the use to which it has been put by others has been in support of a fresh emphasis upon the Church and the Church's supernatural authority such as till recently has been but little known in Protestant circles. The desire for authority is very evident today, nor only in the religious sphere. In politics it is seen in the ready acceptance on the Continent of Fascism and Communism, and in our own country in the much readier acceptance than would have been conceivable fifty years ago of an omnicompetent Government's increasingly totalitarian demands. In religion it is seen in the unparalleled increase, statistically and in influence, of the Roman Catholic Church, which appears as the one lighthouse of authority on the one rock of certainty in a sea of troubles. The Church claims to be *semper eadem* and hence to provide security; but history, if it is process, includes change as well as continuity, with all the dangers to be imagined in a living chiaroscuro. The Church claims infallible guidance into the truth, and is treated even by some modern Protestants as if it were kept holy in the world through being in a kind of insulated vacuum; but history knows only varying approximations to the truth, conditioned always by the interpenetrating contemporary *Zeitgeist* and environment of men. The Church claims a grand objectivity in judgement, yielding an unmistakable certainty; but in historiography the interpretative element introduces an unavoidable subjectivity, and in its most unhesitating judgements a relativity remains. It is no wonder if, in the present intellectual upset, moral chaos and physical danger and destruction, religious men should crave for something more than history can give, and theologians seek the suprahistorical in the Church. In such a context history is almost bound to take a subservient place. Too truly has it been said

[1] M. D. Petre, *op. cit.*, p. 19 (italics hers).

that 'for a mind accustomed to dogmatic schemes history, when it does not fit in with dogma, is as though it did not exist'.[1]

III

The present-day anti-historical reaction is thus intelligible on several counts. It must nevertheless be resisted. The historical character of biblical religion must be affirmed afresh, and the implications of that historical character reconsidered.

For the statement with which we began still stands. Judaism and Christianity are both essentially and distinctively historical religions. Moses *did* bring Israel out of Egypt. Jesus *was* crucified. These things happened. They have, of course, to be interpreted, and the interpretations are important; but, however they are interpreted, the interpretations are of facts, of events which happened. To say that 'even if they never happened at all, the Faith of Israel' or of the Church 'would still have survived the storms of the centuries' is not true. *A* Faith might have survived; but it would not have been *the* Faith. For the Faith of Israel and of the Church depends upon these things having happened: is bound up, that is to say, with particular *events in* history, as well as with the whole process which is history as a framework without which they could neither have happened nor possess meaning. The events may be seen by the inspired writers of Scripture or by us as symbols revealing the character of God in His dealings with men; but without 'the indestructible nucleus of historical reality . . . there would have been neither Scripture, nor symbolism, nor Inspiration'.[2] 'There must be the actual event to be the nucleus of the interpretation and of faith in the divine revelation.'[3]

These events in history, as the cause of the biblical writings, and as the objects of their descriptions, are presented, moreover, in and through those descriptions. They may not be presented prosaically or precisely. The writers may confuse the historical events with mythical happenings and with their own imaginings of what would happen or their ideas

[1] O. Tommasini, *Machiavelli*, II. 601, as quoted by J. H. Whitfield, *op. cit.*, p. 7.
[2] W. J. Phythian-Adams, *The Call of Israel*, pp. 19, 64.
[3] H. Wheeler Robinson, *Inspiration and Revelation in the Old Testament*, p. 189.

of what should have happened. Yet 'however much they may embellish the facts, or even obscure them in the interests of their particular purpose, at the heart of their narrative these facts remain as a solid, resistant core. . . . the facts are *there*'.[1] They are 'there', then, first in the sense of having taken place in history; and secondly in the sense of being at the heart of the biblical narrative. Neither Judaism nor Christianity could be as it is unless these things were so.

The facts, it is true, may not be on the surface of the narrative. At first, they 'may not be by any means recognizable in the form in which they are presented'. Often, indeed, 'we shall not discover them until we have penetrated *behind* the immediate purpose of the individual writer and the garb in which he has clothed it'.[2] This, which has been said by Canon Phythian-Adams of the Old Testament, is no less true of the New Testament, and Christian students of it may not shirk the task of penetration through a mistaken reverence. To apply one set of criteria to the study of the Old Testament and a different set of criteria to the study of the New Testament is false to the historical continuity with the Old Testament writings in which the New Testament writings stand, false also to the historical character which New Testament *religion* has in common with Old Testament religion.

Nor may the task be shirked through timidity, in face of the fact that the biblical writings contain a complex of fact and interpretation. Of course they do; but they 'bear the authentic character of historical documents, not despite but by reason of'[3] this. It is just such documents which historians are accustomed to handling. There is no ground for accepting the competence of the historians in reference to other historical documents only to deny it in reference to the biblical documents; or to accept it so far as is convenient in reference to the biblical documents but not further. Here as elsewhere trained historians may be trusted to sift the written account according to recognized principles and criteria of authenticity; and indeed to do more: for in the historical study of both Testaments they will need at times 'that imaginative

---

[1] W. J. Phythian-Adams, *op. cit.*, p. 64 (italics his).
[2] *Ibid.* (italics his).
[3] N. Sykes, *op. cit.*, p. 30.

insight which will dare to ignore the written words, and to decipher the palimpsest which they have almost obliterated'.[1] The task is difficult; but in the words of Professor T. W. Manson:

> The application of critical principles and critical methods to the Bible can only be set on one side by a sacrifice of intellectual integrity which would infallibly stultify any attempt at theological reconstruction. Biblical criticism has come to stay; and no theological system that rejects it can hope to stand.[2]

Professor C. H. Dodd similarly warns us to 'be suspicious of any suggestion that we can afford to by-pass criticism. The way of advance lies through and not round the critical problem.'[3]

There is next the large and double question of interpretation: double, because we are concerned both with the interpretation combined with the facts in the biblical writings, and with the interpretation of those writings by the biblical critic with historical understanding. Those who feel uneasy about the historical approach are apt to allow the critic freedom so far as the facts are concerned, but to argue that as a historian he neither is nor ought to be concerned with their interpretation; and secondly to insist that he can have no understanding wherewith to interpret them unless he does so from a position within the faith which first dictated the biblical interpretation. To take the last point first, if all that is meant is that the Bible will be more truly interpreted by a Jew or a Christian than by a Hindu or an agnostic, that is an illustration of a position now accepted by those with an understanding of history. For

> the object of historical knowledge must be such that it can revive itself in the historian's mind: the historian's mind must be such as to offer a home for that revival. He must be the right man to study that object. If the historian working against the grain of his own mind tries to master the history of a thought into which he cannot personally enter, instead of writing the

[1] W. J. Phythian-Adams, *op. cit.*, pp. 78f.
[2] T. W. Manson, in *The Interpretation of the Bible*, ed. C. W. Dugmore, p. 101.
[3] C. H. Dodd, *The Bible To-day*, p. 27.

history he will merely repeat the statements that record the external facts of its development, the dry bones which may some day become history when someone is able to clothe them with the flesh and blood of a thought which is both his own and theirs.[1]

This granted, the biblical critic with historical understanding may claim, moreover, that the very nature of his work should aid him in discovering, recovering, and reviving positions within the faith which first dictated the biblical interpretation. He will, however, retain his own standards and criteria, which he shares with those engaged in historical work outside the Bible or the life of Israel or of the Church. It does not look well when, on Dr B. J. Kidd's remark concerning the Council of Nicaea, 'The numbers, character and composition of the Council are matters on which we have sufficient but not absolute information', Professor Norman Baynes can comment, 'A historical student can only wonder at the ease with which a theologian can be satisfied'.[2]

To return to the other point, the historian's concern with the biblical writers' interpretation of the facts. To suppose that the historian is concerned only with the facts and not with the interpretation combined with them in the documents which he studies betrays complete misunderstanding. He is concerned to isolate the facts so far as he can. But he is as concerned with their interpretation, with the meaning attributed to the facts, as with the facts themselves: as concerned with the effect on the Elizabethan mind, say, of the defeat of the Armada as with the facts and figures about the ships which sailed; and all the more so, very likely, if in point of fact 'as a military operation the English victory was *less* glorious than some other less renowned achievements of the British fleet'.[3] For the interpretation of the event is as much a fact, as much a part of the history which he studies, as is the event itself; very often it is a later part, the event's *Nachgeschichte* as it has been called.

[1] N. H. Baynes, *The Thought-World of East Rome*, pp. 4f., paraphrasing R. G. Collingwood, *The Idea of History*, pp. 218, 304f., 327.

[2] N. H. Baynes, *Constantine the Great and the Christian Church*, p. 87, commenting on B. J. Kidd, *A History of the Church to A.D. 461*, II. 23.

[3] *Encyclopaedia Britannica*, 13th edn., *s.v.* Armada (italics mine).

From a religious point of view the historian must consider whether the *Nachgeschichte* of a word or event in the biblical writings, or the *Nachgeschichte* in the Bible itself, is legitimate; whether, that is, 'the spiritual continuity with the original meaning is maintained'.[1] He will not assume that it is maintained. But even where it is not maintained, he will still be concerned with it. For him, even an erroneous interpretation of an event may be illuminating; and so may the erroneous application by a second writer of the first writer's erroneous application. Thus, the historian will not use St Augustine's flagrant mistranslation of *Romans* v. 12 to interpret the Pauline doctrine of sin; but he will to interpret the Augustinian. Nor will he use the Pauline exegesis of the story of Eden in the same chapter to interpret the meaning intended in *Genesis*[2]; but he will to interpret St Paul. His doing so is involved in the principle of allowing the subject studied to interpret itself. Nor would his perception of relevance or irrelevance, according to his universe of discourse, be possible, but for his historical understanding, with its recognition of the inescapable reality of the passage of time in the process of history.

For to the historian it is not only the events and their interpretation which matter, although these, 'the outstanding events in which the voice of God has been heard, or his hand discerned, must be studied' by him, whether a Jewish or a Christian historian, 'with the same passion for accuracy that the scientist gives to a chemical analysis'.[3] For the historian history itself, the process, matters, matters perhaps most of all: the process as combining change with continuity. In Collingwood's phrase, 'What is thought to be a permanent problem P is really a number of transitory problems p 1 p 2 p 3'. To see them as a single problem under the one name P with no internal variations indicates blurred vision, historical myopia.[4]

The passage of time, that is to say, is accepted as a real,

---

[1] H. Wheeler Robinson, *op. cit.*, p. 172.

[2] *Cf. ibid.*, p. 190: 'There is no exegetical warrant for reading back into the story of Eden the Christian dogma of "original sin" '.

[3] T. W. Manson, *op. cit.*, p. 104.

[4] R. G. Collingwood, *An Autobiography*, p. 69.

and conditioning, factor. What men did at one time they *could* not do at another; and what they thought or believed at one time they *could* not think or believe at another. Thus, the Christians of the Middle Ages could not share the early Christians' faith in the Lord's imminent Second Coming; John Wesley could not join St Francis in 'thanking God that the accursed ones will be sent to eternal fire';[1] we cannot share Wesley's implicit belief in witchcraft. And each of these things, if reflected on, may be seen to be of vast importance for the theology of those concerned, which in fact, such things express more vitally than any repetition of traditional credal formulae common to them all. This is not to say that the Christians of successive generations have no faith in common. It is to say that their faith is, inevitably, an historical faith, a faith conditioned by the process of history, precisely as the faith of Israel in the Old Testament is seen to have been conditioned. It is to say that the faith of one generation and of another, like Plato's and Hobbes' political thought, 'are related by a traceable historical process, whereby one has turned into the other; any one who ignores that process, denies the difference between them' and suffers from historical myopia.

An obvious implication here is that patristic doctrine, for instance, can no longer be accepted uncritically. Not only must the confessional formulae established be studied in relation to their historical context, and this in the widest sense, since, had the subject been considered earlier, or later, than was the case, the conclusions reached would have been different. Not only must our ignorance, where we are ignorant, be admitted with the frankness shown by Professor Baynes, when he writes: 'The source of the all-important word ὁμοούσιος—who suggested it?—is unknown. The word is perhaps of eastern—and not western—origin'.[2] The conclusions reached must also be seen as reached by men using the Bible in a way no longer possible for ourselves, because unhistorically. The conclusions may be correct, but they cannot be reached by us along the same road. The same criticism applies equally to the Reformers. The centre of the Reformed

---

[1] *Cf.* C. J. Cadoux, *Catholicism and Christianity*, p. 533.
[2] N. H. Baynes, *Constantine the Great and the Christian Church*, p. 87.

theology was in its biblical interpretation. Yet 'Calvin's view of the Bible,' Dr Dakin has said, 'will never be resuscitated'; for 'there is in his theory no true historic sense'.[1]

That our understanding of history must separate us appreciably from those whose understanding now appears to us as inadequate is something to face which requires courage. The coming of historical understanding and its application in theology has in fact made a break between those who have accepted it and their predecessors comparable with the break with Roman Catholicism effected at the Reformation. By it we are as much separated from Calvin as Calvin was separated from St Thomas by his own principles of biblical interpretation. Such a break is always painful, and many will shun it, as many shunned the Reformation, by seeking refuge in authority of a traditional kind. If the new understanding has come in part from outside religion, like the influence which came to early Protestantism from the Renaissance, that is but a reminder that theology must always be studied in the interplay of its full historical context. Also as at the Reformation, the implications of the new understanding are still painfully to be worked out, and will be worked out only slowly.

One implication is that historical understanding is total in its reference. We cannot get outside history if we would. All our living, thinking and believing, consciously or unconsciously, is within the framework of the historical process. This is as true of the biblical writers as of ourselves; and as true of the Church as of the biblical writers. To claim doctrinal infallibility whether for individuals or for the Church as a whole is as much Ranterism as to claim moral perfectibility. For it is to claim exemption from the limitations of time and place which are of the essence of history: the limitations, as the Jewish and Christian historian must claim, within which it has pleased God to set men's lives. To complain that His setting these limitations is 'unfair' may be permissible if it arises from the aspiration after infinity which God has set within men's hearts, and from the spiritual perception that this life 'cannot be all'; but in reference to *this* life such a complaint is no more than the complaint that men

[1] A. Dakin, *Calvinism*, pp. 245, 193.

234

are not as God. The limitations which God sets must be accepted.

It is still within these limitations, not apart from them, that God inspires men. The divine inspiration and enlightenment is always in reference to the period at which it takes place. Prophecy, speaking for God, proclamation of the faith as taught by Him, though often continuing to live *through* time after its utterance, and, as we have seen, possessing a *Nachgeschichte*, is yet given *in* time, is uttered at a particular moment of time and in a particular period. Poetry offers a helpful parallel here. For poetry, like religious utterance, might seem to escape from time. Yet, however timeless the poetry of any poem may seem to be, on examination, as Mr David Bell has said of the poetry of Dafydd ap Gwilym:

> its clothes, its buttons, its laces, its very features are, by a curious paradox, the fashion and pattern of a particular minute corner of time and space. . . . The contemporaneousness of poetry is one of its essential elements.[1]

Such limitations clearly carry with them a large degree of relativity, and this it is which, among those desirous of certainty and the authority of the absolute, arouses the sharpest, if often a largely latent and even unconscious, antagonism to historical understanding. The perception of historians that there are no absolute thought-forms, that all thought-forms, together with the theories or doctrines in which they are expressed, are 'of their time' (*scripsere suo seculo*), has made the historical method a perpetual solvent. Yet one understands St Thomas better, we may say one only can understand him, if one studies him as a medieval; just as the meaning of Calvin's doctrine becomes clearer if one knows something of the contemporary political scene.

The philosopher may say scornfully that the history of philosophy is not philosophy. The theologian who believes that God reveals Himself in history must be more patient, more chary of dismissing history from his theology. If he is ever to see things *sub specie aeternitatis*, he must be humble enough to study them *sub specie temporis* first.

[1] D. Bell, in *Dafydd ap Gwilym* (Cymmrodorion Soc.), ed. H. I. and D. Bell p. 74.

> They dreamt not of a perishable home
> Who thus could build.

But it is because the 'perishable home', the chapel of King's College, Cambridge, was built in and for its time, by men whose thoughts were directed to a limited purpose, that Wordsworth was thus inspired with

> thoughts whose very sweetness yieldeth proof
> That they were born for immortality.[1]

In applying the understanding of history in theology we are not seeking to exclude the eternal but to discover it in the only place in which it is discoverable, in the temporal. A prime teacher here is Baron von Hügel, the first series of whose *Essays and Addresses* is introduced with the hope that they 'will reveal a deep apprehension of the Unconditioned, the Abiding, the Absolute' not although, but *because* 'not a line printed . . . but is steeped in this sense of Conditions, Growth, Contingencies'.

> Certainly the religion of the Incarnation will be able consistently to despise Happenings, however lowly, and the study of Happenings, however minute, only if and when it does not sufficiently realize its own abiding implications and requirements, its rootedness in the Childhood at Nazareth and in the Cross on Calvary.[2]

The Baron brings us to what for Christians is at once the most central and the most delicate point of our faith. The doctrine of the Incarnation, properly understood, is a historical doctrine: that God revealed Himself uniquely in a particular personality at a particular time. This doctrine is a New Testament doctrine, given within the same historical process as the Old Testament doctrine of divine inspiration and revelation to personalities living within that historical process. Unfortunately the doctrine of the Incarnation has

---

[1] Wordsworth's Sonnet 'On the Extinction of the Venetian Republic' is notable for being instinct with the sense of history as process; on the sense of history in Wordsworth, *cf.*, further, F. M. Powicke, *Three Lectures*, p. 76.

[2] *Op. cit.*, p. xvi.

been torn from its context and interpreted in the light of conceptions of God un-Hebraic and unconcerned with either history or personality. These have produced doctrines accepted by traditional orthodoxy which are so patently unhistorical as the impersonality of Christ's humanity. The recovery of a sense of history, which led the Reformers to repudiate mediaeval sacramental doctrine as unhistorical, is bound to lead also to the repudiation of much traditional Christology as unhistorical. To accept history as the conditioning framework of divine revelation throughout the Old Testament, and to see in Old Testament history an increasing understanding of that revelation, with the promise of yet greater fulfilment, and then to study what we believe to be that fulfilment in the New Testament as if it had undergone a μετάβασις εἰς ἄλλο γένος, is absurd. It is indeed here, in the mode of self-revelation by God, and in its acceptance by men, as in history, that a true continuity between the Testaments is to be found.

To claim, as the Bishop of Derby has done,[1] that, as the source of our highest moral judgements, Christ Himself must be outside history, is as unhistorical a judgement as would be the claim that a source of our finest aesthetic perceptions, such as Shakespeare, must be outside history. Like King's College Chapel, in its place, Christ can reveal to us so effectively something of what is beyond history only because *He* is so firmly rooted *in* history, because He lived and taught and died for, and within the limitations of, His own time. The limitations are as much a condition of the possibility of His being what He was at all as the canvas of a picture or the form of a sonnet is a condition of its being possible to paint the picture or to write the sonnet. His acceptance of the limitations makes Him, like the great artist, greater, not smaller; makes Him, in reference to God, more, not less, divine.

The divine revelation in Christ is visible to men only through what, in reference to the divine revelation in the process of history as a whole, Wheeler Robinson has called, from God's side, 'the kenosis of the Spirit'.[2] 'God *must* anthropo-

---

[1] *Cf.* A. E. J. Rawlinson, *Criticism, History and Christology*, p. 22.
[2] H. Wheeler Robinson, *Redemption and Revelation*, pp. 2ς4f.

morphize Himself in order to be known by man.'[1] The understanding of history will lead us to recognize not only the inevitable anthropomorphic element subjectively in our thought about God, however elevated, however abstract, but the equally inevitable anthropomorphic element objectively in God's revelation of Himself to men. In His teaching Jesus is notably unafraid of expressing His thought about God in anthropomorphic terms. So also the supreme revelation of God in the personality of Jesus exemplifies the divine anthropomorphization.

The conception of Divinity so revealed is bound up with two related Hebraic conceptions: the Hebraic conception, and acceptance, of revelation as given in and through history; and the Hebraic conception of the Holy Spirit of God, personalized through the effects of the personality of Jesus on His friends and their associates. Such a conception of Divine revelation might (ideally) be more acceptable to Jews than is the traditionally orthodox conception. That, surely, should not count against it. It might only mean that it is truer to the Divine purpose and nature as made known to God's ancient people.

'We have this treasure in earthen vessels.' How clearly the Jewish understanding of God's ways rings out in these words of the Apostle! Those earthen vessels were mortal bodies and a mortal face: his own body, enframing the personality through which, by God's grace, the treasure of the gospel was to be brought to others; but also the Face in which he had found the treasure, because in it he had seen shining the glory of God. The understanding of the nature of history and its application in theology is indeed a delicate, hard and even perilous task. At first sight it may seem to involve an undue concentration on the earthen vessels with all their limitations and relativity. On a longer view the surpassing glory of the treasure, so far from being dimmed, shines but the more brilliantly and brightly.

1948

---

[1] *Id., Inspiration and Revelation in the Old Testament*, p. 190 (italics mine).

XXII

THE ECUMENICAL MOVEMENT

THAT this volume[1] represents a vast and imaginative enterprise is at once evident. Simply to record the genesis and development of the Faith and Order and the Life and Work Movements in the present century, with their coalescence in 1948 in the World Council of Churches, would be much. But 'the ecumenical movement is not to be identified with the formation of the World Council'; its story is therefore combined with accounts of 'many other manifestations of the ecumenical spirit', such as, in particular, the International Missionary Council, which is 'in association with' the W.C.C. and the W.C.C. with it, and the World's Alliance of Y.M.C.A.s, the World's Y.W.C.A. and the World's Student Christian Federation, which, themselves 'deeply interdependent', are regarded by the W.C.C. as its 'major allies'. Furthermore, an attempt has been made to provide perspective for these twentieth-century movements through a number of studies of 'the unitive efforts of the Churches' between the Reformation period and the year 1910, when the World Missionary Conference, which was to prove 'in many respects the starting-point of the modern ecumenical movement', was held in Edinburgh. No man could well be expert in all these fields; yet the editors desired 'the production of a History and not of a series of detached essays'. The several writers were therefore asked 'to revise and rewrite in the light of the development of the work as a whole'. This they appear to have been more willing to do than to keep within the limits imposed on them; for each of two chapters has suffered reduction by a third, and another by more than half, of its original length. With the editing no pains have been spared; the various contributions are interconnected by a great number of cross-references; and there are no discrepancies and remarkably little repetition. Forty

[1] *A History of the Ecumenical Movement 1517–1948.* Edited by Ruth Rouse and Stephen Charles Neill. S.P.C.K.

pages of bibliography, ten of glossary and twenty-six of index complete the volume: in these some minor inconsistencies in presentation and a few curious slips may be detected, but none worth recording here. A commendable care with detail, in fact, distinguishes the whole enterprise; though the Dissenting Deputies (150) are laymen, not ministers, and the London Society for the Study of Religion (336) did not come to an end in 1926 but still flourishes. The S.P.C.K.'s exceptionally good proof-reading gives the book a fine finish.

The historical introduction, in which Bishop Stephen Neill surveys 'the search for unity prior to the Reformation', is somewhat weak, perhaps inevitably; it is both more conventional and more disputable than the rest of the book or than *The Divine Society*. There follow chapters on the Reformation period by Professor J. T. McNeill, on the seventeenth and eighteenth centuries in Europe by Professor Martin Schmidt and in Great Britain by Professor Norman Sykes, on the Orthodox Churches prior to 1910 by Dr Georges Florovsky, and on the nineteenth century in America by Professor D. H. Yoder and elsewhere by the Rev. H. R. T. Brandreth. The activity of the Scot, John Durie, on the Continent and the correspondence of Durie's secretary, D. E. Jablonski, with Archbishop Wake and of the English Non-jurors with the Eastern Patriarchs are reminders that the geographical divisions were not absolute. If Professor Schmidt's chapter in places approximates to a catalogue, while Professor Sykes has had difficulty in compressing his spacious periods, these chapters are all good; and for those who have reservations about the possibility of writing 'history' contemporaneously with the events recorded they are the chapters most worth reading. But it is not till with Chapter 7 we come to Dr Ruth Rouse on the Evangelical Alliance, the World Alliance for Promoting International Friendship through the Churches and other 'voluntary movements' (a curious usage?), that we feel the master hand. Vision and imagination here compensate for a tendency to rhetoric, and the book now really gets going, with a momentum it never afterwards loses. Professor K. S. Latourette very properly writes on the International Missionary Council; Canon Tissington Tatlow, in reminiscent vein, on the Faith and Order Movement, with its conference held at Lausanne in 1927 and at Edinburgh in 1937. The Life and Work Movement, with its Conferences held at Stockholm in 1925 and at Oxford in 1937, together with earlier conferences, such as the Neutral Church Conference held at Uppsala in 1917 and the C.O.P.E.C. Conference held at Birmingham in 1924, are the subjects of chapters by two compatriots of Archbishop Söderblom, Dr Nils Karlström and Dr Nils Ehrenström. Dr Ehrenström writes reflectively, as does Bishop Neill in a chapter on 'Plans of Union and Reunion, 1910–1948', which is saved from becoming a 'list' by his wise and thought-provoking comments. Dr Rouse describes with clarity and trenchancy a variety of 'ecumenical manifestations' 'parallel with' the W.C.C., or even 'divergent', among the former being the W.S.C.F. and the World's Y.W.C.A., to both of which she has given long service. In a brief but somewhat repetitive chapter Dr Nicolas Zernov writes of the Eastern Churches in this century. Canon Oliver Tomkins provides an objective, if necessarily detached, account of 'The Roman Catholic Church and the Ecumenical Movement, 1910–1948'. The final chapter, on the genesis of the W.C.C., is by Dr W. A. Visser 't Hooft, the Council's General Secretary. This is not only the end of the story but its climax, and Dr Visser 't Hooft writes triumphantly; but, lest any should think that the movement's leaders claim too much, Dr Neill confesses winningly, in a brief epilogue, that it is, as yet, too Western, too urban and too official.

A study of the ecumenical movement inevitably raises questions on the relation of theology to geography and to history. The extra-territoriality of the Kingdom has always been a stumbling-block; and the 'deeply-rooted prejudice against the West', which, we are told, 'exercises a powerful control' (671) over many Orthodox minds, while intelligible, even excusable, as xenophobia, is theologically worth no more than the anti-semitic objections which are as old as Celsus and Julian, or the still older Jewish particularism which Christians have to learn to overcome. Yet, when the Kingdom's universality in this sense has been accepted, the argument seems to run the other way, as we come to see that it is made known among men in and through the conditions of particular periods and situations. Only when apprehended within its historical context can a theological principle such as justification by faith or the significance of the *Filioque* clause be fully understood; and, before the present birth-pangs of 'one world' (of which, *sub specie temporis*, the ecumenical movement is itself a manifestation), a historical context has of necessity had limits geographically. Here, through impatience with the difficulties of discrimination between the transient and the abiding and through despair over the discrepancies of interpretation there is a recurrent temptation to bypass the history of the Church.

The Christians in South India, for instance, now united in 'one Church, wholly independent and rooted in the soil of India', are described as having been 'separated by Western denominational allegiances' (475). But can any Church be 'wholly independent' without being illiterate? And what is the significance of 'Western' in the argument? In many minds it is equivalent to 'irrelevant'. If so, where does one draw the line? Was the Reformation 'Western'? That it was 'in' the West and 'of' the West need not mean that it was only 'for' the West. The younger Churches must be as willing to learn from the 'Western' Reformation, whatever be the lesson they learn, as Western Christians must be to learn from, say, the Fathers of the Desert. Moreover, if through national or racial xenophobia or through impatience with the faltering pace of earlier generations, the younger Churches cut themselves off from the history of the Church, they are likely to repeat their predecessors' mistakes: if 'rooted in the soil of India' means that the Church of South India is a 'national' Church, owing part of its being to political pressure, it would seem to be reproducing an element in the Reformation fragmentation which many Reformed Christians, no less than Roman Catholics, now regret.

There is the further uncomfortable fact that, when the historical context in which a theological principle is visible has been assimilated, a permanent element in the principle may be apparent to some and be felt by them to be of continuing obligation, independently of its original historical circumstances, while to others this sense of obligation appears mere prejudice. Thus 'the Presbyterian Church in Canada was not established, and there was no reason at all for the Disruption to travel overseas', we are told; 'the disunions were meaningless when transported across the Atlantic' (304). But the desire to witness to a principle, or to be in communion with those Christians who hold it, will not always be affected by geographical conditions such as may limit, or even prevent, its immediate application. The Scot who believed in diocesan episcopacy did not lose his faith in it when in 1689 it was legally extinguished in Scotland and for half a century 'college' episcopacy replaced it. To an Episcopalian the Disruption over voluntaryism may seem trivial in comparison with the earlier Scottish rupture over episcopacy without jurisdiction; but in Bishop Stephen Neill's words, 'if there is one thing more than any other which is made plain by this ecumenical History, it is that no conviction sincerely held by any Christian man may be treated as trivial' (450).

Throughout the book great attention is paid to the Roman Catholic Church and to Orthodoxy. No one would gather from its pages that in the sixteenth and seventeenth centuries very many Protestants regarded Rome not as part of the Church but as Antichrist: a study in the dissolution of that identification would have been a useful introduction to the consideration of the Tractarians' ecumenical ideals. 'If Anglicans ever came to accept a view of reunion which, while embracing the Protestant Churches, excluded the ancient Churches of Rome and the East, the work of the Tractarians would have been in vain' (300); and for Anglican co-operation Archbishop Davidson was willing only if invitations were sent also to the Roman and Orthodox Churches —a course of action on which Archbishop Söderblom also insisted, although personally he 'gave up as hopeless the idea of co-operation with Rome' (534). Since today 'the dogmatic claims of Rome are pressed with an increasing intransigence' (691) and 'there is a deep incompatibility between Roman Catholic ideals of unity and those professed by all the other Churches' (728), most observers would probably accept Professor Latourette's judgement that there is 'no prospect of a unity which would embrace both Roman Catholics and Protestants' (386). That being so, it is the more striking, if it is true, that 'Roman Catholics may claim that their contribution to the ecumenical movement has been, by their abstention, to compel non-Romans to reconsider the meaning of authority, ministry, sacraments, and dogma' (693).

Even without Roman Catholic participation, the W.C.C. is, we are reminded, saved from becoming 'a merely pan-Protestant organization' by the presence in it of the Orthodox, who have insisted on 'the necessity of recognizing the significance of the Blessed Virgin Mary in the work of reconciliation' (673) and at whose instance a section on Mariology appears in the W.C.C. publication, *Ways of Worship*. 'Since they believe themselves to be in possession of all the truth, any doctrinal disagreements can be resolved only by the total surrender of any Church which wishes to enter into fellowship with them' (488). Their co-operation with the ecumenical movement has thus inevitably been of a 'tentative character' (669). Yet they 'serve the whole ecumenical cause by the firmness with which they take their stand on positions from which they are not prepared to depart' (489).

So sympathetic a comment is not made on the attitude of those Baptist Churches who, similarly, hesitate to join the W.C.C., lest they compromise their separate witness (615); while 'the fundamentalist Churches, often revivalist in practice, ultra-conservative in theology' and 'in open opposition to the major Churches' (254) receive but scanty attention. Yet separation from these fundamentalist Churches[1] is no less serious, and should cause an uneasiness and a regret no less keen, than separation from Rome and Orthodoxy. In some ways it is more serious, for *within* the Churches in the ecumenical movement are many whose fundamentalist sympathies make them critical of the W.C.C. Moreover, if this division has been brought about by a new understanding of Scripture, then this new understanding must be seen for what it is, a revolution as great as the revolution of the sixteenth century, and must be faithfully adhered to; in which case the oft-quoted 'that they all may be one', as a dominical saying, may be felt to be as sandy a foundation for an ecumenical

---

[1] It is noteworthy that Dr J. R. Mott owed his 'decision' to J. E. K. Studd, who in turn was 'profoundly influenced' by D. L. Moody (331).

movement as *Matthew* xxviii.19f. is for a missionary movement.[1]

One of the book's most attractive features is its thumbnail sketches of the more recent ecumenical leaders: Charles Brent, to whom 'the vision of a united Church' came at Edinburgh in 1910, and whose 'secret was his unique capacity for giving himself to all kinds of people and for loving them all' (427); Nathan Söderblom, 'a prophet in the guise of an Archbishop', who 'in a most unusual way' *'was* Stockholm 1925' (571, 545); William Temple, whose mind 'did not need to become a closed mind in order to take a firm stand' (713) and whose 'unique gift for irenic formulation' (590) contrasts with A. C. Headlam's liability 'to try to fit others to his own pattern by devising formulas to which all could assent' (427); Henry Lunn, who 'made it his purpose to bring together the unlike-minded' (338); R. H. Gardiner, who 'knew when to act and how to act' and 'never talked about himself' (420); and many others. If two further names stand out as together constituting both the driving-force and the inter-connecting link, they are those of Dr J. R. Mott and Dr J. H. Oldham, both of them, like Lunn and Gardiner, laymen. With Dr Ruth Rouse, to whom, as Editorial Secretary, this *History* owes its direction and detailed planning, as well as her own two chapters, Dr Mott and Dr Oldham were present at Edinburgh in 1910; and in 1948 all three saw the crowning of their, and others', labours in the formation of the W.C.C. at Amsterdam. 'Never before has so short a period seen such rapid progress in thought and action' (731).

1955

---

[1] For the same reason, the W.C.C. might do well to follow the W.S.C.F. and the World's Y.W.C.A. in amending the phrase 'Christ as God' in its doctrinal basis (641).

XXIII

THE MINISTER'S DEVOTIONAL LIFE

I WANT to direct your thoughts to three things which I
believe we should constantly have in mind as Christian
ministers, as we seek to deepen and enrich our devotional
life for the service of others: the large outlook; the ordered
life; and the tender spirit. The opposites of these—the narrow
outlook, the disorderly life and the hard spirit—we all recognize as wrong and to be avoided.

Do you not often feel (as I do) that our lives as ministers
and leaders of churches tend to be small, petty, stuffy, and
confined? taken up with a number of little things which are
unrelated to one another and fail to express any common
principle or reality? Judged by Aristotle's dictum that animals differ from men in having no grasp of universals, how
animal we are much of the time. We need to inquire more
into the meaning of things; to be interested in truth, which
is a big thing; to see how things are related; to perceive laws;
to make generalizations; and to give even abstractions their
proper place. For without these things there can be no ideas,
save of a hazy, lazy and ill-defined kind; and without ideas
there will be no ideals. We need also to be aware, alert,
sensitive to life's imaginative and mystical undertones and
overtones; to see life in its varied levels, moving as cloud-
layers move, towards one another yet without clashing; to
be full of wonder and of awe at the richness and variety of
the universe. We need to pass beyond our contentment with
the sliding-scale of the good, which often so conveniently
coalesces with the expedient, beyond to that which is right.
'Circumstances alter cases,' we say. Of course they do; but
we cannot tell what a thing is a case *of*, unless we have looked
beyond the here and now to the universal and eternal.

If we are to tell people with conviction that Christ calls a
man to say farewell to all that he hath, and that a Christian
must be ready to count all things but refuse, to win Christ,
we must have some sense of the bigness of that *all* as well

as of the greatness of Christ. 'The world is so full of a number of things, I'm sure we should all be as happy as kings': too little of this gets into our meetings. 'A small spirit will never convert the world; the world will only say Sour grapes'. Again, if we are to lead our people, we must come to them from some larger understanding or experience than (in the mass) they possess, to, or through, which we want to lead them: back, if you like, from Moses' mount to Plato's cave. Yet rarely have we either the rays of glory with which Moses wist not that the skin of his face shone or the discomfort (and indeed ill reception) of those who returned from the light of day to the men in the cave. 'Two men looked out of prison bars; one saw the mud, the other the stars': but many of the people in prison we preach to don't even see the bars, they don't know how much of their being still is in prison, they're sitting with their backs to the light. Nor will they turn round unless we bring in 'a *larger* hope, a deeper love', and something still of the freshness of the Breath of God we have felt away on the Mount.

I remember my father telling me, when first I had to wear spectacles, that it would help to counteract my myopia if I looked out across the sea. We must look out across what St Bernard calls the sea of eternal light and luminous eternity, what George Fox calls the ocean of light and love which flows over the ocean of darkness. I hope you will not think that I in any way forget the reading of Scripture, or meditation and prayer, if with the Psalmist I remind you of the heavens. Most of us here in London do not see much of the country. But for all of us, the heavens are always there. 'Stand still and consider the wondrous works of God.' 'The heavens declare the glory of God; and the firmament showeth his handiwork.' 'When I survey the heavens, the works of *thy* fingers, the sun and the moon, which *thou* hast ordained; what is man, that *thou* art mindful of him? and the son of man, that *thou* visitest him?'

This spiritual elation and response to Nature
is Man's generic mark . . .
[writes Robert Bridges]
Thus Rafaël once venturing to show God in Man
gave a child's eyes of wonder to his baby Christ; . . .

>'Tis divinest childhood's incomparable bloom,
>   the loss whereof leaveth the man's face shabby and dull.

'Unless ye become as little children, ye cannot enter into the kingdom of heaven': and this means, not only unless ye become dependent as children, but as full of wonder as they are. 'Seek him that maketh the seven stars and Orion, and turneth the shadow of death into the morning, and maketh the day dark with night: the Lord is his name.' 'I will lift up mine eyes into the hills': fortunate are those who live within sight of the hills, or even of a Salisbury spire or York minster, as I have done; but none of us here, now, do. Then 'Lift up your eyes on high, and behold who hath created these things': for the sky is always there, even for town-dwellers, and it is possible to practise looking at it sometimes, and at the clouds; it is rewarding to lie down occasionally, and just watch them—without waiting till we are ill. George Wyndham said of his mother that she helped people 'unconsciously, as a mountain helps those whose horizon is too confined by leading them to lift up their eyes'. *She* was helped in first being able to look out to the wide Wiltshire downs from the house characteristically called Clouds. Looking up can, similarly, enlarge our personalities, till they reflect the spacious firmament, and even, in time, the Hand that made us as well as it. To bring men into a large place where their spirits may breathe and stretch themselves and grow: in this narrow, crowded, jostling world there is no greater service. 'And at midnight Paul and Silas prayed, and sang praises unto God; and the prisoners heard them. And suddenly the foundations of the prison were shaken; and immediately all the doors were opened, and everyone's bands were loosed.' And that, after all, is our main purpose.

Now to practise keeping our lives open to something of this large outlook is not too difficult, if we are serious in setting about it; but we are not philosophers or poets, we are practical people and ministers; our lives are full of many little things to do, and that's the rub if we also are to seek after the ordered life; for it's in the multiplicity of the little things that the disorder comes. 'God's order and man's disorder': we know the phrase; but we mustn't be content with it. 'The steps of a good man are ordered by the Lord'; and if we are to fulfil our purpose, or God's purpose in us, as men of God, something of God's order in us must be apparent to our people. Putting things in order, arranging them, getting our priorities right, how difficult it is; and, because difficult, how important for us to practise it till we become examples and witnesses in it to our people.

The ordered life implies judging things by a central principle; having a master passion; being men under orders; saying 'This one thing I do'; knowing that 'but one thing is needful'; having our faces set and the compass of our lives fixed in a certain direction, so that our course can be—never fixed and predetermined: Jesus was always ready to be interrupted—but plotted, the things around arranging themselves within reason and falling into a pattern. This means that we must not be afraid to make value-judgements; to have preferences; to be discriminating: 'yea, and why even of yourselves judge ye not what is right?' In a striking phrase in the Epistle to the Hebrews, we are to have our spiritual senses exercised, to discern good and evil: to be able to put things in order: with a good, better, best; and with a bad, worse worst; not to think that, because so much in life is grey, there is nothing black.

All the same, much that is grey must be omitted, even though it is not black but only grey. This is one of the things we find hardest to accept and to practise: to realize that in any ordered life, as in an ordered work of art, a picture or a poem, which is a true whole, with its parts properly integrated, not only will things have been arranged round a central principle but some things will have been omitted altogether, cut out, given up. This asceticism, as it is sometimes called, sometimes by those who do not like it, I find to be a prevailing background tone of the life and teaching of Jesus, who is often much more severe than we are courageous enough to allow, even to ourselves. 'If thine eye offends thee, makes thee to stumble, upsets you, is a cause of disorder, pluck it out; if thine hand offend thee, cut it off', 'Thou knowest the commandments, honour thy father and mother', He would say; but He could also say, 'he that loveth father or mother more than me, is not worthy of me'. 'Let me first go and say goodbye at home'; 'let me first go and bury my father'; but Jesus would not have it: in His service there are *no* other *firsts*. 'Let the dead bury their dead; but go *thou* and preach the kingdom of God.' The dead have to be buried; and the organizations of the Church have to be carried on; with the socials and the outings and the 101 other things which are all good in their way; but do you not sometimes hear those stern words, 'Go *thou* and preach the kingdom of God', and ask pardon for your disobedience to what once you knew was primary in your call, and for the little time proportionately you spend in your study and with the Bible?

It is not that I want us to be less busy, in the right way. The ship that is well loaded keeps a straighter course. Life is short, and we of all men know how true it is that in the midst of life we are in death; and when we have done all, we can say no more than that we are servants and have done some part of what it was our duty to do. But you and I have been satisfied early with the Divine mercy, so that inwardly we may rejoice and be glad all our days, whatever the wear and tear of it—and it comforts me sometimes to remember that 'Jesus, being *wearied, sat* thus on the well'. Then let this also be our earnest prayer, 'So teach us to number our days, that we may apply our hearts unto wisdom'; putting first things first, and, because these take up more time than we expected, letting some things go altogether. It is perhaps because I am a student of history that I am so conscious of the reality and importance of time; but the simple truth is that the right use and arrangement of our time is at the bottom of the ordered life. You may think it is a sudden lapse from the dignities proper to the subject to say that the time of our getting up and the time of our going to bed are closely related to it, but I believe they are. First, because, if each morning we are to ask 'How can I, in the duties and opportunities of this day, fulfil the will of God? O help me to this end', we dare not get up unnecessarily late; but neither dare we go to bed unnecessarily late. It is more than a mistake, it is disgraceful in its revelation of the disorder we let our lives get into, that so often we wake up tired. Of course, sometimes we should be tired; but 'We ought just to be doing what we have to do as well as ever we can, and not forcing more work out of ourselves than we ever were meant to yield. We mustn't spend our capital of strength': not for selfish reasons, but for unselfish; 'because it isn't ours': 'ye are not your own': 'ye were bought with a price'. And secondly, the times of our uprising and our downlying are important, because their rightness and their regularity, or the lack of these, are the clearest index to the regularity, the rhythm, the place of habit within our lives more generally; and all of these, even habit the despised, are closely related to the ordered life which comes of living under orders; to the disciplined life which comes of remembering that we are disciples and serve a Master. It is indeed a great mistake not to take advantage of the ministry of habit: no athlete or musician ever makes it; and only if we develop habits of awareness and obedience, getting up as soon as the alarum clock goes or after we have seen the vision *straightway* endeavouring to go into Macedonia (which for us may be a few streets away), habits of attention and allegiance, are we likely to be awake and ready, with the flesh strong as well as the spirit eager, when we are called to do some great thing that takes everything we have. It is, in any case, the little things which try us; if I may use some wise words of Bishop Paget (whom I quoted just now without acknowledgement), much of our life as ministers and men of God must be spent 'in doing very little things, whose value lies in this, that, if one did not hope in God, one would not do them; in secretly dispelling moods which one would like to show; in saying nothing about one's lesser troubles and vexations; in seeing whether it may not be best to bear a burden before one tries to see whether one can shift it; in refusing for one's self excuses which one would not refuse for others'. Alongside which I would put this, from another bishop, Bishop Creighton: 'Spiritual work is all concerned with details; and he who would work for God must learn never to be in a hurry, must curb his natural impatience, must remember how tenderly God has dealt with him, must regard no time wasted which composes differences, or removes scruples, or resolves doubts, which cheers, consoles or convinces'.

Such is the ordered life; and this last quotation, with its pastoral *motiv* and its remembrance of God's tenderness with ourselves, carries us on to the tender spirit, without which, however large our outlook and however ordered our life, we can never be good ministers of Jesus Christ. The older I grow, the more I am convinced of the prime need in us of delicacy of perception, expectancy, sensitiveness, responsiveness, in our relations with other people, and especially when as ministers we are seeking to awaken and to liberate, or to nurture and to strengthen. The religious impulse, the core of faith, is set very deep within us, and it is only deep that calleth unto deep. Especially in the hearts of the young people whose eager interest and inquiry begin again to encourage us, after so many years when we seemed unable to keep them, it is very small, and tender, and delicate. We are all shy and reserved about our greatest experiences—and there can be no greater experience than the coming of faith—afraid of misunderstanding and mockery: such things are too sacred to be bandied about and made light of. It has to be nurtured tenderly, as a seed, and let grow gradually. 'It commeth not in by the lumpe,' says one of the Puritans; 'the will of God is, to let it in sometimes by little and little'. God forgive us for our blundering! We cannot answer for others; all men must buy for themselves; but we can often hurt them, so that their own answer dies on their lips. The man of God, if he is like his Lord, will not break the bruised reed, nor quench the smoking flax. 'The strongest plants in God's house,' says another Puritan, 'are exposed sometimes to strong winds of temptation, and thereupon meet with bruisings'; and when there come these

> blastings and blightings of hope and love,
> and rude shocks that affray,

the man of God will put his hands round the tender sapling, praying for Christ's hands over his own.

But, unless we have altogether forgotten our own youth, it is not here that our main difficulty lies: there is more evidently something to awaken in the young, and they are so much readier of response, even when the response brings us heartburn and disappointment. Far more difficult are the people in our churches, and how many they are, who are good decent people, and who are in fact living a kinder, cleaner life than they ever would or could if they were not in our churches, but who do not seem to know this or to have come within a telescope's vision of the outgoing, seeking, serving, giving, forgiving, winning, rescuing, saving, redeeming love of God, to which we all, whether ministers or not, are called to witness and live by and show forth. It is to them, for them, above all, that we have to learn to be tender, all the more because in them there is so little tenderness apparent; for them that we have to learn to spend and to be spent, though the more we love the less we be loved, grateful for even a small share in the fellowship of Christ's sufferings; and do you not think His disciples were rather like the people in our churches—not in the end, of course, but in the beginning, before He had been so long time with them? 'O ye of little faith! Perceive ye not yet? How is it that ye do not understand? Are even ye so without understanding? Will ye also go away?' Yes, Jesus knew this difficulty; and yet having loved His own, He loved them unto the end, with unwearying tenderness and permission, indeed encouragement, for them to begin again. That is a mark of the divine tenderness, that we can always begin again: how far have *we* the patience with people, and the unbroken faith in their possibilities or the possibilities of what Christ can make of them, not only to encourage them over and over (knowing we need the same encouragement ourselves) to begin again, but to wait hopefully, and to speak (or be silent) sensitively, when they do not know their need but are quite content to go on as they are?

These people are imprisoned, as I said earlier; and, when we come into our pulpits on Sundays, we need to pray that the Spirit of the Lord God may be upon us, not only to preach good tidings to the meek and to bind up the broken-hearted but to proclaim liberty to the captives and the opening of the prison to them that are bound and *do not know it*. This thought of Christian ministry as release from the prison-house is one which was peculiarly dear to the first Quakers in the days of their own terrible persecutions, when at times it seems almost that there were more of them in prison than outside it. 'Look not at your sufferings,' George Fox would write to Friends, 'but at the power of God, and that will bring some good out in all your sufferings; and your imprison-ments will reach to the prisoned, that the persecutor prisons in himself'; and of his own lot he could say finely, 'There was never any prisons or sufferings that I was in but still it was for the bringing multitudes more *out* of prison'. How won-derful that is! In this country we no longer have the oppor-tunity for such dramatic witness; but our calling is still the same; and, if we are to be worthy, the demand from us for patience and tenderness is all the greater: to go 'pushing on towards a faintly glimmering light, and never doubting the supreme worth of goodness even in its least brilliant fragments'; to be quick to perceive the least tendering, the first softening, in a man's heart, the turning of the tide which at first will always be almost imperceptible. Nor, as a matter of fact, was Fox ignorant of this. 'Patience must get the vic-tory,' he writes, 'and answers to that of God in everyone, and will bring everyone from the contrary.' 'Answering that of God in everyone': will you take this phrase away, and look at it in the light of your ministry and at your ministry in *its* light? It means responding to God's seeking us and speaking to us through others, it also means speaking to that of God in others even when it is imprisoned, concealed, perhaps from their own eyes; still answering that of God which speaks in and through them, though their outer words may be in another tone and tongue; and by answering it, drawing it out; in fact by liberating it, for all practical purposes creating it. Faith often creates in someone else, and so in a situation, what would not otherwise have been there.

1957

XXIV

THE HEIRS OF HEAVEN[1]

> Voi credete
> forse che siamo esperti d'este loco;
> ma noi siam peregrin, come voi siete.
> Dianzi venimmo, innanzi a voi un poco.
>
> Dante, *Purgatorio*, ii. 61–4.[2]

AWAY in a quiet Northamptonshire village churchyard is a tombstone which bears these words:

> They, alone, who Jesus love,
> They whose hearts are fixed above,
> To Him entirely given—
> Whose only trust is in His blood,
> Who live by faith, and live to God,
> They are the heirs of heaven.

There is a boldness, a strength, about the verse, a strength of assurance and a boldness in the claim staked out, more especially in the severity of its limitation, which impressed me when I transcribed the words, some twenty-five years ago, from the tomb of my great-great-great-grandmother, Mary Smeeton, who died in 1829, aged sixty-five. A faith so crystalline, a Christocentricity so adamant, recalls us with some sharpness from our more modern hesitations to the confines which, in the New Testament, considerations of life after death receive as their defining context.

The New Testament begins and ends with Christ: He is the Alpha and the Omega: Jesus Christ the same yesterday, today and for ever. And the Church begins and ends with the Resurrection. It begins with it in a story of heavenly messengers, who say that He is alive: and there is still no

---

[1] The 1956 Drew Lecture on Immortality, delivered in London on 25 October 1956.

[2] The passage quoted at the head of the lecture may be translated:
  'You think perhaps that we are experienced in this place: but we are pilgrims as you are. Just now we came, but a little before you.'

more essentially Christian greeting than 'The Lord is risen!'
—'He is risen indeed!' It ends with it in the sense that it
cannot get beyond it; for of His Kingdom there shall be no
end: Christ being raised from the dead dieth no more, death
has no more dominion over Him. He has the dominion over
death as well as life: He is Lord both of the dead and of the
living.

And of the living, note. His rising from the dead was not
in order to rise to other worlds, this poor one all forgot. Still
He will be Lord of those living in this world. Still there is, or
can be, even as there was before, the closest relation, communication, communion between Himself and those whom
He calls, and makes, His own, those who respond and follow
Him in discipleship, trust and love.

So it had been throughout His ministry. In the beginning
He had chosen twelve, to be with Him; and to be with Him
then had meant letting family ties go, abandoning your way
of living and your livelihood, your security and what measure of comfort you possessed, abandoning it for a hard,
roving, uncertain life, not knowing today what you would do
tomorrow. But how well worth while it was! As Jesus passed
through town and village, preaching and showing the glad
tidings of the kingdom of God, just to be with Him was
abundantly worth while; while to hear Him say 'You are
the folk, who have stuck it through with me in all my times
of trial and testing' was enough to break your heart. Peter and
Thomas only spoke for them all when they said they were
willing to die with Him.

One of the first implications of the resurrection of Jesus is
that this relationship to Him, this being with him, is still
possible: is possible, indeed, in a far wider way than before.
Before, only a few could be with Him. 'Sirs, we would see
Jesus,' they cried. 'If I may but touch His clothes, I shall be
whole.' As many as had diseases pressed against Him for to
touch Him. There was no room, no, not so much as about
the door. They uncovered the roof. But by and large it was
no use. Only a few could be with Him. It was part of the
straitening which at times was an almost unendurable constraint to Him. But now, that is over. The Lord is risen! And
in being risen from the dead, He is released from the

limitations of all that dies: those physical, spatial, temporal limitations which, before, through the divine purpose of self-revelation in a human life, Jesus could no more evade than we can. Now, no longer solely the twelve, not even the ten times twelve met together in Jerusalem, but all who will may come close to Him in discipleship, trust, love and self-abandonment. His ministry is continued; it is on a vastly wider scale, but it is the same ministry, on the same principles, and on the same moral conditions, as before; which means that being with Him is at the heart of it.

That Christ is risen, and is there, with and among His disciples, is in fact what creates the peculiar character and colour of life in the New Testament. When Paul cries that Christ lives in him, or that for him to live is Christ, he is not in an ecstasy, he is not claiming a special experience limited to himself. Equally to others he will write, Christ is among you; your true but hidden life is your life with Him: nay, He is your life. In the words of good Dean Alford, 'The only real life of the Christian is his resurrection life in and with Christ,' 'the new and glorious life of the Spirit begun here below and enduring for ever: the only life worthy of being so called': 'Christ is personally Himself that life, and we possess it only by union with Him and His resurrection.'[1]

Moreover, we can hardly remind ourselves too often that Paul was not among those who had seen Jesus: so far as appears, he had seen Jesus neither before the crucifixion nor after the resurrection, not at least in the way others believed they had seen Him in the weeks immediately after it. Paul stands with us, this side the great divide, not with the twelve. It may be that the cessation of the mortal, corporeal, human element in their relationship to the Lord made it hardest for those who before the crucifixion had been closest to Jesus to accept and enjoy the new conditions. Whether that was so or not, it was left to Paul, above all, to proclaim the gospel of the resurrection, the good news that Christ was risen, and was there: saying, 'I am Jesus, and it is Me that thou art persecuting, so closely am I one with My disciples'; turning Paul aside from his course to Bithynia, not permitting him to

[1] Henry Alford, *The Greek Testament*, 3rd edn., 1862, *ad Col.* iii. 3, *II Tim.* i. 10, *Col.* iii. 4.

enter upon it; persuading him, on the other hand, to stay in Corinth, saying, 'Fear not; for I am with thee,' assuring him, with a 'Be of good cheer!', that he would achieve his purpose to see Rome. 'Be of good cheer! It is I! Be not afraid!': so had the Lord always spoken. It was the same Lord, bringing the same good tidings.

Now it well may be that 'geniuses or creative leaders', such as those among whom Paul, on any reckoning, must be numbered, 'become sensitive organs of direct spiritual impressions and divine revelations which are missed by those who are busy alone with the affairs of time and sense'.[1] But if we suppose that, with all his genius and sensitiveness, nay with all his discipleship and devotedness, Paul saw very much or very far, or even thought that he did, we mistake. Paul's unmistakable greatness,his humbling sincerity and humility, appear in his constant insistence that it is not so. οὐχότι ἤδη ἔλαβον, '*not as though I had already*'—attained the prize or reached the winning-post—was surely suggested by the celestial heralds for Paul's patent of spiritual gentility.

If we miss this, we miss an essential aspect of the nature and burden of faith: the faith to which Paul turns and returns at every juncture, and from which life in the New Testament never strays far. In Protestant Christianity faith has received so much emphasis and attention that it has sometimes been in danger of becoming a towering juggernaut. In truth, of its nature, faith is a limited, partial, immature thing. Apologists remark that all our life rests on faith. That is true; and it is wise to see that it is true and to accept the fact as an implicate of our humanity, or more religiously of our createdness, as a limitation on us that is set by God. It remains, none the less, a limitation; and at no point are we more aware of being limited by it than in our relation to Christ, whom, if we love, we love not having seen, still resting in faith alone. We walk by faith, not by that which is seen, not by any visible form seen directly. There is always a medium; a glass translucent but not transparent; a metallic mirror which reflects but does it imperfectly; a veil, a hint, a parable, an enigmatic element not wholly understood. However close we

[1] R. M. Jones, introd. to W. C. Braithwaite, *The Beginnings of Quakerism*, 1st edn., 1923, p. xxvii.

come to Christ, however sure of Him we are, here this will always be so: it is of the nature of faith.

Here, but not hereafter: not after death. Death brings freedom from restraint and limitation, brings fulfilment of the partial and immature. The restraint and humility of Paul's 'not as though already' is finely, poignantly, counter-balanced by the eager excitement of his 'but then . . .'. As he holds the perspective glass of faith, Paul still sees only something like the glory of the place; but at times its gates appear so near that his spirit faints to reach the land, where he may see the one who gives the place its glory, even Christ, as He is, without mirror, glass or veil. When Paul dares to contemplate this, he can hardly bear the constraint it sets upon him. He is conscious only of the desire to be released and be with Christ. That were far better. With Christ? is he not that already? Christ is his life, here. Yes, but while he is in the body, there is inevitably a degree of mediation, he must still be at a remove from the Lord. Only when at death he puts on immortality will mortality's limitations be broken through. Then, he will not only be with Christ as he is here; he will see Christ, will see Him face to face, will know Christ: know Christ as fully as, he believes, already Christ knows him.

In order to describe an activity possible only after death, when physical limitations are over, Paul writes of *seeing* Christ. Since seeing is itself dependent upon the body's co-operation, this may, logically, be confusing; but it is hard to tell how else he could express himself, not better, but intel-ligibly. At a deeper level than the logical, his doing so is a moving measure of the passion with which, while still in the body, he longs to do just what, so long as he is in the body, he never can do, namely to see Christ. This passion is, in fact, the driving force behind his whole wider conception of a spiritual body after death; and we may understand, and share, the passion without necessarily being tied to, or understanding, the conception. Certainly what Dean Alford calls 'the one expression of a hope in which all other hopes culminate and centre'[1] is a familiar refrain in the hymns we sing.

[1] *Op. cit., ad I John* iii. 2.

Till with the vision glorious
  Her longing eyes are blest . . .
That we may be where now Thou art
  And look upon Thy face.
Until at last our wondering eyes
  Look on Thy glorious face above.
Till, clouds and darkness ended,
  They see Thee face to face.
The rending veil shall Thee reveal
  All glorious as Thou art.
Those eyes, new faith receiving,
  From Jesus shall not move . . .
Then let me on the mountain top
  Behold Thy open face . . .
Not in that poor lowly stable,
  With the oxen standing by,
We shall see Him . . .

The lines are from hymns of different centuries; and when a desire is not only felt so long and so continuously but is regularly accompanied by the assurance that it will be fulfilled, it deserves respect even from those who do not share it. By those who do, the holding together, the delicate balancing, of the longing and the belief that it will be realized is found to be of a piece with much else in Christian experience. On earth we live as children do, by hope, by hints, by promises, by pledges—nothing more. Yet all of these are forward-looking. They have, in fact, no meaning except as things to be fulfilled; no meaning, that is, ultimately, save as they *are* fulfilled. Moreover, we do know in part. So far, hope maketh not ashamed. We have, already, the purchase-price, the deposit, the first instalment of what is to follow, the first-fruits of the harvest to come; and we believe that He is faithful who promised.

Is then the rest of life a static period, to be spent waiting patiently, and in resignation, for release from what is limiting and partial? Not at all. That would be to misunderstand the nature of discipleship and the desire at the heart of it to grow more like the Master. The Christian's course is not only from the death in life, which spiritually is what life without

Christ is, to the deathless life, which is begun in the body but finds fulfilment only after the body's death. It is also a process of transformation into the image, the pattern, given in Christ, nay rather into Christ Himself, as the Christian and He grow together. The Christian remembers how Jesus said that the vision of God is given to the pure in heart; and, strong in the hope to see Christ as He is, he seeks to purify himself even as Christ is pure. The Christian remembers how Jesus rebuked the disciples for setting their mind on the world's level instead of on God's when they should rather seek God's will before all else and centre their heart's desire in heaven, not on earth. He also remembers how Jesus Himself put God's will first, even though it brought Him to the cross; and, knowing something already of the power of Christ's resurrection, he does his utmost to live to God and to seek, and to set his mind on, the things that are above, not on earthly things. Again, the Christian remembers how Jesus overturned the conventional scales and standards of things and would ask what profit there could be in anyone's gaining all there was, if he did so only at the cost of losing himself; and, eager to share in some measure in the fellowship of Christ's sufferings, he tries to learn to be willing for Christ's sake to lose, to give up, what before he counted his richest gain, and towards sin and temptation to be as dead. In all this he brings himself, so far as he may, into conformity with Christ's death, and hopes passionately that he is on the way to the resurrection life. Once more, the Christian remembers how Jesus said that only the man who, in another and a deeper sense, *was* willing to lose himself, to care so little for himself as to give himself, to lose his life even, in love for others would in the end find his truest self, saved, preserved, made alive in the heavenly life. He remembers too how in His own life Jesus practised this pouring Himself out, and how by His death and resurrection He proved it true. Thus the Christian expects to spend himself and to be spent for the sake of others; and, wherever he finds it, whether in others or in himself, he treasures every sparkle of such self-forgetful love as an undeniable token that, in principle, the passage from death to life is made.

Nor is this all, or even the half. For the Christian's Master is the risen Lord, whose ministry remains as constant and living, as effective and transforming, as ever it was in Galilee, when He said these things and lived and died. Still He attaches us livingly to Himself, still He shares with us His mind, His experience, all that His ministry costs Him, even the oft-repeated bitter cup. This is the deeper meaning of those many verbs and adjectives in the New Testament epistles which begin with σύν, words which in English are less easily recognizable because of the variety of renderings used for the affix ('with', 'together', 'together with', 'joint', 'fellow' and sometimes nothing at all). It is not only that in all our afflictions He is afflicted. More wonderful still, He permits, nay draws, us to share in His own ministry of suffering love. To quote Dean Alford once more: 'Every suffering saint of God in every age and position is in fact filling up, in his place and degree, the tribulations of Christ, in his flesh and on behalf of Christ's body. Not a pang, not a tear is in vain.'[1] So, at last, by allowing us a share in His ministry of suffering, Christ will bring us to a share in His glory. Our outward man, our body, will be destroyed; but our inward man, the hidden man of the heart, that life that has been hidden with Him, will spring up in renewal; and whatever of His afflictions we may have been permitted to share, in the love and recovery of others, we shall count a featherweight beside the exceeding great glory of looking at the things which at present, with the body's eye, we cannot see, and, most of all, of beholding Him. For then, transformed by the Lord into His pattern, we shall be joint heirs with Him in all things. We shall be heirs of heaven.

This, or something like it, seems to me a fair account of the faith of the New Testament, and of faith continuing through the Christian centuries where it has been consonant with the faith of the New Testament, so far as concerns this particular aspect of life after death, namely being with Christ. For theologians it is only one aspect, one among many ways of regarding the subject, others of which have received attention in earlier lectures in this series; though it is, I believe, an important aspect and one which we are inclined to neglect.

[1] *Op. cit.*, *ad Col.* i. 24.

From the point of view of Christian piety, of the experience which the theologian analyzes and upon the validity of which he pronounces, often with difficulty, as he finds its elements eluding his most careful formulation, it is less an aspect than the heart of the matter: it springs directly from the first preaching of 'Jesus and the Resurrection'. Being with Christ when He was in this life: being with Him now, while we are in this life: being with Him after death—for our present purpose I have sought to elaborate these concepts into something approaching an argument; but for the first Christians they were less stages in an argument than moments in a single experience, the experience of the presence of the Risen Christ: 'Lo, I am with you alway': 'There is not room for Death.'

Those last bold words come not from the New Testament but from a poem which, while doubtless influenced by a Christian environment, is, rather, Stoic in its defiance and pantheist in its mysticism. The 'God within my breast' whom Emily Brontë apostrophized was hardly the God and Father of Jesus Christ. Yet the poem is triumphant in its conviction: Emily Brontë's confidence in 'the steadfast rock of immortality' is magnificent. I believe, moreover, that her interpretation of her experience is sound. Deathlessness subsists in the very quality of the mystical feeling which informs her poem. Nor is it necessary for us to possess her intense poetic power to be able to enter into something like her experience, which fundamentally is not uncommon. In terms of a lowest common denominator it may be described as a sudden consciousness of heightened significance. We may hardly be able to say *what* is significant: everything, 'the totality of things'. But

> There's a certain slant of light,
> On winter afternoons,
> That oppresses, like the weight
> Of cathedral tunes. . . .
> When it comes, the landscape listens,
> Shadows hold their breath; . . .[1]

and while it lasts, we are lifted strangely out of mortality into a sphere which death cannot touch. Such moments can be

[1] *The Poems of Emily Dickinson*, Boston, Mass., 1932, ed. M. D. Bianchi and A. L. Hampson, pp. 108 f.

precious. I know no valid reason why we should distrust them, if they come to us. A Christian will, rather, welcome them and find God in them: 'The Lord is in this place,' he will say, 'this is the gate of heaven'; or 'Thou art with me; then I will fear no evil, though I walk through the valley of the shadow of death.'

At the same time, these moments, however precious they may be, must not be confused with the Christian's faith in being with Christ and his consequent assurance of life after death. In the first place, such mystical feeling is limited in its incidence. It appears, in fact, to be characteristic of certain types of personality only, and to be undetermined by moral or spiritual considerations: Richard Baxter, for instance, was markedly lacking in it. The Christian's faith in being with Christ, on the other hand, and his assurance of life after death, are something which any Christian may have, and which every Christian should have. His faith does not, indeed, primarily depend upon feeling at all, however naturally it may be accompanied by and give rise to feeling, and however rightly it may control his interpretation of feeling. Nor is there in his faith as such any sense of deathlessness directly and *per se*, such as is present in mystical feeling. Life after death, as the Christian conceives it, is not an indestructible implicate of his being, a right to which he is born, like the fresh air of Haworth moors; it is, rather, the gift of God, the outcome of an encounter between God and each soul, in which God takes the initiative as He did when He 'raised' Christ: theologically, the transitive reference of 'resurrection' is prior to the intransitive. The Christian's assurance of life after death is thus never a sheer *datum*, it is always consequent upon his faith, an inference from it we may say, albeit a necessary inference: 'He that is joined unto the Lord is one spirit'; then, 'God who raised up the Lord will also raise us up.' Thus Baxter, for all his deficiency in 'Sensible Consolations', knew a 'rational satisfaction' and 'doubted not of his Right to Heaven' as a Christian. Again, while limited in its incidence, mystical feeling is unconditioned and undemanding. It is also transient and leaves no lasting impression: the sense of deathlessness present in it passes: 'Cold in the earth . . . cold in the dreary grave!' The Christian's faith in being

264

with Christ, on the other hand, involves him at once, as we have seen, in moral conditions; demands are made upon his personality, and continue to be made; and the gradual transformation of his personality, if he is obedient to these demands, out of love to the One who makes them, in the end provides the best evidence that his faith in Christ and his consequent assurance of life after death are well founded.

> They, alone, who Jesus love,
> They whose hearts are fixed above,
>   To Him entirely given—
> Whose only trust is in His blood,
> Who live by faith, and live to God,
>   They are the heirs of heaven.

'They, alone . . .': do we stick yet at that limit set so sharply? We are eager today for as large a degree as possible of tolerance, understanding, and accommodation. To reserve heaven for the disciples of Jesus will by many not only be thought ridiculous but be felt to be an outrage on the universality of God's love. If God should shut others out, has He not lost His character?

For all its apparent penetration this question is, I believe, a superficial one. The universality it assumes for, or wishes to attribute to, God's love, a relationship undifferentiated and unconditioned, has no foundation either in the Bible or in our experience of any kind of love, divine or human, nor yet in any honest observation of the world in general. Its foundation, if it has one, is rather in that human craving for 'fair shares' which Professor Farmer rightly insists is, while one of the most difficult, also one of the most necessary, things for Christians to grow out of. It was not 'fair' or 'loving' of God to 'shut out' so many from 'knowing' Shakespeare; and, while it is true that for Christian faith 'knowing' Christ is in a different sphere of discourse from 'knowing' Shakespeare, and its 'reward' is 'eternal' life instead of merely a heightening of 'temporal', in relation to God's character the principle is the same. A religion which saved (!) the character of God at the expense of the Incarnation might be highly moral but would no longer be Christianity. A divine love which, in response to man's need, accepts the conditions of humanity and of

265

history for its medium of revelation to man must also accept the implicates of those conditions. 'When *Thou* hadst overcome the sharpness of death, *Thou* didst open the kingdom of heaven to all *believers*.' There, in the *Te Deum*, is the characteristic setting for heaven as the Christian conceives of it, the being with Christ, the relationship of Christ to those who believe, with all the starkness of exclusivity implied which any relationship must imply, and without which any gospel, any good news, must soon evaporate: without his equal insistence on the personal pronouns, Wesley's universalism would have won no one: 'To me, to all, Thy mercies move.' For *believers* there was no other good enough and there is none other name given. Only those who, while in the body, though now they see Him not, yet believing in Him, rejoice with joy unspeakable because, in faith and love, He is with them here, know the passion to see Jesus hereafter. Only they respond to the supremely great words which form the climax to *I Corinthians* xiii and without which half the wonder and glory of Paul's description of *agape*, of Christian love as we are to practise it here in this very difficult present world, would be lost: the words 'but then face to face'. And it is this, as we have reminded ourselves, which is the great glory of heaven in the only sense in which the New Testament knows anything of it. To a passionate conviction about life after death Emily Brontë had her own mystical path; and, if our temperamental make-up permits us to do so, I know no reason why we should not walk with her along it. It can lead us a long way from the things which are seen, temporal and mortal; nor do I think that it is a will-o'-the-wisp which beckons along it; but it will not lead us to heaven. To life after death there may be many paths; but not to the being with Christ in paradise which alone is heaven. If after death there is life of some kind for all, but life of a particular kind for some only, that would at least be consistent with the state of affairs here; and, though ethically men have been inclined to think of life after death more in terms of redress of the state of affairs here, ontologically it may be more convincing to think of it as similar.

I can imagine that the considerations of the last few

minutes have seemed to many somewhat arid and remote. Let us return in conclusion to Sibbertoft churchyard. There is another tombstone there, in memory of a great-grandson of Mary Smeeton's, Sydney Smeeton, who died in 1889. He was a lively, loving boy, the light of his parents' eyes and their only child. When they were fifty-six and fifty-three respectively, he died, aged sixteen. His parents were broken-hearted, as who would not be? But they were Christians. They were people of no note, the father then known in Northamptonshire but long since forgotten. But both of them knew the New Testament and were at home in that divinest atmosphere of it which is timeless. To both, the power of Christ's resurrection was not a phrase but a reality; and now more than ever. In their joy that the Christian, even Christ's little ones, may be with Christ, hereafter no less than here, their grief in the loss of their boy was assuaged; and with a triumph still deeply moving they put this upon his stone:

> Is it well with the child?
>   It is well.
> Praise God! The Shepherd is so sweet,
> Praise God! The country is so fair,
> We could not hold thee from His feet,
> We can but hope to meet thee there.

Sydney Smeeton's parents lived on into this century, his father to the age of eighty, his mother of eighty-five. And, when they both had died, this is what was put upon their stone:

> At eventide Jesus called them to the other side.

*   *   *

> Though wise men better know the way
> It seems no honest heart can stray.

1956

XXV

CHRISTIAN LOVE MANIFESTED IN HISTORY[1]

IN London and elsewhere in England, where the increase in traffic accidents has given rise to serious concern, a number of posters have appeared recently as part of a continuous campaign to ensure safer driving. In England, though not in the United States, it is still permitted to assume that every man desires to be 'better' than the average; and each of these posters begins with the words 'Better drivers . . .'. The variation in what follows is interesting. One poster, for instance, reads 'Better drivers survive'. This appears to be a naked appeal to self-interest. It may be said to express evolutionary ethics and 'the survival of the fittest'. Another poster reads 'Better drivers honour the code'. This may be interpreted as the Judaic appeal to those who think of goodness as the fulfilling of the law. Yet another poster reads 'Better drivers give way'. This, surely, is the Christian poster. Only, I think, in a country influenced to some extent by the Christian ethic of grace, in which a determination to stand on one's own rights is overcome by the desire to help others, could this poster appear. 'Better drivers give way.'

The part of our general subject which has been entrusted to me is the manifestation of Christian love in history. My thesis is that by students of history Christians may be watched in many spheres 'turning the flank of recalcitrant institutions'[2] (to cull a phrase from A. D. Lindsay). By the force of their convictions Christians bring moral pressure to bear on others, including those who do not wholly, or even at all, share those convictions, until institutions and practices found offensive are either transformed or destroyed. I believe that a brief reminder of some of the facts may enhearten us as *we* work so to affect *international* relations that the institution of war may be abolished. My purpose is to describe and to suggest rather than to dispute; but there are three prejudices

[1] An address delivered to the International Fellowship of Reconciliation at Schloss Trautenfels, Austria, in August 1959.

[2] A. D. Lindsay, *The Two Moralities: our duty to God and to Society*, 1940, p. 85.

against my thesis, any of which may be in some of your minds, and I should like to say a word about each of these before proceeding.

First, there are those who doubt the possibility of what I have described, or, if it should be possible, its rightness. In *Christus Victor* for last March the Bishop of Lund in Sweden re-presented the Lutheran doctrine of the two kingdoms: the kingdom of God, of Christ, of the Gospel and of the Word of God; in short, the Church; and the kingdom of the world, of evil, of the Law and of the sword; in short, the State; and never the twain shall meet. 'It is against the will of God,' Dr Nygren writes, 'to try to rule the world by the Gospel. God has ordained an entirely different government to rule the world.' Now certainly we need to guard against making an identification, an easy merging, of the Church and the world, or of the Church and the State; but in fact it has often been those with a lively sense of the *difference* between the Church and the State who have been most active in bringing Christian influences to bear, in order to *transform* the State and its institutions. Certainly, also, we should remember that through Christ new powers are made available for those who believe in Him, and that from those without faith the Christian ethic is not to be demanded. Nevertheless, Christians *can* make their own convictions effective within a non-Christian, or only partially Christian, society. May I give two contemporary examples of what I mean? After the close of the 1939–45 war the British Government ruled that civilians might not in any way fraternize with prisoners of war; and also that food parcels might not be sent to enemy countries. In both matters Christians were active in bringing pressure to bear upon the Government and upon public opinion generally; and *quite soon* prisoners of war were being entertained and shown Christian friendship on church premises, while out of their still very limited rations families were sending food parcels to those officially their enemies, whose need they knew to be even greater than their own. These things can be done; and I never heard that any Lutheran declined a food parcel because it expressed the intrusion of the gospel of love into the alien kingdom of a warring world.

A second objection to my thesis is this. In most, perhaps all of the movements which will come before us not only have other motives and causes besides those which may fairly be called Christian come into play, but prominent Christians have opposed at the time what in retrospect has come to be recognized as Christian action of a transforming or revolutionary type. This is true. However much more it is, the Church itself is, or is embodied in, an institution; and in any institution the force of vested interests and conservatism of outlook are strong. At first, Christians were found to oppose the introduction of anaesthetics or even the use of the umbrella. Nevertheless, the fact is not altered, or its significance reduced, that the pioneers and leaders in the movements we shall consider were themselves deeply committed and concerned Christians.

Thirdly, it is often objected that between social relations, whether within the confines of a single nation or more widely, and political relations internationally between sovereign states, there is a fundamental difference; and that therefore any analogy drawn between demonstrations of Christian love in the former sphere and demonstrations in the sphere with which we have to do in the I.F.o.R., falls to the ground. To reply to this adequately would demand a full consideration of the nature of the State, such as would not be in place in this lecture. I can do no more than mention it, by way of indicating that I am not unaware of it; but we shall return to it at the close.

To proceed, then; and may I say that, if most of my illustrations are taken from the last three centuries and from England, this is not only because these are the period and the country with the history of which I am most familiar, but also because traditionally the Anglo-Saxons, and in particular the Protestant Nonconformists, have been leaders in the sort of movements which concern us? To say this is not to be smug. By those under the influence of Lutheran doctrine the *fact* is recognized, though it is regretted, or condemned.

One of the most striking illustrations of our subject, because its effects have been so far-reaching, is the influence of Christian convictions and experience among the radical Puritans of seventeenth-century England on the theory and practice of parliamentary government and on the resultant concept of the State. One reason why parliamentary government in other countries sometimes appears less effective or secure is that it has been adopted without reference to, even in unawareness of, the Christian principles which have helped to shape it in England. Parliament long antedated seventeenth-century Puritanism, of course (though it has been argued,[1] not very convincingly, that even the beginnings of Parliament in the thirteenth century were influenced by the constitution and practice of the Dominican order); but behind modern parliamentary procedure lies the Puritan conviction of 'the equality of a society in which all count', because 'each in his separate individual existence is dear to God'; in which, in the search to discover the will of God, all are 'equally called on to contribute to the common discussion'; and in which there is a respect for tender consciences and therefore a tolerance for minorities. In the influence of this in the creation of democratic government—and the transference from a religious and a theocratic purpose to a secular and a democratic, though not always observed, is for us precisely the point at issue—A. D. Lindsay draws attention to two matters in particular, each of which is significant for our investigation. From what he calls the 'exaltation of the small society' or congregation, 'in which the individual man in close community with his fellows can find shelter from the pressure of Leviathan, comes', Lindsay says, 'the new view of the function of the state as concerned to cherish and protect the voluntary association, in which the most precious things in society may develop'; and from the experience of a way of church life 'which rested on consent and on the resolution of differences by discussion' comes the concept of government by consent. 'In politics,' Lindsay says, 'government by consent is strictly a contradiction in terms. But because the Puritan tradition started with the experience of a society which rested on consent and abjured the use of force, it tended to conceive the state on the analogy of such a society.'[2]

---

[1] See Ernest Barker, *The Dominican Order and Convocation*, 1913, p. 53; and G. R. Galbraith, *The Constitution of the Dominican Order*, Manchester, 1925, p.5.
[2] A. D. Lindsay, *The Modern Democratic State*, 1943, pp. 77f., 117f.

What, in fact, we are studying is just that: *the abjuring of the use of force*, and its replacement by a more excellent way; by consent, by respect for minorities, by tolerance, by humanity, by tenderness towards sufferers, by the redemption of the wrongdoer: all of them expressions, manifestations, of Christian love. It is good to have this ultimately Christian motivation clearly recognized in the political sphere, in the background of parliamentary procedure and democratic government. Still in this sphere, it is not difficult to see how greatly the new conception of legal toleration by the State, first of religious toleration and then of toleration more generally, was influenced by the Christian tolerance first practised mutually in these same congregations. The radical Puritans not only claimed liberty of conscience for themselves, they granted it to one another, and on positive and Christian grounds. Both Christian faith and Christian practice they perceived to be essentially voluntary things, so that persecution crosses their very nature. Because it is freely given, redemption in Christ demands that those who accept it be free. Compulsion in religion not only makes hypocrites of the unwilling, it bruises and insults the willing mind. Convictions such as these, after many years' endurance of persecution, had their share in bringing about the Toleration Act of 1689; and that Act may be regarded as the beginning of a movement through which the use of force in English law to inhibit, punish or control social practice has been persistently reduced. It would not be fanciful to see some relation between the Toleration Act of 1689 and the fact that in Britain (save, alas, in Northern Ireland) the policeman goes unarmed.

Historically, the growth of toleration is important for us for this reason, that the abandonment of war between States will probably always be preceded by the abandonment of persecution within a State. We shall do well to remind ourselves how recently—by a historian's measurement—persecution has been abandoned (where it has been), and after what painful and long drawn out struggles. The burnings and tortures at Belsen or Auschwitz, or for that matter of

Hiroshima, are less startling, though not less horrible, when we realize that in Britain, though the last heretic to be burned died in 1612, a witch was burned in 1708 and a murderer (a woman) was burned in 1789; that torture was still legal and in use in Baden in 1831; and that in England hanging still took place in public until 1868. The road from mere revenge and vendetta to a justice less wild in retribution, from this to contentment if the wrongdoer can be restrained and potential wrongdoers deterred, and from this to an active concern for the wrongdoer's redemption and for the reform of the social conditions which lead to crime, is a long road; and the end of it is by no means yet in sight. We all too easily, if in one sense properly, tend to be impatient, to fail to see, for instance, that the Nürnberg trials after the last war, with all their faultiness, were, at least in form, an immense advance on any treatment previously meted out to a vanquished enemy. So also 'co-existence' as a newly recognized principle internationally may to some extent correspond to the 'toleration' within a single State during an earlier generation; and the 'token' arming of the United Nations Emergency Force may remind us of the 'unarmed' policeman.

CHRISTIAN HUMANITY

Many secular motives contribute to the recognition of national toleration or international co-existence: indifference, force of circumstances, fear of consequences. The gradual spread, despite many setbacks, of a humaner spirit in much of the world during the last four centuries owes much to our classical heritage and to the Renaissance as well as much to Christianity and the Reformation. Yet, in face of the recent reaction against humanism, as a form of liberalism fundamentally secular rather than religious, I deliberately included 'humanity' in my list, a few moments ago, of manifestations of Christian love. Let me quote from three Puritan tracts all published in London in 1647. Christ's rule, says one, is 'to winne men by instruction, and not to force men by destruction'. 'Compulsion,' says another, 'can no more gain the heart, than the fish can love the fisherman.' A third writer says that he would rejoice more 'to rescue one poor soul (in

273

gentleness and love) out of the prison of a corrupt opinion, than keep all the heretics under heaven, in the ward where Pharaoh's prisoners are bound, till their feet are hurt in the stocks, and the iron enter into their soul'.[1] There is an evangelical, a missionary quality in the writing of these men, one of whom was Solicitor-General to the Commonwealth of England and another Steward to Oliver Cromwell, which is altogether different from merely humanist productions. These men have a humanity which is Christian in inspiration. They are concerned 'to rescue . . . out of . . . prison'. The Quakers, especially, went under a perpetual sense of suffering for, and with, what they called the seed of God imprisoned and suffering within men, and believed God called them to give themselves utterly to working for its release. The early Quakers knew much of the inside of prisons in the literal sense; but George Fox, their leader, wrote to them so to behave that 'your imprisonments will reach to the prisoned, that the persecutor prisons in himself'; and looking back over his own life, he could say triumphantly, 'there was never any prisons or sufferings that I was in but still it was for the bringing multitudes more out of prison'[2]—in a spiritual sense, he means.

PENAL REFORM

It was, perhaps, this inveterate habit of thinking of men as spiritually imprisoned which led the Quakers, some generations later, to concern themselves so deeply with penal reform and the treatment of the insane. Most of us have no conception how great a revolution has taken place in these spheres: a revolution begun, and for long carried on, by a few Christian men and women wholly committed to their work, fearless, unassuming, seeking no reward for themselves, and unwearying in their faith, patience, and endurance. To say this is not to dramatize them. In the vulgar sense there is little dramatic about Elizabeth Fry, her 'Ladies' Prison Committees' and her rules for prisoners' self-government and self-help, rules remarkable in that no penalties were attached

---

[1] See my *Visible Saints: the Congregational Way, 1640–1660*, 1957, pp. 104, 121.
[2] George Fox, *Epistles*, ed. G. Whitehead, 1698, p. 80; *Journal*, ed. N. Penney, 1911, II. 338 (spelling modernized).

to them; or about her less well known predecessor, the tee-total, vegetarian, and Sabbatarian John Howard and his dryly matter-of-fact book on *The State of the Prisons in England and Wales*, which he visited methodically, riding about forty miles a day. What is striking about both these practical reformers, each of them a practising Christian, is their un-remitting persistence and the universality of their humanity. From 1818 till her final illness in 1843 Elizabeth Fry 'visited and organized *every* convict-ship that carried women prisoners to the colonies'.[1] When Acts for the amelioration of prison conditions were passed, John Howard had copies printed and sent, at his own expense, to *every* prison in the country; and on his tomb at Kherson, in Russia, where he died of plague, is (or was) the simple inscription addressed to the reader: 'Who-ever thou art, thou standest at the tomb of thy friend.'

ASYLUM, SCHOOL, AND HOME

The work of penal reform which Howard and Elizabeth Fry set in motion was but one form of the abjuring of force and violence in social relations. It included the abolition of both capital punishment and of corporal punishment, or at least the reduction of the number of offences to be punished by either punishment and the mitigation of corporal punish-ment, when still administered. Nor, of course, does penal reform stand alone. It was, and has continued to be, accom-panied by a concern for the insane, who, when William Tuke founded the Retreat at York in 1796, were prisoners— chained prisoners—of the madhouse, and for children, who, when the Earl of Shaftesbury started the movement from which (after fifty-five years) sprang the National Society for the Prevention of Cruelty to Children, were virtually prisoners of industry. Indeed, alongside the demonstration of Christian love in the treatment of criminals and the insane, the concept and practice of social relations in both family and school have been transformed. If brutality and corporal punishment were to be brought to an end within the prison and within the asylum, they must end no less within the school, which was often too much like a prison, and within

[1] Janet Whitney, *Elizabeth Fry: Quaker Heroine*, 1951 edn., p. 212 (my italics).

the home as well. The relationship of the master to his children, even of the father to his children, had to be altered. Absolute authority, and its expression in brute force, had to give way to tenderness, consideration, a respect for the personalities of the children, an encouragement to freedom. With these changes, revolutionary however gradual, there has also been, inevitably, a change in the position of women, whom, not less than their children, men have had to learn to respect as persons in their own right. Not one of these battles is yet won; many forces besides Christian convictions are at work; but in every case Christian convictions have played an active part both in changing public opinion and in shaping parliamentary legislation to express this.

THE RED CROSS

My illustrations have been from England; but in the centenary year of the battle of Solferino we have all, I imagine, read articles about the Genevese philanthropist, Henri Dunant, and the organization founded by him which has made the Swiss flag with the colours reversed, a white flag with a Red Cross, familiar to multitudes outside Switzerland. Howard and Elizabeth Fry were concerned for civil prisoners, nationally; Dunant, after witnessing the appalling sufferings at Solferino, for prisoners of war, internationally. As a matter of fact, Howard had himself been a prisoner of war for a short time in France; and a generation later the Frenchman, Etienne Grellet, who introduced Elizabeth Fry to the suffering women and children in Newgate prison, was visiting French prisoners of war in England before he entered Newgate. Concern for prisoners, in any case, is the common factor; as is the need for patience in the reformer. Not till 1882 was a branch of the Red Cross organization founded in the United States; as late as 1898 Britain was insisting on the exclusion of Red Cross rules from maritime warfare; in the last war the Red Cross convention for prisoners of war was still not ratified by either Russia or Japan.

The work initiated by Henri Dunant raises a moral problem. The Christian compassion behind the Red Cross we all acknowledge; but a society for the organization of humane laws of war?—for this was its purpose. Whether or not in wartime we have subscribed to the Red Cross, we in the I.F.o.R. are likely to be sensitive to the danger of 'humanizing', and thus in effect perpetuating, an evil institution instead of exposing it in all its viciousness with determination to abolish it. Is not the Red Cross in effect the handmaid of war?

SLAVERY

This is indeed a real issue; but it is not a new one. As we have been reminded, reforms are nearly always brought about piecemeal and by degrees over a very long period. The eventual abolition of capital punishment is gained by agitation to reduce the number of crimes regarded as capital; the possibility of an 'open' prison comes about only as the 'closed' prison is gradually humanized; the 'free' type of education is reached through the reduction of confinement, and of rules and penalties, in the traditional school. If it be said that schools and prisons, while not equally 'good', are neither of them evil in themselves, while war is wholly evil and to be abolished, I agree; but I would point to slavery as another institution now seen to be wholly evil, which, insofar as it was abolished (and in three countries it is still legal: in Saudi Arabia, Oman, and Yemen), was abolished in the same slow and undermining way as were the other evils we have considered, and fundamentally with the same motives and methods. Slaves, too, are 'prisoners'; and it was, again, Christian compassion and humanity which worked against slavery, and kept on working until, little by little, it was abolished. The American Quaker, John Woolman, whose name is outstanding in this matter, was (in a phrase of Rufus Jones')[1] 'palpitatingly sensitive to human suffering'. He was also as 'universal' as John Howard: do you know his noted phrase, 'to turn all we possess into the channel of universal love becomes the business of our lives'?[2] The first American society for the abolition of slavery was founded in 1775; it was eighty-eight years before all slaves in America were at last free. In Britain the pace was quicker, but there also the

[1] R. M. Jones, *The Later Periods of Quakerism*, 1921, I. 316.
[2] Quoted *ibid.*, from John Woolman, *A Word of Remembrance*, sect. iii.

series first of petitions and later of bills presented to Parliament over a period of fifty-five years teaches the same lesson: namely, that if evil is to be overcome by Christian love, it will take a very long time.

But in reference to the question raised by the Red Cross, the many *centuries* which elapsed before Christians began directly to attack the institution of slavery *at all* are what is relevant. We are inclined, if we think about it, to stand aghast that the Christian conscience was insensitive to this evil for so long. But in fact it was not as insensitive as we suppose. 'The essence of slavery,' if I may quote A. D. Lindsay again, 'is that it is based on force, on the denial of the rights and personality of the slave . . . But St Paul says that both slaves and masters are to ignore these assumptions. The slaves are to serve their masters as if they were serving Christ'; and 'Philemon is to receive back Onesimus "not now as a slave but above a slave—a brother beloved both in the flesh and in the Lord".' This was to 'humanize' slavery, was it not, not to abolish it? Yet 'to act like that' was also, as Lindsay comments, 'to undermine the whole institution of slavery . . . accepting it as an institution' but 'giving the lie to the assumptions . . . on which it is based'. It is relevant to note in passing that within ten years of the founding of Quakerism, a whole century before they began to agitate against slavery, it was said by one of them that among Quakers 'the mistress and maid are hail fellow well met'.

'The implication' which Lindsay draws from all this is that 'the best way to reform institutions is to accept their obligations and at the same time to act better than these demand.'[1] I cannot say whether he knew, or remembered, it or not, but he is in fact quoting a second-century anonymous Christian apologist who writes that 'Christians obey the laws prescribed but in their own lives *surpass the laws*'. We are 'to act better than these demand'. 'If ye salute your brethren only, what do ye more than others?' 'If ye love them that love you, what grace, what graciousness is there in that?' 'Better drivers give way.' 'Whosoever shall compel thee to go a mile, go two with him.' The Christian love which 'turns the flank of recalcitrant institutions' always has

[1] A. D. Lindsay, *The Two Moralities*, pp. 81 f.

something of this *two*, this *more*, this *extra*, this *giving way*
'always *abounding* in the work of the Lord' with an abundance, an overflow, which has its origin in the love of God
Himself.

NATIONAL SOVEREIGNTY

If we look at international relations, and the task of the
I.F.o.R. in the world today, in the light of these historical
studies, I believe that one of the next stages for which we
should work is the abandonment of national sovereignty—
eventually in practice but first in theory. In one sense the
theory of sovereignty as an essential mark of the State,
though assumed as self-evident, is relatively new. It is a
'modern doctrine which took its rise in the sixteenth century', 'a product of the times in which it gained pre-eminence'
'an admirable account of the absolutist states of that time . . .
based on the authority of the monarch, not on the authority
of law'.[1] In another sense, as a general idea applied to the
State, it is very old. The husband, the father, the school-
master, the gaoler, the madhouse keeper, the slave-owner
were all held to have absolute authority over the persons
within their control. So in more religious terms, as representing God (though the father also to some extent represented
God), had the abbot, the bishop, the archbishop, the pope;
so, in the sixteenth century, had the monarch—'the king is
in the room of God', said William Tyndale, 'and his law
is God's law,'[2] and so, in process of time, has Parliament or
the modern State: an absolute authority or sovereignty.
'Sovereignty is an exclusive or an all-or-nothing theory.'[3]
Now the States holding the theory most consistently in reference to internal affairs are the totalitarian régimes, and they
have taught us that at this level the theory of sovereignty
within a State must be abandoned. We have yet to learn that
it must be abandoned no less in international relations; and
abandoned not only because it will no longer work, but because here also it is an affront to God, who alone is Sovereign;
to Christ, who alone is Lord.

[1] A. D. Lindsay, *The Modern Democratic State*, pp. 213, 72, 213.
[2] Quoted *ibid.*, p. 73.
[3] *Ibid.*, p. 16.

As members of the I.F.o.R. we should, therefore, welcome paragraphs 53 and 54 of the provisional study document entitled 'Christians and the Prevention of War' issued by the World Council of Churches a year ago. 'Responsibilities which hitherto have been considered exclusively as functions of national sovereignty,' the writers say, 'must be internationalized'; 'the politically autonomous nation-state is no longer the last word in the organization of society'.

In paragraph 66 of the same document the writers recommend that, 'if all-out war should occur, Christians should urge a cease fire, if necessary on the enemy's terms, and resort to non-violent resistance', and in a note appended to the chapter containing this paragraph it is expressly recognized that 'non-violent resistance or non-resistance may mean decades of tyranny and suffering . . . but . . . all-out war . . . might be less justifiable than even the acceptance of defeat under the conditions imposed by a tyrannic victor.'

In a document compiled by a group containing only four pacifists out of fourteen, this is a remarkable admission. How much is implied by the word 'justifiable' is not made clear. It may be intended in a sense merely pragmatic. I should like to see the justification of the acceptance of defeat taken up and given a theological basis. The prophet Jeremiah might contribute to the argument. In the first year of this century a minister of religion in England, Dr Alexander Mackennal, said in a large assembly: 'until our advocates of peace apprehend that . . . martyrdom (of a nation) may be within the counsel of God, their advocacy will lack its final inspiration'. I believe this to be true.

POLITICAL ENSLAVEMENT

The suffering likely to issue from defeat on the enemy's terms (ruling out of consideration, which we have no right to do, its transforming power *if* accepted as a demonstration of Christian love) is now commonly spoken of, in reference to the sort of war envisaged, as slavery rather than martyrdom. It troubles me that to so many Christians enslavement should be a state they cannot contemplate, a state worse than death. No one is likely to regard enslavement with equanimity.

But, after all, very many, possibly even most, Christians in the Church's history *have* been slaves, or something very like it; and in those countries domination by which, it is assumed, would mean enslavement there are still Christians.

When I have made much of the demonstration of Christian love in working for the abolition of slavery, am I now inconsistent in suggesting that the demonstration of Christian love may mean a readiness to accept a form of enslavement? I do not think so. Christians work for the diminution of suffering generally; yet the true Christian knows that he must be willing himself to accept suffering cheerfully, vicariously, and redemptively; and slavery is but a form, albeit a very terrible form, of human suffering. The fact is that the undermining of the institution of slavery in the New Testament goes much further than in those passages which refer to it directly. In the New Testament the Christian ministry is described again and again as a form of enslavement: 'we preach not ourselves but Christ Jesus as Lord, and ourselves your slaves, for Jesus' sake'.

'And Jesus called them to him and saith unto them: Ye know that they who are accounted to rule over the nations lord it over them, and their great ones tyrannize over them. But so shall it not be among you. But whosoever will be great among you shall wait upon you; and whosoever of you will be first shall be everyone's slave. For even the Son of Man came not to be waited on but to do the waiting; and to give His life, to redeem many.' So far as I can see, this contrast between the ways of Christ's disciples and the ways of the rulers of the nations is not meant to be a wall of partition which nothing, not even the transforming power of Christ, can break down. It involves His disciples in a way of life which will be not only towards one another within the Church but eventually towards the rulers of the nations themselves. If that is so, I think we must work for the abandonment of sovereignty internationally as well as within the nation; and if this should bring about enslavement, the acceptance of it willingly and redemptively, would after all, be in line with the main burden of the Christian ethic.

Not that I think that any nation is at present ready to abandon its sovereignty; but no group, in family, school, gaol, what you will, ever has been, at the first; yet Christian love has been demonstrated; and by those faithful to their convictions, in time transformations, revolutions, have been accomplished.

1959

XXVI

THE JUSTIFICATION OF WAR—HOW THE CHURCH'S TEACHING HAS CHANGED

IT IS commonly said that, with the exception of a few small though respected communities such as the Society of Friends, the conviction that Christians are forbidden to go to war is very recent in the Church's history. In the main, this is correct. The Church lives in the world, and its members respond to the varying pressures of their time. The Church as a whole, like its members, has to keep its intelligence open to new light, its conscience sensitive to fresh moral claims. Initial infallibility or perfection was never granted to it.

Even so, after-generations find it surprising that institutions now universally condemned by Christians were so late in receiving the Church's disapproval. Especially has this been the case when the abandonment of an institution seriously undermined the structure of society. Slavery is a case in point. Today the owning of slaves is universally condemned, nor do Christians own slaves in practice. Yet for more than seventeen hundred years the number of Christians who were uneasy about slavery was negligible. The institution of war also is now increasingly, though not universally, condemned by the Church; but the Church still approves the profession of the soldier, and in preparing for war and, in the last resort, in waging war, governments know that they will meet with no effective opposition from the Church.

The slowness in the Church to condemn war, and even in the individual conscience, where social reforms commonly have their origin, becomes less surprising if we pass a number of considerations in review. Despite the deplorable amount of violence in the world today, the impact of which on us is increased by the new speed in communication, life till recently used to be very much harder than it is now (at least in the West). Infant and child mortality was terribly high, and very many of those who survived were cut off suddenly in later life. We forget how modern modern medicine is. The current interest in 'spiritual healing' could hardly have arisen before medicine transformed the conditions of life. The discovery of anaesthetics alone has revolutionized much of our moralizing. The causing of unnecessary pain did not carry the stigma now attaching to it so long as pain played a large and inevitable part in the natural order, and thus for Christians in the divine order. The Church did not condemn the use of torture as wrong.

A corresponding revolution has taken place in many institutions in society, such as the home, the school, the asylum, and the prison. Till recently, in the treatment of women, children, the insane, and criminals *force majeure*, even violence, were commonplace; and the state of fear caused by such treatment, and then encouraging it, was not only fostered but morally justified. Public flogging and public hanging were held to be proper and effective deterrents. The Church played on men's fear of hell to bring about their conversion, and on their fear of the stake to keep them orthodox.

We need, in fact, to recall how universal in the Church the practice of religious persecution was. The conception of the Church as the infallible and conscious possessor of revealed truth provided compassionate pastoral reasons for using force to convert or destroy heretics; but, had this conception been lacking, an authoritarian and hierarchic society such as till lately was to be found in most countries would still have practised compulsion in ways, and to a degree, which since the French and American Revolutions seems unnatural and will no longer be endured.

Furthermore, for by far the greater part of its history the Church itself has been conceived for practical purposes either as *something like* the State (even when seen as standing *over against* the State) or else as forming a single entity with the State in a State-Church or a Church-State. By birth or domicile all men belonged equally to both State and Church; and in return for the State's protection the Church blessed the State's institutions, including war. In the State men were familiar with compulsion, *force majeure*, violence, persecution, war. Until they began to see that even in the State all of these methods should be reduced as far as possible and for the

Church even the way of compulsion was closed, they were not likely to see that the way of war was closed too. That they had some inkling of this appears in their sense that *priests* should not shed blood. The abandonment of such a 'two-level' ethic at the Reformation opened the path to a higher common level, but also to a lower.

Seen in this light, the Church's slowness to condemn war is no longer surprising. What is surprising is that any Christian leaders, still more that any communities, should have stood so far outside the mental and moral context of the world they knew as to query war's justification. The Waldenses, who based their repudiation of war primarily on the prohibitions they found in the Sermon on the Mount, have preserved a tenuous and geographically limited existence since the twelfth century. More effective, continuous and widespread Christian pacifism begins with the Swiss Brethren in Zürich in the 1520's and their successors, the Mennonites. They saw the Church as, by its calling and in its mission, intended and bound to be a suffering Church: submitting to violence, and by submission absorbing and overcoming it, but never resorting to violence, nor *a fortiori* to war. This perception was utterly incompatible with the theory of Church-and-State as reverse and obverse of a single entity, and was therefore regarded as socially disruptive; and the story of the first Swiss Brethren is almost wholly a story of martyrdom. This is their glory. Their genius lay rather in that they worked out and stated their basic principle *before* they were persecuted. 'Neither do they use worldly sword or war, since by them killing is entirely abrogated.'

For in the main it was the experience of persecution from which, at last, men wrung out a sense of the nature of the Church as different from the State. In England the repudiation of the State's right to compel conscience thus preceded the repudiation of war. 'The Lords people is of the willing sorte', 'for it is the conscience and not the power of man that will driue vs to seeke the Lorde's kingdome'. This position had to be maintained by Robert Browne in the sixteenth century before the Quaker George Fox could venture in the seventeenth to universalize for the Church his own experience of 'that life and power that took away the occasion of all war' in the saying 'All dwelling in the light that comes from Jesus leads out of wars.' Earlier leaders, such as Wycliffe and Erasmus, had seen the inconsistency of saying 'Our Father' and at the same time waging war. Fox's special contribution was in his missionary impulse. To the patience, forbearance, and willingness to suffer already exhibited by the Swiss Brethren, Fox added a love 'to them all that had persecuted me' and a 'reaching of God in every man' that might change the evil mind into the right mind. Those whose everyday lives are lived in the light of this costly but rewarding endeavour could not, and cannot, suddenly nullify their faith on the outbreak of war.

Fox also founded a community of Friends who shared his vision and took its application seriously. Since William Penn made his treaty with the American Indians it has been impossible to relegate the vision to the sphere of what politically can have no practical significance. The pacifist witness of the Mennonites and Quakers has slowly but effectively permeated the Church as a whole, till the World Council of Churches has found itself able at least to agree to the theorem that 'war is contrary to the will of God'. But more than this, in their equally unremitting efforts for Christian education, for penal reform, for the care of the insane, for the emancipation of slaves, as well as in their own absorption of persecution, Friends and those who have worked with them have so affected other institutions and practices in Christian ways that war now stands out as the last enemy.

In doing so, they have in effect taken up the Christian task at the point where the early Church laid it down. For, though the interpretation of the facts is disputed, it seems certain that in the first two centuries virtually no Christians served in the army, and that the soldier's profession was not approved for some time longer. In those first centuries the Church was in no position to persuade the State to abandon warfare. What it did was, rather, so far as possible to bring Christian influence to bear upon institutions open to it, such as slavery, and to refuse those which were not, such as war. In 313 Christianity became the religion of the State. Thus began the Church-and-State complex which has persisted, secularizing

286

the Church's institutions and inhibiting the Christian conscience. Its weakening throughout the modern world should make the Church more open to pacifist conviction. Thus in England Dr Ramsey, who is almost the first Archbishop of Canterbury to question the accepted interdependence of Church and State in national politics and ethics, is also the first Archbishop to question the sovereignty of the State in international affairs.

1964

XXVII

THE CHURCH'S MINISTRY OF SUFFERING

*N*o *Cross, No Crown*, says Penn tersely. 'Oh how great a part of Christianity is it to understand and rightly bear the cross!' says Richard Baxter; 'Oh! little, too little, do many honest Christians think how much of their most excellent obedience consisteth in child-like, holy suffering.'[1] Today we think it even less. The purpose of this paper is, first, to recall the prominence of suffering in the ministry of Jesus and in the life and witness to which, in the New Testament, all Christians are called; secondly, to suggest that as the Suffering Messiah Jesus is like an alembic through which the ministry of the Ideal Israel, the Suffering Servant, passes and issues, continuing but transformed, in the ministry of the New Israel, the Suffering Church; and thirdly, to indicate, with special reference to the Swiss Brethren and the English Quakers, that such an interpretation of the Divine revelation and purpose demands the repudiation by Christians of war.

Throughout the Christian centuries the Passion of Jesus has been the object of continuous and intensive study. Often, however, attention has been concentrated on the sufferings involved in His death and in the experiences which immediately preceded His death, to the neglect alike of the element of suffering in His ministry as a whole and of the suffering which both He and St Paul after Him regarded as a distinguishing mark in the lives of His disciples. This neglect may be attributed in part to a mistaken reverence, which has dreaded any tendency to stress His common humanity or to weaken the conviction of His uniqueness; in part to an allied assumption, which has its origins in Greek philosophy rather than in biblical religion, that Divinity cannot suffer; in part also, at certain periods, to the lessening of one form of suffer-

[1] R. Baxter, *Dying Thoughts*, 1683, Appendix.

ing in Christian experience, through the cessation of persecution, whether by pagans or by other Christians. It remains neglect, none the less.

More generally, orthodoxy has looked with disfavour on those who have sought to base their Christology on Jesus' character and personality rather than on philosophical presuppositions regarding the nature of Deity and the nature of unity. Yet unless, first, Jesus had been the sort of person He was, neither the claims nor the problems of Christology would have arisen. Nor is it possible to give even a cursory glance at His ministry without realizing how varied but continuing a factor in it suffering was, suffering so often disclosed, indeed, as to suggest much more left unrevealed. The suffering with which we are concerned in this paper is not the suffering which came to Him, as it comes to us all, in virtue of our humanity—

> The heart-ache and the thousand natural shocks
> That flesh is heir to.

Our concern is with the suffering which came to Jesus through His being the kind of person He was and through His living the kind of life He did live, and which will continue to come to those who seek to live in the power of His endless life. Not that we find that Jesus ever sought suffering or thought of suffering as something good in itself. On the contrary, He sought constantly to relieve suffering, to cure it, or to prevent it. But equally He treated it as something not to be avoided or run away from. For Jesus suffering is something to be accepted and used quietly, patiently, triumphantly, as part of the method, part of the cost, of being allowed by God to be, in filial obedience to Himself, an instrument of His redeeming love towards men.

Outwardly, Jesus' ministry involved suffering from near the outset. It is not necessary to make of Him something so near an automaton as to suppose that He saw the end of His ministry from the beginning. 'Rather should we think of him as sensitive always to the divine direction, from situation to situation, and obedient ever thereto.'[1] Nor need we picture Him as so inhuman as to begin His ministry without hope of a better response than in the event was given to Him; though

[1] E. L. Allen, *The Purpose of Jesus*, 1951, p. 19.

we remember that He knew His Scriptures and the descriptions there of the lot which regularly befell the prophets. But what initial hopes He may have had were quickly dashed. Already in the second and third chapters of Mark's Gospel, not only is He 'drawing on himself hostility, as soon as his purpose is apparent', from the scribes and Pharisees and Herodians, He is also 'in the isolation of love continually misunderstood'[1] by His own family and friends. Such misunderstanding must have been hard; but 'of all his disappointments the greatest must have been when one from the inner circle of his followers went out into the night to betray him'.[2] 'Consider what it meant for our Lord to pray for Simon, that He should not lose all. But when we do consider, we are in depths where all our thoughts are drowned.'[3]

Even apart from this opposition, misunderstanding and betrayal, it is impossible not to see how costing (to use von Hügel's word) Jesus' ministry was. We see Him wrestling all night in prayer to God. We see Him battling with His own will to bring it into conformity with God's will—in Gethsemane but, surely, not only there. Above all, Jesus' ministry is a ministry of suffering simply because it is a true ministry. He is always ready of compassion and sympathy (both of them words implying suffering if their meaning is more than formal), caring so deeply as to weep over the Jerusalem which rejected Him.

'To seek and to save' one single lost character is to set out upon the longest and hardest journey known to human experience, with no guarantee that the search will be rewarded or that our strength will hold out to the end.

Unlike us, Jesus had none of the protection of indifference against the needs of others; nor was it possible for Him at any time to disclaim responsibility or say that any man's need was not His affair. He was more sensitive and discerning than the best of us, and, with 'the most vulnerable heart in the world,'

[1] I venture to apply to Jesus Himself these phrases used in description of the Christian by A. N. Brayshaw, *The Quakers: their Story and Message*, 3rd edn., 1938, pp. 194f.
[2] E. L. Allen, *op. cit.*, p. 19; it is perhaps worth noting that the ὡρισμένον of *Luke* xxii. 22 appears to be no more than Luke's development of γέγραπται in *Mark* xiv. 21.
[3] W. R. Maltby, *Christ and His Cross*, 6th edn., 1948, p. 69.

never faltered in the constancy and courage of His sympathy.

Any man, any woman, who encountered Jesus any day, might leave with Him a fresh burden even to tears.

'To seek and to save that which was lost' imposed a burden upon Him from which His love never drew back, but which the human frame, dependent as it is on brain and nerve, and subject to exhaustion when the due limits are passed, could not indefinitely endure. The records, I believe, indicate that He knew this Himself.

'O faithless generation, how long shall I bear with you! how long shall I be with you!' It is the cry of a nature strained to the utmost limit, and uncertain how long strength will hold out. The cup was not yet full, but it was filling. . . . 'Sorrowful unto death' is His word, and we must not allow it to be weakened to a conventional phrase. . . . While yet no scourge had touched His flesh nor any hand of violence been laid upon Him, He was pressed to the very edge of physical collapse by an inward sorrow which had nothing to do with bodily pain, but only with the sin of men whom it was His to save.[1]

'I have a baptism to be baptized with, and in what constraint I am till I am through with it!'

This ministry of suffering Jesus not only accepted for Himself, He expected it of His disciples likewise. When He asked James and John, 'Can you drink of the cup that I drink of? and be baptized with the baptism that I am baptized with?' they replied, 'We can.' To this He did not reply, as He had said when they had asked for seats in His glory, that they did not know what they were talking about; on the contrary, He accepted their ability and willingness to share His sufferings as part of their discipleship and ministry. Again, 'If Peter had kept his word and gone with his Lord to the death, would Jesus have sent him away, saying he did not want that? I cannot think it. Surely what he hoped was that they would be willing to share his pain and to drink his cup, to continue with him to the very end of his earthly trials.'[2]

Nor dare we limit this narrowly to those sufferings which led to Jesus' death and might have led to the disciples', as in

[1] W. R. Maltby, *op. cit.*, pp. 66, 74, 72, 68f., 76f.

[2] E. L. Allen, *op. cit.*, p. 43. Perhaps this should be amended to 'what he had hoped': by the time of Peter's bold words, and indeed earlier, it appears that Jesus clearly foresaw that He would be forsaken.

later days they often did. 'The fellowship of his sufferings', as it came to be called, was to be far wider than that. Those who had continued with Him as His friends in His own temptations He called to watch and pray, that they entered not into temptation themselves; to agonize to enter into the kingdom as He had agonized in the pangs of its coming-in. Above all, He called them to be Good Samaritans, showing compassion to any in need, going the extra mile, praying for their persecutors, washing the feet of those who betrayed them—in short, to live as He lived and consequently to expect, to accept at God's hand and to use the suffering inseparable from such a life of ministry.

After His own death and resurrection much of what Jesus asked for came to pass. To the apostles outward persecution came soon, as it had come to Him, and they rejoiced that they were counted worthy to suffer shame for His name. Stephen was stoned to death, but dying prayed forgiveness for his murderers. So, when Ananias sought the divine reassurance that he was not mistaken in welcoming the persecutor Saul into the fellowship, 'I will show him,' it was said, 'how great things he must suffer for my name's sake'—not *do*, but *suffer*—strange words, but fulfilled throughout Paul's ministry.

For to Paul, as to Jesus, came, outwardly, perils, losses and persecutions such as are described by him in his second letter to the Corinthians. 'We are made as the filth of the world and the offscouring of all things.' 'I am ready not only to be bound but even to die for the name of the Lord Jesus.' Inwardly, too, Paul knew the suffering involved in the tireless bodily discipline required if power over the will is to be gained and retained, knew the experience of what he can call being crucified to the world and dying to sin. And for Paul, as for Jesus, suffering, both outward and inward, could have redemptive character. 'If we are afflicted, it is for your comfort and salvation.' 'Now I rejoice in sufferings on your behalf.' It is because he accepts persecution on behalf of others that he can write, 'I am exceeding joyful in all our tribulations.' 'Longsuffering with joy' is a strange combination, hardly to be found or even expected outside the society of Christ's redeemed and redeeming ones, but it is what Paul knows in his own experience and can pray for in his converts.

No one will seek persecution; but if it comes, it is to be welcomed as a means of ministry, of witnessing to Christ before those who do not believe and also of strengthening and encouraging the faith of those who do, especially when they are still babes in Christ.

To the suffering not put upon him from without by persecutors, but present as an integral element in the ministry of seeking, saving, and serving, Paul makes many references no less telling. 'The love of Christ constrains us!'—it is the same word as in Jesus' cry, 'In what constraint I am!' 'I seek not yours, but you!' 'My little children, of whom I am in birth-pangs again till Christ be formed in you.' 'Very gladly will I spend and be spent for you! And if the more abundantly I love you, the less I am loved, what matter!' Paul even says that he is willing to enslave himself to everyone that he may gain the more for Christ. And he expects others to do likewise. 'For we that are strong ought to bear the infirmities of the weak, and not to please ourselves. Christ did not please himself.' 'Bear one another's burdens, and so fulfil Christ's law.' These exhortations are familiar, but we do not always appreciate that they mean suffering. True, all is to be done, these sufferings too are to be accepted, with joy, in the power of the risen and triumphant Lord; but they would not be accepted at all, were not that risen and triumphant Lord one with the patient and suffering Jesus of Nazareth, who came to minister, to seek and to save, who loved us and gave Himself for us, not only in His dying but in the way He lived.

One of the insights given to biblical scholars of recent years has been a recovered sense of the unity within the Bible as a whole and of the continuity of the People of God as a community with its own life and character. The old question 'Did Jesus found the Church?' has lost much of its meaning. The Church as an institution, with all the detailed organization which has developed in the course of the centuries, was no doubt not in His thought; but the Church as a Divine Fellowship He did not need to found, it was there already in the ideal purified Israel, the holy remnant, of which the Christian Church is the continuation, the new Israel. The two friends on the road to Emmaus have not been alone in being slow of heart and lacking in understanding. The idea of a Suffering Messiah, of Christ Crucified, was something not only new but horrible, a distracting obstacle, as to an orthodox Jew it still remains. Yet deep in the tradition of the ideal Israel, there can be no denying, is suffering: outward suffering and inward suffering, suffering borne in filial obedience and suffering accepted for the help and salvation of others. 'The prophet is a fool, the spiritual man is mad.' 'So persecuted they the prophets which were before you.' 'Ye do always resist the Holy Ghost.' Over the sufferings put upon the prophets, as over the sufferings of Israel more generally, there is no need to linger. Saintliness in a sinful world is bound to be abnormal and to suffer the pains of abnormality. But near the beginning of Israel's story is one figure to whom it is worth calling attention. The story of Abraham and Isaac it has become customary for Christian preachers to expound in terms of Abraham's faith and obedience; but for Jewish piety, at least equally with Abraham, Isaac has been the story's hero, Isaac the protomartyr, offering himself so meekly and willingly, in absolute filial trust, though found guilty of no sin. Rembrandt, it would seem, here as elsewhere reveals the influence of his Jewish contacts: in more than one of his paintings of the scene it is on Isaac the self-sacrificing that the unearthly light falls.[1] This story Jesus knew. We cannot tell how far it influenced Him; but later Christian interpreters have not been altogether fanciful in taking Isaac as a type, or forerunner, of Jesus.[2] Willingness to suffer, to die even, is a mark of the Only Son, the Beloved,[3] in the Old Testament too.

[1] *Cf.* Richard Hamann, *Rembrandt*, 1948, pp. 26of., on the painting of this scene in the Hermitage at Leningrad, and p. 370 on a drawing of it: 'Im klar geformten Körper Isaaks mit seiner in Knicken sich abspielenden Beugung kommt gespannte Erwartung und Ergebung, Gehorsam und Freiwilligkeit grossartig zum Ausdruck. Er ist sich der Grösse des Opfers bewusst, opfert sich selbst.'

[2] *Cf.* David Lerch, *Isaaks Opferung christlich gedeutet, eine auslegungsgeschichtliche Untersuchung*, 1950. Isaac as a type of Jesus may be found in seventeenth-century English hermeneutics, in *e.g.* Thomas Goodwin, *Works*, 1863 edn., V.225, and Stephen Charnock, *Works*, 1866 edn., V. 45.

[3] The word יָחִיד in *Gen.* xxii. 2 is translated ἀγαπητός in the LXX, but μονογενής by Aquila, both of them words treated as *termini technici* in relation to Jesus.

The figure which undoubtedly did deeply affect the vision and purpose of Jesus is the Isaianic figure of the Servant of the Lord. Part of the message of Israel's prophets is that 'a human "sympathy" with the "pathos" or emotion of God' is possible. 'The prophet so far shares in the whole personal relation of God to His people and the world, and by this fellowship in experience the mind and heart of God are made known to him.'[1] This message finds its finest expression in the Servant of the Lord, who like Isaac is brought as a sheep to the slaughter, and into whose sufferings the vicarious, redemptive element enters prominently, adding a depth of meaning at first sight[2] absent from Isaac's sacrifice. The suffering Servant does not break the bruised reed or quench the smoking flax: he bears our griefs and carries our sorrows. This ideal figure influenced Jesus so profoundly that, in the words of T. W. Manson, 'his life and death can only be understood as the deliberate and consistent working out of these ideals'.[3] Moreover, as we noted earlier in a similar connexion, it is not for Himself alone that Jesus adopts the ideal. 'He calls on his disciples to accept it as he accepts it, and to be prepared to share this destiny with him. This is the way the Rule of God works: there is no alternative way.'[4] He could do so the more naturally in that the figure of the Servant of the Lord itself 'portrays the life of a community, a community which realizes its destiny as the people of God in the measure in which it accepts the burden of service and sacrifice'.[5]

This feeling of oneness with others and of concern for their deepest good, this willingness to share in the consequence of

[1] H. Wheeler Robinson, in *Congregational Quarterly* for July 1937 (xv. 3), p. 384, reviewing Abraham Heschel, *Die Prophetie*, 1936. Dr Robinson adds: 'Such a position, of course, involves the complete rejection of the doctrine of divine impassibility, which we owe to Greek thought; this is all to the good.'

[2] But 'l'exégèse judaïque du récit [du sacrifice d'Isaac] se cristallise autour de l'idée de la puissance rédemptrice du sacrifice, de la souffrance et de la mort, quand le juste les accepte volontairement' : Harald Riesenfeld, *Jésus Transfiguré*, 1947, p. 87 (from a chapter on 'Le Messie Souffrant').

[3] T. W. Manson, *The Beginning of the Gospel*, 1950, p. 23. For criticism of too narrowly relating Jesus' consciousness to the Suffering Servant in particular, see M. D. Hooker, *Jesus & the Servant*.

[4] T. W. Manson, *op. cit.*, p. 60, in comment on *Mark* viii. 34 ff. Professor Manson adds : 'And it does work. The Crucified Messiah is the great undefeated figure in world history.'

[5] *Ibid.*, p. 22.

others' wrongdoing in a ministry of suffering is thus deep in biblical religion as a whole. It is so because the God of the Bible as a whole, not only the God of Jesus, has these characters. 'In all their affliction he was afflicted, and the angel of his presence saved them; in his love and in his pity he redeemed them; and he bore them, and carried them all the days of old.' Nor only of old, but still: 'Even to your old age I am he; and even to hoar hairs will I carry you; I have made, and I will bear; even I will carry, and I will deliver you.' That is the gospel of the Old Testament; and it is because God is like that that, having loved His own which were in the world, having compassion on them as sheep without a shepherd, Jesus loved them unto the end.

We have already looked forward into the life of the primitive Church and have seen how, under St Paul's inspiring leadership, the life of the community did, at first, contain and continue something of the ideal, of the ministry of suffering, as this had been actualized in Jesus the Suffering Servant. Outwardly, persecution continued to be the Christians' lot, and the martyrs' blood proved a seed; while within the fellowship was a mutual ministering care, with all the suffering this never fails to carry with it, care of a quality to evoke the wondering words, 'See how these Christians love one another!' We see now how this willingness to suffer, while inspired by Jesus, was true to the earlier biblical tradition. When Paul writes to Philemon of the runaway slave Onesimus, 'If he oweth thee anything, put that on my account' he is in the line of Judah, who said to his father of Benjamin, 'If I bring him not unto thee, and set him before thee, then let me bear the blame for ever.' Or at a deeper level, when Paul cries, 'I could wish that myself were accursed, separated from Christ, for the sake of my brethren the Jews', standing beside, or before, him is the sublime figure of Moses beseeching God for Israel's forgiveness and adding, 'If thou wilt not forgive them, then blot me out of thy book of life.'

But all too soon, as the Church became an established and triumphant institution, with the power of the State behind it, the situation changed completely. 'The history of the Fourth Century is . . . largely taken up with Court-bishops, theological controversy, and a lowering of Christian standards

whether of worship or of morals.'[1] 'Few Councils but were
disgraced by violence and party spirit.'[2] In monasticism the
old martyr spirit found a place, and an honoured place, as
'the religious life' *par excellence* within the Church; but asceticism, however excellent as self-discipline, is not identical
with suffering borne on others' behalf. In early monasticism
at least, 'the social selfishness' which he finds there is described by one writer by no means unsympathetic to monastic
ideals as 'so complete that at times it becomes sublime'.[3] In
later centuries the ministry of suffering was part of the attraction of the Little Poor Man of Assisi, as well as of sporadic
movements less successfully kept within the fold; but any
penetration behind the existing ecclesiastical framework of
comfort and power, any return to the conception of a Church
which as part of its nature expected and accepted suffering
by all its members, was hardly possible without a revolution.
From Constantine's time onward, 'the alliance of Church
and State, bringing with it huge benefits . . . had brought
also its notorious penalty, nominal churchmanship'.[4] Moreover, 'when Church and State had become co-extensive, the
corporate sense, which had in part depended upon the naked
opposition between Church and society and the protest of
the Church against society, begins to fade, perhaps never
fully to be recovered until the recognition of the modern age
that Christian and citizen are no longer synonymous terms'.[5]
Not until the revolution of the Reformation, partly because
not until then could ordinary men freely study the Bible for
themselves in their own language, was there any effective
attempt to go behind the Constantinian façade of the State-
Church and to recover a Church which might be free from
association with the State to live according to its own, often
different, principles. Even then the perception that by its
nature the Church should be a suffering Church was granted
but to a few extremists, such as one group of the Anabaptists,

[1] B. J. Kidd, *A History of the Church to A.D. 461*, 1922, II. 190 (the word
omitted is 'so'). There were, of course, redeeming features, which Dr Kidd is at
pains to point out.

[2] *Ibid.*, II. 27.

[3] H. B. Workman, *The Evolution of the Monastic Ideal*, 1913, p. 58.

[4] Owen Chadwick, *John Cassian: a study in primitive monasticism*, 1950, pp. 3f.

[5] *Ibid.*, p. 180.

more properly known as the Swiss Brethren, and in the following century, here in England, to the radical group known as the Quakers.

'The Anabaptist vision', as a leading Mennonite historian, Professor Harold S. Bender, has recently presented it,

> included three major points of emphasis; first, a new conception of the essence of Christianity as discipleship; second, a new conception of the church as a brotherhood; and third, a new ethic of love and nonresistance.
>
> An inevitable corollary of the concept of the Church as a body of committed and practicing Christians pledged to the highest standard of New Testament living was the insistence on the separation of the church from the world, that is nonconformity of the Christian to the worldly way of life.
>
> A logical outcome of the concept of nonconformity to the world was the concept of the suffering church. Conflict with the world was inevitable for those who endeavored to live an earnest Christian life.
>
> The church would always be a suffering church.[1]

On the basis of our earlier analysis it would seem difficult to deny that these convictions, including the last of them, are nearer to the ideal Israel or Church of God in Scripture, with its Crucified Messiah, than more conventional Christianity has been or is.

It is probably true, as Dr Bender suggests, that the Swiss Brethren were assisted in the formation of their revolutionary teaching by the persecution which they endured, the fact that they were persecuted by a State-Church, for instance, leading them to repudiate the conception of a State-Church on principle. It is no less true that a State-Church and a Suffering Church would seem to involve a contradiction *in adjecto*. Again, an unsympathetic observer might remark that in their

[1] H. S. Bender, *The Anabaptist Vision* (reprinted from *The Mennonite Quarterly Review* for April 1944), 1949, pp. 13, 18, 23; *cf.* H. S. Bender, *Conrad Grebel, c. 1498–1526: The Founder of the Swiss Brethren Sometimes Called Anabaptists*, 1950, p. 276, n. 77, quoting Grebel's words, 'Rechte glaubige Christen sind schaff mitten under den wölffen, schaff der schlachtung, müssend in angst und nott, trübsal, verfolgung, liden und sterben getoufft warden' and 'Und ob du darumb liden müsstest, weist wol, dass es nit anderss mag sein. Christus muss noch mer liden in sinen glideren.'

acceptance of suffering the Swiss Brethren were doing no more than making the best of difficult circumstances:

quicquid erit, superanda omnis fortuna ferendo est.

It is certainly possible to practise the gospel of love for the brethren within the Church and still to show nothing warmer than resignation towards persecutors, accepting the suffering inflicted by them as the will of God but not seeing in it an opportunity of ministry towards them, of reconciliation, redemption and victory. Even this, however, is a notable advance on the resentment and retaliatory spirit towards those who do us wrong which mars too much of Christian history, whether past or contemporary. It is at least nearer to the endurance and longsuffering which Paul practised and advocated, to the meekness of the Servant of the Lord who 'shall not strive, nor cry'. But it still does not go far enough.

The English Quakers, like the Swiss Brethren, were bitterly persecuted. They also repudiated the State-Church in favour of a Suffering Church. But from the beginning they accepted suffering not with resignation but gladly and willingly as part of the ministry of reconciliation laid upon all Christians. 'Look not at your sufferings but at the power of God,' wrote their leader, George Fox, 'and that will bring some good out in all your sufferings; and your imprisonments will reach to the prisoned, that the persecutor prisons in himself.'[1] Early in his *Journal* Fox tells how, after a violent attack upon him by a mob, 'I was in the love of God to them all that had persecuted me.'[2] Another Friend, Isaac Penington, records similarly how in prison he was filled 'with love to, and prayers for, those who had been the means of outwardly afflicting me and others upon the Lord's account'.[3]

> When people came to smash up Friends' meetings, sometimes with shocking cruelty, the men, while uttering their protest against the wrong, did not put up a fight and the women did not call on the men to protect them, because what they cared most about was the bringing home to those people a sense

[1] George Fox, *Epistles*, ed. G. Whitehead, 1698, p. 80.
[2] George Fox, *Journal*, ed. N. Penney, 1911, I. 58 (spelling modernized).
[3] Isaac Penington, *Works*, 1681, I. 406.

of their evil-doing, 'reaching that of God in them,' as they put it, and sometimes they were successful. . . . It was this result and not their own safety that those men and women held to be the more important. They could not compel their persecutors to refrain from evil, but they took the *most likely* way to bring home to them a sense of it.[1]

Sometimes, it is important to notice, they were successful. ' "Here is gospel for thee," ' said Fox once to a man who threatened him, ' "here is my hair and here is my cheek and here is my shoulders," and turned it to him . . . and the truth came so over him that he grew loving.'[2] This kind of thing happened, indeed, so often that, looking back, Fox could write, 'And there was never any persecution that came but we saw it was for good, and we looked upon it to be good, as from God; and there was never any prisons or sufferings that I was in but still it was for the bringing multitudes more out of prison.'[3]

Now it is only honest to observe that both the Swiss Brethren and the English Quakers also insisted on the repudiation of war by Christians, and that they were impelled to such insistence by their interpretation of the Gospel of the Redeemer and by their experience of His power. Christians, wrote Conrad Grebel, the leader of the Swiss Brethren, 'use neither worldly sword nor war, for among them killing is done away with altogether'.[4] Grebel had been much influenced by Erasmus, but a comparison between Erasmus' teaching with regard to war and Grebel's teaching reveals a sharp difference between them.[5] Again, 'much has been said and written about "a Sermon on the Mount ethic" among the Anabaptists'; but Grebel never quotes it. 'Grebel bases his rejection of the sword and war and of killing as a whole,

[1] A. N. Brayshaw, in *A. Neave Brayshaw: Memoir and Selected Writings*, ed. R. Davis and R. C. Wilson, 1941, pp. 133f.
[2] George Fox, *Journal*, II. 4.
[3] *Ibid.*, II. 338.
[4] 'Sy gebruchend weder weltlichs schwert nach krieg, wann by inen ist dass töten gar abgetan': H. S. Bender, *Conrad Grebel*, pp. 179 and 276, n. 75.
[5] 'The Erasmian pacifism was primarily humanitarian in character and not theological and biblical. The one argument against participation in war which Grebel used in his letter to Müntzer, the argument of "the suffering church", is not only not found in Erasmus, but is at the opposite pole from his position': *ibid.*, p. 201.

not upon the specific teaching of the Sermon on the Mount but upon the thought of the suffering church.'[1] It springs directly from his major insight.

Much the same is true of George Fox and the Quakers. Like the Swiss Brethren, the Quakers applied in the sphere of warfare what they had learned to practise in the school of persecution. Their repudiation of war springs, at least in part, from their perception that suffering remains an integral part of Christians' mission, ministry and witness to the world.

> The Quaker testimony concerning war does not set up as its standard of value the attainment of individual or national safety, neither is it based primarily on the iniquity of taking human life, profoundly important as that aspect of the question is. It is based ultimately on the conception of 'that of God in every man' to which the Christian in the presence of evil is called on to make appeal, following out a line of thought and conduct which, involving suffering as it may do, is, in the long run, *the most likely* to reach to the inward witness and so change the evil mind into the right mind. This result is not achieved by war.[2]

It is well to note the words italicized in this and in an earlier passage, *the most likely*. The italics are not the present writer's. They represent the honest realism of the Quaker writer, who would not claim too much, and who could also write, 'If you are on the side of Christ in His work for the world's healing, you will know far more defeats than victories if you are only going to count the number of times':[3] words which may remind us again that ' "To seek and to save" one single lost character is to set out upon the longest and hardest journey known to human experience, with no guarantee that the search will be rewarded or that our strength will hold out to the end.' The way of the Suffering Church, that is to say, remains, as it should, a way of faith.

[1] *Ibid.*, p. 179.

[2] A. N. Brayshaw, *op. cit.*, p. 131. I owe to this work some of the Quaker quotations in this paper.

[3] A. N. Brayshaw, in *Memoir*, p. 59. It should be remarked that it is not because the ministry of suffering is the most likely to be successful that it is right, as if it were a matter of expediency. On the contrary, it is because it is right that, in the long run, it is the most likely to be successful.

'But,' the Quaker writer continues, 'once in a while you will have your share in a victory which makes up for many defeats.' And with this we may return to the New Testament. For Jesus, when speaking of His sufferings, nearly always speaks also of His resurrection. If we are to suppose that He did not know just when or how the sufferings would come which would lead to His death, the same must have been even truer of His resurrection; yet clearly He has faith that He will come through. The suffering is not, in the Divine purpose, the end. For the joy that was set before Him He endured the cross. The way of the cross is the way of glory: *via crucis via lucis*. The very quality of the love which drew Him to suffer also brought Him back in risen glory and made Him Lord in the hearts of men, by His Spirit still redeeming them from evil and drawing them to Himself till the end of time. In an image drawn from slave-emancipation, we were bought with a price, and what a price, but the purpose was achieved, and we are free! The Suffering Messiah is also *Christus Victor* as in no other way He could have been. So for us, His followers, *No Cross, No Crown*; but, if we accept His way, God's way, of the love which is willing to suffer, we are *most likely* 'once in a while' to have the share in His victory which will be our noblest crown.

The reason why so far, in the history of the world, the Church's ministry of suffering has never been practised on the national level, where wars are fought and lost, is simple. It is because it is a ministry which none will dare to attempt save Christians in the power of their Lord, and no nation, as a nation, is, or has been, Christian. Yet most nations today, including our own, have Christians within them; and even in war-time, as William Temple had the courage to remark, Christians remain Christians first and nationals second. The Suffering Israel: The Suffering Servant: the Suffering Messiah: the Suffering Church. If in truth there is a continuity here which is vital to the Gospel of the Redeemer, and if we are constrained to honour as true to its message the attitude towards persecutors adopted by the Swiss Brethren and the Quakers, are we not bound to weigh more seriously the rightness of what to them has seemed but the next step, hardly indeed so much? Are we not bound, with them, to refuse to take part in war, whatever suffering this may involve, and whether or not the Lord deliver us or, like Israel of old, we are carried into captivity? In the noble words of Isaac Penington:

> I could say in the joy of my heart, and in the sense of the good-will of my God to us, who suffereth these things to come to pass; *Go on; try it out with the Spirit of the Lord; come forth with your laws and prisons and spoiling of our goods and banishment and death (if the Lord please), and see if ye can carry it.* For we come not forth against you in our own wills, or in any enmity against your persons or government, or in any stubbornness or refractoriness of spirit; but with the Lamb-like nature which the Lord our God hath begotten in us, which is taught and enabled by Him, both to do His will and to suffer for His namesake. And if we cannot thus overcome you (even in patience of spirit, and in love to you), and if the Lord our God please not to appear for us, we are content to be overcome by you.[1]

1954

---

[1] Isaac Penington, *loc. cit.*

XXVIII

A CORNISH CHILDHOOD

I HAD the leisure yesterday between dawn and dusk to read *A Cornish Childhood*[1] from cover to cover. Autobiographies benefit more than most books from being read thus uninterruptedly. The bird's eye view gives the reader a sense of integration which, in the nature of the case, is not recoverable by the author.

A Cornish Childhood is perhaps the best autobiography of its kind—going no further, that is, than earlier adolescence—since Joyce's *Portrait*. In recent years autobiographies of childhood have not been few. They tend, however, to concentrate, finely but excessively, on the childly side of childhood; a particular phase which commends itself to the author's adult imagination is made definitive and is used as a single starting-point for several descriptive excursions; there is no sense of growth; it is all looking back, however disguised. It is the distinction of *A Cornish Childhood*, as of *Portrait of the Artist*, that there is no amused adult gaze, riveting, freezing development; childhood and adolescence are here, not only in all their seriousness but with the atmosphere of growth and expectation which is of their essence, and which is so difficult to recapture. Mr Rowse has been helped in its recapture by his exceptional memory and by the historical temperament; perhaps also by something more Celtic which he shares with Joyce, namely the feeling that what took place thirty years ago is as *real* as what is happening today, and that the mere passage of time is no reason for either forgetting or forgiving.

It is just this which makes *A Cornish Childhood* so live; so bitter (though too conscious of triumph to be embittered) and so scornful, but so live. The story is of an unwanted child in a working-class home and in a house without water laid

[1] A. L. Rowse, *A Cornish Childhood*, Cape, 1942. This essay was written on 5 November 1942 and has not been previously published. Meanwhile A. L. Rowse has continued his autobiography in *A Cornishman at Oxford*, Cape 1965.

304

on, who, without a particle of encouragement or even of understanding from his family, wins an open scholarship to Christ Church (and, eventually, a Fellowship at All Souls); and of the child's grim struggle, despite everything, to remain true to himself and to the abilities of which he cannot but be conscious. Mr Rowse is Satanically proud of his victory—and with more justification, perhaps, than Satan had; but he is even more resentful that he had thus to struggle against such unfair disadvantages.

For disadvantages they were; Mr Rowse makes no doubt about that: disadvantages which inevitably he has not been able wholly to overcome, because they affected *him*. The twisted sapling will never grow into a graceful tree; and the *novus homo* in intellectual (as in any other) society can barely rid himself of his inferiority-superiority complex. Doubt may be cast at times, indeed, on the objective value of the narrative for future educators and child welfare workers; for Mr Rowse so evidently enjoys 'getting his own back' at the 'idiot people' from whom he comes, and who had neither the wish nor the ability to understand him. There is a good deal of 'fouling his own nest', as it is called in the kind of *cliché* which he contemptuously records in his own *Dictionnaire des Idées Reçues*. 'His consistent attitude' in adolescence, he says, 'was one of loathing his lot in having been born into a working-class family'; nor is his mother, for whom, in her old age, he has made a home, and to whom, with the memory of his father, the book is dedicated, shielded from the 'realism' of his portrayal: 'Gid along—taakin' up all that time to write a few little ole verses'. In estimating his fairness, one must also take into account the inescapable bias of the *émigré*, the *déraciné*; for in every way except in his devotion to the *land* of Cornwall Mr Rowse is very noticeably *déraciné*.

His devotion to the land was a large part of 'my one consolation'—'my life to myself'. One of the book's qualities is that it tells us a great deal about his life to himself. We learn his favourite walks and retreats, Carn Grey and the Luxulyan Valley, where he took only his best friends as 'a sign of great confidence'; his favourite books, Daudet, Q., Hardy, Swift, 'my schoolboy admirations to which I have remained constant ever since', with a natural preference for the Brontës against Jane Austen; the things which brought tears to his eyes, sixteenth-century music ('I think I would rather have been a great musician, or just a pianist, than anything'), the name of Nelson; the dream from which, still, 'I wake up to find myself crying as when I was a lad of sixteen': his 'automatic mnemonics' *à la* Proust. One of the key-words to his book and life, indeed, is *nostalgia*, and it is this, partly, which creates the tension existing in both. Autobiography implies nostalgia; but one would hardly expect to find so much of it in a work also so full of scorn for the imprisoning conditions of a life now finally burst through.

For a considerable period of his childhood Mr Rowse was a choirboy, full of enthusiasm for Anglo-Catholicism; he even intended from the age of five to become Primate of All England. He now regards the Church's influence as part of the imprisonment; despite his continuing fondness for church bells and Cranmer's liturgy, he came to see at Oxford 'how impossible was the intellectual foundation'. He now, it seems, has two religions, one for his heart and the other for his head. The first is 'the sum of those moments of ecstasy which is my real inner life. They constitute my revealed religion—a revelation of the world as beauty'. He makes it clear that in his experience such moments reach beyond the aesthetic to the mystical, 'as one felt time standing still'; but he is content to regard them as 'a protest of the personality against the realization of its final extinction'—and a vain protest. For his head, secondly, there is genius: 'I regard it as the one redemption of the world—it is my religion, what I worship . . . (Hobbes, Swift, Beethoven, Newman, even Frederick the Great)'. Newman is the one religious genius whose name recurs (more often than the index suggests); it is a significant choice, wholly suited to the nostalgia of a *déraciné*.

One may surmise that it was not only 'the intellectual foundation' of Christianity which troubled Mr Rowse. Here is a sentence which goes deeper: 'I never for a moment understood why humility should be regarded as a virtue: I thought it contemptible': like A. E. Housman, if without his European reputation, 'I am deliberately and deeply arrogant'. *Si Maria non humilis fuisset, non descensisset Spiritus super illam,* says St

306

Bernard; and one thinks of her working-class home, from which another boy, also little understood, had to break free, and of the unique combination in Him of 'But I say unto you' with 'I am among you as one that serveth'. Perhaps one difference, humanly speaking, was that Jesus was taken annually up to Jerusalem. Mr Rowse did not even cross the Tamar till he sat for a scholarship at Oxford.

But even more crippling than the lack of anyone or anything greater than himself, to admire and look up to, was the lack of anyone to be fond of, and to be fond of him. At home there was complete misunderstanding; at school 'friendship was the one thing wanting'. 'I had an extremely affectionate nature as a child'; it was 'denied, turned away, unwanted'. Consequently (it is not Mr Rowse's consequence) ' "God is love" conveyed nothing, for I could attach no meaning to either term in the equation'. In such a case how could he know whether 'the intellectual foundation' was impossible or not? *A Cornish Childhood* is the story of a triumph, and a triumph which commands one's admiration; but it is a triumph in which the underlying tragedy still persists.

1942

XXIX

VIRGINIA WOOLF

Ma vie, à moi, s'use à lutter contre la fragilité des choses

THE words are Loti's; but they might well be Virginia Woolf's, and are essential to a sympathetic understanding of her. The brittleness of things: many people, even most, are not conscious of it; but to those who are even a little conscious of it there is endless delight and excitement and inspiration to be found in Virginia Woolf's novels. It means, of course, that she has to assume, in all her main characters, a sensibility as acute as her own. Lily Briscoe, in *To The Lighthouse*, is representative, when she could 'see, as in an X-ray photograph, the ribs and thigh bones of the young man's desire to impress himself lying dark in the mist of the flesh'; while for Mrs Ramsay, it was 'as if she had antennae trembling out from her, which, intercepting certain sentences forced them upon her attention'. It may be argued that in this universalizing by Virginia Woolf of her own peculiar powers, at once receptive and penetrating, is a simplification which is false; but it must be accepted as part of her technique.

Rightly understood, it can be willingly accepted; for her technique is in the articulation of the subconscious, where in fact we are all more receptive and more penetrating, though we often are quite unaware of it. 'Never children spake like these children,' wrote the Editor of the *Congregational Quarterly*, in comment on the earliest pages of *The Waves*; but no one supposes they are speaking; they are thinking, or not even thinking, they are dreaming, imagining, reacting to what is before them on the subconscious level of symbolism.

> Images, metaphors of the most extreme and extravagant twined and twisted in his mind. He called her a melon, a pineapple, an olive tree, an emerald, and a fox in the snow all in the space of three seconds; he did not know whether he had heard her, tasted her, seen her, or all three together.

Thus with Orlando in love; and so it is with all the characters.

> While James the lawgiver, with the tablets of eternal wisdom laid open on his knee (his hand on the tiller had become symbolical to her), said, Resist him.

In a later work the phrase in brackets would be omitted; partly because it prosaicizes the image, partly because of an increasing passion to penetrate to reality, to which metaphor seems nearer than does simile:

> 'Like' and 'like' and 'like'—but what is the thing that lies beneath the semblance of the thing?

A vrai dire, M. Delattre has well said of Virginia Woolf's characters, *ce sont moins leurs pensées et leurs sentiments qu'ils nous communiquent que l'écho, presqu'informulé encore, éveillé au fond de leur conscience par le choc de sensations qui résonnent à la surface, 'comme un gong qui frappe'.* It would be a grievous mistake, however, to assume that her writing is mere chiaroscuro, subjective imagination-spinning. It is the greatness of her work that it is tied fast to ordinary happenings; the imaginative creation is connected with, even conditioned by, particular places.

> But can this last? I said to myself, by a lion in Trafalgar Squre, by the lion seen once and for ever.
> The strangeness of standing alone, alive, unknown, at half-past eleven in Trafalgar Square overcame him.

The recurrence of Trafalgar Square here (from two different novels) is indicative. This binding together of imaginativeness and hard fact, this articulation of the mind's working on various levels at the same time is one of Virginia Woolf's most striking characteristics, and is a noteworthy achievement in itself. The commonest realization of it by the ordinary mortal is perhaps when travelling, 'as one raises one's eyes from a page in an express train and sees a farm, a tree, a cluster of cottages as an illustration, a confirmation of

something on the printed page to which one returns, fortified, and satisfied'; but her characters do it all the time, as
when telephoning:

> He saw her at the end of the line, Greek, blue-eyed, straight-
> nosed. How incongruous it seemed to be telephoning to a
> woman like that. The Graces assembling seemed to have joined
> hands in meadows of asphodel to compose that face. Yes, he
> would catch the 10.30 at Euston.

or at the tea-table:

> And all the time she was saying that the butter was not fresh
> one would be thinking of Greek temples, and how beauty had
> been with them there.

It is the reflection in her style of this double articulation—
what Miss Rose Macaulay has called the to and fro of the
shuttle in her work—which makes her style so exquisite: she
has succeeded in uniting form and content. *Shimmering* Lord
David Cecil calls her style, and there seems no better word:

> Up in the sky swallows swooping, swerving, flinging them-
> selves in and out, round and round, yet always with perfect
> control as if elastics held them; and the flies rising and falling;
> and the sun spotting now this leaf, now that, . . .
> Our commonest deeds are set about with a fluttering and
> flickering of wings, a rising and falling of lights.

This last quotation may also introduce something which
is constantly recurring in Virginia Woolf: the sense of endless
adventure, of undreamed-of possibilities, in the simplest of
happenings.

> Every single thing, once he tried to dislodge it from its place
> in his mind, he found thus cumbered with other matter like the
> lump of glass which, after a year at the bottom of the sea, is
> grown about with bones and dragon-flies, and coins and the
> tresses of drowned women.
> To speak, about wine even to the waiter, is to bring about an
> explosion. Up goes the rocket. Its golden grain falls, fertilising,
> upon the rich soil of my imagination. The entirely unexpected

nature of this explosion—that is the joy of intercourse. I, mixed with an unknown Italian waiter—what am I? There is no stability in this world. Who is to say what meaning there is in anything? Who is to foretell the flight of a word? It is a balloon that sails over tree-tops. To speak of knowledge is futile. All is experiment and adventure.

Yet we are never left merely with the *choc de sensations*—the whole fun of the game is that we have a mind there to resolve them and to make them into a unity which is its own creation.

That woman sitting there, writing under the rock resolved everything into simplicity; made these angers, irritations fall off like old rags; she brought together this and that and then this, and so made out of that miserable silliness and spite (she and Charles squabbling, sparring, had been silly and spiteful) something—this scene on the beach for example, this moment of friendship and liking—which survived, after all these years, complete, so that she dipped into it to re-fashion her memory of him, and it stayed in the mind almost like a work of art.

Love had a thousand shapes. There might be lovers whose gift it was to choose out the elements of things and place them together and so, giving them a wholeness not theirs in life, make of some scene, or meeting of people (all now gone and separate), one of those globed compacted things over which thought lingers, and love plays.

Virginia Woolf's work is, in fact, as deeply metaphysical as an artist's can well be: she is for ever on the verge of discovering the ultimate meaning of things and of people:

Then, for that moment, she had seen an illumination; a match burning in a crocus; an inner meaning almost expressed. But the close withdrew; the hard softened. It was over—the moment.

What was the spirit in her, the essential thing, by which, had you found a glove in the corner of a sofa, you would have known it, from its twisted finger, hers indisputably?

But to go deeper, beneath what people said (and these judgements, how superficial, how fragmentary they are!) in her own mind now, what did it mean to her, this thing she called life?

Again and again we are presented with the old problems of

the one and the many, of time and eternity, only posed with all the poignancy of experience:

'This is here,' said Jinny, 'this is now. But soon we shall go. Soon Miss Curry will blow her whistle. We shall walk. We shall part. . . . This is only here; this is only now.'

Here was one room; there another. Did religion solve that, or love?

What she loved was this, here, now, in front of her; the fat lady in the cab.

But she said, sitting on the bus going up Shaftesbury Avenue, she felt herself everywhere; not 'here, here, here'; and she tapped the back of the seat; but everywhere.

Resulting naturally from this combination of extreme sensibility with a passion half mystical, half metaphysical, is a recurrence of moments of intense happiness and even ecstasy, which to the reader are sheer joy. Life itself, its simple process, is enough to yield such ecstasy, and with it the vain yearning to preserve the wondrous moment for all time.

In people's eyes, in the swing, tramp, and trudge; in the bellow and the uproar; the carriages, motor cars, omnibuses, vans, sandwich men shuffling and swinging; brass bands; barrel organs; in the triumph and the jingle and the strange high singing of some aeroplane overhead was what she loved; life; London; this moment of June.

She rammed a little hole in the sand and covered it up, by way of burying in it the perfection of the moment.

'In a world which contains the present moment,' said Neville, 'why discriminate? Nothing should be named lest by so doing we change it.'

The torments, the divisions of your lives have been solved for me night after night, sometimes only by the touch of a finger under the table-cloth as we sat dining—so fluid has my body become, forming even at the touch of a finger into one full drop, which fills itself, which quivers, which flashes, which falls in ecstasy.

For their keenest appreciation Virginia Woolf's novels need, in keeping with their subject, to be read as incantation and half consciously. Then not only do the connexions between the sentences, which are imaginative, not logical, imperceptibly make themselves apparent, but the value of the dreamlike rhythm is fully felt.

> She could see the words echoing as she spoke them rhythmically in Cam's mind, and Cam was repeating after her how it was like a mountain, a bird's nest, a garden, and there were little antelopes, and her eyes were opening and shutting, and Mrs. Ramsay went on saying still more monotonously, and more rhythmically and more nonsensically, how she must shut her eyes and go to sleep and dream of mountains and valleys and stars falling and parrots and antelopes and gardens, and everything lovely, she said, raising her head very slowly and speaking more and more mechanically, until she sat upright and saw that Cam was asleep.

That is a key to all Virginia Woolf's work, in which her favourite figure is a simple anaphora.

> And there is my father, with his back turned, talking to a farmer. I tremble. I cry. There is my father in gaiters. There is my father.
> Look how the willow shoots its fine sprays into the air! Look how through them a boat passes, filled with indolent, with unconscious, with powerful young men.

Virginia Woolf's style is emphatically her own. It is not difficult, however, to trace the influence on her of one writer, not only in his love of anaphora and in his skilful use of brackets to suggest the interweaving of consciousness' strands, in his punctuation even, but for something nowhere better described than by herself in *The Common Reader*:

> The first quality that attracts us is not his meaning, charged with meaning as his poetry is, but something much more unmixed and immediate; it is the explosion with which he bursts into speech . . . we do not merely become aware of beautiful remembered lines; we feel ourselves compelled to a particular attitude of mind. . . . In this power of suddenly surprising and subjugating the reader, Donne excels most poets. It is his characteristic quality.

Listen to Donne on Christ's love for men:

Them, who by nature are not able to love him at all; and when by grace they are brought to love him, can expresse their love no other way, but to be glad that he was betrayed, and scourged, and scorned, and nailed, and crucified; and to be glad, that if all this were not alreadie done, it might be done yet; and to long and to wish, if Christ were not crucified, to have him crucified now (which is a strange manner of expressing love) those men he loved, and loved to the end; men, and not Angels.[1]

And he that stands in the highest subordinate heighths, nay in the highest supreme heighth in this world, is weighed downe, by that, which is nothing; for what is any Monarch to the whole world? and the whole world is but that; but what? but nothing.

There we recognize the master.

It is a matter for keen regret that we can have no more works from her imaginative genius; matter for regret perhaps rather than surprise. For

> For each ecstatic instant
> We must an anguish pay
> In keen and quivering ratio
> To the ecstasy.

Absorbing, mysterious, of infinite richness, this life.

Yes, but

Was there no safety? No learning by heart of the ways of the world? No guide, no shelter, but all was miracle, and leaping from the pinnacle of a tower into the air? Could it be, even for elderly people, that this was life?—startling, unexpected, unknown?

---

[1] With this style, which is not a common one, the following from Sidney's *Apologie for Poetrie* may be compared:

But grant loue of beautie to be a beastlie fault (although it be very hard, sith onely man, and no beast, hath that gyft to discerne beauty); grant that louely name of Loue to deserue all hatefull reproches (although euen some of my Maisters the Phylosophers spent a good deale of theyr Lamp-oil in setting foorth the excellencie of it); grant, I say, what soeuer they wil haue granted; that not onely loue, but lust, but vanitie, but (if they list) scurrilitie, possesseth many leaues of the Poets bookes: yet thinke I, when this is granted, they will finde theyr sentence may with good manners put the last words foremost, and not say that Poetrie abuseth mans wit, but that mans wit abuseth Poetrie.

For the most part, oddly enough, she must admit that she felt this thing that she called life terrible, hostile, and quick to pounce on you if you gave it a chance.

To such a spirit there must often have been times when death spelt release, and a release to be welcomed:

And that was what now she often felt the need of—to think; well not even to think. To be silent; to be alone. All the being and the doing, expansive, glittering, vocal, evaporated; and one shrunk, with a sense of solemnity, to being oneself, a wedge-shaped core of darkness, something invisible to others. . . . This core of darkness could go anywhere, for no one saw it. They could not stop it, she thought, exulting. There was freedom, there was peace, there was, most welcome of all, a summoning together, a resting on a platform of stability. Not as oneself did one find rest ever, in her experience (she accomplished here something dexterous with her needles), but as a wedge of darkness. Losing personality, one lost the fret, the hurry, the stir; and there rose to her lips always some exclamation of triumph over life when things came together in this peace, this rest, this eternity.

1941

REFLECTIONS ON THE LIFE OF
WILLIAM TEMPLE

W HEN a great man dies, his biography seems a poor compensation. Yet a good biography is a great compensation, especially to those who have known and admired him only from a distance. The English-speaking world is immeasurably indebted to the Dean of Lichfield for his biography[1] of his old friend and companion-in-arms, William Temple. The Dean has borne it in mind that 'in dealing with the career of an Archbishop of Canterbury, the biographer cannot avoid making some contribution to Church history'; but in portraying the public figure he has never allowed himself to lose the man. As Temple's life became increasingly filled with speeches, committees and causes, the temptation must have been great for his biography to be made inhuman. It is not the least of Dr Iremonger's services, in conveying Temple's spirit and in carrying on his influence, that his writing never strays far from the reverent study of personality.

He has been helped in this by his bold rejection of a purely chronological order. The framework retains a temporal sequence—Rugby, Balliol, Queen's, the W.E.A., Repton, St James', Piccadilly, the 'Life and Liberty' movement, Westminster, Manchester, York, Canterbury—with Copec, the Prayer Book controversy, the Oecumenical movement, the Malvern Conference and other outstanding subjects appearing (more or less) where one would expect them. But where, in studying any of these phases of interests of Temple's life, the Dean has found light in a letter or pronouncement from another period, he has not hesitated to introduce it. Such a method was undoubtedly made the easier by the clear lines of Temple's life, which was marked by strong continuity and coherence. There is a lovely story of the future philosopher's

[1] *William Temple, Archbishop of Canterbury: His Life and Letters.* By F. A. Iremonger. Oxford University Press.

complaining at the age of eight that, in 'The Cat sat on the Mat', 'It does not say *which* cat'! And his handwriting changed little in fifty years.

Temple was the first Archbishop of Canterbury to be the son of an Archbishop of Canterbury. Frederick Temple died when his son was still an undergraduate; but his influence on him 'is beyond compute'. Dr Iremonger even asks, in seeking to understand why Temple went to Repton—the only sphere where there was no resounding success—'Is it possible that he had an almost superstitious reverence not only for the Archbishop's character and example, but even for the sequence of stages in his father's career?'—for Frederick Temple had been Headmaster of Rugby. William decided to be an archbishop like his father, 'in the nursery'! There is a further parallel in their lives in the devotion of each of them to his mother. Frederick Temple's mother, who was left a widow when he was still a boy, lived with him always, nor was it till after her death that he married, at the age of fifty-four. William Temple wrote, and heard from, his mother *daily* when he was at Rugby; when an undergraduate, he walked arm in arm round Oxford with her, and 'That needed some doing in those days'; he had her with, or near, him wherever he lived; nor did he, either, marry until after her death. Besides this close relation with his parents and the advantage—as students of genius consider it—of an elderly father, all but sixty at his birth, there was a contrast in Temple's heredity so striking as to be worth noting. His mother was a grand-daughter of the sixth Earl of Carlisle (with all her family's rabid teetotalism). His father's mother was a plain Cornishwoman.

Whatever the home and hereditary influence, it is clear that from his childhood Temple was brilliant, one who in mental activity found the breath of life and was marked out for future leadership. At Rugby he could do two hours' prep. in half an hour, and he 'read the whole of 7 English poets' in the time gained. 'I think *anything*[1] is possible to him', wrote the Headmaster in his latest report. At Balliol his work was comfortably alpha, and 'all were agreed that . . . whatever career he adopted, nothing could keep him from the

[1] The Headmaster's italics.

317

top of it'. This pre-eminence he owed in part to his exceptional memory. From his father he inherited the photographic memory which retains perfectly, and permanently, what has been read. He could also, when dictating, 'break off in the middle of a sentence in a complicated letter with the utmost tranquillity and proceed ten minutes later from the exact point where he had left off', and indeed 'would be careful' to adopt this procedure if interrupted when writing a book; and once, when at a public address 'the shorthand writer failed to appear, he dictated the address a week later walking up and down in his room, without a note'.

He also all his life used odd moments as faithfully as any pupil of Samuel Smiles. At seventeen he read Kant's *Critique of Pure Reason* in a boat on holiday in the Lakes, while the others were fishing or rowing. Bosanquet's *Logic* he read on a three-legged stool in his lodgings at the Oxford Medical Mission in Bermondsey. Croce's *Philosophy of History* he would take for the train. Equally, he would write articles in railway-station waiting-rooms, and work in odd half-hours at his devotional or philosophical writing—not always with the best effect: Professor Dorothy Emmet, who contributes a chapter on Temple as philosopher, says frankly that his *Mens Creatrix* 'is a curiously disjointed book'. The ability to behave in this way demands an unusual power of detachment, which Temple evidently possessed. He could sleep at any time in the train, and hardly ever lay awake at night.

All this indicates exceptional powers of concentration and endurance, and exceptional control of those powers. Certainly one outstanding character of his life is his steadfast, unwavering purposiveness and assurance. Before he became Bishop of Manchester he spent a number of short periods in a variety of avocations; yet never did a great figure sail more surely and serenely over the sea of life. Even at Rugby 'he had a sort of quiet purpose that was recognized'. He was not nineteen when he wrote to a friend, 'I have been determined to be ordained longer than I can remember.' Six years later he wrote revealingly, 'I emphatically say that a man who has no serious purpose as the backbone of his life cannot be a Christian.'

'My interpretation of Subject as primarily Will', as he

wrote of his Christological contribution to *Foundations*, though couched in philosophical terms, points clearly to the source of his own purposiveness. It was in the adoring effort to bring his own will into line with the Will of God that he gained the fixity of purpose which nothing could shake. 'I have never known what it is to doubt the existence of God,' he once confessed. Philosophically, this was a drawback. 'His writing leaves the impression,' Miss Emmet complains, 'that he is never very seriously puzzled.' But religiously it enabled him, like Newman, to speak with the conviction which commands a hearing. 'Sure of God and of God's universe as he was from the beginning . . . he grew, as a result, to be sure of himself.'

'And that goes a long way in Lancashire.' These words follow the words 'sure of himself' in another context. Was Temple's assurance altogether founded on faith in the Unseen? Or was it flecked at least with something earthier, with what Carlyle called (in the very different case of George Fox) an 'enormous sacred Self-confidence', based on the consciousness, which he could not help having, of ability and soaring achievement? As an undergraduate he carried the 'self-confident, even cocksure' air of Balliol. At times he was misled by his 'gift of ready and lucid speech,' his tutor noted, 'to think that he had found a solution, when he had found a phrase.' There is a similar suggestion in the question of Bishop Brilioth 'whether Temple's extraordinary ability did not carry with it a certain lack of depth in his thinking'.

Something of a parallel to this is to be detected in his emotional life. Again and again in discussing moral questions, 'he took his stand firmly on certain Christian principles, the first and greatest of which was the sacredness of personality' (Miss Emmet, indeed, holds that his interpretation of moral obligations is 'too exclusively personalist'); and on one occasion he wrote, 'I suppose that no sermon preached to a crowd ever did much good. . . . Good spiritual work is done on[1] one person or a dozen people at a time.' Yet, though 'never shy with childen,' 'he lacked facility for small talk with strangers'; at Repton he admitted he would feel more comfortable 'if only he could always address individual

[1] Note *on*, not *to*.

parents or boys as if they were a public meeting'; when preaching, 'he gave the impression of thinking more of the message he had come to deliver than of the people to whom he was giving it'; and he defended a cope as 'curiously effective in obliterating the sense of individuality in the wearer' (though earlier 'he preferred not to wear vestments'). When he became engaged to be married, 'You have seemed so strong and αὐτάρκης,' wrote a friend, 'one wondered whether you were independent of these things.' To the end, says his biographer, he 'remained inappropriable,' seeming to many 'a man without close friends.' This is as much as to suggest a certain lack of depth here also.

In reading his life, in fact, one is from time to time brought up against something which cannot be called superficiality and yet which fails to reach beneath the upper levels down to the fountains of the spirit. Intellectually, part of the price paid for his brilliance was that he was so consciously conscious. While allowing that 'all my decisive thinking goes on behind the scenes', he had all his generation's antipathy to, almost unbelief in, the subconscious. There is no evocative dreaminess about the expression of his thought, all is clear and clear cut. And in the emotional sphere the reader feels, as Dr Iremonger says his contemporaries felt, that 'the note of tragedy was missing from Temple's life, that he had never been "up against it".' The element of struggle seems strangely lacking.

But is this last judgement true? It needs qualifying. If tragedy, *la douleur fertilisante*, was a stranger to Temple, he knew at least the weariness of ill-health and the trial to faith which acute pain can bring. In all his reading 'he read entirely through one eye' and 'always read slowly'; and all his life his activities were hindered by this poor sight. All his life, also, he was 'very susceptible to heat' and prone to hay fever. Moreover, he had a 'thorn in the flesh' which attacked him first when he was two, and finally (though it was not the immediate cause) killed him: gout. It rarely left him for long and sometimes attacked him with (in a characteristic phrase) 'prodigious violence'. Against this torturing and inhibiting complaint his life *was* one long struggle. But 'he never lost heart'.

There was also one moment, if only one, when Temple received a slap in the face; and it was an occasion which affected the deepest places of his life. We have seen his early 'determination' to be ordained. 'I had hoped to do useful work as a parson, and thought my gifts(!)[1] peculiarly suited to that kind of work.' His only doubt was whether his acceptance of the Church's 'formulae would be so deceptive as to be impossible'. At the age of twenty-four he sought ordination from the Bishop of Oxford, stating his belief that 'the helping men to reach the living Presence of Christ is the noblest work in the world'. The Bishop refused to ordain him—on the ground that Temple could accept the Virgin Birth only 'very tentatively' and the Physical Resurrection 'with rather more confidence'. This must have been a turning-point in Temple's life. His sense of a Divine call to the ministry was evidently not strong enough to counter the Bishop's refusal: he was too loyal an Anglican for that. Within two years the Archbishop of Canterbury, whom Temple described *at the time* as 'the essence of kindness and sanity— without a glimmer of inspiration', found him '*in all essential particulars,*[2] an orthodox believer' in both doctrines; and he was accordingly ordained. In respect of the Virgin Birth, his biographer states that Temple later 'experienced absolute certitude of its truth—at a second of time during a symphony concert at the Queen's Hall'. One may make what one will of this: for 'mystical' content it stands alone; but one has no right to question Temple's sincerity. One may, however, wonder what would have happened had he not become 'an orthodox believer', and had he continued to feel as he wrote after the Bishop had refused him: 'The Church must be purged, I think, from without . . . More and more I come to regard "Churchiness" as a sign of the useless . . . If the Church turns one out one must go on outside.'

One may also imagine the caustic comment he would have made on words which, as it worked out, in 1942 Temple was to write himself: 'I shall be surprised if just at this moment the "powers" select me for Canterbury. Some of my recent utterances have not been liked in political circles. . . .' 'The

[1] Temple's exclamation mark.
[2] Davidson's italics.

"powers" . . . political circles'! Long before this, as, frankly and sorrowfully, his biographer notes, the question of disestablishment, which in their 'Life and Liberty' movement had loomed so large in the eyes of both of them, for Temple had 'ceased to be a moral issue'. As early as 1925 he had pronounced it a question 'in which the Church need take no interest at all'. In this matter 'Temple made no attempt to disguise the complete *bouleversement* of his earlier convictions'. Dr Iremonger's feelings appear in his placing in this context (without date) a phrase from a letter in which Temple wrote, 'I often wonder, sometimes with real torment of mind and soul, whether I have not been turning my back on the light.' This is the one occasion on which Temple permits us to see a tiny puncture in his otherwise unfailing self-confidence. To Free Churchmen the context of disestablishment provided by Dr Iremonger is less unimportant than it will be to most of his Anglican readers. We are left to wonder whether the original context was a wider one.

If depth in Temple's character is sometimes open to question, the breadth of his humanity is never in doubt. One of the many excellencies of this biography is that it tells the little personal things. 'In later life cats were among his favourite companions.' Browning was his favourite poet; Botticelli his favourite painter; *Lear* his favourite Shakespeare play, though Hamlet his favourite character; *Karamazov* 'the greatest novel'; *Emma* his favourite Jane Austen. We also see him reading *Winnie-the-Pooh* and reading *Alice* aloud; Bradshaw's *Timetable* was 'one of his favourite books'. He read the *Republic* 'eight times in his life' and thought himself probably the only English clergyman who had read Aquinas' *Summa* from cover to cover. Spinoza (read at Jena) 'is the greatest of all of them—there!' We learn which were his favourite *Psalms* (103, 23, 104, 107, 139 were the first five) and some of his favourite hymns. 'With St John I am at home.' We are told his specially loved holiday places at home and abroad. 'For cricket he had neither taste nor talent,' but 'eternally hopeful, he nearly always brought a tennis racket' to conferences. 'Before 1937 he had only seen two films in his life.' 'He knew the names of no racehorses.' 'He was a non-smoker and a teetotaller.' We are also treated to a number of pen-pictures such as 'I thought old Lord Halifax would shake to pieces in his rage at what I said' or 'Laski amuses me. He dislikes the Church intensely, and his net is spread too visibly in the sight of the birds.' All these touches, and many more, fill out the picture of the man and help us to know him with an intimacy which would have been possible to few before his death.

To sum up, the spiritual quality which was God's gift to us in Temple would seem to have had two main aspects. In the first place, he held fast to the roots of religion in experience. Of religion he said that 'in its essence it is an experience . . . an experience of the power of the love of God in Christ changing our hopes and desires'. He believed in 'the real and objective presence of our Lord in the sacramental elements', but evidently not only there. 'I am entirely convinced that prayer is the chief thing,' he said more than once, and his people at Manchester he asked to 'pray for me chiefly that I may never let go of the unseen hand of the Lord Jesus and may live in daily fellowship with Him.' From this daily fellowship came the serenity which overcame his physical ailments and torments, came the stillness even of body as he stood preaching, an 'atmosphere of stillness and peace (which yet seemed charged with power) that pervaded' even his study.

Secondly, he was unwearying and fearless in relating religious experience and conviction to ordered thought. A prime influence here was Edward Caird, and Dr Iremonger justly applies to Temple words written of Caird: 'Nothing could content him but to be a man of coherent convictions.' Of one of his own books Temple wrote that he sought to show that 'Epistemology, Aesthetic, Ethico-politics, and Philosophy of Religion are moving on converging lines'. Metaphysics, sociology, economics, whatever it might be, were all to be related to fundamental Christian principles and to find their point of unity and ultimate intelligibility in the Incarnation. He spent his life in showing a sceptical and scornful generation that it is possible to be a Christian and still to be enlightened. For the increase of late in serious-mindedness among thoughtful people the war has been largely responsible, but Temple hardly less so. Where, one wonders, would he have led us next? To what new line of thinking would he have turned to break fresh ground? 'I think I shall write a book about the Holy Spirit,' he said to his wife a month or two before he died; 'I have always wanted to have a try at that.'

1949

XXXI

THREE BENEFACTORS

(I) WILLIAM BOOTHBY SELBIE

HIS PERSONALITY

IT is perhaps impertiment of me to say much, for I was never a pupil of Selbie's; but I have asked myself to do so because I knew him well for the last sixteen years of his life, and for eight of the sixteen with some degree of intimacy, having regard to the difference of generation. Let that excuse my recording some things which we all know, and others more *à la* Aubrey.

I do not think Selbie had genius, in the sense of integrating what in lesser men would be inconsistencies, such as appears, for instance, in Joan Evans' account of Sir Arthur Evans or in Lucy Cohen's memoir of Montefiore. What he did achieve was something almost as rare as genius, namely a combination of being 'always the same' ('I like Headlam. You can always tell where you are with him') with being lovable. When you talked with him about people, places or books, he seemed to know everyone, to have been everywhere and to have read everything; yet he was never in a whirl, he remained himself, taking his own course, a middle course nearly always. Nor had his knowledge and experience turned his head or spoiled his humour. I think his not infrequent acidity and biting criticisms were part of the detachment which enabled him to retain a surprised amusement at finding himself in some of the *galères* he adorned. To the end he remained human and was all the more influential for neither being, nor appearing to be, faultless. Something of the *enfant terrible* visible in early portraits still hung about him. One sometimes felt more confidence in his judgement than in his prudence.

Selbie was always a conventional Greats man, deeply influenced by Greek culture as well as Hebrew. When he first sailed in sight of the Acropolis and in imagination saw Pericles and his generation ἁβρὸν βαίνειν through the bright

Athenian air, he could not, he told me, keep the tears back; and I remember his introducing me on a visit to the crocuses in Addison's Walk to

par levibus ventis volucrique simillima somno.

He was also a Lancashire lad, fond of his pipe and his cup of tea, who never lost his understanding of the common man. When he left Mansfield, I helped to tie up parcels of hundreds of detective stories to be sent to the Wingfield Orthopaedic Hospital and elsewhere. In his late sixties he could still put up a lively game at tennis. Earlier he used to have holidays with Silvester Horne. We did not realize perhaps how much Horne's death meant to him; the way he talked sometimes recalled the proverb, οὐθεὶς φίλος ᾧ πολλοὶ φίλοι.

Reference has been made to his pastoral genius. During the day perhaps thirteen people would come to his study one after another, and then in the night he would be called up to see some hysteric needing immediate attention. He found time for everyone only by 'redeeming the time' at great cost to himself. For his guests breakfast was at 8 a.m. ('with a tendency to mercy'), but he had been up long before. During the years when he had charge of *The British Congregationalist*, the whole of his editorial work was finished before breakfast. Nor did he allow himself to read the newspaper until evening. It was this personal austerity which gave weight to his perennial warning against the minister's besetting sin, laziness.

George Eliot he regarded as the greatest English novelist, but his own favourite was Trollope, whose influence on his pulpit style is worth recording. The simplicity, forthrightness and persuasive common sense of that voice which seemed to place him just beside you in the pew can be recovered to a remarkable extent from a perusal of Trollope's *Autobiography*. For the note of passionate caring Richard Baxter's style is more evocative. His practice, he told me, was to think out his sermon for forty-eight hours beforehand, and then shoot it forth and let it be forgotten: 'think what you are going to say, but not what words you will use'. The burning ethical purpose provided the words.

To preach as if we could do everything ('What are you

going to do about it?') and to **pray** as if we could do nothing ('help us to help them') may be wrong-headed logically and theologically and yet be justifiable psychologically and homiletically, especially if the preaching is preceded by praying. Some of us will remember Selbie's prayers even more than his preaching. *La prière, c'est l'homme.* In Selbie's praying were revealed the broken heart and contrite spirit which except before God he was too English not to hide. One was conscious then not only of the divine presence but of the *consecrated personality* which makes 'the man of God'. In what was perhaps his last published writing before his death, Selbie praised Principal Curtis' *Jesus Christ the Teacher* because it 'reveals a personality . . . . self-consistent and self-authenticating'. He believed that through the refractions of the evangelists the white light of the glory of God in the face of Jesus Christ may be recovered; and his obedient consecration to that integrated, living Personality made him the man he was. He had not chosen the life he lived: his advice to keep out of the ministry if you possibly could had deep roots in his own experience. Christ, he believed, had chosen him, and it was as Christ's servant that, little like Paul, he could walk with Princes of the Church.

1944

(II) ARTHUR DAVIS MARTIN

THE death of A. D. Martin (as he always signed himself), at the age of seventy-one deprived the Congregational churches of one of those scholar-ministers who, we like to think, are a special characteristic of ours, yet for whom one searches far in days when Christianity must be 'practical' or it is nothing. Though his interests were less specialized, Martin reminded one of F. J. Powicke, who had the same combination of spiritual and intellectual earnestness with Christian gentleness. His conversation could recall Dr Horton's: how few have that gift of expressing personality as they talk, so that with the first sentence you know you are in touch with something vital; his choice of words might seem at first a trifle precious, but soon you saw they were not chosen self-consciously but were the fruit of a reflection deep and disciplined. In Edinburgh, indeed, some came to listen to his sermons drawn in the first instance by admiration for his English. There, as at Southampton, Buxton, and Chelmsford, his name is held in warm affection and respect. In his churches, as in his home life, he was a truly happy man. Even the ill health, which in youth had prevented him from the higher education, and which often dogged him later, was accepted and used and made a blessing.

Those who know Martin's books think so highly of them that it is a pity they are not known and read more widely. The number of our ministers who, with no degree from any university, have had a six shilling work published by the Cambridge Press, must be small, if it exceeds the number one: *Aspects of the Way: being meditations and studies in the life of Jesus Christ* (C.U.P., 1924) is perhaps Martin's most distinguished contribution. It was followed by *The Prophet Jonah: the Book and the Sign* (Longmans, 1926); and by *Foreshewings of Christ: Old Testament Studies in the Preparation for the Advent* (S.P.C.K., 1930), in which are to be found the same scholarly 'openings' of familiar texts and scenes, the same delicacy of touch and spiritual perception, as in the larger book. Meanwhile our own leaders knew their man, and for the Congregational Union he wrote his admirable book, *The Principle of the Congregational Churches* (1927), which has chapters on the principle's devotional and business applications as well as on its historical evolution; while for the L.M.S. he wrote of *Doctor Vanderkemp* (Livingstone Press, 1931), the Society's pioneer missionary to S. Africa. A short appreciation of one of his 'great ones' appeared as *The Religion of Wordsworth* (Allen & Unwin), which he told me, significantly, was really on the religion of gratitude, as illustrated by Wordsworth. Earlier he had tried his hand at a seventeenth-century novel, *Una Breakspear*. Increasingly, however, his mind turned to Jesus Himself, and 1934 saw the publication of a larger work, *The Holiness of Jesus* (Allen & Unwin). In the last year of his life he wrote to me, 'I feel that this Supreme Figure is more to me than ever. It would be a good thing if *every* Christian disciple in his old age would try to write the Life of his Master, though no eye other than his own ever saw it.' Happily the MS. of his attempt was completed a few weeks before he died, and is at present with the printer.

Martin's temperament was a poetic and imaginative one—
Vaughan, Wordsworth, and Francis Thompson were among
his hierarchy—and it is the combination of this with his
scholarly carefulness (he knew and could interpret *cruces* in
both the Bible's original tongues) which gives character and
quality to his writing. While deeply grateful for all the help
towards understanding which modern scholarship has given,
he yet insisted that Jesus Christ was a poet, not a logician,
and that the intuitive, imaginative approach to Him needs
tender nurturing. Then 'sometimes we come suddenly upon
a hidden blossom where we had never before discerned a
bud, though we had thought we knew all the buds'.

Martin was no pacifist—he felt too keenly, he said, the
individual's undischarged debt to Society—but he had the
eirenic temper which all pacifists must desire. It sprang from
his child-like trust in a Father-God. 'Two texts often ring in
my memory', he wrote in his last letter to me; ' "All things
are Thy servants' (*Ps.* cxix. 91) and "Of Him and through
Him and unto Him are all things" (*Rom.* xi. 36). Here I
anchor and find tranquillity.'

1941

(III) A. G. MATTHEWS

A.G.M., as he was known to his familiars—Mat to a favoured
few—was the most distinguished historian among us, and his
death on 6 December 1962, is a sensible loss to our Society.
As long ago as 1916 he spoke at our autumnal meeting on
early Nonconformity in Staffordshire, in preparation for his
small book on the Congregational churches in that county,
where he was assistant minister at Queen Street, Wolverhampton; and in 1932, when the autumnal meetings of the
Congregational Union were held at Wolverhampton, he
presented additions and corrections for the book in 'Some
Notes on Staffordshire Nonconformity'. This threefold thoroughness over many years was characteristic of him. Without
it he would never have attempted, certainly he could never
have carried through, the enormously laborious work necessary to produce his two great volumes, *Calamy Revised* (Oxford, 1934) and *Walker Revised* (Oxford, 1947).

The titles of both are really misnomers arising from his
modesty, for the material copied (or often corrected) from

Calamy or Walker is far less than what, over the years, Matthews gathered from widely dispersed MS. sources as well as books; but only a fundamentally modest man would have devoted himself to work of this kind in the first place, content to provide bricks for others to build with rather than to construct an interpretation of his own. For a scholar to go on to give the same attention to Walker's clergy sequestered by the Puritans as to Calamy's ministers ejected by the Anglicans was also a remarkable object-lesson; in his unassuming way Matthews was a worker in the ecumenical field as well as the historical. Failing energies prevented him from complying with the editors' desire that he should contribute to the recent symposium *From Uniformity to Unity, 1662–1962*; but the frequency of reference to him by name, as well as to *Calamy Revised* and *Walker Revised*, in its pages is an index of the extent to which all students of later seventeenth-century English religion, Anglicans as much as Free Churchmen, now lean on him and trust his work as unprejudiced and reliable.

Some who have occasionally referred to one or other of these lists of names may not have suspected Matthews' breadth of outlook. This in fact went far beyond the seventeenth century or ecclesiastical history in any century. Among the books in his sitting-room there were Greek and Latin and French writers (including Proust) as well as English, tastefully bound but not for show. In his latter years he read Homer steadily, in Greek of course. Another of his enthusiasms was Gothic architecture. He spent many holidays abroad and amassed a magnificent collection of postcard views of French Cathedrals with which to adorn the summer-house in the garden where he did much of his writing. Indoors, representations of modern art had places of honour, along with oil paintings of his ancestors and a portrait of Cromwell. These and other interests, such as music or the ways of birds, overflowed into his conversation and made him a charming companion, once the persistent shyness which would ice over even quite close relationships had worn off, as after a few hours it always did; while until her death at a very advanced age his home was redolent of his utter devotion to his mother.

On a Sunday summer evening he would often choose to walk across the fields to Evensong at Tandridge parish church. Yet he was a convinced and faithful Congregationalist. He had a lovely pride in 'The Peace', as he called the church at Oxted of which he had been minister and, after his early retirement, secretary; and he was always ready to help men who had neither the financial security nor the New College, Oxford, and Mansfield *cachet* which were in the air he breathed. If his manner sometimes suggested an Olympian uncommittedness more natural in an undergraduate or a country gentleman than in a Christian minister, at other times the flame shot forth from his blue eyes or in his gentle but decisive voice, revealing an affectionateness, a severity, a fury for truth and decency, which self-protection and good manners normally veiled.

With his wide culture A.G.M. combined the historian's judicial cast of mind, but he could only with difficulty be persuaded to consecutive writing. His friendship with H. C. Carter produced an essay in a slim volume on Emmanuel church, Cambridge, and a pamphlet written around the diary of one of its ministers, Joseph Hussey; his friendship with K. L. Parry produced an essay for the *Companion to Congregational Praise* and his loyalty to his old Principal an essay on Puritan worship for the *Festschrift* in honour of W. B. Selbie, *Christian Worship* (Oxford, 1936). With this should be read his study 'The Puritans at Prayer' in the collection not very happily called after its opening essay, *Mr. Pepys and Nonconformity* (1954), which first appeared in these *Transactions*. Matthews published here a small number of other articles, besides a valuable bibliography of Richard Baxter (later printed separately), an occasional review and a few documents, including the will of Robert Browne. In 1959 he provided a tercentenary edition of the Savoy *Declaration* with a characteristic introduction; but his last contribution to our own pages was his paper on 'Church and Dissent in the Reign of Queen Anne' which he read to us in May 1951 on becoming the Society's President. At its close he called on the historian of 'English religious life during the Interregnum . . . to give his most careful consideration' to the *unejected*; 'these men were faithful to the Englishman's inveterate belief that the religion of all sensible men is always one of compromise. That is all'. For A.G.M. this was *not* all. More of the man of faith comes through in the delicate assessment, which he read to us nine years earlier, of 'B. L. Manning, the Historian'. 'The main value of history is for the heart', he quoted from Manning. 'It keeps the heart tender, as only a study of our own poor humanity can.'

1963

XXXII

CHARTRES IN MAY

Oh, to be in England
Now that April's there . . .

but there is something to be said for being in France in May; and it was not many hours after the choristers had finished their singing from Magdalen Tower that my train drew up at Chartres. Already as we rounded the bend into the station, 'See Naples and die', I thought; and it was with a gladness reminiscent almost of Simeon that I stepped out into the quiet *place*, dominated, as all else is in Chartres, by the cathedral. Here one could walk in the road, with one's eyes on the cathedral, untroubled by the tearing, hooting motors of the city. In the study of what is great I love the oblique method, and, steadfastly declining the invitation to enter by either West or North portal, I therefore began my pilgrimage with a visit to the terrace by the former episcopal palace, turning my back on the cathedral's mounting *chevet*. It was not impudence, for that terrace is part of the continuity of Chartres: there of old *in hortulo juxta capellam* St Fulbert used to walk, holding *vespertina colloquia* with the boys he loved, and there that day was a priest in tonsure and cassock playing at simple games with the boys from the cathedral school.

A little later the great West door of the cathedral was flung open for a funeral, and following the mourners I left the sunshine, which the stonework so delicately reflects, and went within, as into a mighty cave: *cassis spelunca latebris. Ibant obscuri*, I thought, . . . *perque domos Ditis vacuas et inania regna;* for the emptiness of the cathedral is perhaps one's first impression. Here are no disfiguring monuments or tombs to divert the eye from its architectural glory; in honour of Our Lady, as M. Houvet has felicitously phrased it, *cette terre devait rester Vierge de toute sépulture humaine.* As my eyes grew more accustomed to the muted light, the symmetry and proportions of the building became plainer; but at Chartres it is the windows which hold one spellbound. Of the blue so lavishly used one can only say it is as incredible and inimitable as the blue of the Mediterranean, though quite another blue; indeed one had hardly realized before how many varied shades of blue there are. Here in the windows is what outside one finds in the sculptures—the stories of the Bible and the legends of the Saints repeated in endless variations, yet every time with the individual touch of the great artist, satisfying alike as separate lights or as part of the whole window. I sat before *Notre Dame de la Belle Verrière*, before each of the three great rose windows, before the windows in the West Front with their absorbing, overpowering blue, and in every case I marvelled at their richness and at the genius of the artist. To their peaceful appreciation there was only one sad hindrance: the whole building resounded to the echo of many hammers. Precautions were being taken to fit the windows into frames, that in the event of war they might all be removed within two hours. By day this, and by night the searchlight from a neighbouring aerodrome flashing restlessly on the spires, ill accorded with the atmosphere of the place; yet perhaps its essential peace was but the more marked thereby.

Out in the sunshine again I noticed the wallflowers, which at Chartres flower as wallflowers should, on any wall that offers, the older the better: far away up on the buttresses one could see the homely yellow. I noticed too the largeness of the stones with which the cathedral is built, and wondered afresh at the fervour which in that moment of religious enthusiasm inspired peasants and noblemen alike to draw the wagons bearing the stone, when beasts of burden were scarce. It is surely because its building proceeded from a wedding of religious impulse and creative activity which was unique even in the Middle Ages, that the cathedral today is so living and still possesses such creative power. The soaring vertical emphasis of later Gothic is not here, there is almost a heaviness about the building commoner in England than in France, but it is a resilient heaviness, by which a massive equilibrium is preserved, there is not a trace of stolidity or undue weight. In the curving arcades which decorate the buttresses—flung rather than flying across the aisles—there

334

is evident a delight in the sheer force of opposing masses, which yields a sense of movement felt more often in the articulation of music or a great poem than in architecture; it carries the mind back to the Pont du Gard, and makes Salisbury, Chartres' younger contemporary, seem the inhabitant of another world.

In the imagery, more perhaps than in the building, of the cathedral one sees the first flowering of the Gothic spirit. Beside the West door the figures are still formalized, massive, monumental; but on the North they are more natural, they have begun to unbend, they are conversing: in Professor Hamann's words *sie machen einander den Hof*, and we see the true *Höflichkeit* or *courtoisie* of the Middle Ages. Medieval affectionateness is revealed in the figure of 'the disciple whom Jesus loved', who is generally represented as a youth of Leonardesque, not to say feminine, features; among the Apostles at the South door he is the only one to be beardless. The same direction of medieval emotion appears in one of the loveliest of all the sculptures, the one which crowns the outermost arch of the North porch. Here in the creation of Adam the Creator is no 'ancient of days' but a youthful Christ, the incarnation of love and gentleness, tenderly fondling the new-created man; the artist must have been thinking, surely, of St Fulbert and his *charitas Christi, qua sicut filios amplectebatur*. Every type of temperament seems represented in these statues, from the mournful, ascetic severity of the Baptist to the alluring gracefulness of St Modeste—for so M. Houvet calls her, one would think, were it not for the accompanying *puits* of her martyrdom, on the *lucus a non lucendo* principle; I privately named her Héloïse. How conscious one is in this imagery of the grand universality of the Middle Ages! Scenes from the Gospels or the Apocrypha mingle unselfconsciously with figures representing the pagan virtues and vices or the animals of the Zodiac; Nature and Learning join with piety in bringing their treasures, for all things are of God. There near the Christ in Judgement sits Aristotle, fearlessly poring over his book, his eyes heavy with much reading—at least M. Houvet says it is Aristotle; but St Fulbert's pupils called *him* Plato, so I have my doubts.

Apart from the cathedral, the city of Chartres has every

right to the phrase it claims, *joyau du Moyen-Age*. Nowhere have I seen so many unspoiled streets and narrow alleys, with a jewel of a house in nearly all and hardly a building without some trace of bygone art; many of the doors are original and retain their ancient knockers. The church of St Pierre, where one may study the lovingly stumbling evolution from an irregularly groined vault to the true *ogive*, with a correspondingly halting development in types of capital, is worth a visit to Chartres on its own account; and there are several other churches, though once there were far more, as witness the names of the streets. Many of these names are rare in having preserved unchanged the older *au* form instead of *de*, as in the *Rue aux Prêtres* or the *Rue au Lait*. Then, if one descends to the lower town by one of the many wall-flowered *tertres*, one finds not one but many medieval bridges over the Eure, by which the women do their washing; and from each of them one looks back up at the cathedral, majestic over all, whether in sunshine or by starlight.

By nine under a full moon the very houses seem asleep; the doors are bolted, the windows fast shuttered, the streets deserted save for a couple of stray cats. But it is at night that the spirit of Chartres is most awake, especially down there by the bridges; for then there is nothing to disturb the old town and its memories. 'The streets are full of his genius', wrote an English monk of Fulbert a hundred years after his death, and Miss Waddell is not alone in having felt they are so still. Yet not of Fulbert only, for the hill of Chartres was a Druid centre centuries before St Fulbert's Christian creation. No wonder that before nightfall the North transept of the cathedral had been crowded with listeners to a sermon in which, as befitted the first day of Mary's month, was urged the presence and blessing of Our Lady and All Saints about the cathedral and the town. The cloud of witnesses, the communion of saints, it is easy to believe in them at Chartres.

1939

XXXIII

UNIVERSITY SERMONS

(1) LEEDS

delivered on 22 October 1950

"Yea, and why even of yourselves judge ye not what is right?"

(*Luke* xii. 57)

WHAT an alleviation it is to have, from Jesus, this robust expression of faith in ordinary men, at least in the possibilities of ordinary men! How different it sounds from much current, as well as traditional, insistence in religion on our *in*ability to judge; whether or not with the effect, perhaps sometimes with the ulterior motive, of pointing us to the Church as the one unmuddied source of judgement. 'Yea, and why even of yourselves—ἀφ' ἑαυτῶν—judge ye not what is right?' The text might well be taken—though I am not sure that it has been—as a foundation-stone for the doctrine of the right of private judgement.

But, although the right of judgement may be implied here, it is not with that right that Jesus is concerned. He seems to take that, rather, for granted. What He is concerned with is less men's right than their *responsibility* to judge. The words are phrased in the form of a remonstrance. They are addressed to people who are not doing what they ought to do, and express the speaker's dissatisfaction with them for not doing so. I want to use the words, I want us to hear them, as if they were addressed to ourselves. We who are here this morning are met as Christian men and women whose business it is to learn and to teach in a university. The subject to which I want to direct your attention is our responsibility in this position to *make judgements*.

Those of us who are teachers are constantly being brought to the point where we are called upon to make judgements, and to make them openly, in public pronouncements, in speaking or in writing. To those of us who are students, one of the things our time at the university should give us, indeed one of the more important elements in education, is the

337

ability, learning as we go, to judge, to distinguish, between truth and falsehood; and also between right and wrong. The distinction between truth and falsehood is not the same as the distinction between right and wrong, true—but between the *acts of distinguishing* in the two spheres there is, clearly, a relatedness. We who are here are called, moreover, to make judgements in *both* spheres. As members of the university we are concerned primarily with truth and falsehood, and with intellectual judgements. As Christians we are also at least equally concerned with right and wrong, and with moral judgements. The fact that we are *Christians in a university* makes it impossible for us to concern ourselves exclusively either with intellectual or with moral judgements. We are bound to be concerned with both. In any case, the intellectual judgement, that something is true or false, often has implications affecting practice and of a moral nature; and even where it has not, even where it is more purely theoretical or academic, our *act of judging* has moral repercussions; for it is the act of a person, of ourselves; and it affects ourselves, if not others as well.

This making of judgements, and the learning to make them, and *how* to make them, may be allowed to be one major occupation of those engaged in the work of a university. Yet it is a commonplace in university circles that those who teach are often notably disinclined to make such judgements. They will say what A, B and C thought; but not what they think themselves. The more learned they are, the less able, or willing, they appear ever to commit themselves. It is perhaps an equally common experience for the parents of undergraduates who are at home during the vacation, to find that their children seem less, rather than more, able to make up their minds, and are irritatingly unable to give a definite answer even to an apparently simple question. Life in a university thus appears to have the opposite effect of what it is intended to have: in that both those who teach and, at least for the time being, those who learn, instead of becoming trained in the making of judgements, too often lose the faculty of doing so. As a result, the truth is not proclaimed, or even stated; right goes by default; and the leadership in things of the mind and of the spirit, which men rightly expect from the universities, tends to be lacking. On us who as Christians have been entrusted with a message to give and a witness to make, in the university as much as anywhere else, the responsibility lies doubly heavy. Woe to us if we have to bow our heads under the condemnation of Jesus: 'Ye took the key of knowledge, ye entered not in yourselves, and them that were on the threshold ye hindered'.

Now I speak to you this morning as one of yourselves. I do not come as a critic from outside. I am engaged in university work myself. You may take it for granted that I have some understanding, because some experience, of the factors which go to the making of this unwillingness to commit ourselves; and that in the critical activity of the mind I value a proper caution and circumspection. A. D. Lindsay used to tell us, when we read essays to him at Balliol, that, if we thought we were perfectly clear what was the answer to any question which we were tackling, we might be pretty sure that we hadn't understood the question. That piece of advice, with its reminder of the greatness of the universe and of the smallness of our own minds, is one which I often recall and for which I remain grateful. Things *are* complicated and inter-related, and have endless ramifications. Only the ignorant are dogmatic. Because we begin our time at the university with (relative!) ignorance, we often begin by being dogmatic. Then, because we tend to swing to extremes, we go on to being sceptical. And such a period of scepticism may be a healthy corrective. The pity is that too often we *remain* sceptical; that, having learned the folly of a permanently closed mind, we not only learn to open our mind to receive new truth but keep it open so long that we forget how to close it again, for a time of reflection and assimilation, when the new truth has been seen and received by us. 'Seek, and ye shall *find*,' said Jesus.

Now the universe *is* great; and truth is many-sided and far greater than we ever comprehend, or can; but our growing realization that this is so should lead us as Christians not to scepticism but to humbleness of mind. We see the panorama of history opening out. We come to look with some tenderness, indeed, at men's stumbling efforts as they grope after the truth which God is ever seeking to reveal in and through history, sending His servants the prophets, 'rising early and sending them, saying, Oh, do not this abominable thing which I hate'. 'I taught Ephraim also to walk, taking them by their arms; but they knew not that I healed them.' God is *there*. Yes, *God* is there; but on earth there is no infallibility. Men's thinking changes. The very forms and setting of our thinking change. The one thing which does not change is the conditioning framework of history itself, with all the relativity which by its nature history introduces. And this I say not as an unbeliever, but as a Christian who accepts that distinctively historical nature of our faith; and who therefore accepts the framework of history, with all its relativity,as a condition and limitation within which it has *pleased God* to set our lives. This is as true for ourselves as for any other generation. *We* cannot get outside history. We too are bound to use our *own* thought-forms, the best that we can find, as those before us were bound to use theirs; and *our* ways of thinking are no more final or perfect than were theirs. We are men, not God. To seek after intellectual infallibility, at *any* time, is as much a form of Ranterism as it is to seek after moral perfection. We have to recognize and to accept our limitations, humbly. Happy are we if, because we are at a university, we gain some insight into the nature of our intellectual limitations, our limitations as *men* as well as those which are more personal to ourselves; and happy are we if, because we are Christians, we learn some glad and humble willingness to accept them at God's hands. This is a very different state of mind from scepticism. The *truth* remains in all its greatness and richness, unfathomable, inexhaustible.

I said just now that we are bound to use our *own* thought-forms. But I want, you see, also to say that we are bound to *use* them. It is our duty to do so not only with our contemporaries in mind, who have a right to look to us for guidance, but because of those who will come after us. How incomparably poorer *we* should be if those who are now dead had timidly refrained from passing judgement on any subject, because they did not see the whole truth. It may be true that in earlier generations there was more naïveté: that men thought making judgements was a simpler matter than we do, and believed that the judgements they made were more final than we think, or can think, either theirs or our own to be. Yet of many great Christian thinkers that is not true. It is not true, for instance, of the seventeenth-century English Puritan, Richard Baxter, with whom I have been living much of late. Baxter could saunter, or sally, round a question with a remarkable grasp of its labyrinthine complications; he could draw up a long list of pros and cons, and put both sides with telling insight; but this did not inhibit him from knowing *where he stood,* or from saying on which side he was. He was no more free than the best of us from error or prejudice; but he was ready to change his mind, and he would admit to mistakes and withdraw. *At the time* he did his best to judge what was true and what was right, and, having come to a decision, he did not hesitate to make it known.

Now I have been forced to ask myself why is it that, in comparison, we are so faltering and ineffective? So far as sheer knowledge is concerned, we cannot pretend that we are in a worse position than Richard Baxter. Though it is hardly possible to be more aware than he was of the anfractuosities of thought and of things, we *know,* I suppose, *more* than he did. The reason why we are so much less ready than he was to make up our minds and pass judgement is, I think, twofold. It is not because we know less, but because we *believe* less, and so *care* less; and it is also because we are more concerned for ourselves and our own reputation. Richard Baxter was never afraid of tackling controversial subjects; and one result was that he had some scores of books written against him by angry opponents, who often attacked his *bona fides* as well as his intelligence. *That* he did not mind (much!). What he cared about was not his own reputation but the truth; and, incidentally, *because* he cared more about the truth, in the long run his own reputation has stood the strain. Of the pusillanimity which holds us back from committing ourselves because of what people will say about us, if, as may well be, we turn out, with the coming of more light, to have been mistaken, there is only one thing to be said. We should be ashamed of it.

But the other inhibiting cause which I mentioned is the more powerful; and of it we ought to be more keenly ashamed still. It is not our lack of knowledge but our lack of faith which is the trouble. The more we learn, in any deep sense, the more we find that the truth about the things which matter most we cannot *know*, in the sense that we may know that two and two make four. The more we learn, the more we find ourselves driven back, in the last resort, upon *faith*, upon intuitions which are not patient of proof in an intellectual sense, intuitions which we can prove, if at all, only in the pragmatic sense that we can try them (or their implications) out by *living by them*.

Now if we are not Christians, or if we are nominal or weak Christians, and so not used to living by faith, this is a sorry outcome for the expectations with which we come to a university. It seems a sort of blank wall against which we are brought up dead. We find in time that we do not *know* what we thought we knew; and we find also, later, that we do not know what we hoped we might learn to know; and we have no faith, or are not used to its exercise. Consequently, we are tempted to take refuge in a cleverly, or sarcastically, or sceptically *negative* attitude, which may cloak our disappointment and feed our self-conceit but in no way alters, or even hides, our ineffectiveness. We become what in the rude world is known as academic ditherers.

Whether there is any solution of such a problematic situation for those who are not Christians, except for them to become Christians, I do not know. I doubt it. But for us who are Christians the problem should not, really, arise. If we are Christians, we live by faith in the Son of God, Who loved us and gave Himself for us; and all the things we care most about—the living God, His relations with us men and His way of running the world, His revealing of Himself in Jesus, His love and forgiveness and willingness to suffer, in order to redeem us, to win us back to the blessedness of sonship, in a life of joyous obedience to His will, a life transcending the material and death itself—all these things are the subject of *faith*. 'We walk by faith, not by sight.' Consequently, if we are Christians, to find *faith*, not logical knowledge or mathematical certainty, at the heart of our studies is not a sorry outcome at all. It is, rather, a discovery in line with our Christian experience, and one which helps to strengthen our confidence in it.

As Christians, moreover, we are not afraid to say, not what we *know*, but what we *believe* to be true and right, because we *care* about it; and also because we care about *other people*. What has been given to us is precious to us in itself. We also want others to share it with us. Genuine Christians are thus always concerned with preaching, or proclaiming, what they believe to be the truth; are always conscious of being missionaries, people sent to bear witness to Christ in the presence of others. Παρρησία, freedom or frankness of speech, boldness of utterance, is a characteristic of New Testament Christianity, nowadays no less than in the days which the New Testament describes. And it is so just as much within the university as outside it.

Let me put it this way. When the Spirit of the Risen Christ comes among us, His effect is the same as it has always been: that is one way of telling who it is. *He sharpens* our perception of the difference between truth and falsehood, and between right and wrong. He makes us more sensitive to their presence, and He insists on our judging: first in the intellectual sense of deciding *what* is true or right and *what* is false or wrong, and then in the moral sense of deciding *where we stand*. He demands, as always, a free decision. He never forced men to His way by compulsion; or by false promises; or by fear; or by misunderstanding. He treated men as *men:* as moral beings, that is: their minds marred by error and their consciences by sin, true; but still as beings who *must* make their *own* choices and decisions. 'Yea, and why even of yourselves *judge ye not* what is right?' We *must* decide. And we have enough light. We do know that there is good and that there is evil: not that there is *only* black and *only* white, and no grey; but that there *is* black and there *is* white, and that most grey things are either *more* black or *more* white. And still we have to judge and to decide. We are to acknowledge that we may be mistaken. We are to remember our finiteness and creatureliness, and to seek the spirit of true humbleness. But still decision is called for.

The strange thing about Jesus is that, where He comes, men find that a decision about what is true and what is right is not enough. It leads on into, they find themselves constrained to, the making of a decision about *Him*. 'Follow me.'

343

In the simplicity and directness of Jesus' call, both qualities are demanded: decision and humility. And both were called out when, as is written of one man who heard Him, 'And he left all, and rose up, and followed him.'

To return, in conclusion, to the intellectual sphere, with which we here are peculiarly concerned. We saw earlier that as Christians who live by faith, we shall not be dismayed when we find faith at the heart of our studies, where we expected to find knowledge. We see now that our finding that here also we must depend on faith does not excuse us from the responsibility of making up our minds. Just as in the moral sphere we have learned on a basis of faith to judge what is right, so here we must be ready to judge what is true. Our Christian faith will provide us with no short-cuts in the sphere of our studies. At the same time, the serenity and fearlessness, the liberation from self-concern and self-regard, which it should bring, may well help us towards a greater objectivity in our search for truth than would otherwise be in our range. The cultivation of sensitiveness to what is right can itself, moreover, foster sensitiveness to what is true. Humility, and with humility decision, are no less necessary in intellectual than in moral judging. Humility, and with humility decision, are, in fact, qualities without which in its members no university can really live. They are qualities which *in combination* are hardly to be found outside the company of those who are learning them in discipleship to Jesus Christ. To bring them into the common life of the university to which we belong is one of the duties laid upon us here, at whatever stage in our studies we may be. We cannot in honesty escape it. With God's help, we may fulfil it.

1950

344

delivered on 26 October 1958

"As the hart panteth after the water-brooks,
so panteth my soul after Thee, O God.
My soul thirsteth for God, for the living God."

(*Psalm* xlii. 1–2)

'My soul thirsteth for God, for the living God.' In these few words—and in the original they are far fewer—we touch a nerve-centre of true religion. *The living God*: God is not an idea, or an ideal, or a wish-fulfilment, or merely the subject of theological or profane discourse; He is some *one*, there before us, to be encountered, to be addressed, to be listened to, to be obeyed, to be loved. So in the New Testament Jesus Christ, though put to death, is very far from dead: He is the living Christ, who by the power of His endless life brings life and immortality to light, and whose words still shake the country round. Likewise a quality of the Bible as a whole— a quality which it shares indeed with other great literature, but which it possesses surpassingly—is its continuing power to penetrate and affect the spirit of man, κριτικός, discerning, revealing, discriminating, judging the thoughts and intents of his heart: so great a power that some readers reverence it as if it had a life of its own, almost forgetting the living God to face whom it should bring them. *We* are more likely to be in the state one was in who in 1652 first heard the Quaker George Fox preach: when, cut to the heart, she cried, 'We are all thieves; we are all thieves; we have taken the Scriptures in words, and know nothing of them in ourselves'. Yet the Spirit who gave them forth is still one and the same, the living and life-giving Spirit of the living God and of the living Christ, inspiring and gifting men, inspiring *us* if we will let Him and giving us gifts both of understanding and of holiness.

My soul thirsteth: in these words too we touch a nerve-centre. 'The thirst that from the soul doth rise Doth ask a drink divine': Ben Jonson may have been too free in classi-

345

cizing and materializing the assertion for his own purposes; but that he could use it so calmly as a foil for the love of a man for a woman means that the thirst of the soul for God is a human experience no less universal or shattering. True, it can more easily be repressed, or overlaid. But the Bible's readers are not long allowed to forget it. That God is the living God, before ever man thirsts for Him, comes first; but that the soul does thirst for God is a fact expressed so often in its pages, now in this image, now in that, that anyone who does so pant as the hart panteth, and with his soul desire God in the night, and hunger and thirst after righteousness, and long for the courts of the Lord, and cry out for the living God, must know that he is not alone, or peculiar, or eccentric, but is quite normally, and properly, knowing a human experience which he was made, and meant, to know. If he reads on, he will find also that his thirst is not just a sublimation of his sexual impulses, or a projection of his unsatisfied finitude on to an uncomprehending universe, or even a pathetic crying 'I want! I want!', like the figure William Blake drew standing at the foot of a ladder, the top of which reaches to heaven; for he will find that God satisfieth the longing soul and filleth the hungry soul with goodness; that those who seek God early are satisfied early with His mercy, that they may rejoice and be glad all their days; that those who hunger and thirst after righteousness are blessedly filled; that One comes down the ladder who may wrestle with him and bruise him, but who at least is real, even the living God, whose nature and whose name are Love. If he reads on, I say, he will find this: and find it, not only as stated in the Bible but as true in his own experience; and then he will rejoice with great joy; for that— when filled out—is the Gospel, the good news which is as cold waters to a thirsty soul.

'My soul thirsteth for God, for the living God.' Here already in the Psalms, we have foreshadowed what Professor Farmer has called 'the radical personalism of the Christian viewpoint': which 'does not shrink from ascribing personal quality to God'; and which believes that 'God's purpose with men is that they should, under the conditions set by their finite earthly life as persons, have personal fellowship with Himself' (*God and Men*, pp. 54, 35, 128). Such state-

346

ments spring from an experience the expectancy, receptive-
ness and interpretative canons of which have been formed by
an intense and reverently reflective study of the Bible. From
the same source springs the current emphasis on the Divine
transcendence and the Divine initiative. Though there is
much in the Bible about man's search for God, there is far
more about God's search for man; or rather, about God's
refusal to let man go. 'How shall I give thee up, O Ephraim?'
'I taught Ephraim also to go, taking them by the arms; but
they knew not that I healed them.' 'We love, because He
first loved us,' the God who 'loved us even when we were
dead in trespasses'. 'How often would I have gathered you
. . . ' 'Even to hoar hairs will I carry you . . .' 'He loved them
unto the end.' For the reader of the Bible these sentences,
and many more, beat cumulatively upon the heart, now surprising, now confirming, its insights and intuitions, till at
last they break and tender his heart into an acknowledgement that they are true.

The acknowledgement, like the acknowledgement of a
human love greater than our own, often comes abruptly because God will not force Himself upon us. Those who rightly
stress the Divine initiative sometimes forget this concomitant
of the Divine forbearance. To quote Professor Farmer again,
'just because God's dealings with men are always in the last
resort personal, and never merely manipulative and over-
riding', His fashioning of us is 'always through freedom and
for freedom' (p. 130). In this perception is involved the truth
that God not only leaves us free not to accept Him but requires us to seek Him. He will be found only of those who
seek Him, not, as might once have been argued, to keep His
pearls from the swine, His holiness from the dogs, but because our seeking Him is the measure of our wanting Him,
and He wants us to want Him. The principle of the Divine
initiative is preserved; for it is He who put eternity in our
hearts and gave us our thirst for Him; but we still have to
seek Him. Go down into the chapel as early as you like, says
St Bernard, you will always find God there before you; so
you will, but you will not find Him there if you do not go
there, eager to find Him.

So, once again, 'my soul *thirsteth*'. I have sometimes thought

347

that the (as it is) somewhat flat consequence, or promise, in Jesus' words, 'Seek, and ye shall find' may be owing to a misunderstanding of the Semitic original, which would convey rather the urgent exhortation, 'Seek, that ye may find': much as the (in *Matthew*) neighbouring words, 'Judge not, that ye be not judged', may be more authentic than their Lucan 'parallel', 'Judge not, and ye shall not be judged'. However that may be, there is no question of the urgency with which Jesus exhorts men to seek God: to seek Him *first*: which, again, perhaps represents the picturesque Semitic verb from the root meaning *dawn*, as of those who watch for the morning, which in the Psalms is rendered, 'O God, Thou art my God, *early* will I seek Thee: my soul thirsteth for Thee'. It is only those who keep *awake* who see the morn, in russet mantle clad, walk o'er the dew of yon high eastern hill; or who see the transfiguring glory of God in the face of Jesus Christ. 'Ye shall seek me, and ye shall find me, when ye shall search for me with all your heart.' It is notable how closely in *Matthew*—even if the adjacency is due only to the evangelist's arrangement—there follows on the exhortation, 'Seek, and ye shall find', the warning, 'Strait is the gate, and narrow is the way, which leadeth unto life, and few there be that find it'. 'Lord, are there few that be saved?' Jesus was asked once; and all He would reply was 'Strive to enter in'. It is only those that hunger and thirst after righteousness who will be filled.

Perhaps this is why we find such people often so objectionable and offensive; so uncomfortable to be with, especially in a university. Many of them are people in whom feeling is developed more strongly than intellect, often because they have not much intellect. This would offend us less if they knew they lacked intellect; but lacking it, they do not. They think things are much clearer and more intelligible than in fact they are; they forget that here the best of us knows only in part. So scornful an assurance, so narrow a dogmatism are out of place in a community properly given to inquiry and the suspended judgement, where 'what's beyond is wide'. To trust in ourselves that we have the answers and to despise others is foolish and wrong, soul-searing and harmful, in whomever it is found: whether in them *or* in ourselves, when *we,* equally, despise *them.* Can we not see that, however faulty and inadequate their psychology, however ineffectual their intellectual understanding, exposition and apologia, however offensive their infallibility of manner, these ardent seekers have often found at least something of God which we have not found, because we have not sought or else have given up the search? 'He that hath *both* the spirit of sanctification *and* acquired gifts of knowledge together,' says Richard Baxter, 'is the complete Christian, and likely to know much more than he that hath either of these alone'; and while some are not capable of 'acquired gifts of knowledge', there is none of us who, if we will, may not have 'the spirit of sanctification' which these tiresome enthusiasts possess. 'Many a man,' as H. M. Gwatkin used to say, 'has been conquered by the winning goodness of his intellectual inferiors.'

If we will; but that is the difficulty, and often the real reason why we despise them: not so much that they are 'intellectual inferiors'—and no one would use the phrase of St Bernard or Baxter or Newman, to name but three thirsters after God—as that we do not want to be conquered or won, least of all by anyone's goodness; for goodness makes claims, and we do not want them. There is no finding God without finding not only His goodness but its claims. Those who thirst after God may not begin by thirsting after goodness; but they find there is no quenching of their thirst apart from goodness. Again, they often interpret its claims in an offensively narrow or negative way, largely missing its joyous, outgoing, helpful character; but they do not try to escape the spirit of sanctification and the claims of goodness, saintliness, righteousness, holiness. It is a weakness in Ronald Knox's *Enthusiasm* that he never seems to realize the passion for holiness which inspired the peculiar people of whom he writes. It is, equally, a strength of Bishop Stephen Neill's *Anglicanism* that whether it is the Reformers of whom he writes, or Laud and the Puritans, or the Cambridge Evangelicals, or the Oxford Tractarians, 'what these men were more concerned about than anything else,' he says, 'what they were primarily interested in,' 'what they cared about above all else was holiness' (pp. 50, 143, 193, 239, 257). In

349

the concluding chapter of that book the aim of the churches of the Anglican Communion is described as that of 'gradually building up a settled resolute will to holiness' (p. 418). Members of other churches also would accept this as a description of their aim no less. A man's 'conviction of a Divine Presence', Newman remarks, varies in direct relation to 'his advance in holiness'; and it is true.

'My soul thirsteth for God, for the living God': as, but only as, we seek Him freely, with all our heart, and with all our mind, and as, but only as, we accept and fall into His will made known in Christ that we shall be holy, good and loving, will that thirst be quenched.

1958

Among the author's writings which carry further some of the subjects discussed in this volume are the following:

Richard Baxter (Nelson)

Richard Baxter and Philip Doddridge : a study in a tradition (Oxford University Press)

The Holy Spirit in Puritan Faith and Experience (Blackwell: out of print)

Visible Saints : the Congregational Way, 1640–1660 (Blackwell)

The Welsh Saints, 1640–1660 : Walter Cradock, Vavasor Powell, Morgan Llwyd (University of Wales Press)

James Nayler : a fresh approach (Friends' Historical Society)

Studies in Christian Enthusiasm illustrated from Early Quakerism (Pendle Hill, Philadelphia, Pa.)

Howel Harris : the last enthusiast (University of Wales Press)

Christian Pacifism in History (Blackwell: out of print)

The Holy Spirit and Ourselves (Epworth Press)

Better Than Life : the loving kindness of God (Independent Press)

INDEX

Saintsbury, George, 157
Salt, William, 179
Saravia, Hadrian à, 85
Savonarola, Girolamo, 12–13, 19–20
Schmidt, Martin, 240
Scott, Sir Walter, 17
Scotus, *see* Duns Scotus
Secker, Thomas, Archbishop of Canterbury, 156
Sedgwick, John, 88
Seeley, Sir John, 222
Selbie, W. B., ch. XXXI(1); pp. 118, 151, 331
Seymour, Edward, Duke of Somerset, 134
Shaftesbury, Earl of, *see* Cooper
Shakespeare, William, 17, 237, 265, 322
Shaw, G. B., 144
Shaw, John, 134
Sheldon, Gilbert, Archbishop of Canterbury, 59
Shubotham, Daniel, 205
Sibbes, Richard, 59
Sidney, Sir Philip, 314
Sippell, Theodor, 119, 170, 176, 195
Smeeton, Mary, 255, 265, 267
Smeeton, Sydney, 267
Smith, Preserved, 48, 129
Smyth, John, 73, 125
Söderblom, Nathan, Archbishop of Uppsala, 241, 243, 245
Some, David, 148
Somerset, the Protector, *see* Seymour
Spinoza, Baruch, 322
Sprigg, Joshua, 120, 125
Stadion, Christopher of, Bishop of Augsburg, 45
Stanford, Charles, 160
Stanley, A. P., 109
Stephens, Nathaniel, 192
Stevenson, R. L., 143
Stonhouse, Sir James, Bt., 158, 162
Storey, John, 194, 203
Stoughton, John, 61, 76–7, 137
Strauss, D. F., 222, 226
Studd, J. E. K., 244
Swift, Jonathan, 305–6
Sykes, Norman, 222, 229, 240
Sylvester, Matthew, 84, 105, 111, 162

Tacitus, 216
Talon, H. A., ch. XIV
Tatlow, Tissington, 240
Taylor, Dan, 74
Temple, Beatrice B., 317
Temple, Dorcas, 317
Temple, Frederick, Archbishop of Canterbury, 317–18

Temple, William, Archbishop of Canterbury, ch. XXII; pp. 101–2, 245, 302
Thomas Aquinas, St., 34, 39, 234–5, 322
Thompson, A. Hamilton, 173
Thompson, Francis, 329
Thornborough, John, Bishop of Worcester, 105
Thucydides, 216
Thurloe, John, 91, 173
Tombes, John, 69
Tomiczski, Peter, Bishop of Cracow, 43, 45
Tomkins, O. S., Bishop of Bristol, 241
Trench, R. C., Archbishop of Dublin, 113
Troeltsch, Ernst, 65
Trollope, Anthony, 326
Tuke, William, 275
Tyndale, William, 279

Vanderkemp, J. T., 328
Vaughan, Henry, ch. XIX; p. 329
Vaughan, Thomas, 195
Vermuyden, Sir Cornelius, 74
Vico, Giambattista, 216–17
Visser 't Hooft, W. A., 241

Waddell, Helen, 336
Wake, William, Archbishop of Canterbury, 157, 240
Walker, John, 329–30
Washington, George, 48
Watts, Isaac, 15, 152, 166, 178
Wernle, Paul, 82, 100
Wesley, Charles, 77, 157, 160, 208
Wesley, John, 39, 67–8, 73–8, 114, 156–7, 160, 165, 167, 233, 266
Wesley, Samuel, 74–7
Wesley, Susannah, 75–6
Whalley, Edward, 106
Whitefield, George, 156
Whitgift, John, Archbishop of Canterbury, 59
Whitley, W. T., 73, 79
Wickstead, Richard, 105
Widders, Robert, 193
Wightman, Edward, 177
Wilkinson, J. T., ch. XX; p. 107
Williams, Edward, 78
Williams, Roger, 71
Wilson, Thomas, 196
Winter, Charles, 71
Wollstonecraft, Mary, 183, 191
Wood, E. F. L., Earl of Halifax, 323
Woolf, Virginia, ch. XXIX
Woolman, John, 277
Wordsworth, William, 15, 21, 236, 328

357